Professional Exami

Strategic Level

Paper P3

Management Accounting Risk and Control Strategy

Exam Kit

CIMA

KAPLAN PUBLISHING

British Library Cataloguing-in-Publication Data

A catalogue record for this book is available from the British Library.

Published by Kaplan Publishing UK
Unit 2
Business Centre
Molly Millars Lane
Wokingham
Berkshire
RG41 4QZ

ISBN 978- 1-84710-443-4

Printed and bound in Great Britain

Acknowledgements

We are grateful to the Chartered Institute of Management Accountants, the Association of Chartered Certified Accountants and the Institute of Chartered Accountants in England and Wales for permission to reproduce past examination questions. The answers have been prepared by Kaplan Publishing.

INTRODUCTION

We have worked closely with experienced CIMA tutors and lecturers to ensure that our Kits are exam-focused and user-friendly.

This Exam Kit includes an extensive selection of questions that entirely cover the syllabus – this ensures that your knowledge is tested across all syllabus areas. Wherever possible questions have been grouped by syllabus topics.

All questions are of exam standard and format – this enables you to master the exam techniques. Section 1 contains Section A-type questions you will come across in your exam; Section 2 contains Section B-type questions.

May and November 2007 exams are at the back of the book – try these under timed conditions and this will give you an exact idea of the way you will be tested in your exam.

CONTENTS

INDEX TO QUESTIONS AND ANSWERS

Section A-type questions

Section B-type questions

Management control systems

Risk and internal control

Review and audit of control systems

Management of financial risk

Risk and control in information systems

SYLLABUS AND LEARNING OUTCOMES

Learning aims

This syllabus aims to test the student's ability to:

- evaluate and advise on management and internal control systems for a range of risks;
- plan a review process, including an internal audit, of such systems;
- evaluate alternatives and advise on the management of financial risks;
- advise on the development of information systems that support the risk control environment.

Learning outcomes and syllabus content

A - MANAGEMENT CONTROL SYSTEMS - 15%

Learning outcomes

On completion of their studies students should be able to:

- evaluate and recommend appropriate control systems for the management of organisations;
- evaluate the control of activities and resources within the organisation;
- recommend ways in which the problems associated with control systems can be avoided or solved;
- evaluate the appropriateness of an organisation's management accounting control systems and make recommendations for improvements.

Syllabus content

- The ways in which systems are used to achieve control within the framework of the organisation (e.g. contracts of employment, policies and procedures, discipline and reward, reporting structures, performance appraisal and feedback).
- The application of control systems and related theory to the design of management accounting control systems and information systems in general (i.e. control system components, primary and secondary feedback, positive and negative feedback, open- and closed-loop control).
- Structure and operation of management accounting control systems (e.g. identification of appropriate responsibility and control centres within the organisation, performance target setting, avoiding unintended behavioural consequences of using management accounting controls).
- Variation in control needs and systems dependent on organisational structure (e.g. extent of centralisation versus divisionalisation, management through strategic business units).
- Assessing how lean the management accounting system is (e.g. extent of the need for detailed costing, overhead allocation and budgeting, identification of non-value adding activities in the accounting function).
- Cost of quality applied to the management accounting function and 'getting things right first time'.

B - RISK AND INTERNAL CONTROL - 20%

Learning outcomes

On completion of their studies students should be able to:

- define and identify risks facing an organisation;
- explain ways of measuring and assessing risks facing an organisation, including the organisation's ability to bear such risks;
- discuss the purposes and importance of internal control and risk management for an organisation;
- evaluate risk management strategies;
- evaluate the essential features of internal control systems for identifying, assessing and managing risks;
- evaluate the costs and benefits of a particular internal control system;
- discuss the principles of good corporate governance for listed companies, particularly as regards the need for internal controls.

Syllabus content

- Types and sources of risk for business organisations: financial, commodity price, business (e.g. fraud, employee malfeasance, loss of product reputation), technological, external (e.g. economic and political), and corporate reputation (e.g. from environmental and social performance) risks.
- Risks associated with international operations (e.g. from cultural variations and litigation risk, to loss of goods in transit and enhanced credit risk). (***Note:*** No specific real country will be tested.)
- Quantification of risk exposures (impact if an adverse event occurs) and their expected values, taking account of likelihood.
- Minimising the risk of fraud (e.g. fraud policy statements, effective recruitment policies and good internal controls, such as approval procedures and separation of functions, especially over procurement and cash).
- Fraud related to sources of finance (e.g. advance fee fraud and pyramid schemes).
- Minimising political risk (e.g. by gaining government funding, joint ventures, local finance).
- The principle of diversifying risk. (***Note:*** Numerical questions will not be set.)
- Purposes of internal control (e.g. safeguarding of shareholders' investment and company assets, facilitation of operational effectiveness and efficiency, contribution to the reliability of reporting).
- Issues to be addressed in defining management's risk policy.
- Elements in internal control systems (e.g. control activities, information and communication processes, processes for ensuring continued effectiveness, etc).
- Operational features of internal control systems (e.g. embedding in company's operations, responsiveness to evolving risks, timely reporting to management).
- The pervasive nature of internal control and the need for employee training.
- Costs and benefits of maintaining the internal control system.
- The principles of good corporate governance for listed companies (the Combined Code) (e.g. separation of chairman and CEO roles, appointment of non-executive directors, transparency of directors' remuneration policy, relations with shareholders, the audit committee). Examples of recommended good practice may include The King Report on Corporate Governance for South Africa, Sarbanes-Oxley Act in the USA, The Smith and Higgs Reports in the UK, etc).
- Recommendations for internal control (e.g. The Turnbull Report).

C - REVIEW AND AUDIT OF CONTROL SYSTEMS - 15%

Learning outcomes

On completion of their studies students should be able to:

- explain the importance of management review of controls;
- evaluate the process of internal audit;
- produce a plan for the audit of various organisational activities including management, accounting and information systems;
- analyse problems associated with the audit of activities and systems, and recommend action to avoid or solve those problems;
- recommend action to improve the efficiency, effectiveness and control of activities;
- discuss the principles of good corporate governance for listed companies, for conducting reviews of internal controls and reporting on compliance;
- discuss the importance of exercising ethical principles in conducting and reporting on internal reviews.

Syllabus content

- The process of review (e.g. regular reporting to management on the effectiveness of internal controls over significant risks) and audit of internal controls.
- Major tools available to assist with such a process (e.g. audit planning, documenting systems, internal control questionnaires, sampling and testing).
- Detection and investigation of fraud.
- Role of the internal auditor and relationship of the internal audit to the external audit.
- Operation of internal audit, the assessment of audit risk and the process of analytical review, including different types of benchmarking, their use and limitations.
- The principles of good corporate governance for listed companies, for the review of the internal control system and reporting on compliance.
- Relationship of the above to other forms of audit (e.g. value-for-money audit, management audit, social and environmental audit).
- Particular relevance of the fundamental principles in CIMA's Ethical Guidelines to the conduct of an impartial and effective review of internal controls.
- Application of CIMA's Ethical Guidelines on the resolution of ethical conflicts in the context of discoveries made in the course of internal review.

D - MANAGEMENT OF FINANCIAL RISK - 30%

Learning outcomes

On completion of their studies students should be able to:

- identify and evaluate financial risks facing an organisation;
- identify and evaluate appropriate methods for managing financial risks;
- evaluate the effects of alternative methods of risk management and make recommendations accordingly;
- calculate the impact of differential inflation rates on forecast exchange rates;
- explain exchange rate theory;
- recommend currency risk management strategies.

Syllabus content

- Sources of financial risk, including those associated with international operations (e.g. hedging of foreign investment value) and trading (e.g. purchase prices and sales values).
- Transaction, translation, economic and political risk.
- Minimising political risk (e.g. gaining government funding, joint ventures, obtaining local finance).
- Quantification of risk exposures and their expected values.
- Operation and features of the more common instruments for managing interest rate risk: swaps, forward rate agreements, futures and options. (***Note:*** Numerical questions will not be set involving FRAs, futures or options. See the note below relating to the Black Scholes model.)
- Illustration and interpretation of simple graphs depicting cap, collar and floor interest rate options.
- Theory and forecasting of exchange rates (e.g. interest rate parity, purchasing power parity and the Fisher effect).
- Operation and features of the more common instruments for managing currency risk: swaps, forward contracts, money market hedges, futures and options. (***Note:*** The Black Scholes option pricing model will not be tested numerically, however, an understanding of the variables which will influence the value of an option should be appreciated.)
- Principles of valuation of financial instruments for management and financial reporting purposes (IAS 39), and controls to ensure that the appropriate accounting method is applied to a given instrument.
- Internal hedging techniques (e.g. netting and matching).

E - RISK AND CONTROL IN INFORMATION SYSTEMS - 20%

Learning outcomes

On completion of their studies students should be able to:

- evaluate and advise managers on the development of IM, IS and IT strategies that support management and internal control requirements;
- identify and evaluate IS/IT systems appropriate to an organisation's needs for operational and control information;
- evaluate benefits and risks in the structuring and organisation of the IS/IT function and its integration with the rest of the business;
- evaluate and recommend improvements to the control of information systems;
- evaluate specific problems and opportunities associated with the audit and control of systems which use information technology.

Syllabus content

- The importance and characteristics of information for organisations and the use of cost-benefit analysis to assess its value.
- The purpose and content of IM, IS and IT strategies, and their role in performance management and internal control.
- Data collection and IT systems that deliver information to different levels in the organisation (e.g. transaction processing, decision support and executive informative systems).
- The potential ways of organising the IT function (e.g. the use of steering committees, support centres for advice and help desk facilities, end user participation).
- The arguments for and against outsourcing.

- The criteria for selecting outsourcing/Facilities Management partners and for managing ongoing relationships, service level agreements, discontinuation/change of supplier, hand-over considerations.
- Methods for securing systems and data back-up in case of systems failure and/or data loss.
- Minimising the risk of computer-based fraud (e.g. access restriction, password protection, access logging and automatic generation of audit trail).
- Risks in IS/IT systems: erroneous input, unauthorised usage, imported virus infection, unlicensed use of software, theft, corruption of software.
- Risks and benefits of Internet and Intranet use by an organisation.
- Controls which can be designed into an information system, particularly one using information technology (e.g. security, integrity and contingency controls).
- Control and audit of systems development and implementation.
- Techniques available to assist audit in a computerised environment (computer-assisted audit techniques e.g. audit interrogation software).

REVISION GUIDANCE

Planning your revision

Begin by asking yourself two questions:

How much time do I have available for revision?

Remember to take into account:

- times of the day when you work most effectively
- other commitments
- time definitely unavailable (e.g. holidays)
- relaxation time.

What do I need to cover during my revision?

Remember to take into account that:

- all syllabus areas are equally examinable
- you need more time when revising areas of the syllabus you feel least confident about
- question practice is the best form of revision.

Make a timetable/plan to remind yourself how much work you have to do and when you are free to do it. Allow some time for slippage.

Revision techniques

- Go through your notes and textbook **highlighting the important points**
- You might want to produce your own set of **summarised notes**
- **List key words** for each topic to remind you of the essential concepts
- **Practise exam-standard questions**, under timed conditions
- **Rework questions** that you got completely wrong the first time, but only when you think you know the subject better
- If you get stuck on topics, **find someone to explain** them to you (your tutor or a colleague, for example)
- **Read recent articles** on the CIMA website and in *Financial Management*.
- **Read** good newspapers and professional journals.

THE EXAM

Format of the exam

	Number of marks
There will be a written exam paper of three hours, with the following sections:	
Section A	
A maximum of four compulsory questions all relating to a single scenario.	50
Section B	
Two questions, from a choice of four, each worth 25 marks. Short scenarios will be given, to which some or all questions relate.	50
Total:	100
Total time allowed: 3 hours	

About the exam

- You are allowed 20 minutes' reading time before the examination begins.
- Where you have a **choice of question**, decide which questions you will do.
- Unless you know exactly how to answer the question, spend some time **planning** your answer.
- **Divide the time** you spend on questions in proportion to the marks on offer. One suggestion is to allocate 1½ minutes to each mark available, so a 10-mark question should be completed in 15 minutes.
- Stick to the question and **tailor your answer** to what you are asked. Pay particular attention to the verbs in the question.
- If you do not understand what a question is asking, **state your assumptions**. Even if you do not answer in precisely the way the examiner hoped, you should be given some credit, if your assumptions are reasonable.
- If you **get completely stuck** with a question, leave space in your answer book and **return to it later.**
- Spend the last **five minutes** reading through your answers and **making any additions or corrections**.
- You should do everything you can to make things easy for the marker. The marker will find it easier to identify the points you have made if your **answers are legible**.
- **Essay questions**: Your essay should have a clear structure. It should contain a brief introduction, a main section and a conclusion. Be concise. It is better to write a little about a lot of different points than a great deal about one or two points.
- **Computations**: It is essential to include all your workings in your answers. Many computational questions require the use of a standard format: company income statement, balance sheet and cash flow statement for example. Be sure you know these formats thoroughly before the examination and use the layouts that you see in the answers given in this book and in model answers.
- **Scenario-based questions:** read the scenario carefully, identify the area in which there is a problem, outline the main principles/theories you are going to use to answer the question, and then apply the principles/theories to the scenario.
- **Reports, memos and other documents**: some questions ask you to present your answer in the form of a report or a memo or other document. So use the correct format – there could be easy marks to gain here.

MATHEMATICAL TABLES AND FORMULAE

Area under the normal curve

This table gives the area under the normal curve between the mean and a point *Z* standard deviations above the mean. The corresponding area for deviations below the mean can be found by symmetry.

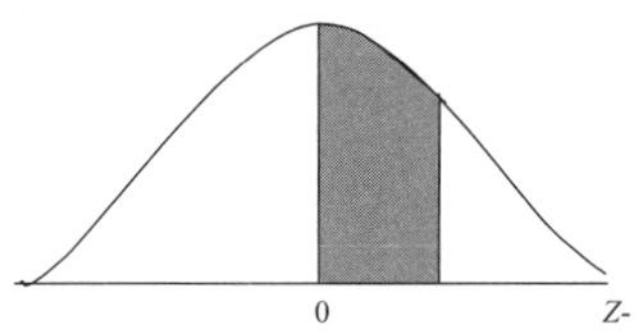

$Z = \frac{(x - \mu)}{\sigma}$	Interest rates (*r*)									
	0.00	0.01	0.02	0.03	0.04	0.05	0.06	0.07	0.08	0.09
0.0	.0000	.0040	.0080	.0120	.0159	.0199	.0239	.0279	.0319	.0359
0.1	.0398	.0438	.0478	.0517	.0557	.0596	.0636	.0675	.0714	.0753
0.2	.0793	.0832	.0871	.0910	.0948	.0987	.1026	.1064	.1103	.1141
0.3	.1179	.1217	.1255	.1293	.1331	.1368	.1406	.1443	.1480	.1517
0.4	.1554	.1591	.1628	.1664	.1700	.1736	.1772	.1808	.1844	.1879
0.5	.1915	.1950	.1985	.2019	.2054	.2088	.2123	.2157	.2190	.2224
0.6	.2257	.2291	.2324	.2357	.2389	.2422	.2454	.2486	.2518	.2549
0.7	.2580	.2611	.2642	.2673	.2704	.2734	.2764	.2794	.2823	.2852
0.8	.2881	.2910	.2939	.2967	.2995	.3023	.3051	.3078	.3106	.3133
0.9	.3159	.3186	.3212	.3238	.3264	.3289	.3315	.3340	.3365	.3389
1.0	.3413	.3438	.3461	.3485	.3508	.3531	.3554	.3577	.3599	.3621
1.1	.3643	.3665	.3686	.3708	.3729	.3749	.3770	.3790	.3810	.3830
1.2	.3849	.3869	.3888	.3907	.3925	.3944	.3962	.3980	.3997	.4015
1.3	.4032	.4049	.4066	.4082	.4099	.4115	.4131	.4147	.4162	.4177
1.4	.4192	.4207	.4222	.4236	.4251	.4265	.4279	.4292	.4306	.4319
1.5	.4332	.4345	.4357	.4370	.4382	.4394	.4406	.4418	.4430	.4441
1.6	.4452	.4463	.4474	.4485	.4495	.4505	.4515	.4525	.4535	.4545
1.7	.4554	.4564	.4573	.4582	.4591	.4559	.4608	.4616	.4625	.4633
1.8	.4641	.4649	.4656	.4664	.4671	.4678	.4686	.4693	.4699	.4706
1.9	.4713	.4719	.4726	.4732	.4738	.4744	.4750	.4756	.4762	.4767
2.0	.4772	.4778	.4783	.4788	.4793	.4798	.4803	.4808	.4812	.4817
2.1	.4821	.4826	.4830	.4831	.4838	.4842	.4856	.4850	.4854	.4857
2.2	.4861	.4865	.4868	.4871	.4875	.4878	.4881	.4884	.4887	.4890
2.3	.4893	.4896	.4898	.4901	.4904	.4906	.4909	.4911	.4913	.4916
2.4	.4918	.4920	.4922	.4925	.4927	.4929	.4931	.4932	.4934	.4936
2.5	.4938	.4940	.4941	.4943	.4945	.4946	.4948	.4949	.4951	.4952
2.6	.4953	.4955	.4956	.4957	.4959	.4960	.4961	.4962	.4963	.4964
2.7	.4965	.4966	.4967	.4968	.4969	.4970	.4971	.4972	.4973	.4974
2.8	.4974	.4975	.4976	.4977	.4977	.4978	.4979	.4980	.4980	.4981
2.9	.4981	.4982	.4983	.4983	.4984	.4984	.4985	.4985	.4986	.4986
3.0	.49865	.4987	.4987	.4988	.4988	.4989	.4989	.4989	.4990	.4990
3.1	.49903	.4491	.4991	.4991	.4992	.4992	.4992	.4992	.4993	.4993
3.2	.49931	.4993	.4994	.4994	.4994	.4994	.4994	.4995	.4995	.4995
3.3	.49952	.4495	.4995	.4996	.4996	.4996	.4996	.4996	.4996	.4997
3.4	.49966	.4997	.4997	.4997	.4997	.4997	.4997	.4997	.4997	.4998
3.5	.49977									

Present value table

Present value of £1 i.e. that is $(1 + r)^{-n}$ where r = interest rate; n = number of periods until payment or receipt.

Periods	Interest rates (*r*)									
(*n*)	1%	2%	3%	4%	5%	6%	7%	8%	9%	10%
1	0.990	0.980	0.971	0.962	0.952	0.943	0.935	0.926	0.917	0.909
2	0.980	0.961	0.943	0.925	0.907	0.890	0.873	0.857	0.842	0.826
3	0.971	0.942	0.915	0.889	0.864	0.840	0.816	0.794	0.772	0.751
4	0.961	0.924	0.888	0.855	0.823	0.792	0.763	0.735	0.708	0.683
5	0.951	0.906	0.863	0.822	0.784	0.747	0.713	0.681	0.650	0.621
6	0.942	0.888	0.837	0.790	0.746	0705	0.666	0.630	0.596	0.564
7	0.933	0.871	0.813	0.760	0.711	0.665	0.623	0.583	0.547	0.513
8	0.923	0.853	0.789	0.731	0.677	0.627	0.582	0.540	0.502	0.467
9	0.914	0.837	0.766	0.703	0.645	0.592	0.544	0.500	0.460	0.424
10	0.905	0.820	0.744	0.676	0.614	0.558	0.508	0.463	0.422	0.386
11	0.896	0.804	0.722	0.650	0.585	0.527	0.475	0.429	0.388	0.350
12	0.887	0.788	0.701	0.625	0.557	0.497	0.444	0.397	0.356	0.319
13	0.879	0.773	0.681	0.601	0.530	0.469	0.415	0.368	0.326	0.290
14	0.870	0.758	0.661	0.577	0.505	0.442	0.388	0.340	0.299	0.263
15	0.861	0.743	0.642	0.555	0.481	0.417	0.362	0.315	0.275	0.239
16	0.853	0.728	0.623	0.534	0.458	0.394	0.339	0.292	0.252	0.218
17	0.844	0.714	0.605	0.513	0.436	0.371	0.317	0.270	0.231	0.198
18	0.836	0.700	0.587	0.494	0.416	0.350	0.296	0.250	0.212	0.180
19	0.828	0.686	0.570	0.475	0.396	0.331	0.277	0.232	0.194	0.164
20	0.820	0.673	0.554	0.456	0.377	0.312	0.258	0.215	0.178	0.149

Periods	Interest rates (*r*)									
(*n*)	11%	12%	13%	14%	15%	16%	17%	18%	19%	20%
1	0.901	0.893	0.885	0.877	0.870	0.862	0.855	0.847	0.840	0.833
2	0.812	0.797	0.783	0.769	0.756	0.743	0.731	0.718	0.706	0.694
3	0.731	0.712	0.693	0.675	0.658	0.641	0.624	0.609	0.593	0.579
4	0.659	0.636	0.613	0.592	0.572	0.552	0.534	0.516	0.499	0.482
5	0.593	0.567	0.543	0.519	0.497	0.476	0.456	0.437	0.419	0.402
6	0.535	0.507	0.480	0.456	0.432	0.410	0.390	0.370	0.352	0.335
7	0.482	0.452	0.425	0.400	0.376	0.354	0.333	0.314	0.296	0.279
8	0.434	0.404	0.376	0.351	0.327	0.305	0.285	0.266	0.249	0.233
9	0.391	0.361	0.333	0.308	0.284	0.263	0.243	0.225	0.209	0.194
10	0.352	0.322	0.295	0.270	0.247	0.227	0.208	0.191	0.176	0.162
11	0.317	0.287	0.261	0.237	0.215	0.195	0.178	0.162	0.148	0.135
12	0.286	0.257	0.231	0.208	0.187	0.168	0.152	0.137	0.124	0.112
13	0.258	0.229	0.204	0.182	0.163	0.145	0.130	0.116	0.104	0.093
14	0.232	0.205	0.181	0.160	0.141	0.125	0.111	0.099	0.088	0.078
15	0.209	0.183	0.160	0.140	0.123	0.108	0.095	0.084	0.079	0.065
16	0.188	0.163	0.141	0.123	0.107	0.093	0.081	0.071	0.062	0.054
17	0.170	0.146	0.125	0.108	0.093	0.080	0.069	0.060	0.052	0.045
18	0.153	0.130	0.111	0.095	0.081	0.069	0.059	0.051	0.044	0.038
19	0.138	0.116	0.098	0.083	0.070	0.060	0.051	0.043	0.037	0.031
20	0.124	0.104	0.087	0.073	0.061	0.051	0.043	0.037	0.031	0.026

Cumulative present value of £1

This table shows the Present Value of £1 per annum, Receivable or Payable at the end of each year for n years $\frac{1-(1+r)^{-n}}{r}$

Periods (n)	Interest rates (r)									
	1%	2%	3%	4%	5%	6%	7%	8%	9%	10%
1	0.990	0.980	0.971	0.962	0.952	0.943	0.935	0.926	0.917	0.909
2	1.970	1.942	1.913	1.886	1.859	1.833	1.808	1.783	1.759	1.736
3	2.941	2.884	2.829	2.775	2.723	2.673	2.624	2.577	2.531	2.487
4	3.902	3.808	3.717	3.630	3.546	3.465	3.387	3.312	3.240	3.170
5	4.853	4.713	4.580	4.452	4.329	4.212	4.100	3.993	3.890	3.791
6	5.795	5.601	5.417	5.242	5.076	4.917	4.767	4.623	4.486	4.355
7	6.728	6.472	6.230	6.002	5.786	5.582	5.389	5.206	5.033	4.868
8	7.652	7.325	7.020	6.733	6.463	6.210	5.971	5.747	5.535	5.335
9	8.566	8.162	7.786	7.435	7.108	6.802	6.515	6.247	5.995	5.759
10	9.471	8.983	8.530	8.111	7.722	7.360	7.024	6.710	6.418	6.145
11	10.368	9.787	9.253	8.760	8.306	7.887	7.499	7.139	6.805	6.495
12	11.255	10.575	9.954	9.385	8.863	8.384	7.943	7.536	7.161	6.814
13	12.134	11.348	10.635	9.986	9.394	8.853	8.358	7.904	7.487	7.103
14	13.004	12.106	11.296	10.563	9.899	9.295	8.745	8.244	7.786	7.367
15	13.865	12.849	11.938	11.118	10.380	9.712	9.108	8.559	8.061	7.606
16	14.718	13.578	12.561	11.652	10.838	10.106	9.447	8.851	8.313	7.824
17	15.562	14.292	13.166	12.166	11.274	10.477	9.763	9.122	8.544	8.022
18	16.398	14.992	13.754	12.659	11.690	10.828	10.059	9.372	8.756	8.201
19	17.226	15.679	14.324	13.134	12.085	11.158	10.336	9.604	8.950	8.365
20	18.046	16.351	14.878	13.590	12.462	11.470	10.594	9.818	9.129	8.514

Periods (n)	Interest rates (r)									
	11%	12%	13%	14%	15%	16%	17%	18%	19%	20%
1	0.901	0.893	0.885	0.877	0.870	0.862	0.855	0.847	0.840	0.833
2	1.713	1.690	1.668	1.647	1.626	1.605	1.585	1.566	1.547	1.528
3	2.444	2.402	2.361	2.322	2.283	2.246	2.210	2.174	2.140	2.106
4	3.102	3.037	2.974	2.914	2.855	2.798	2.743	2.690	2.639	2.589
5	3.696	3.605	3.517	3.433	3.352	3.274	3.199	3.127	3.058	2.991
6	4.231	4.111	3.998	3.889	3.784	3.685	3.589	3.498	3.410	3.326
7	4.712	4.564	4.423	4.288	4.160	4.039	3.922	3.812	3.706	3.605
8	5.146	4.968	4.799	4.639	4.487	4.344	4.207	4.078	3.954	3.837
9	5.537	5.328	5.132	4.946	4.772	4.607	4.451	4.303	4.163	4.031
10	5.889	5.650	5.426	5.216	5.019	4.833	4.659	4.494	4.339	4.192
11	6.207	5.938	5.687	5.453	5.234	5.029	4.836	4.656	4.486	4.327
12	6.492	6.194	5.918	5.660	5.421	5.197	4.988	7.793	4.611	4.439
13	6.750	6.424	6.122	5.842	5.583	5.342	5.118	4.910	4.715	4.533
14	6.982	6.628	6.302	6.002	5.724	5.468	5.229	5.008	4.802	4.611
15	7.191	6.811	6.462	6.142	5.847	5.575	5.324	5.092	4.876	4.675
16	7.379	6.974	6.604	6.265	5.954	5.668	5.405	5.162	4.938	4.730
17	7.549	7.120	6.729	6.373	6.047	5.749	5.475	5.222	4.990	4.775
18	7.702	7.250	6.840	6.467	6.128	5.818	5.534	5.273	5.033	4.812
19	7.839	7.366	6.938	6.550	6.198	5.877	5.584	5.316	5.070	4.843
20	7.963	7.469	7.025	6.623	6.259	5.929	5.628	5.353	5.101	4.870

Formulae

Annuity

Present value of an annuity of £1 per annum receivable or payable for n years, commencing in one year, discounted at r% per annum:

$$PV = \frac{1}{r}\left[1 - \frac{1}{[1+r]^n}\right]$$

Perpetuity

Present value of £1 per annum, payable or receivable in perpetuity, commencing in one year, discounted at r% per annum:

$$PV = \frac{1}{r}$$

Growing Perpetuity

Present value of £1 per annum, receivable or payable, commencing in one year, growing in perpetuity at a constant rate of g% per annum, discounted at r% per annum:

$$PV = \frac{1}{r - g}$$

Section 1

SECTION A-TYPE QUESTIONS

1 CRASHCARTS (PILOT PAPER)

Crashcarts IT Consultancy is a £100 million revenue business listed on the London Stock Exchange with a reputation for providing world class IT consultancy services to blue chip clients, predominantly in the retail sector. In 20X1, Crashcarts acquired a new subsidiary for £2 million based on a P/E ratio of 8, which it renamed Crashcarts Call Centre. The call centre subsidiary leased all of its hardware, software and telecommunications equipment over a five-year term. The infrastructure provides the capacity to process three million orders and ten million line items per annum. In addition, maintenance contracts were signed for the full five-year period. These contracts include the provision of a daily backup facility in an off-site location.

Crashcarts Call Centre provides two major services for its clients. First, it holds databases, primarily for large retail chains' catalogue sales, connected in real time to clients' inventory control systems. Second, its call centre operation allows its clients' customers to place orders by telephone. The real-time system determines whether there is inventory available and, if so, a shipment is requested. The sophisticated technology in use by the call centre also incorporates a secure payment facility for credit and debit card payments, details of which are transferred to the retail stores' own computer system. The call centre charges each retail client a lump sum each year for the IT and communications infrastructure it provides. There is a 12 month contract in place for each client. In addition, Crashcarts earns a fixed sum for every order it processes, plus an additional amount for every line item. If items are not in inventory, Crashcarts earns no processing fee.

Crashcarts Call Centre is staffed by call centre operators (there were 70 in 20X2 and 80 in each of 20X3 and 20X4). In addition, a management team, training staff and administrative personnel are employed. Like other call centres, there is a high turnover of call centre operators (over 100% per annum) and this requires an almost continuous process of staff training and detailed supervision and monitoring.

A summary of Crashcarts Call Centre's financial performance for the last three years:

	20X2	*20X3*	*20X4*
	£000	£000	£000
Revenue			
Contract fixed fee	400	385	385
Order processing fees	2,500	3,025	3,450
Line item processing fees	600	480	390
Total revenue	3,500	3,890	4,225

Expenses			
Office rent and expenses	200	205	210
Operator salaries and salary-related costs	1,550	1,920	2,180
Management, administration and training salaries	1,020	1,070	1,120
IT and telecoms lease and maintenance expenses	300	310	330
Other expenses	150	200	220
Total expenses	3,220	3,705	4,060
Operating profit	280	185	165

Non-financial performance information for the same period is as follows:

	20X2	*20X3*	*20X4*
Number of incoming calls received	1,200,000	1,300,000	1,350,000
Number of orders processed	1,000,000	1,100,000	1,150,000
Order strike rate (orders/calls)	83.3%	84.6%	85.2%
Number of line items processed	3,000,000	3,200,000	3,250,000
Average number of line items per order	3.0	2.9	2.8
Number of retail clients	8	7	7
Fixed contract income per client	£50,000	£55,000	£55,000
Income per order processed	£2.50	£2.75	£3.00
Income per line item processed	£0.20	£0.15	£0.12
Average number of orders per operator	15,000	15,000	15,000
Number of operators required	66.7	73.3	76.7
Actual number of operators employed	70.0	80.0	80.0

Required:

(a) Discuss the increase in importance of risk management to all businesses (with an emphasis on listed ones) over the last few years and the role of management accountants in risk management. **(10 marks)**

(b) Advise the Crashcarts Call Centre on methods for analysing its risks. **(5 marks)**

(c) Identify and quantify (using appropriate methods) the major risks facing Crashcarts at both parent level and subsidiary level. **(20 marks)**

(d) Explain the components of a management control system and recommend the main controls that would be appropriate for the Crashcarts Call Centre. **(15 marks)**

(Total: 50 marks)

2 EPM FINANCE HOUSE

Overview

EPM is a finance house with nearly 100 branch offices situated throughout the country. The company provides financial advice to customers. Financial advice includes recommending different savings accounts through to pension and retirement planning for individual customers. Customers vary from private individuals with relatively high net worth to companies planning specific pension schemes for their staff. Advice provided may vary, almost on a daily basis, given the volatile nature of the savings products on offer and changes in share prices on the stock exchange. However, other areas such as pension schemes tend to be more stable as the investments are longer term.

EPM has built up a good reputation for supplying appropriate products for its customers, although recently there has been some adverse publicity resulting from poor investment advice due to delays in customer service staff at branches obtaining appropriate financial information on the products offered by EPM.

EPM has also benefited from relatively informal anti-money laundering legislation in its host country, meaning that background checks on customers have been limited. Also, in many cases, evidence confirming the customer's identity has been filed incorrectly, making retrieval difficult. New Anti-Money Laundering legislation is due to be implemented in two months, which will require appropriate documentation to be retained on all customers, not just new customers. At present, EPM does not meet the regulatory requirements of this new legislation.

A new product 'Pensions4You', a flexible pension product which takes account of recent deregulation in the pensions industry, has not been advertised due to delays in setting the marketing budget. EPM's competitors are known to be preparing similar products with marketing starting in the near future.

Information systems

EPM has a centralised data processing function at its head office. Each week, significant volumes of information are distributed from head office to each branch. Information transferred includes internal financial information as well as confidential customer details, which is used to update and maintain customer databases at each of the branches. This information is used by staff in each branch to provide advice to customers regarding the suitability of different financial products for the specific requirements of each customer.

The board of EPM has recognised the need to establish some form of wide area network to be able to share information between head office and the different branches.

Receivables

There are many reasons for maintaining internal control systems. These include the need to ensure that:

(i) transactions are properly authorised;

(ii) transactions are promptly and accurately recorded;

(iii) access to assets and records is properly authorised;

(iv) recorded assets represent actual assets.

In the absence of internal controls, errors, omissions and misappropriation of assets are likely and external and internal auditors pay particular attention to both the design and operation of internal control systems.

Receivables are an area in which most organisations expect internal controls to be operating effectively. In EPM, customers pay for financial services provided and also make payments to be credited to different pension funds and other financial products recommended by EPM.

Clerks in EPM record these payments, and where necessary transfer the funds on to specialist companies providing the financial products recommended by EPM. EPM always raises a sales invoice for payments due; customers pay by cheque or credit or debit card. Cash payments are also received, mainly where the customer is new to the country in which EPM operates and bank accounts etc. have not been set up by the customer.

Required:

(a) Identify and discuss the risks that could affect EPM, briefly explaining how each risk can be overcome. **(14 marks)**

(b) Describe two different methods for distributing information between the branches of the company, and suggest how the use of each of these distribution systems might be preferable to the existing system. **(12 marks)**

(c) (i) In the context of receivables, list and describe the types of error, omission and misappropriation of assets that can occur in practice where internal controls are weak or non-existent.

(ii) Explain why even a good system of internal control will not necessarily prevent or detect errors, omissions and the misappropriation of assets in a receivables system, and explain why a good system of internal control is important.

(iii) Discuss the main internal controls that you would expect to be in operation in the receivables system in EPM. **(16 marks)**

(d) Explain the risks of using a wide area network to transfer personal data, and briefly explain the controls that can be used to mitigate those risks. **(8 marks)**

(Total: 50 marks)

3 STAND

Stand is a UK-based company that sells financial software to customers all over the world. From a small beginning nearly 20 years ago, Stand has grown into a large company with an extensive international client base. About 75% of its income is now earned from clients in other countries.

The chief executive officer of Stand is aware that the company has experienced some difficulties with its foreign business, and that profit margins have been adversely affected by foreign exchange volatility. A large proportion of the contracts to provide software are won after a competitive bidding process involving rival software companies. Rival bidders are invited to submit proposals to the customer, who then selects the preferred bidder to do the work. The process from making a bid for a contract and the awarding of the contract can take up to six months.

Contracts to provide software to foreign customers are priced either in US dollars or the customer's domestic currency. When Stand is awarded a contract, it is usual for the customer to make an initial payment immediately, usually for about 50% of the full contract price, with the remaining payment on satisfactory completion of software testing. The duration of contracts is typically about six months to one year.

The Chief Executive Officer (CEO) has consulted you about the foreign exchange problems the company has experienced. He is particularly concerned about a contract with a customer in Eastland, that Stand has just started working on. Stand is expecting to receive 2 million Eastland dollars (E$) in about six months' time, when the contract is expected to finish. The current spot rate of exchange is 2.5 Eastland dollars to £1. Current six-month interest rates are 5% per annum in the UK and 8% per annum in Eastland. The CEO thinks that it would be appropriate to hedge the currency exposure in the forward foreign exchange market, although he is not sure just how significant currency risk is for the company. He is aware that risk assessment is an element of good corporate governance, and that it would be inappropriate to ignore currency risk.

Required:

(a) Calculate how much Stand would receive if it hedged the currency exposure in the forward market. You may assume that the forward rate of exchange simply reflects the interest differential in the two countries (i.e. it reflects the Interest Rate Parity analysis of forward rates). Compare hedging with a forward contract with leaving the exposure unhedged. **(8 marks)**

(b) Explain the nature of the currency risk exposures faced by Stand. Explain how forward FX contracts, currency futures and currency options might be used to hedge currency exposures for Stand's business, but explain the problems that there might be with using them. **(20 marks)**

(c) Discuss other ways in which Stand might reduce its currency exposures, without using forward contracts, currency options or currency futures. **(6 marks)**

(d) With reference to a corporate governance code with which you are familiar, explain an appropriate organisation and management structure that Stand might use to assess the scale of its currency risks and control the risk. **(16 marks)**

(Total: 50 marks)

4 POOL PUBLISHING

(a) POOL Publishing is a publisher of books with a listing on the national stock exchange of the country in which it is based. The company has been profitable in recent years. However, although total annual profits have been growing at a good rate, the directors are searching for a strategy that will enable the company to achieve even better growth.

One proposal is to grow through acquisition. The directors believe that growth opportunities in book publishing in their country are limited. They also take the view that the company should be diversifying to reduce risk and should therefore be developing into a conglomerate organisation operating a range of different businesses in different industries. They have therefore been looking at four potential takeover targets:

(1) a foreign book publisher in a country where the same language is spoken;

(2) a magazine publisher;

(3) a company operating a chain of internet cafes;

(4) a company operating a chain of restaurants.

The last three companies in the list all operate in the same country as POOL.

The chairman has reported, however, that several of the major shareholders in the company have expressed strong misgivings about the strategy of the board. They believe that a diversification strategy of the kind proposed would be inadvisable and unnecessary.

Required:

(i) Explain how diversification reduces risk.

(ii) Explain why the diversification strategy of the POOL board might be inappropriate. **(15 marks)**

(b) The books that POOL Publishing publishes are specialist titles that have a short 'shelf life' and the demand for a new title occurs in the few weeks following publication. One of the major problems faced by POOL Publishing when they publish a new book is to decide how many copies to print. If they print too few copies to meet the demand, they will lose sales and profits, because there will be insufficient time for a reprint. If they print too many copies, they will be left with unsold inventories.

The managing director would like to use risk analysis to make decisions about how many copies of a new edition to print, but is not sure how this might be done.

The company plans to publish a new book in the next few weeks, and has to make a decision soon about the print quantity. The following information is available:

Print costs: The costs of printing and distribution will be fixed cost of $40,000 plus $1.50 variable costs for each book printed.

The book will be sold to the retail bookshops for $10 per copy.

Sales demand has been estimated as follows:

Demand quantity units	*Probability*
2,000	0.3
8,000	0.4
12,000	0.2
24,000	0.1

Required:

(i) If the company uses expected values to decide on the print quantity, calculate the expected profit or loss from publishing this book.

(ii) Recommend an alternative approach to the assessment of the risk and use your recommended approach to suggest how many copies should be printed.

(10 marks)

(c) POOL has a large number of customers. Almost five years ago, it outsourced its accounting to an external service provider, ITW. The accounting system is fully computerised, and is a bespoke system developed several years ago for POOL, and updated occasionally since that time.

The service from ITW has operated fairly well until recently, but ITW now appears to have difficulty in dealing with the rapidly-growing accounting requirements of POOL, as its business has expanded.

A decision has therefore been taken that the contract with ITW will not be renewed when it expires in six months' time. The accounting work will be given to a different outsourcing firm.

As management accountant and internal auditor for POOL, you have been asked to plan the changeover from ITW to the new outsourcing firm. In addition, in accordance with the contractual agreement with ITW, you will be required to carry out an audit of the accounts system before the changeover occurs.

Required:

Describe the potential risks that need to be considered in the changeover from ITW to the new outsourcing firm, and recommend measures to limit those risks. **(13 marks)**

(d) Explain the reasons for wanting to audit the system operated by ITW before the changeover, and suggest how computer-assisted audit techniques can be useful in carrying out such an audit. **(12 marks)**

(Total: 50 marks)

5 GHI GROUP (MAY 06 EXAM)

The GHI Group is a major listed travel company based in the UK, with a market capitalisation of £200 million, that specialises in the provision of budget-priced short and long haul package holidays targeted at the family market. The term 'package holiday' means that all flights, accommodation and overseas transfers are organised and booked by the tour operator on behalf of the customer.

The GHI Group encompasses a number of separate companies that include a charter airline, a chain of retail travel outlets, and several specialist tour operators who provide package holidays. Each subsidiary is expected to be profit generating, and each company's performance is measured by its residual income. The capital charges for each company are risk adjusted, and new investments are required to achieve a base hurdle rate of 10% before adjustment for risk.

The package holiday market is highly competitive, with fewer than five main players all trying to gain market share in an environment in which margins are continually threatened. The key threats include rising fuel prices, last minute discounting and the growth of the 'self managed' holiday, where individuals by-pass the travel retailers and use the Internet to book low cost flights and hotel rooms directly with the service providers. Also, customer requirements regarding product design and quality are continuously changing, thereby increasing the pressure on travel companies to devise appropriate strategies to maintain profitability.

Sales of long haul packages to North America are relatively static, but the number of people travelling to South East Asian destinations has fallen substantially following the 2004 tsunami disaster. Africa, New Zealand, Australia and certain parts of the Caribbean are the only long haul growth areas, but such growth is from a small base. Sales within the European region are shifting in favour of Eastern Mediterranean destinations such as Cyprus and Turkey as the traditional resorts of Spain and the Balearic Islands fall out of favour. Short 'city breaks' are also growing rapidly in popularity, reflecting higher spending power particularly amongst the over 50s.

The shift in patterns of demand has created some problems for GHI in a number of Eastern Mediterranean resorts over the last two summer seasons. There are not many hotels that meet the specified quality standards, and consequently there is fierce competition amongst travel operators to reserve rooms in them. In 2002 GHI took out a three-year contract (2003 – 2005 inclusive) for 10,000 beds in four major hotels over the peak holiday season of mid July – end of August. The contract terms required GHI to pay a 20% refundable deposit at the start of each calendar year, in return for the right to cancel unwanted rooms without penalty at just one week's notice. These contract terms were selected in preference to an alternative which required a 5% guarantee payment at the start of the calendar year, but with two weeks' notice for all cancellations, and the payment of a flat fee of £20 per week per cancelled room.

On three occasions in 2003, and six occasions in 2004, approximately 150 holidaymakers booked through GHI arrived at their hotels only to find that their rooms were already occupied by clients from a rival company. GHI's resort representative had severe problems relocating their customers, and over half of them were forced to move to inland hotels because all of the beach resorts were fully booked. The total compensation paid out by GHI to dissatisfied customers amounted to £135,000 in 2003 and £288,000 in 2004, and these payments were categorised as exceptional costs in the published accounts.

The problems encountered by GHI received extensive coverage in the UK media, a popular television travel programme provided assistance to holidaymakers to compile compensation claims. As a result of all of this adverse publicity, GHI decided in early 2005 to invest £8 million in purchasing two new hotels in the affected resorts. Sales forecasts indicate demand will grow at approximately 15% per year in the relevant resorts over the next five years. It is anticipated that the hotels will supply 70% of the group's accommodation requirements for the 2006 season. The package holidays to the GHI owned hotels will be sold as premium all-inclusive deals that include all food, soft drinks and local beers, wines and spirits. Such all-inclusive deals are not currently offered by other hotels in the target resorts.

Required:

(a) Identify and briefly discuss two risks that are likely to be faced by the GHI Group under each of the following categories:

- Financial
- Political
- Environmental
- Economic. **(16 marks)**

(b) Identify and evaluate risk impact upon GHI's financial statements and cash flow management of choosing to purchase its own overseas hotel properties as opposed to block booking rooms from local suppliers under the terms of the 2003 – 2005 contract. **(15 marks)**

(c) Identify and comment upon the changes in risks to GHI Group that might arise from the decision to sell premium all-inclusive deals, and suggest methods by which these risks might be monitored and controlled. **(8 marks)**

(d) Explain, using the investment in the new hotels as an example, how strategic decisions can simultaneously affect both performance measurement and capital allocation across a number of different companies within a group such as GHI. **(6 marks)**

(e) List the tasks that the internal audit department of GHI should have performed to ensure that the risks associated with the new hotel purchases are managed effectively. You should assume that its involvement commenced immediately the strategic decision was made to purchase overseas property – in other words, prior to identification of target sites. **(5 marks)**

(Total: 50 marks)

6 BLU (NOV 06 EXAM)

BLU is a stock market listed manufacturing company that has historically invested in computer numerical control (CNC) equipment to manufacture a range of electronic components for the telecommunications industry. BLU's strategic objective is to increase shareholder value through an annual increase in sales revenue of 15% and an annual increase in after-tax profits of 17.5%, both of which have been achieved over the past three years. This objective is strongly promoted within BLU and senior management bonuses are linked to the achievement of those targets.

In early 2006, the following financial justification was presented to the Board of Directors of BLU to support a proposal for capital investment in new CNC manufacturing equipment:

Projected cash flows for new equipment

	2007	*2008*	*2009*	*2010*	*2011*
all figures in £000					
Additional sales income	12,000	13,000	14,000	15,000	16,000
Additional variable costs	3,600	3,900	4,200	4,500	4,800
Additional fixed costs	1,500	1,500	1,500	1,500	1,500
Additional operating profit	6,900	7,600	8,300	9,000	9,700
Less taxation		2,070	2,280	2,490	2,700
Additional operating cash flow	6,900	5,530	6,020	6,510	7,000
Less additional working capital	1,000	300	400	500	600
Additional cash flow	5,900	5,230	5,620	6,010	6,400

Cost of capital	15%
Present value of future cash flows	19,398
Less capital cost of new equipment	17,500
Net present value	1,898

It is company policy to evaluate investments over the first five years only.

In March 2006, the Board approved the capital investment as it met its minimum criterion of a positive NPV using a cost of capital of 15%. There was one other project that was competing for funds at that time. This was for a new distribution system. However, this project was rejected by the Board because the NPV was lower than that of the CNC equipment.

Later in 2006, the audit committee asked a firm of consultants to review BLU's capital investment approval process and the information system that informs that process. As part of the first stage of the consultants' review, a draft report has been received by the Board that describes the process but as yet does not make any recommendations. The following are extracts from the consultants' draft report:

- BLU has a Market Research Department that looks at economic, industry and competitive factors affecting the market demand for its products in order to forecast market growth and likely market share during BLU's strategic planning horizon of five years. As part of its assessment, the Market Research Department asks the Sales Department to liaise with its largest customers to determine their likely requirements. The Sales Department forecasts sales based on its own knowledge of its market, including information from existing customers and its plan to win new customers. Having collated the available information, the Market Research Department provides the Production Department with annually updated forecasts of market demand for the next five years.

- The Production Department compares the Market Research Department's forecasts with its production capacity based on past experience of volumes, product mix and cycle times. The Production Department then determines the 'capacity gap' over the next five years, which it defines as the difference between the capacity required to satisfy forecasts of market demand and its existing practical capacity.
- Based on the capacity gap, the Production Department conducts a search for new CNC manufacturing equipment that will satisfy projected sales. A range of alternative suppliers is considered and prices for the equipment are compared, after which the Production Department identifies the supplier and the equipment deemed most suitable to bridge the capacity gap. The capital costs of new equipment and the capacity of this new equipment are calculated by the Production Department.
- The Finance Department accepts the forecasts of market demand from the Market Research Department and the cost and capacity information from the Production Department. It then uses historical cost information to update standard costs of labour and materials, with advice from the Human Resources and Purchasing Departments respectively about likely increases in the price of labour and materials. The Finance Department makes its own assessments about the additional working capital requirement.
- The Finance Department then completes a discounted cash flow calculation to assess the investment in new capital equipment, which is then presented to the Board of Directors as part of the annual budget cycle. BLU uses a cost of capital of 15% for the assessment of new capital expenditure proposals. This is the benchmark figure used by the Board, which has been in use for several years. Proposals that show a positive net present value are likely to be approved and where there are competing proposals for limited capital funds, the project with the highest NPV is usually selected. The Board's capital investment approval criteria are well known by BLU's managers.

Required:

***Note*: No calculations are required to answer this question.**

(a) Analyse the risks facing BLU in relation to:

(i) its investment appraisal and approval process; and

(ii) the information system feeding that process. **(20 marks)**

(b) Explain how, as an internal auditor, you would plan an audit of BLU's existing capital investment process (and the information system feeding that process), highlighting those elements of the process that you would pay particular attention to under a risk-based approach. **(10 marks)**

(c) Recommend to the Board of BLU the internal controls that should be introduced to improve BLU's capital investment process (including the information system feeding that process) and explain the benefits of your recommended controls.

(20 marks)

(Total: 50 marks)

7 Q FREEZE

Q Freeze (QF) is an autonomous division of MegaFoods. QF produces frozen foods which it sells and distributes to supermarket chains. It has an annual sales revenue of $80 million and some 2,000 employees located at its central factory and its regional distribution centres. QF currently operates in a stable market where there is excess production capacity. It is now about to launch a major strategic initiative by moving the bulk of production capacity into the relatively new but very fast growing market for frozen pre-cooked gourmet meals. The new products will be sold to supermarkets but have a much larger potential market, including delicatessens and restaurants. The marketing team at QF see the key success factors in the gourmet meals strategy as product innovation, quality, range and choice of product, responsiveness to changing consumer preference, fast, adaptive and efficient distribution, and flexible pricing policies.

Below is an extract from an information brochure, which is given to prospective recruits to the QF computer centre.

'QF has had computerised systems for many years. Systems are centralised at the QF computer centre and cover a typical range of applications; sales order entry, production control, distribution scheduling, procurement, sales and purchase accounting, monthly management accounting and payroll. Hardware is configured on the computer centre mainframe operating batch-based processing with some on-line access from terminals located in finance, production operations and at the regional distribution centres. There are a number of standalone personal computers (PCs) installed in the finance and marketing departments utilising PC based spreadsheet and database application software.

The computer centre is allocated an annual revenue budget based on the previous year plus or minus a percentage to cover cost inflation to finance operations and systems development. In addition, it receives a capital budget to cover hardware upgrades. Computer centre costs are charged out to departments based on apportionment rates for development, processing and on-line access. Proposals for new systems projects are vetted and prioritised by a steering committee chaired by the computer services manager. Projects that cannot be accommodated in the current year's budget have every opportunity to re-submit to the steering committee in the following budget year. PCs and associated equipment acquisition by user departments must be agreed by the steering committee.

The computer centre manager reports directly to the divisional managing director. The 70 full-time computer centre staff are organised into two units: (i) data processing operations and (ii) systems development and maintenance. All systems development is undertaken by the computer centre development team.'

Required:

(a) Advise the managing director at Q Freeze of the implications of embarking on the proposed 'frozen pre-cooked gourmet meal' strategy with the present structure of information technology. **(10 marks)**

(b) Explain how Q Freeze's information technology strategy might be adapted to align it to its new business strategy. **(12 marks)**

(c) Traditional management accounting activities have had their original scope broadened by the development of a variety of techniques that incorporate a growing recognition of the cost and quality issue in the management decision making process.

Required:

Explain how contemporary management accounting/management techniques such as Total Quality Management, Just In Time, Value Analysis, Activity Based Costing and The Balanced Scorecard could contribute towards the analysis of the relationship between costs and quality. **(15 marks)**

(d) A common approach to control theory for organisations is to look at the model of a cybernetic system, such as a thermostat mechanism.

Required:

(i) Explain the limitations of a cybernetic system as a feedback control model for organisations.

(*Note:* A diagram of a control system is **not** required.)

(ii) Explain the required conditions (pre-requisites) for the existence of control in an organisation, which are often derived from this approach to control theory.

(13 marks)

(Total: 50 marks)

8 ZZ BANK

ZZ Bank is a bank that is engaged in both a commercial banking and investment banking operations. Its investment banking division specialises in the provision of financial advice to corporate clients on mergers and acquisitions (M and A). It is also involved in a variety of trading activities in the equities, bonds and financial derivatives markets. Like many other investment banks, ZZ Bank seeks to attract high-quality staff with large basic salaries and very attractive incentive schemes. Annual cash bonuses are based on performance for the previous year, and are often well in excess of 100% of basic salary for successful individuals.

Having attended a banking conference recently on risks in banking, the bank's chief executive is concerned about risk management generally, including reputation risk and business continuity risk (disaster recovery risk).

He is particularly concerned about a lack of adequate internal control in the bank. Some trading activities have incurred large losses, and others have been investigated by the financial services regulator following suspicions of malpractice by traders. The chief executive is concerned that adverse reports about the bank in the press might damage the bank's reputation, and result in the loss of some M and A clients to other banks.

He is aware that the bank's internal control system is not as effective as it should be. As a first step towards addressing the problem, he has asked for an assessment of the scope of the potential problems.

Required:

(a) As internal auditor of ZZ Bank, prepare a report for the chief executive explaining the factors that might contribute towards a weak internal control system and a breakdown in controls. **(20 marks)**

(b) Explain the nature of disaster recovery risk (or business continuity risk) in banking, and explain the measures that the bank might take to address this risk. **(10 marks)**

(c) Explain how the bank might classify its risks for the purpose of control and monitoring. **(10 marks)**

(d) The bank's major shareholders have persuaded the bank to produce an annual social and environmental report, as a matter of good corporate governance. Explain the purpose of a social and environmental report and what it might contain, and suggest why it might contribute to good corporate governance. **(10 marks)**

(Total: 50 marks)

9 MAKERS

Makers is a large company in the building and construction industry. One of its largest divisions is engaged in large construction projects in many countries. It also has divisions that operate in the residential house-building industry, and in the manufacture of building materials, such as windows and doors.

The construction division has received an invitation from a foreign customer to submit a fixed price quotation for building an extension to a power plant. The management accountant has been asked to assist with the preparation of a cost estimate, in order to quote a price for the contract. The team responsible for preparing the cost estimate are well aware of the risks of construction difficulties and delays, and have tried to allow for these risks in their estimates.

The three major risks that have been identified are delay in starting the project, site clearance difficulties, and delays in construction work after site clearance. The estimated costs are as follows:

Cost item	*Expected cost*	*Extra cost if start is delayed*	*Extra cost if site clearance difficulties*	*Extra cost if delay in construction*	*Worst possible cost*
	$ million	$ million	$ million	$ million	$ million
Materials	6.0	1.0	0.5	0.0	7.5
Own labour	8.0	2.0	2.0	0.5	12.5
Sub-contractors	9.0	1.0	3.0	1.0	14.0
	23.0	4.0	5.5	1.5	34.0
Estimated probability		0.20	0.10	0.20	

When quoting for fixed-price contracts, the company likes to add 25% to cover overheads and provide a profit.

However, at east two other contracting firms have been invited to tender for the contract, and it is almost certain that if the company submits a quotation of $42.5 million to do the work (the worst expected cost of $34 million plus 25%), it will not be awarded the contract. The contract would take about three years to complete.

Required:

(a) Discuss the factors to consider in deciding on a price for the contract and recommend a price to quote, giving your reasons. **(20 marks)**

(b) If the contract is awarded to the company, there will be a risk of costs exceeding the expected amount. Discuss the measures the construction division should take to limit these risks. **(15 marks)**

(c) If the company wins the contract, it will be paid in dollars, but a large proportion of its costs will be incurred in the domestic currency of the customer's country.

There is some concern about the credit risk and foreign exchange risk in the contract.

Required:

Explain the nature of these risks and suggest measures that might be taken to limit them. **(10 marks)**

(d) Makers has a division that manufactures windows and doors. Its management applies a philosophy of continuous improvement (or kaizen). Competition within the industry is intense, and net profit margins are low.

It has been suggested that target costing would be an appropriate technique within this manufacturing environment, as a means of protecting profit margins.

Required:

Explain with reasons whether you consider that target costing would be appropriate for the division, and whether it would contribute towards continuous improvement.

(5 marks)

(Total: 50 marks)

10 RG

RG manufactures industrial glues and solvents in a single large factory in the UK. Approximately 400 different inputs are used to produce the 35 specialist outputs, which range from ultra-strong glues used in aircraft manufacture to high-impact adhesives that are required on construction sites.

Two years ago, with the company only just breaking even, the directors recognised the need for more information to control the business. To assist them with their strategic control of the business, they decided to establish a MIS. This is now operational but provides only the following limited range of information to the directors via their networked computer system:

(1) A summary business plan for this and the next two years. The plan includes details of the expected future incomes and expenditure on existing product lines. It was produced by a new member of the accounting department without reference to past production data.

(2) Inventory balances on individual items of raw materials, finished goods etc. This report is at a very detailed level and comprises 80% of the output from the MIS itself.

(3) A summary of changes in total demand for glues and solvents in the market place for the last five years. This information is presented as a numerical summary in six different sections. Each section takes up one computer screen so only one section can be viewed at a time.

The company's treasurer has a cash forecasting and treasury management system, separate from the MIS. The company trades with entities in several European countries. Trade deals over the next three months are shown below. Assume that it is now 20 April.

	Two months time		*Three months time*	
	Receipts	*Payments*	*Receipts*	*Payments*
France	–	€393, 265	€491, 011	€60,505
Germany	–	–	€890, 271	€1,997,651
Denmark	–	–	Kr 8.6m	–

Foreign exchange rates

	DKroner/£1	*Euro(€)/£1*
Spot	10.68 – 10.71	1.439 – 1.465
Two months forward	10.74 – 10.77	1.433 – 1.459
Three months forward	10.78 – 10.83	1.431 – 1.456

Annual interest rates (valid for 2 months or 3 months)

	Borrowing %	*Investing* %
United Kingdom	7.50	5.50
Euro zone	5.75	3.50
Denmark	8.00	6.00

Futures market rates:

Three-month euro contracts (125,000 euro contract size)

Contracts are for buying or selling euros. Futures prices are in £ per euro.

June	0.6964
September	0.6983
December	0.7013

Required:

(a) (i) Comment on the weaknesses in the information currently being provided to the directors of the company by the MIS.

(ii) Suggest how the information may be improved, with particular reference to other outputs which the MIS might usefully provide to the directors. **(16 marks)**

(b) Explain briefly the risks to which the company would be exposed in each of the following situations, including any currency risk exposures.

(i) The company issues an annual price list for its products in euros during January each year, for its customers in Europe.

(ii) A Japanese competitor has just begun to distribute its products in Europe and the UK.

(iii) RG is planning to move one half of its production capacity to Spain. **(9 marks)**

(c) Explain how the forward market, money market and currency futures market could be used to devise a foreign exchange hedging strategy for RG for its currency exposures.

Note: Denmark is not a member of the eurozone.

Transaction costs and margin requirements may be ignored for this part of the question. Basis risk may be assumed to be zero at the time the contracts are closed out. Futures contracts may be assumed to mature at the month end. **(15 marks)**

(d) Successive daily prices on the futures market for a June contract which you have SOLD are:

Selling price	0.6916
Day 1	0.6930
Day 2	0.6944
Day 3	0.6940

Initial margins are £1,000 per contract. Variation margin is 100% of the initial margin.

Spot exchange rates may be assumed to not change significantly during these three days.

Required:

(i) For each of the three days, show the effect on your cash flow of the price changes of the contract.

(ii) Discuss the advantages and disadvantages of forward contracts and currency futures for hedging against foreign exchange risk. **(10 marks)**

(Total: 50 marks)

11 IDAN (MAY 05 EXAM)

Company overview

IDAN is a large banking and financial services group that is listed on both the London Stock Exchange and the New York Stock Exchange. The group has over 20 million customers throughout the world and operates in 35 countries on four continents. The IDAN Group is composed of a mix of retail and commercial businesses that include corporate and investment banking, private banking and commercial banking.

Trends within the Financial Services Sector

The Board of Directors of IDAN is aware that a number of trends within the sector will require the bank to substantially re-design a number of its operating and information systems and review the nature of the interface between the internal audit and risk management functions. Current issues that are having an impact on the financial services sector include:

- A new European Union law requiring banks to provide details of interest paid on personal savings accounts held by non-residents. A withholding tax of 15% is to be imposed on such income and details must be sent by the bank to the tax authorities in the EU country where the recipient resides.
- Forecast rises in interest rates over the next two years.
- The elimination within the UK of the use of personal signatures as the authorisation method for credit and debit card transactions and their replacement with personal identification (PIN) numbers.
- The increasing use, by personal customers, of both telephone and internet banking services. Over 40% of bill payments, standing order amendments and balance transfers by such customers were processed in this way during the last 12 months compared with 28% the previous year.
- A growth in the number of cases being sent to the financial ombudsman or the financial industry regulator relating to claims of mis-selling or incorrect advice on the part of financial services companies in the supply of a range of savings and investment products.
- As a result of threats of terrorist activity, money laundering legislation has been introduced or tightened in all of the countries in which IDAN has banking operations.

Analysis by type of business

(i) Net assets

	Year ended	
	31 December 20Y0	*31 December 20X0*
	£m	£m
Corporate and investment banking	15,824	12,286
Personal financial services	9,250	6,400
Private banking	2,320	1,755
Commercial banking	11,186	9,364
	38,580	29,805

(ii) Profit on ordinary activities before tax

	Year ended	
	31 December 20Y0	*31 December 20X0*
	£m	£m
Corporate and investment banking	3,416	2,949
Personal financial services	2,427	1,684
Private banking	116	85
Commercial banking	3,356	3,558
	9,315	8,276

(iii) Within the commercial banking portfolio, the allowance for credit losses equalled one per cent of the assets compared with two and a half per cent in personal financial services and private banking.

(iv) Profits from Private Banking are viewed as being influenced by a range of factors including the state of the world economy and sentiment and performance in the equity markets. The current outlook for the global economy remains uncertain and depressed equity markets are expected to recover slowly over the coming financial year.

Required:

(a) Discuss the main categories of risk that are faced by a bank such as IDAN and the advantages of risk categorisation in the design of a risk management system. **(10 marks)**

(b) For every one of the six issues identified in the question, recommend the controls that might be introduced to minimise IDAN's exposure to such risks. **(15 marks)**

(c) Compare and contrast the roles played by internal audit and risk management in organisations. Discuss the likely nature of the interaction between these two activities. **(10 marks)**

The performance of the Managing Directors of the four types of business within IDAN is evaluated on the basis of the profits of their individual businesses. It has now been suggested by the Board that the strategy of the group, future investment opportunities and the profitability of each business should be evaluated against a risk-adjusted hurdle rate.

Required:

(d) Critically discuss this suggestion by making reference to the information provided in the question. **(15 marks)**

(Total: 50 marks)

12 VCF (NOV 05 EXAM)

VCF is a small listed company that designs and installs high technology computer numerical control capital equipment used by multinational manufacturing companies. VCF is located in one Pacific country, but almost 90% of its sales are exported. VCF has sales offices in Europe, Asia, the Pacific, Africa, and North and South America and employs about 300 staff around the world.

VCF has annual sales of $200 million but the sales value of each piece of equipment sold is about $2 million so the sales volume is relatively low. Sales are always invoiced in the currency of the country where the equipment is being installed. The time between the order being taken and the final installation is usually several months. However, a deposit is taken when the order is placed and progress payments are made by the customer before shipment and upon delivery, with the final payment being made after installation of the equipment.

The company has international patents covering its technology and invests heavily in research and development (R&D, about 15% of sales revenue) and marketing costs to develop export markets (about 25% of sales revenue). VCF's manufacturing operations are completely outsourced in its home country and the cost of sales is about 20%. The balance of costs is for installation, servicing and administration, amounting to about 15% of sales revenue. Within each of these cost classifications the major expenses (other than direct costs) are salaries for staff, all of whom are paid well above the industry average, rental of premises in each location and travel costs. Area managers are located in each sales office and have responsibility for achieving sales, installing equipment and maintaining high levels of after-sales service and customer satisfaction.

Although the head office is very small, most of the R&D staff are located in the home country, along with purchasing and logistics staff responsible for liaising with the outsource suppliers and a small accounting team that is primarily concerned with monthly management accounts and end of year financial statements.

VCF has a majority shareholding held by Jack Viktor, an entrepreneur who admits to taking high risks, both personally and in business. The Board of four is effectively controlled by Viktor who is both Chairman and Chief Executive. The three other directors were appointed by Viktor. They are his wife, who has a marketing role in the business, and two non-executive directors, one an occasional consultant to VCF and the other a long-time family friend. Board meetings are held quarterly and are informal affairs, largely led by Viktor's verbal review of sales activity.

Viktor is a dominating individual who exercises a high degree of personal control, often bypassing his area managers. Because the company is controlled by him, Viktor is not especially concerned with short-term profits but with the long-term. He emphasises two objectives: sales growth to generate increased market share and cash flow; and investment in R&D to ensure the long-term survival of VCF by maintaining patent protection and a technological lead over its competitors.

Viktor is in daily contact with all his offices by telephone. He travels extensively around the world and has an excellent knowledge of VCF's competitors and customers. He uses a limited number of non-financial performance measures, primarily concerned with sales, market share, quality and customer satisfaction. Through his personal contact and his twin objectives, Viktor encourages a culture committed to growth, continual innovation, and high levels of customer satisfaction. This is reinforced by high salary levels, but Viktor readily dismisses those staff not committed to his objectives.

The company has experienced rapid growth over the last 10 years and is very profitable although cash flow is often tight. A high margin is achieved because VCF is able to charge its customers premium prices. The equipment sold by VCF enables faster production and better quality than its competitors can offer.

Viktor has little time for traditional accounting. Product costing is not seen as valuable because the cost of sales is relatively low and most costs incurred by VCF, particularly R&D and export marketing costs, are incurred a long time in advance of sales being made. R&D costs are not capitalised in VCF's balance sheet.

Although budgets are used for expense control and monthly management accounts are produced, they have little relevance to Viktor who recognises the fluctuations in profit caused by the timing of sales of low volume but high value capital equipment. Viktor sees little value in comparing monthly profit figures against budgets because sales are erratic. However, Viktor depends heavily on a spreadsheet to manage VCF's cash flow by using sensitivity analysis against his sales and cash flow projections. Cash flow is a major business driver and is controlled tightly using the spreadsheet model.

The major risks facing VCF have been identified by Viktor as:

- competitor infringement of patents, which VCF always meets by instituting legal actions;
- adverse movements in the exchange rate between the home country and VCF's export markets, which VCF treats as an acceptable risk given that historically gains and losses have balanced each other out;
- the reduction in demand for his equipment due to economic recession;
- a failure of continued R&D investment to maintain technological leadership; and
- a failure to control costs.

Viktor considers that the last three of these risks are addressed by his policy of outsourcing manufacture and continuous personal contact with staff, customers and competitors.

Required:

(a) Identify and evaluate the existing controls within VCF (including those applied by Viktor). **(20 marks)**

(b) Write a report to the Board of VCF recommending improvements to the company's corporate governance, risk management strategy and internal controls.

Note: You should use examples from the case to illustrate your answer. **(20 marks)**

(c) Identify the exchange risks faced by VCF and recommend the methods that could be used to manage those risks. **(10 marks)**

(Total: 50 marks)

Section 2

SECTION B-TYPE QUESTIONS

MANAGEMENT CONTROL SYSTEMS

13 SMILE TRAINING

Smile Training is a training organisation specialising in training sales and marketing executives and purchasing executives for a number of professional examinations. The company has four regional offices, but its main operations are in the capital city, where it also has its head office and administration team. The CEO of Smile Training is himself an experienced trainer, who takes a personal interest in each of the trainers employed by the company. He believes that the key to profitability is to deliver successful training programmes to a standard level of a high quality.

There is a risk to the company's reputation and business from unsatisfactory training programmes. The CEO is aware of several different problems that have affected quality. He has been told that many trainers employed by the company also do some training work for other organisations at weekends and during evenings, although these organisations are not direct competitors of Smile Training. There have also been instances where a trainer has failed to turn up for a course, subsequently claiming to have been ill but unable to contact head office at short notice. Although much of the feedback from students is favourable, there are occasions when a course has been unpopular and the level of complaints has been high.

You are the management accountant of Smile Training. During a recent meeting of the risk management committee which you attended, the consensus view of the meeting was that the risks from poor quality training were unacceptably high and getting worse. You expressed the view that quality could be improved within the framework of a control system for the management of the organisation. The CEO is interested in your views, and has asked for a report on the subject.

Required:

Prepare a report for the CEO, setting out the features of a control system you would recommend for managing the organisation, explaining how you think that each of your recommendations should help to improve training quality standards and reduce the risk from poor quality. **(25 marks)**

14 WAL

You have recently been appointed to lead the management accounting department of WAL, a small engineering company engaged in the manufacture of precision parts. The market in which the company sells its products is small, and WAL faces severe competition. Owing to the production facilities available, the company is able to undertake only small-scale engineering work. Large-scale engineering jobs are turned away, as the company does not possess the manufacturing facilities to undertake them. At best it can act only as agent for another contractor to do the work.

The board of WAL is aware that there has been an increase in the volume of work being turned away. This is particularly frustrating as the company is unable to utilise its capacity to the fullest extent all the time. The profitability of WAL has increased steadily over the last few years. Nevertheless, the board of directors believes that it could increase profitability still further by expanding operations to carry out the larger-scale work that is currently being turned away.

Budgetary control and standard costing information has for many years been provided as the sole output of the management accounting department. The previous management accountant prided himself on the punctuality and comprehensiveness of the reports produced. Each job is priced by adding a percentage to its total cost, calculated in accordance with the company's standard costing procedures. The annual cost budget is split into monthly parts and flexed to take account of a particular period's actual production. Monthly cost variances, comprising those for direct materials, direct labour, variable and fixed production overheads, are produced and provided to the relevant manager. In addition, sales price and volume variances are produced each period by the management accounting department.

The company does not have a marketing department, although new customers are obtained from advertising within professional engineering journals and by attendance at trade shows.

Required:

(a) Comment critically on the current management accounting system as an information system for providing control information to management and information for the directors to assist with strategic decision making. **(13 marks)**

(b) State and justify what changes you would make in providing information, which facilitates strategic planning in the company. Within your answer, describe what financial and non-financial information you would supply which is different from that already provided. **(12 marks)**

(Total: 25 marks)

15 CDE (MAY 06 EXAM)

CDE is a manufacturer of almost 100 hundred different automotive components that are sold in both large and small quantities on a just-in-time (JIT) basis to the major vehicle assemblers. Business is highly competitive and price sensitive. The company is listed on the stock exchange but CDE's share performance has not matched that of its main competitors.

CDE's management accounting system uses a manufacturing resource planning (MRP II) system to control production scheduling, inventory movements and inventory control, and labour and machine utilisation. The accounting department carries out a detailed annual budgeting exercise, determines standard costs for labour and materials, and allocates production overhead on the basis of machine utilisation. Strict accounting controls over labour and material costs are managed by the detailed recording of operator and machine timesheets and raw material movements, and by calculating and investigating all significant variances.

While the information from the MRP II system is useful to management, there is an absence of integrated data about customer requirements and suppliers. Some information is contained within spreadsheets and databases held by the Sales and Purchasing departments respectively. One result of this lack of integration is that inventories are higher than they should be in a JIT environment.

The managers of CDE (representing functional areas of sales, production, purchasing, finance and administration) believe that, while costs are strictly controlled, the cost of the accounting department is excessive and significant savings need to be made, even at the expense of data accuracy. Managers believe that there may not be optimum use of the production capacity to generate profits and cash flow and improve shareholder value. CDE's management wants to carry out sensitivity and other analyses of strategic alternatives, but this is difficult when the existing management accounting system is focused on control rather than on decision support.

Required:

(a) (i) Outline the different types of information system available to manufacturing firms like CDE.

(ii) Recommend with reasons the information system that would be appropriate to CDE's needs. **(10 marks)**

(b) Given the business environment that CDE faces, and the desire of management to reduce the cost of accounting:

(i) critically evaluate the relevance of the current management accounting system; and

(ii) recommend how the system should be improved. **(15 marks)**

(Total: 25 marks)

16 MOVE

MOVE is a transport company that operates train and bus services. Both services rely on large subsidies from the government, and profitability is low.

The train services are mainly long-distance services across the country. MOVE provides the trains, but pays another national rail service company for the hire of the rail network that it uses (tracks, signalling equipment and railway stations). There are several train service companies such as MOVE that make use of the same network. These companies also pay hire charges.

The bus services are national express services that operate between major cities and towns. MOVE owns or leases its buses, and pays a rental to local government authorities for the bus stations that it uses.

The company's senior management have set performance targets for each division that attempt to balance financial and non-financial targets, and short-term and longer-term objectives. Both divisions are given annual profit targets. Both divisions also have targets for the volume of passengers. This is expressed as a target for the number of passenger-miles carried as a percentage of full capacity. The railway services division also has a minimum target for the percentage of train services operated that reach their destination on time. This is regarded by the government as a key target of performance for all train services that it subsidises. MOVE's managers are rewarded with an annual bonus for achieving or exceeding their targets.

The management accounting system is based at the company's head office. Monthly control reports for each division show the full cost of each service operated, and the profit or loss of each service, compared with the budget.

Required:

(a) Discuss the factors to consider in deciding whether the management accounting system of MOVE should be re-located out of head office, and replaced by two separate management accounting systems in each of the divisions. **(7 marks)**

(b) Discuss the behavioural problems that might arise with the bonus system. **(8 marks)**

(c) The Finance Director believes that the current full costing system is inadequate for management's requirements, and that it would be more appropriate to introduce an activity based costing (ABC) scheme. Evaluate whether an ABC scheme might be appropriate for the company. **(5 marks)**

(d) Many of the costs incurred by MOVE are regarded as fixed costs. The marketing director has therefore argued that the main focus of monthly management control reports should be on revenues, and not costs. Discuss, giving your reasons whether you agree or disagree with this view. **(5 marks)**

(Total: 25 marks)

17 SPECIFIC PERFORMANCE MEASURES

To focus on specific performance measures may lead employees or managers to take action which is not in the best interests of the organisation. Examples of problems which may occur are:

(i) over-emphasis on the short term;

(ii) over-emphasis on the achievement of specific measures;

(iii) over-simplification of the meaning of specific measures;

(iv) deliberate distortion.

Required:

(a) Expand briefly on each of the above problems, giving a specific example to illustrate how each may occur. **(12 marks)**

(b) Identify and comment on any FOUR actions which may be implemented in order to overcome problems in the operation of a performance measurement system. **(6 marks)**

(c) Explain the issues to consider when structuring a management accounting control system so that it identifies the appropriate control centres within the organisation. **(7 marks)**

(Total: 25 marks)

18 JKL

JKL is planning to introduce a new computer system throughout the organisation, designed around an intranet and shared databases. One of the features of the new system currently under discussion is the new management accounting module.

The CEO believes that the new system offers an opportunity to cut back the costs of the accounting department, particularly in management accounting. He argues that:

(1) all inputs to the management system can be either extracted from the financial accounting system or entered directly into the system by non-accounting staff;

(2) costs can be analysed automatically, without the need for manual intervention;

(3) standard management reports and control reports can be produced automatically;

(4) the system will enable managers to interrogate the files directly, and obtain all the information they require on demand;

(5) budgets can be prepared using standard spreadsheets that will be available to management.

He believes that the costs of the management accounting function are too high, and that the system fails to produce information of a sufficiently high quality.

He has challenged you to explain why a management accounting function might still be necessary when the new computer system is designed and introduced.

Required:

(a) Prepare a memo for the CEO giving your views, with reasons, about whether the management accounting function will continue to be needed. **(13 marks)**

(b) Explain the cost of quality as it can be applied to a management accounting system. **(12 marks)**

(Total: 25 marks)

19 SUNDOWN SUPERMARKETS

Sundown Supermarkets is experiencing trading difficulties; its profits are falling and it is losing market share to rival supermarket companies. These rival companies are able to offer lower prices to customers, and a wider range of products, or have a better reputation for good-quality products.

Sundown has also suffered from severe operating difficulties with the introduction of a new computerised distribution system for scheduling the delivery of goods from the central warehouses or depots to the stores. As a result, most stores suffer frequently from non-availability of product items on the shelf.

The CEO of Sundown believes the way forward is to get prices down in order to compete more successfully. In addition, he recognises the need to resolve the problems with the distribution system, and for many stores to improve their image. Market research has shown that for many customers, their 'experience' in Sundown's stores compares badly with the stores of rival supermarkets. In Sundown, they experience a shortage of shopping trolleys, a shortage of in-store assistants and long waits at the check-out desks.

The CEO also believes that spending on advertising and in-store sales promotions must be monitored carefully, to ensure that it remains effective. Sundown has four major operating divisions: stores, distribution and warehousing, buying and marketing. The marketing department is responsible for advertising and in-stores promotions (which are operated on a national scale).

The current management accounting system does not provide management with all the control information needed to manage all these aspect of the business effectively.

Required:

Describe the features of a management accounting system that would provide management with the control information needed to improve the performance of Sundown Supermarkets, in both the short-term and the long-term. **(25 marks)**

20 TRADITIONAL MANAGEMENT ACCOUNTING

The modern manufacturing environment is characterised by more flexibility, a readiness to meet customers' requirements, smaller batches, continuous improvements and an emphasis on quality. In such circumstances, traditional management accounting performance measures are, at best, irrelevant and, at worst, misleading.

Required:

(a) Discuss the above statement, providing specific examples to support or refute the views expressed. **(12 marks)**

(b) Explain in what ways management accountants can adapt the services they provide to the new environment. **(13 marks)**

(Total: 25 marks)

RISK AND INTERNAL CONTROL

21 DOCTORS' PRACTICE (NOV 05 EXAM)

A large doctors' practice, with six partners and two practice nurses, has decided to increase its income by providing day surgery facilities. The existing building would be extended to provide room for the surgical unit and storage facilities for equipment and drugs. The aim is to offer patients the opportunity to have minor surgical procedures conducted by a doctor at their local practice, thus avoiding any unfamiliarity and possible delays to treatment that might result from referral to a hospital. Blood and samples taken during the surgery will be sent away to the local hospital for testing but the patient will get the results from their doctor at the practice. It is anticipated that the introduction of the day surgery facility will increase practice income by approximately 20%.

Required:

(a) Identify the additional risks that the doctors' practice may expect to face as a consequence of the introduction of the new facility, and explain how a model such as CIMA's risk management cycle might be used to understand and control such risks. **(12 marks)**

(b) Explain the meaning of the term 'risk appetite' and discuss who should take responsibility for defining that appetite in the context of the scenario outlined above. **(5 marks)**

(c) Critically discuss the role of systems-based internal auditing in relation to the assessment of risk management procedures in any organisation. **(8 marks)**

(Total: 25 marks)

22 QUANTIFYING RISK EXPOSURES

Entity V is an international company that is growing rapidly. Annual sales volume has been increasing at the rate of over 20% each year for the last six years, and strong growth is expected to continue in the future. The management of the company is concerned, however, about the increasing risks from irrecoverable debts. In order to increase sales growth, Entity V is offering more generous credit terms and giving credit to higher-risk customers.

The company assesses its credit risk using probabilities. It has estimated that the risks of non-payment by customers are as follows:

Probability	*Irrecoverable debts*
0.2	0.5% of monthly sales
0.5	2.0% of monthly sales
0.2	3.0% of monthly sales
0.1	6.0% of monthly sales

These probabilities are reviewed regularly. They are used to estimate the expected value of irrecoverable debts each month, and this expected value is included as an expense in the monthly budget.

The Finance Director believes that this is a satisfactory method of quantifying credit risk and the company's exposure to risk. The chairman of the risk committee disagrees. He believes that expected values on their own are not a suitable way of assessing and monitoring risks.

Required:

With reference to Entity V assess the value of using expected values to quantify and monitor risk exposures, and suggest additional methods of credit risk assessment that might be used to improve the credit risk management system. **(20 marks)**

23 LANDMASS PLC

Landmass plc is a UK property company that is planning to obtain a listing for its shares on the London stock market. The directors are aware, however, that the company will be required to comply with the corporate governance requirements including an annual review by the directors of the adequacy of its risk management systems.

At the moment, the company does not have any formal risk management system, and the directors need advice on how such a system might be established. They have been informed that the risks of the business should be categorised, but they do not know how this might be done.

The company operates in three different areas:

(1) It manages business property which it rents to business customers under short-term and medium-term lease arrangements.

(2) It buys and re-sells office property and property used by retail businesses (such as shopping arcades).

(3) It has a subsidiary that specialises in building high-quality residential property.

Required:

(a) Explain how risks might be categorised by companies, and suggest the risk categories that might be used by Landmass. **(9 marks)**

(b) Recommend how Landmass might establish a risk management system prior to its listing and the introduction of its shares to trading on the stock exchange. **(16 marks)**

(Total: 25 marks)

24 DRUM

As internal auditor of DRUM, you have identified the following items likely to have a bearing on your assessment of risk and internal control.

(1) On the recommendation of its non-executive chairman, DRUM has invested a substantial amount of money in buying a minority stake in STK, a private company of which the chairman is the chief executive officer and major shareholder.

(2) A development project XC34 is behind schedule. Unexpected problems have arisen which increase substantially the cost of development and the production costs of the new product that is being developed. In the balance sheet at the end of the last year, $150,000 of development costs were recognised as an asset for the project. A further $75,000 has been spent in the year just ended. The original budget for the project was $180,000.

(3) A new performance-related bonus scheme was introduced for senior management in the current year. In total, 25% of the increase in company's reported profits before tax, in excess of the previous year's profits, will be set aside to provide for bonuses for management. No bonus, however, will be paid if profits in the current year do not exceed the previous year's profits.

(4) To finance investment in new projects, DRUM has taken out a large bank loan. The loan agreement states that the company's gearing ratio (the proportion of loan capital to equity capital) must not exceed 30%. Last year's financial statements showed a gearing ratio of 20% and the latest monthly management accounts show a gearing ratio of 25%.

Required:

For each of the items (1) to (4) above:

(a) explain the nature of the actual or potential risk; **(12 marks)**

(b) explain how you might propose to carry out audit checks or investigations on the effectiveness of controls. **(13 marks)**

Assume each item is potentially material. Consider each item separately. **(Total: 25 marks)**

25 EXPORT-LED GROWTH

RED is a successful company manufacturing electronic equipment. Until recently, most of its sales were to customers in its domestic market, with just a few export sales. Recently, however, the board of directors of RED have approved a new export-led strategy for growth. The company is planning to grow sales and profits substantially by targeting new markets in other countries.

The targeted markets are:

(1) the US and countries in Western Europe;

(2) countries with developing economies.

The finance director of RED is concerned about the large amount of working capital required to finance the increase in trade. He has estimated that for every $1 of working capital needed to finance domestic sales, the company will need $2.50 to finance the same volume of export sales. He has also expressed concerns about the lack of experience of the credit assessment team in the accounts department in carrying out credit assessments on customers in other countries. He believes that credit risks will be much higher with customers in the new markets.

The risk management committee of RED will consider various risks associated with export sales at its next meeting, and as management accountant you have been asked to provide a discussion paper for the meeting.

Required:

Prepare a discussion paper for the meeting in which you:

(a) explain why credit risks might be higher with export sales; **(8 marks)**

(b) recommend methods of reducing these credit risks; **(10 marks)**

(c) describe other risks associated with an export sales strategy, that the company should evaluate, control and monitor. **(7 marks)**

(Total: 25 marks)

26 REGIONAL POLICE FORCE

A regional police force has the following corporate objectives:

- to reduce crime and disorder;
- to promote community safety;
- to contribute to delivering justice and maintaining public confidence in the law.

The force aims to achieve these objectives by continuously improving its resources management to meet the needs of its stakeholders. It has no stated financial objective other than to stay within its funding limits.

The force is mainly public-funded but, like other regional forces, it has some commercial operations, for example policing football matches when the football clubs pay a fee to the police force for its officers working overtime. The police force uses this money to supplement the funding it receives from the government.

Required:

(a) Discuss the risks to the achievement of the corporate objectives of the regional police force. **(12 marks)**

(b) Discuss the risks associated with a regional structure for the national police force. **(7 marks)**

(c) Describe the types of internal controls that might be applied by the police force in order to assist with the achievement of its objectives. **(6 marks)**

(Total: 25 marks)

27 FRANCHISING AGREEMENTS (PILOT PAPER)

ZX is a UK-based retailer and manufacturer that also owns a limited number of outlets in the USA, but is anxious to expand internationally via the use of franchising agreements. The enterprise plans to open five franchised shops in each of France, Italy, Germany, Belgium and Holland over the course of the next twelve months. ZX will provide loan finance to assist individuals wishing to purchase a franchise, the average cost of which will be €100,000. Loans will also be available (up to a maximum of 50% of the purchase price) to cover the cost of the franchisee acquiring suitable freehold or leasehold premises. The total sum required for the property loan facility is estimated by the treasurer of ZX to equal €4.8 million. The opportunity cost of capital in the UK is 10% per annum but, in recognition of the lower rates of interest available in the Eurozone, ZX will only charge the franchisees a fixed rate of 7.0% each year on all loans. Repayments will be made in equal Euro-denominated instalments.

ZX charges commission to the franchisees at a rate of 1% of sales revenue, and also earns a net margin of 12% (of retail value) on the products supplied to the outlets from its UK manufacturing plant.

Planned sales from the new European outlets equal €26 million over the next twelve months, but the enterprise recognises that its profits are dependent upon both sales revenue and the extent of loan defaults amongst franchisees (if any). Estimates of the likelihood of a range of scenarios are detailed below:

Probability	*Sales*	*Number of loan defaults*	*Comment*
0.1	10% below plan	Two	Economic difficulties reduce sales and cause problems for some franchisees
0.3	20% below plan	Four	Severe economic problems lead to low sales and higher loan defaults
0.4	As per plan	Zero	'Base case'
0.2	As per plan	One	The weak German economy causes problems for one franchisee

Loan default is assumed to mean total write-off and ZX expects 80% of the new franchisees to take full advantage of the loan facilities offered to them.

The current Euro: Sterling exchange rate is €1.3939/£1 and the Euro is expected to strengthen against Sterling by 5% over the next 12 months.

In addition to the cash required to fund the foreign loan facility, a further £3.65 million of working capital will be required for the expansion project and the Treasury Department of ZX requires a minimum annualised return of 15% on all overseas projects.

Required:

(a) Use the table of possible scenarios given above to calculate the expected Sterling value of the additional profit that ZX will earn if all the store openings are completed as planned and the foreign exchange rate forecast is fulfilled. (You should use the average exchange rate over the year for the calculation.)

You should evaluate whether this profit yields the return required for international operations. **(7 marks)**

(b) Discuss the risks that ZX might face in choosing to expand into Europe via the use of franchising. **(8 marks)**

(c) Evaluate methods of managing/minimising the risks involved in granting Euro denominated loans to the franchisees. **(10 marks)**

(Total: 25 marks)

28 POLITICAL RISK

The finance department of Beela Electronics has been criticised by the company's board of directors for not undertaking an assessment of the political risk of the company's potential direct investments in Africa. The board has received an interim report from a consultant that provides assessment of the factors affecting political risk in three African countries. The report assess key variables on a scale of –10 to + 10, with –10 the worst possible score and +10 the best.

	Country 1	*Country 2*	*Country 3*
Economic growth	5	8	4
Political stability	3	–4	5
Risk of nationalism	3	0	4
Cultural compatibility	6	2	4
Inflation	7	–6	6
Currency convertibility	–2	5	–4
Investment incentives	–3	7	3
Labour supply	2	8	–3

The consultant suggests that economic growth and political stability are twice as important as the other factors.

The consultant states in the report that previous clients have not invested in countries with total weighted score of less than 30 out of a maximum possible 100 (with economic growth and political stability double weighted). The consultant therefore recommends that no investment in Africa should be undertaken.

Required:

(a) Describe the nature of political risk for business investment. **(4 marks)**

(b) Discuss whether or not Beela Electronics should use the technique suggested by the consultant in order to decide whether or not to invest in Africa. **(7 marks)**

(c) Discuss briefly how Beela might manage political risk if it decides to invest in Africa. **(6 marks)**

(d) In addition to political risk, what other risks might a company face when engaging in foreign trade, and how might these risks be managed? **(8 marks)**

(Total: 25 marks)

29 ROLES AND RELEVANCE

Many countries have developed best practice guidelines for corporate governance, although the details of what constitutes best practice varies from one country to another. There are also differences between statutory and regulatory corporate governance, as in the US, and voluntary codes of practice, as in Europe.

In all countries with a corporate governance regime, the composition of the board of directors is a key issue. In some countries, the remuneration of directors is another important aspect of corporate governance.

Required:

(a) Explain why it is considered appropriate for the positions of chairman and chief executive officer of a company to be held by different individuals. **(5 marks)**

(b) Describe the roles of non-executive directors, and suggest why there might be tension in these roles between contributing to strategy development and monitoring executive activity. **(8 marks)**

(c) Explain the reasons why directors' remuneration might be regarded as an important issue in corporate governance, and explain the principles that should be applied by a remuneration committee when negotiating a remuneration package with an executive director. **(12 marks)**

(Total: 25 marks)

30 CORPORATE GOVERNANCE (NOV 05 EXAM)

Required:

(a) Identify the key reasons for the emergence of corporate governance regulations around the world. **(5 marks)**

(b) Explain the core principles that underpin corporate governance regulations. **(10 marks)**

(c) Discuss the role and responsibilities of audit committees as laid down in the Combined Code. **(10 marks)**

(Total: 25 marks)

31 GOVERNANCE (PILOT PAPER)

You have recently been appointed as Head of the Internal Audit function for a large UK listed company that trades internationally, having worked within its finance function for two years prior to your new appointment.

Your company has also appointed a new Chief Executive, headhunted from a large US corporation where she had held the post of Vice President, Finance.

Required:

As part of the new Chief Executive's orientation programme, you have been asked to prepare a detailed report which provides key information on the principles of good corporate governance for UK listed companies.

You should address the following in your report, remembering that her background is in US governance and procedures.

(a) The role and responsibilities of the Board of Directors. **(5 marks)**

(b) The role and responsibilities of the audit committee. **(10 marks)**

(c) Disclosure of corporate governance arrangements. **(10 marks)**

(Total: 25 marks)

32 LMN (MAY 06 EXAM)

LMN is a charity that provides low-cost housing for people on low incomes. The government has privatised much of the home building, maintenance and management in this sector. The sector is heavily regulated and receives some government money but there are significant funds borrowed from banks to invest in new housing developments, on the security of future rent receipts. Government agencies subsidise much of the rental cost for low-income residents.

The board and senior management have identified the major risks to LMN as: having insufficient housing stock of a suitable type to meet the needs of local people on low incomes; making poor property investment decisions; having dissatisfied tenants due to inadequate property maintenance; failing to comply with the requirements of the regulator; having a poor credit rating with lenders; poor cost control; incurring irrecoverable debts for rental; and having vacant properties that are not earning income. LMN has produced a risk register as part of its risk management process. For each of more than 200 individual risks, the risk register identifies a description of the risk and the (high, medium or low) likelihood of the risk eventuating and the (high, medium or low) consequences for the organisation if the risk does eventuate.

The management of LMN is carried out by professionally qualified housing executives with wide experience in property development, housing management and maintenance, and financial management. The board of LMN is composed of volunteers with wide experience and an interest in social welfare. The board is representative of the community, tenants and the local authority, any of whom may be shareholders (shareholdings are nominal and the company pays no dividends). The local authority has overall responsibility for housing and social welfare in the area. The audit committee of the board of LMN, which has responsibility for risk management as well as internal control, wants to move towards a system of internal controls that are more closely related to risks identified in the risk register.

Required:

For an organisation like LMN:

(a) Discuss the purposes and importance of risk management and its relationship with the internal control system. **(8 marks)**

(b) Explain the importance of a management review of controls for the audit committee. **(5 marks)**

(c) Discuss the principles of good corporate governance as they apply to the Board's role:

(i) in conducting a review of internal controls; and

(ii) reporting on compliance. **(12 marks)**

(Total: 25 marks)

33 BJP (MAY 05 EXAM)

BJP is an organisation involved in making business-to-business sales of industrial products. BJP employs a sales team of 40 representatives and assigns each a geographic territory that is quite large. Sales representatives search for new business and follow up sales leads to win new business, and maintain contact with the existing customer base.

The sales representatives spend almost all their time travelling to visit clients. The only time when they are not doing this is on one day each month when they are required to attend their regional offices for a sales meeting. Sales representatives incur expenses. They have a mobile telephone, a fully maintained company car and a corporate credit card which can be used to pay for vehicle expenses, accommodation and meals and the cost of entertaining potential and existing clients.

The performance appraisal system for each sales representative is based on the number and value of new clients and existing clients in their territory. All sales representatives are required to submit a weekly report to their regional managers which gives details of the new and existing clients that they have visited during that week. The regional managers do not get involved in the daily routines of sales representatives if they are generating sufficient sales. Consequently, sales representatives have a large amount of freedom.

The Head Office Finance department, to whom regional managers have a reporting relationship, analyses the volume and value of business won by sales representatives and collects details of their expenses which are then reported back monthly to regional managers. At the last meeting of regional managers, the Head Office Finance department highlighted the increase in sales representatives' expenses as a proportion of sales revenue over the last two years and instructed regional managers to improve their control over the work representatives carry out and the expenses they incur.

Required:

(a) Advise regional managers as to the risks facing BJP as a result of the lack of apparent control over sales representatives and their expenses and recommend the controls that should be implemented by regional managers to rectify this situation.

(12 marks)

(b) Explain what an internal control system is, how it relates to the control environment and its likely costs, benefits and limitations. **(8 marks)**

(c) Recommend how analytical review could be used in the internal audit of BJP's sales representatives' expenses. **(5 marks)**

(Total: 25 marks)

34 COMPANY A AND B (NOV 06 EXAM)

The following information relates to two companies based in the United States of America, both of which are listed on the New York stock exchange. Each company had an annual sales revenue of approximately $800 million in 2005.

Company A

This company sells into a mix of business-to-business and end-user markets across a total of 15 countries in North America and Europe. Business-to-business sales predominate and 40% of sales revenue comes from two key European customers.

Manufacturing, assembly and delivery is managed geographically rather than by product type, via three separate subsidiaries with their own CEO based in Canada, France and the UK respectively. Research and all Treasury operations for the arrangement of loan finance and hedging of foreign exchange risk are both fully centralised.

The company has a diverse shareholder base that includes two major pension funds, one of which has a representative entitled to be present as an observer at the board meetings of Company A.

Company B

This company operates in the same product market as Company A, but earns most of its income from end user sales, many of which are initiated by on-line direct orders. 80% of the internet sales originate in the United States of America. Company's B's largest single customer, a Canadian company, represents 15% of its annual sales revenue, but no other customer exceeds 1% of total sales revenue. Research and sales facilities are based at the US headquarters, but manufacturing and assembly is all undertaken by separate subsidiaries in China, where the company also has a joint venture business that manages all the global distribution. Treasury operations are fully decentralised, but run as cost rather than profit centres.

The company was started ten years ago, and the Board of Directors remains dominated by members of the founding family. The CEO and the Finance Director are husband and wife, and together own 35% of the company's shares.

Required:

Using the information contained in the above scenario to develop your arguments, answer each of the following questions:

(a) Discuss how decisions about company structure, market types and location can impact upon the risk profile of a company. **(12 marks)**

(b) Compare and contrast the risks associated with the differing approaches to the Treasury function adopted by the two companies in the above scenario. **(4 marks)**

(c) For **either** Company A **or** Company B as described in the scenario, taking into account its current structure and size, recommend **one** example of **each** of financial, non-financial quantitative, and non-financial qualitative controls that may be useful tools in monitoring exposure to either strategic or operational risks. You should briefly justify your choices. **(9 marks)**

(Total: 25 marks)

REVIEW AND AUDIT OF CONTROL SYSTEMS

35 REVIEW OF INTERNAL CONTROL

You are the internal auditor of Gash, a listed company. The company has recently appointed a new non-executive director, who is being given induction to the company and some training for carrying out his role on the board of directors. You have been asked to give him some information and guidance about the annual review of internal control, which is a requirement of best practice in corporate governance. (As a listed company, Gash applies best practice.)

He presents you with a list of questions about the review, which he would like you to answer. The questions are as follows:

(1) What aspects of the company's operations and activities will be covered by the review?

(2) What is the responsibility for the review and evaluation of internal control of (i) senior management, (ii) the audit committee and (iii) the board of directors?

Required:

(a) Provide an answer to the questions of the non-executive director. **(5 marks)**

(b) Describe a method for carrying out a review of the internal control system that you believe would be consistent with the guidelines for best practice. **(12 marks)**

(c) The non-executive director is aware that it is company policy for the internal auditors to carry out regular checks on internal controls, outside the annual review. He is rather surprised that the internal auditors, who report to the Finance Director, should be asked to do this work, due to ethical issues that could arise. He is not certain that the internal auditors could conduct an impartial and effective review of controls.

Explain the ethical issues that could arise for the internal auditor, and the relevance of the fundamental principles in CIMA's Ethical Guidelines to the conduct of an impartial and effective review of internal controls. **(8 marks)**

(Total: 25 marks)

36 HIJ (MAY 06 EXAM)

HIJ is a new company that provides professional services to small businesses. Apart from the Principal, a qualified accountant who owns 100% of the business, there are four professionally qualified and two support staff. The business model adopted by HIJ is to charge an annually negotiated fixed monthly retainer to its clients in return for advice and assistance in relation to budgeting, costing, cash management, receivables and inventory control, and monthly and annual management reporting. The work involves weekly visits to each client by a member of staff and a monthly review between HIJ's Principal and the chief executive of the client company. In delivering its client services, HIJ makes extensive use of specialist accounting software.

The Principal continually carries out marketing activity to identify and win new clients. This involves advertising, production of brochures and attending conferences, exhibitions, and various business events where potential clients may be located.

The management of HIJ by its Principal is based on strict cost control, maximising the chargeable hours of staff and ensuring that the retainers charged are sufficient to cover the hours worked for each client over the financial year.

Required:

(a) Recommend management controls that would be appropriate for the Principal to have in place for HIJ. **(12 marks)**

(b) Discuss the need for various types of audit that are appropriate for HIJ. **(8 marks)**

(c) Discuss the costs and benefits for HIJ that are likely to arise from a system of internal controls. **(5 marks)**

(Total: 25 marks)

37 CARPETS AND FLOOR COVERINGS

BK is a company specialising in the sale of carpets and floor coverings to sports clubs, sports halls and social centres around the country. It obtains its carpeting and other materials directly from suppliers in Eastern Asia.

When it provides new carpeting to a customer, BK also undertakes to remove and dispose of the old carpeting or floor covering, but charges a fee for the service. The old carpets are taken to waste disposal sites or occasionally burned.

You have recently been appointed as an internal auditor to the company, and you are discussing your plan of work for the next 12 months with the finance director. The following points arise in your discussion.

(1) The work of the internal audit section has so far been largely restricted to audits of elements of the financial accounting system, although there have been occasional management audits. You suggest that it might be appropriate to carry out some value for money audits.

(2) The board of directors has come under pressure from its major shareholders to publish an annual Social and Environmental Report for inclusion in the annual report and accounts. You suggest that it might be appropriate to check and verify the contents of this report before publication.

(3) There has been considerable publicity in the national press recently about the use of child labour and slave labour in certain parts of the country from which BK purchases its carpets. The finance director expresses the view that BK benefited from low purchase costs for carpets and floor coverings, but he would be disappointed if BK's suppliers were associated with these labour practices.

(4) The Finance Director informs you that your predecessor as internal auditor resigned from the company after a dispute with the executive director concerning a department where the auditor had carried out a management audit. Apparently, the internal auditor had criticised the director and his department severely for lax controls and inefficiency. The director had argued that the internal auditor had not discussed any of the criticisms before preparing the report, had been deceitful in asking questions and was probably not qualified to do the audit work. On being told that the auditor was a CIMA member, you express the view that this seemed to be a matter where the Institute's Ethical Guidelines should have been followed.

Required:

(a) Explain the difference between a value for money audit of the accounts department and an audit of the accounting system. **(7 marks)**

(b) Suggest how you might plan a social and environmental audit of the company and what you would consider to be the main social and environmental risks facing BK. **(8 marks)**

(c) From the information available about the dispute between the previous internal auditor and the executive director, suggest how CIMA's Ethical Guidelines might have been relevant to the way in which the auditor acted, or ought to have acted. **(10 marks)**

(Total: 25 marks)

38 ROXY HOTELS

Roxy Hotels is a listed company which runs about 40 hotels. The company has an established internal audit department which is based at the head office and which makes regular visits to the hotels.

The hotels provide business and tourist class accommodation. They also provide restaurants, bars, and conference and leisure facilities which are open to the general public as well as residents. The company operates a computerised central booking and billing system and an inventory and asset control system, both of which can be accessed via terminals in the hotels. Access to the system is restricted by the use of passwords and all significant expenditure is authorised through head office. The payroll is operated through head office. Hotel and regional managers are actively involved in the setting of budgets and cash flow forecasting. On average, throughout the year, the chain has a 65% occupancy rate.

Required:

(a) Explain the significance of the system of internal control in ensuring that organisations achieve their corporate and business objectives and explain briefly the role of internal audit. **(5 marks)**

(b) Explain the types of activities normally carried out by an internal audit department. **(5 marks)**

(c) Discuss situations where the internal audit department at Roxy Hotels might check detailed transactions and balances. **(9 marks)**

(d) Discuss areas where the internal audit department at Roxy Hotels might perform reviews of systems or operational performance. **(6 marks)**

(Total: 25 marks)

39 SPQ (NOV 05 EXAM)

As a CIMA member, you have recently been appointed as the Head of Internal Audit for SPQ, a multinational listed company that carries out a large volume of internet sales to customers who place their orders using their home or work computers. You report to the Chief Executive, although you work closely with the Finance Director. You have direct access to the Chair of the Audit Committee whenever you consider it necessary.

One of your internal audit teams has been conducting a review of IT security for a system which has been in operation for 18 months and which is integral to internet sales. The audit was included in the internal audit plan following a request by the Chief Accountant. Sample testing by the internal audit team has revealed several transactions over the last three months which have raised concerns about possible hacking or fraudulent access to the customer/order database. Each of these transactions has disappeared from the database after deliveries have been made, but without sales being recorded or funds collected from the customer. Each of the identified transactions was for a different customer and there seems to be no relationship between any of the transactions.

You have received the draft report from the Internal Audit Manager responsible for this audit which suggests serious weaknesses in the design of the system. You have discussed this informally with senior managers who have told you that such a report will be politically very unpopular with the Chief Executive as he was significantly involved in the design and approval of the new system and insisted it be implemented earlier than the IT department considered was advisable. No post-implementation review of the system has taken place.

You have been informally advised by several senior managers to lessen the criticism and work with the IT department to correct any deficiencies within the system and to produce a report to the Audit Committee that is less critical and merely identifies the need for some improvement. They suggest that these actions would avoid criticism of the Chief Executive by the Board of SPQ.

Required:

(a) Explain the role of internal audit in internal control and risk management. **(5 marks)**

(b) Analyse the potential risks faced by SPQ that have been exposed by the review of IT security and recommend controls that should be implemented to reduce them. **(8 marks)**

(c) Discuss the issues that need to be considered when planning an audit of activities and systems such as the one undertaken at SPQ. **(5 marks)**

(d) Explain the ethical principles you should apply as the Head of Internal Audit for SPQ when reporting the results of this internal review and how any ethical conflicts should be resolved. **(7 marks)**

(Total: 25 marks)

40 BRIDGEFORD PRODUCTS

You are the chief internal auditor of Bridgeford Products, a listed company, and you are planning your audit programme for the next 12 months for the year ended 31 January 20X5. You are looking in particular at the following aspects of operations.

During a recent visit to the company you obtained the following information.

(i) The management accounts for the 10 months to 30 November 20X4 show sales of $130 million and profit before tax of $4 million. Sales and profits accrue evenly throughout the year. In the year ended 31 January 20X4 Bridgeford Products had sales of $110 million and profit before tax of $8 million.

(ii) The company installed a new computerised inventory control system which has operated from 1 June 20X4. As the inventory control system records inventory movements and current inventory quantities, the company is proposing:

- to use the inventory quantities on the computer to value the inventory at the year end; and
- not to carry out an inventory count at the year end.

(iii) You are aware there have been reliability problems with the company's products, which have resulted in legal claims being brought against the company by customers, and customers refusing to pay for the products.

(iv) The sales increase in the 10 months to 30 November 20X4 over the previous year has been achieved by attracting new customers and by offering extended credit. The new credit arrangements allow customers three months credit before their debt becomes overdue, rather than the one month credit period allowed previously. As a result of this change, receivables age has increased from 1.6 to 4.1 months.

(v) The purchasing manager was dismissed on 15 August. A replacement purchasing manager has been appointed but it is not expected that she will take up her position until 1 January 20X5.

Required:

(a) Describe the reasons why it is important that auditors should plan their audit work **(5 marks)**

(b) Describe the actions you will take as internal auditor concerning the matters listed in (i) to (v) above. **(20 marks)**

(Total: 25 marks)

41 GRAPE

As an internal auditor for Grape, you have been asked to apply analytical procedures to the information produced by the management accounting system. You have no reason to expect significant differences from previous years. As a result of your review, you identify the following as requiring further investigation.

Ratio		*20X5*	*20X4*	*20X3*	*20X2*
(i)	Days sales in accounts receivable	55 days	39 days	40 days	37 days
(ii)	Inventory turnover	8 times	11 times	13 times	11 times
(iii)	Plant and machinery depreciation expense as a percentage of cost	7%	11%	10%	12%
(iv)	Repairs and maintenance expense to sales revenue	4.2%	1.8%	1.4%	2.0%

You are concerned that the deterioration in these ratios has occurred without the managers responsible apparently having attempted to discover the reasons for the changes. You are concerned that this might indicate weaknesses in the management accounting reporting system.

However, you begin by trying to establish, by asking the managers responsible, whether there is any satisfactory explanation for the changes.

Required:

(a) For each ratio, explain why the change could have occurred. **(8 marks)**

(b) Explain how adverse changes in these ratios might be of different significance to the external auditors and the internal auditors. **(8 marks)**

(c) Explain the weaknesses in the management accounting control system that might be indicated by the fact that these ratios indicate a deterioration in efficiency but management have done nothing about correcting the underlying problem. **(9 marks)**

(Total: 25 marks)

42 AL & CO. (MAY 05 EXAM)

AL and Co. is a London-based building contractor, with an annual sales revenue of almost £15 million. The company employs 50 people, the majority of whom are skilled tradesmen or apprentices in the areas of plumbing, electrical work, plastering, carpentry, glazing and hard landscaping. AL and Co. specialises in renovation work for private clients by offering a fast 'all service' facility that suits busy professional people seeking to renovate properties either for their own occupation or for investment purposes. As a result of the property boom, sales revenue has grown by over 30% in the last two years.

Day-to-day management of the business is shared by two executive directors, one of whom manages the financial and legal aspects of the business (Director X), while the other is responsible for operational activities including work scheduling, agreeing quotes with the sales staff, and all procurement (Director Y). The two directors have a mutual respect and trust for one another and therefore do not check or verify each other's work.

As a medium-sized company, AL and Co. is subject to an annual external audit, but it has no internal audit function and both its internal control and management accounting systems are very basic. Management accounting procedures record the costs of materials associated with all contracts via a job costing system, but other costs are not charged to individual contracts.

The system is thus unable to identify whether any specific contract is profitable, and can only compute aggregate profit. One consequence of this system is that the company profitability depends on there being a close match between the actual time taken to complete jobs and the sales team's estimate of the times required: however, the time variances are neither calculated nor monitored.

The systems have never been questioned or refined because, to date, an average gross markup of 25% has always been achieved. This margin has ensured that both directors earn high salaries which have risen year on year, and there has therefore been little incentive to improve controls and manage costs.

Two staff are employed to issue written quotes in response to customer enquiries, with prices being calculated on the basis of estimated labour and material costs plus 25%. The quotes are reviewed by Director Y before they are sent to customers. All payments are due on completion of the work.

In drafting the work schedules Director Y has full knowledge of which quotes are accepted by customers. Additionally, given his role of supervising procurement, he regularly gives administrative staff the names of new suppliers for inclusion in the accounting system.

Six months ago, Director Y found himself over-committed financially, and devised a way of diverting company funds from AL and Co. for his own personal use. He began adding 10% to the figures quoted for all jobs requiring the use of more than three separate services (plastering, electrical, etc), thereby raising the gross markup to 37.5% in such cases. The intention was to fraudulently redirect the additional income for his personal use. This was achieved by the submission to AL and Co., on the completion of a job, of an invoice (for the 10% additional charge) in the name of a fictitious supplier of small tools and consumables. Director Y would code the associated costs as variable overhead in the accounting system. The timing of the invoices could easily be matched to the job completion dates in view of his knowledge of work schedules, and he set up a separate bank account in the fictitious name to receive these payments.

You are an accountant in AL and Co. and have been assigned responsibility for liaison with the external auditors. You find that you are unable to resolve their concerns about the escalation in variable overhead expenses over the course of the last year, most of which have been charged to a non-local supplier's account. You are having difficulty clarifying the precise nature of the expenses incurred because telephone calls to the business number always request that a message be left but no calls are ever returned. All other aspects of the audit are satisfactory.

Required:

Write a report for the Directors of AL and Co. that:

- Details the inadequacies of the current 'internal control' system within the company and possible changes that could be made to improve the system **(10 marks)**
- Explains why the rise in variable overhead costs is a matter of concern from both an external audit and an internal control perspective, and thus requires immediate agreement on a co-ordinated response to investigate the possibility of fraud **(5 marks)**
- Briefly explains the limits of the responsibility of external auditors to detect fraud **(5 marks)**
- Explains why the company should prepare a fraud response plan, and outlines the issues to be considered in drafting such a plan. **(5 marks)**

(Total: 25 marks)

43 INTERNAL CONTROLS (NOV 06 EXAM)

Required:

Write a report advising the Board of Directors of a stock market listed company on:

- the key responsibilities of Board members in relation to ensuring the effectiveness of internal controls;
- the methods used to assess such effectiveness; and
- the regulations that govern the reporting to the stock market of the results of internal control reviews.

An indicative mark allocation for the three points above are 5, 10 and 5 marks respectively.

(Total: 25 marks)

(includes 5 marks for report format and style)

MANAGEMENT OF FINANCIAL RISK

44 LIABILITIES (PILOT PAPER)

A listed services group with a UK Head Office and subsidiaries throughout the world reports in UK £ and has the following liabilities:

Liabilities All figures are in £million	*Total liabilities*	*Floating rate liabilities*	*Fixed rate liabilities*	*Weighted average interest rate*	*Weighted average years for which rate is fixed*
£ Sterling	98	98			
US$	41	8	33	7.25%	5
Euro	4	4			
Total	143	110	33		

Maturity All figures are in £million	*Total*	*Maturing within 1 year*	*Within 1 – 2 years*	*Within 2 – 5 years*	*Over 5 years*
£ Sterling	98	73	3	18	4
US$	41				41
Euro	4	1	1	1	1
	143	74	4	19	46

Interest rates are currently about 5%.

Required:

(a) (i) Discuss the main sources of financial risk for this group (assuming there are no offsetting assets that might provide a hedge against the liabilities).

(ii) Discuss the transaction risk faced by the group if the UK £ were to depreciate against the $US and Euro by 10%.

(iii) Explain the elements of currency risk in the context of the above example.

(13 marks)

(b) Discuss the use of exchange traded and Over The Counter (OTC) derivatives for hedging and how they may be used to reduce the exchange rate and interest rate risks the group faces. Illustrate your answer by comparing and contrasting the main features of appropriate derivatives. **(12 marks)**

(Total: 25 marks)

45 SK CONSORTIUM

SK Consortium is an international Public Relations (PR) and marketing agency. Its shares are listed on an international stock exchange. The company is based in London, but has offices throughout Europe, the Far East and India. Many members of staff are recruited locally. They are supplemented by members of staff based in corporate headquarters in London, but who work worldwide.

SK Consortium generally invoices in the customer's currency. For many years it followed a policy of not hedging currency risks, and has generally profited from this. The Finance Director, who was widely credited with successfully managing the treasury function, has retired. However, the 'no hedging' policy was not without its critics among major investors and financial analysts.

The SK Consortium Board is now concerned about currency volatility and the potential effect on its market value and wishes to evaluate different hedging mechanisms. The recently-appointed new Finance Director has suggested using either currency futures or forward contracts. She proposes to demonstrate to the directors how futures and forward contracts would have worked if a forthcoming transaction had been hedged. The details are as follows:

Receipt of US$875,000 is due on 1 June 20X5. The company has known since the end of February 20X5 that this receipt is to be expected.

Market information at 1 March 20X5

Exchange rates **US$/£**		**US$ futures** **US$/£, contract size £62,500**	*Price*	*Initial margin*	*UK interest rate (% per annum)*
Spot	1.6132				
One month forward	1.6100	March	1.6022	£1,000	3.38
Three months forward	1.6038	June	1.5950	£1,500	3.41

Required:

(a) 'Despite its success, the 'no hedging' policy was criticised.'

Discuss the basis for such criticism among investors and analysts and explain why and to what extent this policy, if continued, might affect the market value of the company's shares. **(8 marks)**

(b) (i) Assume it is now 1 June 20X5. The spot rate US$/£ is 1.6080 and the June 20X5 currency futures rate is 1.6085. Calculate the net receipts in sterling that would have been expected on 1 March and today (1 June) under the two alternative hedging methods and comment on which would have been the most financially advantageous.

Assume the profit (or variation) margin would be settled on the maturity or disposal of the futures contract.

(ii) Discuss the main features of these two hedging instruments and comment on their suitability for a company such as SK Consortium. **(17 marks)**

Notes: Marks are distributed roughly equally between the two sections of requirement (b). A report structure is not required for this question.

(Total: 25 marks)

46 IOU

IOU Inc is a large company based in the United States that trades mainly within the US and with the UK. It has a significant amount of borrowing in £ sterling. Debt interest of £725,000 is due to be paid on 31 October and a further £530,000 on 31 December. IOU's policy is to hedge the risks involved in all foreign currency transactions.

Assume it is now 30 September. The company's bank quotes the following rates of exchange, US$ per £1:

Spot	*1 month forward*	*3 months forward*
	(mid-rate)	*(mid-rate)*
1.5584 – 1.5590	1.5601	1.5655

Prices for a £/US$ option on a US Stock Exchange (cents per £, payable on purchase of the option, contract size £31,250) are:

Strike price	*Calls*		*Puts*	
(US$/£)	*October*	*December*	*October*	*December*
1.56	2.02	3.00	1.00	2.16
1.57	1.32	-	-	-
1.58	0.84	2.12	2.18	3.14

The Treasurer is considering two methods of hedging the risk, fixed forward or option contracts. Market expectations, based on current published economic forecasts, are that sterling will appreciate against the US$ over the next three months. The Treasurer thinks it might weaken or at least remain stable against the $. He suggests that if options are to be used, one-month options should be bought at a strike price of 1.57 and three-month options at a strike price of 1.58.

Ignore transaction costs.

Required:

(a) Recommend, with reasons, the most appropriate method for IOU Inc to hedge its foreign exchange risk on the two interest payments due in one and three months time. Your answer should include appropriate calculations, using the figures in the question, to support your recommendation and a discussion of the factors to consider when choosing between the two hedging mechanisms. **(15 marks)**

(b) Assume you are a financial manager with the nationally-owned postal and telecommunications company in Zorro, a country in Asia. In organisations such as this, periodic settlements are made between local and foreign operators. Net receipts or payments are in US$.

Required:

Explain the main types of foreign exchange risk exposure that are likely to affect the organisation and advise the company on policies it could consider to reduce exposure to these risks. **(10 marks)**

(Total: 25 marks)

47 PONDHILLS

Pondhills Inc is a US multinational company with subsidiaries in the UK and Africa. The currency of the African country is pegged against the dollar, with a current exchange rate of 246.3 dinars/$US1. In recent months political unrest and an increasing inflation rate has led the finance director of Pondhills to become concerned about a possible devaluation of the dinar. He believes that the dinar could devalue by up to 15% relative to the dollar during the next few months.

Summarised financial data for the African subsidiary, Ponda SA are shown below:

	Million dinars
Sales revenue	2,300
Non-current assets	510
Current assets	
Cash	86
Trade receivables	410
Inventory	380
	876
Short-term payables	(296)
Long-term loans	(500)
	590
Shareholders' equity	590

Current exchange rates are:

$US/£1	1.5780
Dinar/$US1	246.3

Notes:

(i) All sales from the African subsidiary are denominated in US dollars, and all receivables are therefore in dollars.

(ii) 50% of payables are debts owned in sterling to the UK subsidiary by Ponda SA.

(iii) Long-term loans are in dinars from an African bank, at an interest rate of 12% per annum.

(iv) The cost of goods sold and other operating expenses (excluding interest) for Ponda SA are 70% of sales revenue. 40% of this is payable in dollars or sterling and 60% in dinars.

(v) No significant changes in exchange rates are expected between the dollar and other major currencies.

Required:

(a) Calculate the balance sheet translation exposure of Pondhills Inc, AND the potential profit or loss on translation of the balance sheet using the current or closing rate method where all EXPOSED assets and liabilities are translated at the current exchange rate. **(10 marks)**

(b) Calculate the expected impact on the dollar value of Ponda SA's annual cash flow in the first full year after devaluation. The time value of money may be ignored. **(7 marks)**

(c) Comment upon whether or not Pondhills Inc should hedge against the exposures estimated in (a) and (b). **(3 marks)**

(d) Discuss, giving examples, the possible longer term economic/cash flow implications of the possible devaluation for Pondhills Inc. **(5 marks)**

(Total: 25 marks)

48 TREASURER OF AB

(a) Assume you are the Treasurer of AB, a large engineering company, and that it is now May 20X4. You have forecast that the company will need to borrow £2 million by the end of September 20X4 for at least 6 months. The need for finance will arise because the company has extended its credit terms to selected customers over the summer period. The company's bank currently charges customers such as AB plc 7.5% per annum interest for short-term unsecured borrowing. However, you believe interest rates will rise by at least 1.5 percentage points over the next 6 months. You are considering using one of three alternative methods to hedge the risk:

(i) forward rate agreements; or

(ii) interest rate futures; or

(iii) an interest rate guarantee (a borrower's option or short term cap).

You can purchase an interest rate cap at 7% per annum for the duration of the loan to be guaranteed. You would have to pay a premium of 0.1% of the amount of the loan. As part of the arrangement, the company will agree to pay a 'floor' rate of 6% per annum.

Required:

Discuss the features of each of the three alternative methods of hedging the interest rate risk and advise on how each might be useful to AB, taking all relevant and known information into account. **(12 marks)**

(b) You are contacted by AB's bank and informed that another of the bank's clients, a smaller company in the same industry, is looking for a swap partner for a similar amount of borrowing for the same duration. This company, RO, would prefer variable rate finance whereas the bank knows that AB would prefer fixed rate. The borrowing rates applicable to AB and RO are as follows:

	Floating	*Fixed*
AB	LIBOR + 0.3%	7.5%
RO	LIBOR + 0.5%	8.5%

Required:

(i) Comment briefly on why swaps may be used and recommend how the two companies here could cooperate in a swap arrangement to their mutual benefit, including the option of changing the type of loan normally preferred. Support your recommendation with appropriate calculations.

(ii) Discuss the advantages and disadvantages of arranging a swap through a bank rather than negotiating directly with a counterparty. **(13 marks)**

Note: A report format is NOT required in answering this question.

(Total: 25 marks)

49 YZ

YZ is a specialist food manufacturing company based in the south of England. It trades with companies within the European common currency area (eurozone). The following receipts and payments are due within the next three months:

	Euros (€)
Due in 1 month:	
Payments to suppliers	600,000
Receipts from customers	400,000
Due in 3 months:	
Payments to suppliers	800,000
Receipts from customers	1,200,000

Exchange rates as at today:	€/£1
Spot	1.6186 – 1.6202
1 month forward	0.0002 – 0.0006 premium
3 months forward	0.0008 – 0.0013 premium

Interest rates (annual):	*Borrowing*	*Lending*
£ sterling	4.25%	3.75%
Euro	3.50%	3.00%

Required:

(a) Calculate the *net* £ currency receipts or payments that YZ might expect for *both* its one month and three month transactions if it:

(i) hedges the risk using the forward market;

(ii) hedges the risk using the money market;

(iii) does not hedge the risk and the €/£ spot exchange rates in one and three months' time are 1.6192 – 1.6208 and 1.6200 – 1.6220 respectively. **(12 marks)**

(b) Discuss the advantages and disadvantages of the three courses of action being considered in (a) and recommend which you consider to be the most appropriate for YZ.

[***Note:*** Alternative (iii) is *not* to hedge. You would not of course know what the actual exchange rates will be when you offer this advice.] **(13 marks)**

Note: A report format is NOT required in answering this question.

(Total: 25 marks)

50 LXN (NOV 05 EXAM)

(a) LXN is a large book retailer in France and, as a result of recent rapid sales growth, has decided to expand by opening six new branches in the south of France. The estimated set up cost per branch is €250,000 and LXN wishes to raise the required funding (plus an additional 20% for increased working capital requirements) via borrowing. The Treasurer at LXN is concerned about interest rate risk, however, and is unsure about whether to opt for a fixed or floating rate loan. LXN's Board of Directors has indicated that it wishes to maximise the company's use of opportunities to hedge interest rate risk.

LXN currently has €2,000 million of assets and the following long-term debt in its balance sheet:

€15 million [(6% fixed rate) redeemable 20Y0]

£18 million [(Sterling LIBOR plus 3%) redeemable 20X7]

All rates are quoted as an annual rate. The current exchange rate is €/£0.684.

Required:

Discuss the factors that should be taken into account by the Treasurer of LXN when deciding whether to raise fixed rate or floating rate debt for the expansion project and whether to hedge the resulting interest rate exposure. **(10 marks)**

(b) LXN's Treasurer has negotiated a fixed rate of 6% or a variable rate of Euro LIBOR plus 1.5% for the required borrowing. In addition, a counterparty (MGV) has offered to convert any new fixed rate debt that LXN takes on into synthetic floating rate debt via a swap arrangement in which the two companies will share the quality spread differential equally.

MGV, the counterparty, can borrow at a fixed rate of 7.2% or at a variable rate of Euro LIBOR plus 2.5%.

Euro LIBOR is currently 5%. All rates are quoted as an annual rate.

Required:

(i) Briefly discuss the advantages and disadvantages of interest rate swaps as a tool for managing interest rate risk. **(5 marks)**

(ii) Draw a diagram to illustrate how the transactions between LXN and MGV and the two lenders will operate if the swap is agreed. **(4 marks)**

(iii) Calculate the interest rate terms payable by LXN. Evaluate the potential annual saving resulting from borrowing at a fixed rate and engaging in an interest rate swap, as against a straightforward floating rate loan. **(6 marks)**

(Total: 25 marks)

51 EXPOT

Expot is an importer/exporter of textiles and textile machinery. It is based in the UK but trades extensively with countries throughout Europe. It has a small subsidiary based in Switzerland. The company is about to invoice a customer in Switzerland for 750,000 Swiss francs, payable in three months' time. Expot's treasurer is considering two methods of hedging the exchange risk. These are:

Method 1

A money market hedge

Method 2

A three-month forward exchange contract with the company's bank.

The spot rate of exchange is SFr 2.3824 – 2.3834 to £1.

The 3-month forward rate of exchange is SFr 2.3674 – 2.3688 to £1.

Annual interest rates for three months' borrowing are: Switzerland 3%, UK 6%.

Required:

(a) Advise the treasurer on:

(i) which of the two methods is the most financially advantageous for Expot; and

(ii) the factors to consider before deciding whether to hedge the risk using the foreign currency markets.

Include relevant calculations in your advice. **(16 marks)**

(b) Assume that Expot is trading in and with developing countries rather than Europe and has a subsidiary in a country with no developed capital or currency markets. Expot is now about to invoice a customer in that country in the local currency. Advise Expot's treasurer about ways in which the risk can be managed in these circumstances.

Note: No calculations are required for this part of the question. **(9 marks)**

(Total: 25 marks)

52 WARREN BUFFETT (MAY 06 EXAM)

(a) Warren Buffett, the stock market investor, views derivatives as a 'time bomb', but many corporate treasurers clearly perceive them as very useful tools for reducing risk.

Required:

Explain and discuss the reasons for such divergent viewpoints. **(13 marks)**

The International Accounting Standard on Financial Instrument Recognition and Measurement (IAS 39) includes a fair value option that permits a company to designate certain types of financial instruments as ones to be measured at fair value on initial recognition, with changes in fair value recognised in profit or loss. The designation is irrevocable. Additionally, all financial assets and liabilities held for trading are measured at fair value with the associated changes in value passing through profit and loss.

This method of accounting is defended on the grounds that it ensures that the disclosures better reflect the risks that are being taken, thereby improving the information available to the stock market.

Required:

(b) Explain the additional risks arising from these rules that may be faced by companies which choose to exercise the fair value option and/or regularly trade derivatives for profit. **(5 marks)**

(c) An investor owns a portfolio of shares that has varied in value over the last 12 months between £1.5 million and £1.8 million. All stock is highly liquid and can be sold within one day. The daily profit and loss distribution is assumed to be normally distributed with a mean of zero and a standard deviation of £60,000.

Required:

(i) Explain the meaning of the term 'value at risk' from the perspective of a fund manager. **(4 marks)**

(ii) Calculate and comment upon the value at risk of the portfolio, assuming a 95% confidence level and a one-day holding period. **(3 marks)**

(Total: 25 marks)

53 JAPANESE EXPORTER

A company which imports electronic equipment into the United States will have to pay 14.4 million yen to a Japanese exporter in three months' time.

A survey in the financial press states that the trading range of the Japanese yen against the dollar during the previous year was 159.45 to 134.20. Last month's average rate was 143.27.

Current quotations are:

Spot	136.45 – 136.55
One month forward	0.35 – 0.32 yen premium
Three months forward	1.12 – 1.08 yen premium

Required:

(a) Discuss the reliability of forward rates as estimates of future spot rates. **(7 marks)**

(b) If the importer were to arrange a three-month forward exchange contract with his bank, calculate the cost to him (ignoring commission and expenses) of the required 14.4 million yen. **(3 marks)**

(c) Discuss whether a forward exchange contract would be advantageous or not, if the spot rate after three months might be at either extreme of last year's range? (Give calculations.) **(5 marks)**

(d) Discuss what alternative actions might be taken if, as a result of some change in the order specification, the goods had not been received by the end of the three months, and payment would therefore not be made until a later date. **(5 marks)**

(e) Explain how to distinguish between:

(i) a forward exchange fixed contract;

(ii) a forward exchange option contract. **(5 marks)**

(Total: 25 marks)

54 MNO (NOV 06 EXAM)

MNO is a UK-based company that has delivered goods, invoiced at $1,800,000 US dollars to a customer in Singapore. Payment is due in three months' time, that is, in February 2007. The finance director of MNO is concerned about the potential exchange risk resulting from the transaction and wishes to hedge the risk in either the futures or the options market.

The current spot rate is $1.695/£. A three-month futures contract is quoted at $1.690/£, and the contract size for $/£ futures contracts is £62,500.

A three-month put option is available at a price of $1.675.

Required:

(a) Assuming that the spot rate and the futures rate turn out to be the same in February 2007, indicating that there is no basis risk, identify the lowest cost way of hedging the exchange rate risk (using either futures or options) where the exchange rate at the time of payment is:

(i) $1.665/£

(ii) $1.720/£

Note: Your answer should show all the calculations used to reach your answer, including the extent (if any) of the uncovered risk.

(10 marks)

(b) Briefly discuss the problems of using futures contracts to hedge exchange rate risks.

(6 marks)

(c) Identify and explain the key reasons why small versus large companies may differ in terms of both the extent of foreign exchange and interest rate hedging that is undertaken, and the tools used by management for such purposes. **(9 marks)**

(Total: 25 marks)

55 ABC

ABC is a UK-based construction company that operates internationally, mainly in the Middle and Far East. It has recently obtained a contract to build a number of Electricity Generating Stations (EGSs) in an Eastern Europe country (EE). The EGSs will be paid for by the EE government at a fixed price of 2,000 million EE marks 12 months after the start of the contract. ABC will need to spend 750 million EE marks immediately and an additional 750 million EE marks in six months' time. The company has not worked in Eastern Europe before and has no other business in this region. Its opportunity cost of capital in the UK is 15% each year.

The treasurer of ABC is discussing the possibility of a fixed rate currency swap with an EE-based company that trades in the UK. The swap would be taken out immediately for the full expected expenditure of 1,500 million EE marks at a swap rate of 15 EE marks to £ sterling.

Interest of 20% each year would be payable on the full 1,500 million EE mark swap by ABC to the EE-based company. Payment would be in EE marks. The EE-based company will pay interest to ABC on the sterling value of the swap at 12%. Payment would be in £ sterling. Assume interest payments are made annually at the end of the year.

There are no formal capital markets in the EE country and therefore no forward rates are available for the EE mark against the £. Forecasts of inflation rates for next year are 3% in the UK and 25% in the EE country.

Assume the value of the EE mark is allowed to float freely by the EE government. The current spot rate is 18 EE marks to the £.

Required:

(a) Explain the procedure for a currency swap, and recommend, with appropriate supporting calculations, whether ABC should enter into the currency swap with the EE-based company. **(15 marks)**

(b) Discuss the advantages and disadvantages to a company such as ABC of using swap arrangements as part of its treasury management strategies, in general and in the circumstances of the proposed contract. Explain, briefly, the risks involved in using swap techniques. **(10 marks)**

(Total: 25 marks)

56 PS

(a) Explain the five input variables involved in the Black-Scholes pricing model and discuss how a decrease in the value of each of these variables is likely to change the price of a call option. **(10 marks)**

(b) PS is a medium-sized UK-based company that trades mainly in the UK and the US. In the past, PS has not hedged its currency risks but movements in the exchange rate have recently become more volatile. Assume it is now 30 September. The company expects net cash inflow in US$ (sales receipts less purchases) on 31 December of US$2,350,000.

The current quoted spot rate of exchange is US$1.4180 – 1.4220 to the £1.

The US$ discount on the three-month forward rate of exchange is 0.36 to 0.46 cents.

Option prices (cents per £, payable on purchase of the option, contract size £31,250):

Strike price	*September contracts*	
$	*Calls*	*Puts*
1.41	2.28	1.69
1.42	1.77	2.19
1.43	1.36	2.68

Assume there are three months from now to the expiry of the September contracts.

The company is risk averse and plans to hedge the risk using either a fixed forward contract or a European currency option. Ignore transaction costs.

Required:

Recommend, with reasons, the most appropriate methods for PS to use to hedge its foreign exchange risk for the next three months. Your answer should include appropriate calculations to support your recommendation. **(15 marks)**

(Total: 25 marks)

57 FRAP

FRAP is a large international mining group. Its treasury operations are managed centrally, and the group expects that it will need to borrow $20 million in two months' time, to cover a liquidity shortage for three months. The company can borrow at US dollar LIBOR + 0.5%.

The head of the treasury department is concerned about the possibility of a large increase in interest rates and he is interested in hedging the exposure.

A 2v5 FRA is currently priced at 5.05 – 5.09.

The following premiums are also available for options (interest rate guarantees) on a notional principal amount of $20 million for three months, with an exercise date in two months' time:

Exercise rate	*Call premium*	*Put premium*
4.5%	$118,000	$45,000
5.0%	$60,000	$68,000

Required:

(a) Explain how an FRA would be used to hedge the interest rate risk for FRAP in this situation, and calculate the effective cost of borrowing if, when the FRA reaches its settlement date, the actual three-month US dollar LIBOR rate is:

(i) 7%

(ii) 4% **(6 marks)**

(b) Explain how an option might be used to hedge the interest rate risk for FRAP in this situation, and calculate the effective cost of borrowing if, when the option reaches its expiry date, the actual three-month US dollar LIBOR rate is:

(i) 7%

(ii) 4% **(6 marks)**

(c) Recommend how FRAP might use options to hedge the risk but reduce the overall premium cost, and show the effective borrowing cost using your recommended approach if, at expiry date, the three-month US dollar LIBOR rate is:

(i) 7%

(ii) 4% **(6 marks)**

(d) Explain the differences and similarities between an FRA and an interest rate swap. **(7 marks)**

(Total: 25 marks)

58 NETTING, MATCHING AND POOLING

BNM International is a multinational company, based in the UK, with subsidiaries operating in 14 different countries and 8 different currencies. There is a substantial amount of decentralisation of authority within the group and subsidiaries are treated as investment centres, for management reporting purposes. Each subsidiary operates its own cash management systems, although if additional capital is required, the subsidiary must apply to the central treasury unit in the Netherlands. This treasury unit is responsible for raising new capital for the group as a whole and for managing the group's debt.

In the past few months, there has been an increase in the volatility of exchange rates, and subsidiaries are reporting significant gains or losses on foreign exchange transactions. At a recent meeting of the finance committee, it was suggested that the foreign exchange risk needed to be kept under control, and that techniques such as netting, pooling and matching would help to reduce the risk.

A dissenting view at the meeting was that since exchange rates fluctuate up and down, gains and losses usually cancel each other out: the FX risk was therefore immaterial.

Required:

(a) Explain the factors that a group such as BNM International might take into consideration when deciding whether it should control its foreign exchange risks.**(5 marks)**

(b) Describe the following techniques:

(i) netting;

(ii) matching;

(iii) pooling.

Suggest whether any of these techniques would be appropriate for hedging foreign exchange risk. **(10 marks)**

(c) Suggest other methods that the group might use to manage its foreign exchange risk, if the board of directors has already decided on a policy of avoiding the use of financial derivatives for foreign exchange risk management. **(4 marks)**

(d) Suggest why the group might use a central treasury department to raise capital for the group, instead of delegating the responsibility for raising their own capital to the individual subsidiaries. **(6 marks)**

(Total: 25 marks)

59 XCV

XCV is a large international company based in the UK, with a listing on the London Stock Exchange. The company has extensive borrowings, both from banks and in the form of bonds issued in the domestic bond market and the international bond market. It is also highly profitable, and has a substantial amount of surplus funds, much of which is invested in financial instruments, such as money market investments, government bonds and shares in other companies.

The company's Treasurer has recently moved on to another company, and his replacement is carrying out a review of the company's treasury policies and procedures. He is particularly surprised at the large amount the company spends each year on interest rate caps. He does not have an accountancy qualification, and he is also concerned about the effect that the many different financial assets and liabilities of the company might have on reported profits, due to the requirements of IAS 39**:** *Financial instruments: recognition and measurement*, which XCV is implementing in full.

Required:

(a) Explain the nature and purpose of an interest rate cap, and suggest ways of reducing the costs without exposing XCV to additional risk or requiring XCV to borrow less. **(10 marks)**

(b) Prepare a report for the Treasurer setting out the principles of valuation of financial instruments for financial reporting purposes, and suggest what controls might be applied to ensure that the appropriate accounting treatment is applied to each type of instrument. **(15 marks)**

(Total: 25 marks)

60 SDT PLC (MAY 05 EXAM)

SDT plc is a UK based manufacturer of a wide range of printed circuit boards (PCBs) that are used in a variety of electrical products. SDT exports over 90% of its production to assembly plants owned by large multinational electronics companies all around the world. Two companies (A and B) require SDT to invoice them in a single currency, regardless of the export destination of the PCBs. The chosen currencies are the Japanese Yen (Company A) and the US$ (Company B) respectively. The remaining export sales all go to European customers and are invoiced in Euros.

The variable cost and export price per unit PCB are shown below.

Market	*Unit variable cost (£)*	*Unit export sales price*
Company A	2.75	Yen 632.50
Company B	4.80	US$ 10.2678
Europe	6.25	Euro 12.033

Goods are supplied on 60 day credit terms.

The following receipts for export sales are due in 60 days:

Company A	Yen 9,487,500
Company B	US$ 82,142
Europe	Euro 66,181

The foreign exchange rates to be used by SDT in evaluating its revenue from the export sales are as follows:

	Yen/£	*US$/£*	*Euro/£*
Spot market	198.987 – 200.787	1.7620 – 1.7826	1.4603 – 1.4813
2 months forward	197.667 – 200.032	1.7550 – 1.7775	1.4504 – 1.4784
3 months forward	196.028 – 198.432	1.7440 – 1.7677	1.4410 – 1.4721
1 year forward	188.158 – 190.992	1.6950 – 1.7311	1.4076 – 1.4426

The Managing Director of SDT believes that the foreign exchange markets are efficient and so the likelihood that SDT will make foreign exchange gains is the same as the likelihood that it will make foreign exchange losses. Furthermore, any exchange risk is already diversified across three currencies, each from countries in very different economic regions of the world. The Managing Director has therefore recommended that the Treasury Department should not hedge any foreign exchange risks arising from export sales.

Required:

(a) Critically comment on the validity of the views and recommendations expressed by the Managing Director and explain how currency hedging might nevertheless be beneficial to SDT. **(6 marks)**

(b) Calculate the sterling value of the contribution earned from exports to each of the customers (A, B and Europe) assuming that SDT

(i) hedges the risk in the forward market; **(3 marks)**

(ii) does not hedge the risk and the relevant spot exchange rates in two months' time are as follows:

Two-month spot
Yen/£ 200.18 – 202.63
US$/£ 1.7650 – 1.7750
Euro/£ 1.4600 – 1.4680 **(3 marks)**

(iii) aims to maximise its contribution to sales ratio, calculate the average contribution to sales ratio in each of the above scenarios and advise SDT accordingly on whether to hedge its foreign exchange exposure. **(3 marks)**

(c) Comment on why (based on relative risk analysis) a company might seek to generate higher rates of return from export sales compared to domestic sales. **(6 marks)**

(d) If the payment from Company B is received late, briefly explain what risk SDT is taking in hedging B's payment in the forward market, and how this risk could be avoided. **(4 marks)**

(Total: 25 marks)

RISK AND CONTROL IN INFORMATION SYSTEMS

61 ERPS AND EIS (PILOT PAPER)

The Information Systems strategy within the MG organisation has been developed over a number of years. However, the basic approach has always remained unchanged. An IT budget is agreed by the board each year. The budget is normally 5% to 10% higher than the previous year's to allow for increases in prices and upgrades to computer systems.

Systems are upgraded in accordance with user requirements. Most users see IT systems as tools for recording day-to-day transactions and providing access to accounting and other information as necessary. There is no Enterprise Resource Planning System (ERPS) or Executive Information System (EIS).

The board tends to rely on reports from junior managers to control the business. While these reports generally provide the information requested by the board, they are focused at a tactical level and do not contribute to strategy formulation or implementation.

Required:

(a) Compare and contrast Information Systems strategy, Information Technology strategy and Information Management strategy and explain how these contribute to the business. **(10 marks)**

(b) Advise the board on how an ERPS and EIS could provide benefits over and above those provided by transaction processing systems. **(10 marks)**

(c) Recommend to the board how it should go about improving its budgetary allocations for IT and how it should evaluate the benefits of ERPS and EIS. **(5 marks)**

(Total: 25 marks)

62 OUTSOURCING RENEWAL

The GH Company designs and manufactures signalling control systems for railways. The company is over 100 years old and produced the first railway signal, which had to be moved by hand and was located by the side of the railway track, for one of the last major railways to be built in England in the 19th century. Since then, signalling systems have become more complex, with the latest signals being controlled by computers run by the railway company.

The latest prototype system being developed by the GH Company is able to determine the precise location of railway engines on a railway using sensors built into the track. An onboard display in the railway engine informs the driver of the estimated safe speed, removing the need for any form of signals beside or over the track completely.

A contracting company building a new railway in the USA has expressed interest in this system as it would significantly reduce construction costs for the railway. Part of the proposal is to monitor the location of trains from a branch of the GH Company in the USA, issuing instructions on recommended speed direct to trains using GH computer systems.

The GH Company entered into an outsourcing agreement with DF six years ago. Under the terms of the agreement, DF was to provide maintenance and upgrades to all hardware and software on a timely basis. The contract has worked well, with the Board of GH in particular being pleased not to have to monitor internal IT expenditure. The contract is for a fixed price every year.

The outsourcing contract with DF is due for renewal in six months' time.

Required:

Advise the Board of GH, with justification, whether or not to renew the outsourcing agreement with DF. **(25 marks)**

63 HZ HOSPITAL

The HZ hospital has recently invested in the most up-to-date computer systems to assist its doctors in making assessments of patients' illnesses. Two of the software packages now available to doctors are:

- a Management Information System which provides information on the medical history of each patient. It includes detailed factual information on past illnesses and any recurring symptoms as well as the patient's name, address and other personal information;
- an Expert System which is used to assist in the diagnosis of current illnesses. The Expert System is linked to the MIS to obtain details on each patient's medical history. From this information, and symptoms of the current illness, the Expert System provides an initial diagnosis, which the doctor uses in making his recommendation for the treatment of the patient. The diagnosis is stated in terms of probabilities of what the illness could be, rather than giving definite conclusions.

Both systems are accessed and updated via a series of on-line terminals located at key points around the hospital. All terminals are linked directly to a central file server; there are no external communications links due to the sensitive nature of the information being held.

Required:

(a) Explain the differences in the characteristics of information being provided by the two systems. **(10 marks)**

(b) Describe three general conditions, which must exist in order for an Expert System to be appropriate. **(8 marks)**

(c) Describe three advantages of using Expert Systems (other than speed and accuracy). **(7 marks)**

(Total: 25 marks)

64 MEASURING COSTS AND BENEFITS

A systems analyst must be prepared to carry out both cost-benefit calculations and risk analysis as part of the proposal for a new computer system.

Required:

(a) Describe two methods for demonstrating the costs and benefits of such a system over a period of time. **(8 marks)**

(b) Explain the specific problems associated with the measurement of information systems costs and benefits. **(7 marks)**

(c) Explain the factors you would take into account when undertaking a risk analysis of the costs and benefits of a proposed computer project. **(10 marks)**

(Total: 25 marks)

65 Q COMPANY

The Q Company ('Q') is an information provider. It has been in existence for three years and has grown relatively rapidly, but in response to customer demand rather than following any specific strategy.

Companies and individuals approach Q and ask it to research and provide information on a wide variety of topics. Topics range from weather forecasts for specific regions or cities to complete case histories of individuals including their names, directorships, addresses, telephone numbers, family and any other details that can be obtained legally on the Internet.

To provide this service, Q employs a team of 20 staff: 4 receptionists/administrators, 6 software engineers and 10 information managers. The information managers use Q's specialist software to search the Internet to obtain the information requested by clients. Information is returned to the client within 48 hours, normally by an encrypted attachment to an e-mail.

The cost incurred and revenue received per customer by Q for this service are shown graphically below. To encourage new business, Q tends to offer an initial consultation and the first 500 words of information free to any customer. Revenues increase steeply after this, although most customers specify a maximum amount of information required and therefore the revenue curve becomes horizontal.

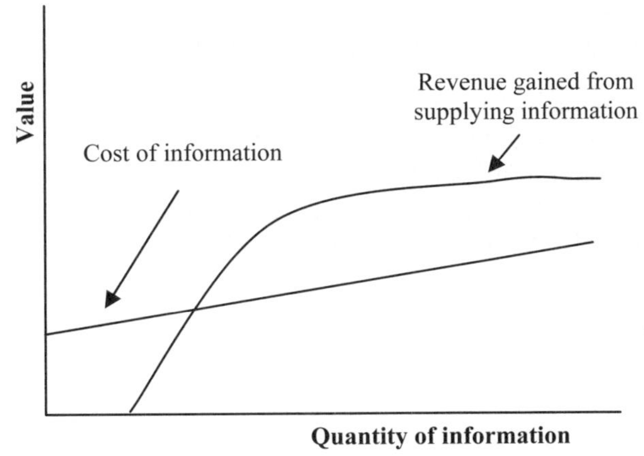

After considerable discussion within Q, various suggestions were put forward to try and increase the company's profits.

- Decrease fixed costs by decreasing the number of software engineers and administration staff.
- Make Q's specialist software available to third parties under a licence agreement by an annual fee or one-off payment.
- Provide information in graphical format, not just text, and make this available to customers.
- Upgrade Q's Internet connection to 'state of the art' to allow more rapid searches of the Internet, significantly decreasing the amount of time spent waiting for information.

No agreement was reached on a course of action, so an independent Management Accountant has been asked to provide a recommendation.

Required:

(a) Prepare a report for Q, evaluating the four suggestions with a recommendation on which suggestions, if any, to follow. **(16 marks)**

(b) Advise Q on how to develop an IS/IT/IM strategy. **(9 marks)**

(Total: 25 marks)

66 RBT

RBT manufactures tractors, harvesting machinery and similar farm equipment. It operates from one integrated office and factory near the capital of the country in which it is based. Due to restricted demand and the cost of manufacture of individual items, all equipment is manufactured to specific orders from clients. No inventories of finished goods are maintained although inventories of spare parts are available for sale.

The farm equipment is sold to farm owners by one of 20 sales representatives. The general procedure for making a sale is for the representative to visit the farm owner to discuss the owner's requirements. Basic price and model specification information are obtained from printed manuals that the representative carries. The representative then telephones the RBT office and confirms with production staff that the order can be made, checks the price and receives an estimated delivery date. An order confirmation is written out and the representative moves on to the next appointment. The farmer pays for the equipment on receipt.

As the country in which RBT operates is large, representatives cannot often visit RBT's office, so their price and model specification manuals may be out of date.

The Board of RBT is considering the introduction of a new information system. Each representative will be given a portable PC. Information on such things as products and prices will be kept on an Intranet and downloaded by telephone line when needed by the representative. Access to production managers and sales representatives will also be made via the Intranet. The voice telephone system will be discontinued and e-mail is thought to be unnecessary.

Required:

(a) Evaluate the proposed use of the Intranet within the RBT Company showing whether it would provide an appropriate communication channel for the sales representatives. Suggest ways in which any problems you have identified with the new systems may be resolved. **(16 marks)**

(b) Identify and evaluate any information systems that can be used to provide clients with information on the progress of their orders with RBT while they are being manufactured. **(9 marks)**

(Total: 25 marks)

67 PRINTING COMPANY

Some time ago, a printing company designed and installed a Management Information System that met the business needs of a commercial environment which was characterised at that time by:

- a unitary structure with one profit centre;
- central direction from senior managers;
- 100% internal resourcing of ancillary services;
- the employment exclusively of permanent full-time employees;
- customers holding large inventories who accepted long delivery times;
- most of the work concerned with long print runs for established large publishing houses.

A radical change in the business environment has resulted in the following outcomes:

- the development of a divisionalised structure with four profit centres that utilise each others services;
- empowerment of team leaders and devolved decision making;
- considerable outsourcing of activities;
- a significant proportion of the employees work part-time and/or on temporary contracts;
- customers now commonly operate JIT systems requiring immediate replenishment of inventories;
- the typical customer requires specialist low volume but complex high value printing.

Required:

Recommend the significant changes in the Management Information Systems that would probably be required to meet the needs of this new situation. Explain the reasons for your recommendations.

Note: Your answer does not require a consideration of technical matters. **(25 marks)**

68 STU (NOV 06 EXAM)

STU is a large distribution business that provides logistical support to large retail chains. A significant problem currently faced by STU is the number of legacy systems[1] in use throughout the organisation. The various legacy systems, each of which tends to be used by a single business function, hold data that is inconsistent with other systems, leading to an inconsistent approach to decision making across the business. The problem is made worse by many managers having developed their own PC-based databases and spreadsheets because of the lack of suitable information produced by the legacy systems.

STU's Board of Directors has recently approved the feasibility study presented by the Finance Director for the in-house development of a new Strategic Enterprise Management (SEM) system. The SEM system will use real-time data entry to collect transaction data from remote sites to maintain a data warehouse storing all business information which can then be accessed by various analytical tools to support strategic decision making. The SEM system will be developed and implemented over a three-year period within a budget approved by the Board. Three phases have been identified: design of the new system; development of the software; and delivery of the finished system into business units. The Board considers that designing, developing and delivering the SEM system will be crucial to business growth plans in a competitive environment.

[1]***Note:*** A legacy system is a computer system which continues to be used because the information it provides is critical to a business. However, the high cost of replacing or redesigning the system has led to it being retained by the business. It is typically an older design, is not compatible with more up-to-date software and, because of its age, provides information that is not as complete or reliable as it should be.

Required:

(a) Assuming that you are STU's Head of Internal Audit, recommend the actions that should be taken in connection with the design, development and delivery of the SEM system. **(13 marks)**

(b) Advise the audit committee of STU about:

(i) possible approaches to auditing computer systems; and

(ii) the controls that should exist in an IT environment. **(12 marks)**

(Total: 25 marks)

69 AMF (MAY 05 EXAM)

AMF is a market leading, high technology manufacturing organisation producing components for the computer industry. AMF has adopted a 'lean' approach to all its functions and has already made a decision to implement a new enterprise resource planning system (ERPS) to support the management of its customers, suppliers, inventory, capacity planning, production scheduling, distribution and accounting functions. The Board of AMF is considering the outsourcing of the design, delivery, implementation and operation of the ERPS to a specialist contractor that has an excellent reputation within the computer industry. A team would be set up within AMF to manage the transition.

Required:

Write a formal report to the Board of AMF that:

- discusses the advantages and disadvantages of outsourcing the ERPS system as suggested above; **(5 marks)**
- identifies the main risks involved in outsourcing the ERPS and suggests how these risks might be mitigated through internal controls and internal audit; **(13 marks)**
- recommends the processes and controls that AMF should adopt to manage a project for successful transition to a chosen outsource supplier should that be the decision of the Board. **(7 marks)**

(Total: 25 marks)

Section 3

ANSWERS TO SECTION A-TYPE QUESTIONS

1 CRASHCARTS (PILOT PAPER)

(a) Risk management should always be important, but it has gained wider recognition in recent years following the development of corporate governance frameworks in many countries, such as the Combined Code in the UK and the Sarbanes-Oxley legislation in the US.

In the UK, the Combined Code recognised the need for a sound system of internal control and risk management, and specified that it was a responsibility of the board of directors to carry out an annual review of the internal control and risk management systems. The basic view is that the objectives of a company should be to achieve a return for its shareholders consistent with the risk to which the shareholders wish to be exposed to achieve that return. Greater risk as well as lower returns can destroy shareholder value.

In the UK, the board of directors of a listed company should be responsible for maintaining a sound system of internal control, and for carrying out an annual review of the system of internal control. This review should cover all material controls, including financial, operational and compliance controls, and risk management systems.

However, it is the responsibility of executive management to devise the system of internal controls and to implement it. Such a system should include arrangements for identifying risks, implementing risk controls, monitoring performance and taking control measures where appropriate. The effectiveness of control systems depends to a very large extent on the quality of its information and communication systems.

The extent to which management accountants are involved in risk management will vary between different organisations, but the management accounting system is an essential element in the management information systems of an organisation. An essential feature of control systems is that targets need to be established, together with risk limits, and actual performance needs to be monitored and compared with these targets. This requires systems for planning and forecasting, and for monitoring performance through systems of feedforward control or feedback control.

Management accountants are closely involved in the design and implementation of such systems. For example:

- Within a system of budgeting and budgetary control, management accountants are involved in the preparation of budgets, and in monitoring actual performance against budget, or revised forecasts against budget, and reporting variances.

- Management accountants are often involved in the provision and analysis of information for strategic planning and control, including risk assessment (for example, through risk modelling and analysis of forecasts).
- Management accountants are often involved in the operation of systems for reporting non-financial performance, including reporting systems based on a balanced scorecard or Key Performance Indicators.
- In the role of internal auditors, management accountants are involved in monitoring the effectiveness of controls.

(b) The Call Centre should establish methods for risk analysis within an organised control framework. To do this, it is necessary to identify the objectives of the Call Centre (for example to achieve growth in annual profits), because risks need to be considered in the context of failing to achieve objectives. In addition, a management framework should be established, with individual managers or risk management committees given the responsibility for risk analysis.

A variety of methods should be used to identify and assess or measure risks. These include brainstorming by a group of managers, environmental analysis (PEST or SLEPT analysis), scenario analysis and modelling (for example, simulation or forecasting models). All recognisable risks should be considered. In the case of a Call Centre, these will include business continuity risks and breach of security risks, as well as commercial, business and financial risks.

Where possible, the analysis of risks should include an attempt to measure them, in terms of both the probability that they will occur and the potential losses or consequences when they do occur. A record should be kept of all the assessed risks, and risk mapping could also be used as a comparative analytical tool.

(c) An appropriate method of identifying the major risks at both parent level and subsidiary level might be brainstorming.

(i) At the subsidiary level, it seems clear that the Call Centre is essentially a fixed cost operation. Variations in profit depend on controlling fixed costs and ensuring that there is sufficient revenue. Major risks that might be identified from the information provided are:

(1) excessive growth in annual fixed costs;

(2) a fall in operator productivity;

(3) the loss of a client (or several clients) at the year end;

(4) a fall in the number of processed orders: this could be caused by either a fall in the total number of incoming calls received or a fall in the order strike rate (conversion of calls to processed orders);

(5) possibly, a fall in the number of line items for each order;

(6) resistance to further price increases from clients;

(7) problems with the computer system and back-up, such as a fraud.

The probability of each of these adverse events occurred might be assessed, and divided simply into 'likely' or 'not likely', as a first step towards risk mapping.

(ii) At the parent company level, the risks would appear to be strategic, and therefore more difficult to measure. A brainstorming approach to risk identification could be used. Potential risks might include:

(1) The risks from diversifying into an unfamiliar business over which management at the parent company level has little or no experience.

(2) The different risk profile of the Call Centre business compared with the consultancy business might result in a change in the risk profile, and the market value, of the Crashcart group.

(3) If any of the Call Centre clients are either clients of the consultancy business, or keen competitors of the consultancy business clients, there could be adverse consequences for customer relations.

(4) The parent company could be exposing itself to a greater risk to its reputation, if the Call Centre performs badly or attracts bad publicity.

The risks for the parent company cannot be measured from the information available. However, some of the risks facing the subsidiary can be quantified.

Tutorial note:

The extent of the quantified analysis you can provide in an answer will depend on the time you have available. There is no single 'correct' answer to this question, but having selected the risks you wish to quantify, present your argument – and your figures – clearly.

Risk: fixed costs become excessive

Between 20X1 and 20X3, annual revenue increased by £725,000 but the total annual salaries and salary-related costs of operators, management and administration staff rose by £730,000. If salary costs continue to rise at a faster rate than annual income, annual profits will be eroded. Operating profit in 20X3 was equal to just 5% [165/(2,180 + 1,120)] of salary costs.

Risk: fall in processed orders

Since the business has few, if any, variable costs, profitability is affected directly by variations in revenue.

Revenue from each processed call:	£
Income per order processed	3.000
Income from line items (2.8 items × £0.12)	0.336
	3.336

The breakeven point for processed orders in 20X3 was therefore 49,460 orders (£165,000/£3.336 per order). This is 4.3% (49,460/1,150,000) less than the actual number of processed orders in the year.

The risks to the number of processed orders include:

- a fall in the total number of calls, which is possibly a low risk;
- a fall in the number of incoming calls that turn into actual orders, possibly due to a greater frequency in out-of-inventory responses from clients' inventory systems;
- a fall in the number of clients.

Risk: loss of a client

This is likely to be a major risk in terms of probability. It would also have a major effect on profitability. In 20X3, the average number of processed orders per client was about 164,000 (1,150,000/7). The loss of revenue would be, in terms of 20X3 revenue:

	£000
Loss of fixed contract income	55
Loss of revenue from processed orders (164,000 × £3.336)	547
Total loss of revenue	602

Although there would be some savings in fixed costs, it seems probable that the loss of a further client would damage profits significantly.

Risk: fall in operator productivity

In view of the rapid staff turnover, there is probably a fairly high risk of some loss in operator productivity. However, in 20X3, 80 operators were employed when only 76.7 operators were required.

The excess capacity might be due to the risk of sudden staff reductions, or the need to employ large numbers temporarily whilst new operators are being trained. However, on the basis of the figures available, productivity in 20X3 could have been worse by 4.3% [(80 – 76.7)/76.7)] without affecting staffing requirement levels.

Since productivity has been unchanged for three years, the risk of such a fall is probably remote.

Risk: fall in line orders for each processed order

Income from processing line items was just £390,000 in 20X3. To reduce profitability significantly, there would have to be a very large fall in the average line entries per processed order. Although there has been some decline between 20X1 and 20X3, the probability of a large fall seems unlikely.

Conclusion

Each measured risk could be placed on a 2 × 2 risk map, with high/low likelihood on one axis and serious/not serious consequences on the other axis. This would indicate, for example, that the risk of a loss of a client is a major risk (high probability/major consequence) whereas the risk from a fall in productivity is a much smaller risk (fairly low probability/ probably a limited consequence). Other risks could be placed on the map in the same way. Management must then identify those risks that need the most urgent control measures or monitoring.

(d)

Tutorial note:

This question is in two parts. The first part of the question asks generally about the components of a management control system. The elements of a control systems should make you think about feedback systems and (hopefully) feedforward systems too. Our solution provides the component elements in a diagram as well as in narrative form; however a diagram is not essential, since it is not required specifically by the question.

The second part of the question goes on to the more specific issue of the main controls for the Call Centre. To answer this part of the question, it is probably necessary to specify the control information required and the controls that might follow from the information obtained. The question also specifies 'main' controls. The main controls are presumably basic controls to keep the system functioning, and controls that apply to the main risks – for example, the risk of a loss of a client.

Solution

A management control system might include elements of both feedforward control and feedback control.

(1) Feedback control involves a comparison of actual results with a plan, measuring differences or variances, investigating their causes and taking control action.

(2) Feedforward control involves using information about actual results or from external sources to revise forecasts for the future, comparing the revised forecast with the plan, measuring differences, investigate their causes and taking control measures as appropriate.

The components of these systems are illustrated in the simple diagram below:

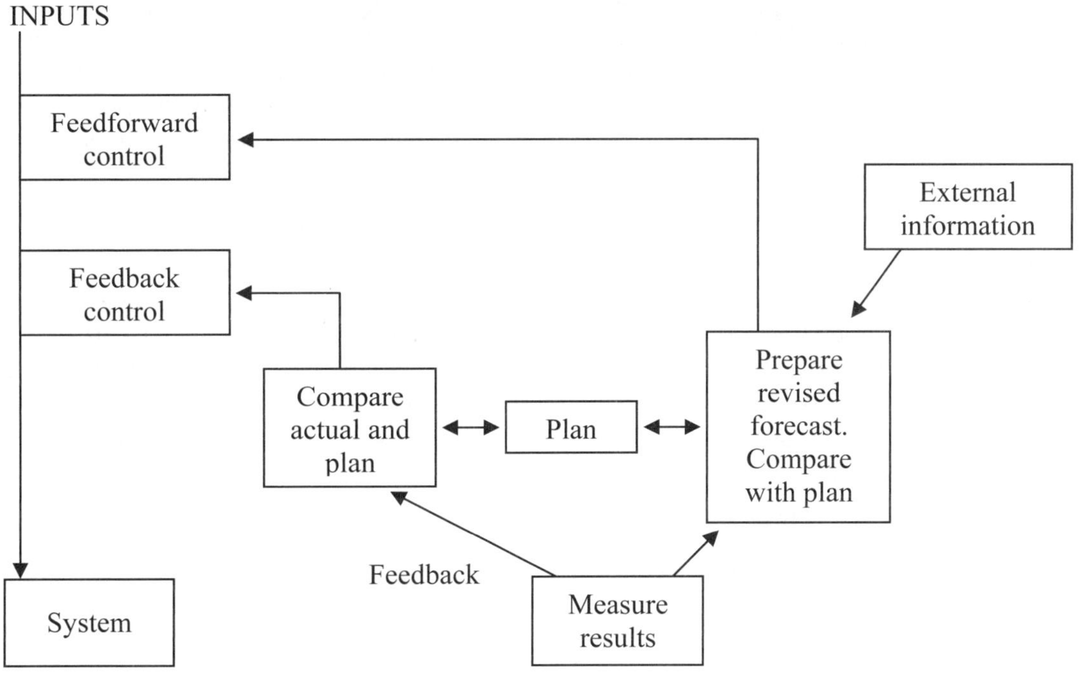

The components are as follows:

(1) Outputs from the system are measured, to provide control information.

(2) In a feedback system, these measured outputs (actual results) are compared with the budget or plan, and differences or variances are measured.

(3) On the basis of this control information, the controller responsible for results takes suitable control measures to change inputs to the system.

(4) In a feedforward system, revised forecasts are prepared, using information from measured actual results or from other (external sources).

(5) On the basis of this information, the controller responsible takes suitable control measures.

(6) Where appropriate, the original plan is replaced with a revised plan or revised forecast as the basis for future control comparisons.

Main controls for the Call Centre

(1) There must be all necessary system and security controls in the Call Centre and the Call Centre's computer system, to minimise the risks of unauthorised access by hackers and the risks of system down-time.

(2) A major risk is the loss of a client, and controls should be applied that contain or reduce this risk. Control information might include client feedback (for example, information obtained from discussions with each client's management team), and measures of operator performance, in terms of quality of service to customers as well as speed and productivity. Control measures to ensure client and customer satisfaction might be applied by means of supervision and refresher training.

(3) Another potentially significant risk is a change in the total number of processed orders, both a fall in total calls for reasons other than the loss of a client and also an increase in calls due to a growth in business volume. Feedforward information can be provided at regular intervals, comparing the current forecast of total calls volume with the original plan. Where necessary, suitable control measures might be to reduce or increase operator staffing levels.

(4) Controls over salary levels should be applied through the annual salary review process.

(5) Operator productivity does not appear to be a major risk at the moment, but productivity (measured by orders taken per operator or line items processed per operator) could be checked by means of productivity and idle time measures. Improvements in productivity might be achieved through better training, supervision, or by reducing staff levels to reduce inactivity/ idle time.

2 EPM FINANCE HOUSE

(a) **Data distribution Systems**

The current IT systems involve significant transfers of data from head office to the branches. As there is no network in place, data transfer presumably is by paper or electronically on CD. Either way, courier or postal systems must be used to transfer the data. This gives rise to risks of loss of data and, more seriously, the loss of confidential or sensitive company data, which could be used by competitors.

Implementing a secure network will help to decrease this risk as data will not have to be couriered between different locations.

Proposed IT systems

Implementation of a new network system will help to alleviate loss of data, as noted above. However, there is an additional risk in that EPM does not currently have any wide area network and therefore expertise in establishing or maintaining this type of system. There are various risks associated with the proposed system:

- Risk from system development. The new system may be incorrectly planned and may not meet business objectives.
- Risks from the project itself in terms of cost and time overruns.
- Risk that data may not be transferred to the new system correctly.

All these risks need to be managed by following a recognised system development technique and employing staff with appropriate experience in system design and development.

Operational risk

Currently, it takes a significant amount of time to transfer data between the different branches within the EPM Company. There is an operational risk in that these processes may be inadequate and do not provide the information needed for basic customer-facing transactions. EPM will therefore lose customers to similar companies where the standard of service or provision of information is of a higher standard.

Implementing a network system will remove this risk as information will be provided on a more timely basis.

Reputation risk

EPM appears to rely to a certain extent on its brand image and has built up a reputation of providing good financial advice to its customers. However, its reputation is at risk from negative publicity provided by some incorrect advice. While these instances of poor advice may be relatively few, if the brand image of EPM is tarnished, then the company could start to lose customers and sales rapidly; provision of financial advice is normally dependent on an element of 'trust' in the finance house.

EPM needs to ensure that information systems provide the necessary product information to staff at branches in a timely manner – another reason why the new network is essential.

Product risk

There is a risk that customers will not buy the new 'Pension4You' product simply because information about the product has not been distributed to the branches. Even though the product fits well into EPM's product portfolio, if staff and customers are not aware of its availability, then it cannot be sold.

Information about Pension4You needs to be made available as soon as possible before other companies market their own competing products. The marketing budget needs to be agreed and details of the product provided to the branches.

Regulatory risk

There is a risk that EPM will be unable to meet the new regulatory regime suggested for finance houses. Records of EPM's customers are not complete, and appropriate records of identification have either not been obtained or in some cases have been filed incorrectly. The effect of this is that EPM's control systems may not be able to identify money laundering and similar activities.

To overcome this risk, EPM needs to appoint a Money Laundering Reporting Officer (MLRO) as soon as possible. This person will then be responsible for establishing and monitoring appropriate control systems to ensure that evidence of customer identity is obtained for all new and existing customers. If this action is not taken then there is an additional risk that EPM will not be granted the necessary approval to continue to give financial advice, effectively causing the closure of the company.

(b) **Information and distribution**

When an organisation has a centralised data processing function, this might indicate that it also has a centralised management structure, with significant amounts of authority retained at head office and relatively little authority delegated to the branches. In an organisation such as a finance house, this might be an appropriate structure, given the need for standardised treatment of customers nationwide and the need to ensure compliance with financial regulations.

However, alternative IS/IT systems might be more appropriate, which delegate much more of the data processing to the local branches.

(i) **Extraction and processing of data by local offices from central files**

A distributed data processing arrangement could provide for local offices to be linked to the head office computer by telecommunications link. Branches could then extract the information they require, at times of their own choosing, from the head office files. The data could also be further processed or manipulated by the branch offices concerned, into a form or format better-suited to their requirements.

The advantage of this arrangement would be to give local management greater discretion in the choice of information they require and use. For this arrangement to be worthwhile, local managers should also have the authority to take certain initiatives at a branch level; for example, localised initiatives for increasing sales of products to customers.

There is also the advantage that much day-to-day transaction data can be distributed for local processing, instead of processing at head office, which is more remote from operations.

Control could be maintained by head office management through the production of regular control reports that are sent to both branch management and head office management. This control information will be much smaller in volume.

(ii) **Local data processing systems**

Instead of having most of the data processing carried out at head office, the processing could be done at branch office level. Each branch office could operate its own IS/IT system, with its own local server. Transaction data would then be input locally and processed locally.

The local servers would be linked to a head office computer, and management data could then be transmitted to head office for processing, or might be extracted from branch systems by head office staff.

The advantage of this system is that transaction data is dealt with entirely at a local level, where staff are probably more familiar with the details of the transactions. This might improve the service of the finance house branches to their customers.

At the same time, localised files give local managers the opportunity to develop their own reporting systems, whilst at the same time giving head office access to branch files to extract the management information it requires.

(c) **Receivables**

(i) If there are weak or non-existent controls, the types of error, omission or fraud that might occur are as follows:

- Invoices or credit notes might be issued for the wrong amount, or to the wrong customer.
- Invoices or credit notes might not be issued at all.
- Invoices might not be issued promptly.
- Invoices and credit notes might be issued but not recorded in the accounting system.
- Invoices and credit notes might be recorded in the accounting system, but for the wrong amount or the wrong customer.
- Receipts from customers might not be banked.

- Receipts from customers might not be properly recorded.
- Customers who are late with payment might not be chased for payment.
- Customers might be allowed more credit than their formal credit limit permits.

(ii) No internal control system is perfect, but a good system of control reduces the likelihood of errors and the opportunities for fraud.

The reasons that errors, omissions and fraud might occur even in a good control system are:

- Human error. Individuals make mistakes, even when they are skilled and knowledgeable in their job. Human error can occur due to tiredness or lack of attention, or because of a misunderstanding. Unless there are controls whereby the work of one individual is checked by someone else, human errors might escape unnoticed.
- Abuse of authority. A manager might choose to use his or her authority to over-ride controls. This would be an abuse of authority, and its effect would be to negate the control and make fraud or error more likely.
- Collusion. When two or more individuals collude to commit a fraud, they might be able to avoid controls in the system. For example, in a receivables system, two individuals might collude over the fraudulent issuing of credit notes to a customer or the improper recording of non-existent receipts.

(iii)

- With EPM, there should be segregation of duties. Different individuals should authorise requests for payments for financial services and payments to be credit to pension funds etc, record invoices and receipts in the accounts, and receive and bank payments.
- There should be a receivables ledger control account, and regular reconciliations should be carried out between the balance on this control account and the sum of the balances on the individual customer accounts in the receivables ledger.
- Regular (monthly) statements should be sent to customers, so that customers can check and verify the amounts recorded as outstanding on their account.
- There should be some data validation controls in the accounts software to identify and report errors in the data input by the accounts clerk.
- There should be a system for authorising invoices for issue, and invoices should not be recorded in the accounts before they have been authorised. In the case of EPM, there needs to be a system whereby financial advisors can record exactly which products have been recommended to customers, what the fee relating to the advice is, and when payments are due into the different pension funds etc.
- A regular report of overdue payments should be prepared, and the manager of the debt collections team should be held responsible and accountable for late payments.
- There should be independent authorisation of irrecoverable debts, and the authorisation of irrecoverable debts should not be made by anyone with access to the accounts system.
- A credit control system should be established, possibly with a full-time credit controller.

(d) **Risks of wide area network**

Access to data

Transferring any data over a wide area network increases the risk that the data will be accessed by unauthorised third parties, and then either copied, amended or deleted before it reaches its intended destination. An additional problem relates to the fact that, if electronic data is copied, it may not be possible to identify that copying has taken place.

Transferring personal data across a wide area network has increased risk that the data will be intercepted by third parties, in other words the data has not been kept secure. There is a potential breach of Data Protection legislation regarding the security of data.

Various controls can be implemented to limit access to date on the wide area network including:

- Use of passwords – the appropriate password being needed to access the WAN.
- Encryption of data in transit – so if the data is accessed it cannot be read.
- Use of private telephone lines or virtual private networks to limit the possibility of data being intercepted.

Access to network

Use of a network means that third parties may gain access to EPM's computer systems. The risk is then that a hacker could introduce viruses into the computer to stop hardware working correctly or corrupt data files. This type of attack would relate to all data stored on the computers, not simply personnel data.

The threat from hackers can be reduced by using firewalls to attempt to identify unauthorised access to systems and passwords to ensure users accessing the system have appropriate authority.

Operational risk

EPM will be significantly increasing its use of computer systems, placing additional reliance on moving data using the wide area network. With more complex systems there is an increased risk of system failure, for example from the wide area network being unavailable to network servers breaking down at head office.

There is also the risk that data could be lost or corrupted as it is transmitted over the network due to 'noise' on the network, or hardware becoming unavailable during data transfer.

Operational risk can be mitigated by:

- Ensuring backup systems are in place and tested – so, if data is lost or corrupted, copies are available.
- For critical systems, having alternative hardware available to use should the main network become unavailable.
- Ensuring that a support contract to maintain hardware is in place, with agreed service levels regarding restoration of service should the network become unavailable.

3 STAND

(a) The interest for six months is 2.5% for the £ and 4% for the Eastland dollar. The six-month forward rate will therefore be:

E$2.50 × 1.04/1.025 = E$2.5366 to £1.

A forward contract to sell E$2 million at 2.5366 would provide income in sterling of £788,457 (to the nearest £1).

At the current spot exchange rate of 2.5, E$2 million is worth £800,000. At the forward rate, the Eastland dollars are worth £11,543 less. However, this is not the amount that Stand would 'lose' by hedging the currency exposure.

Hedging with a forward contract and leaving the exposure un-hedged can only be compared when the forward contract reaches maturity and the foreign currency income is sold. The income from the forward contract can be compared with what the sterling income would have been at the spot rate at this future time.

(b) Currency risk exposures arise for Stand in two ways.

(1) When the company bids for new contracts, it quotes prices in a foreign currency without knowing whether it will be awarded the contract. There is a potential currency exposure between the time the bid is submitted and the time that the work is awarded.

(2) When Stand does win a contract with a foreign customer, a transaction exposure arises for the foreign currency income that it will eventually receive at the end of the contract.

The company has economic exposures to currency risk, arising from the fact that the company's expenses are incurred mainly in sterling, whereas 75% of its revenue is in foreign currencies. The risk is that sterling will strengthen against other currencies, and Stand will either have to raise its contract prices in other currencies (to maintain the same prices in sterling), or will have to reduce its contract prices and suffer a cut in profit margins. As a consequence, it would become less competitive compared with rival companies in other countries, because of the strength of sterling.

Forward contracts can be used to hedge transaction exposures. However, although the amount of currency income from each contract is known, there may be some uncertainty about the timing, due to uncertainty about when contract work will end. Forward contracts can be arranged giving the company the option of arranging settlement at any time between an earliest and a latest date, but if the contract is not completed by the latest date, the forward contract would have to be rolled forward, and the hedge for the currency risk would lose its effectiveness.

Currency futures are similar to forward contracts, but are exchange-traded in standardised contracts. An advantage of currency futures might be that there is greater flexibility about the settlement date, because a position can be closed at any time. However, hedging with currency futures is not perfect due to basis risk (arising from the difference between the spot rate and the futures price). Currency futures are available for some currencies (such as sterling/US dollar), but might not be available for many of the currencies in which Stand receives income.

Forward contracts and currency futures are both unsuitable for hedging potential exposures during the tender-to-contract period, because arranging a forward contract during the tender-to-contract period or opening a position in currency futures would be potentially speculative, and expose the company to risk rather than provide a hedge against risk.

Buying currency options would give Stand the right to sell a quantity of a foreign currency in exchange for sterling at a future date, at a fixed exercise rate. Options can be used to hedge transaction exposures, and allow the company to benefit from favourable movements in the exchange rate as well as providing a hedge against adverse exchange rate movements. However, currency options can be expensive, and the cost of the option premium might exceed the benefits from the hedge.

Currency options might be useful for hedging potential currency exposures, during the tender-to-contract period. For the cost of the option premium, Stand could fix a worst-possible exchange rate for any income it will receive at the beginning of the contract, if it is awarded the work. However, Stand might consider that using options to hedge potential exposures is too expensive, and the cost might exceed the benefits.

(c) Stand might consider managing its currency exposures in the following ways:

- It might insist on pricing its contracts in sterling. This would transfer the currency risk to Stand's customers. However, this would create a further risk, that customers would be less willing to award Stand contract work because of the currency risks to which they would be exposed.
- Stand could try to switch some of its expenses from sterling to the foreign currencies in which it receives income. To some extent, this might be possible by using foreign suppliers for sub-contract work and supplies (IT equipment).
- Stand's management need to be aware of the strategic business risks facing the company by having a UK base when most income is in foreign currencies. These risks can be mitigated by re-locating some operations into other countries, so that there is much more matching of revenues and expenses in the same currencies.

(d) If Stand complies with the Combined Code in the UK, it would be required to take suitable measures to ensure that an adequate risk control system is in place. The Combined Code includes a requirement that the board of directors should review the system of internal controls each year, and report to the shareholders that they have done so. The Combined Code also requires the audit committee (or a board risk committee consisting of independent directors, or the board as a whole) to review the company's internal control and risk management systems.

The Smith Guidance states that it is the responsibility of the company's executive management to identify, assess, manage and monitor risk, and for developing, operating and monitoring the system of internal control. Management should be accountable for this to the board and the audit committee

Within the UK system of good corporate governance, the operational responsibility for risk management should be given to executive management. The organisation and management structure will differ between companies, but a suitable system for internal control should include processes for assessing risk, designing and implementing internal controls, reporting on risk and monitoring the effectiveness of controls.

In the case of Stand, a risk committee of executive managers might have the responsibility for identifying and assessing the major risks, and prioritising them in a risk mapping process. Management should assess on a regular basis the scale of Stand's currency risk exposures. Suitable methods or techniques for assessing the scale of currency risks might be used. Presumably, the assessment of currency risks should be based on an analysis of actual currency revenues in the past or budgeted revenues, and an analysis of how income will be affected if exchange rates move adversely.

If the risks are considered significant, policies and systems for controlling the risk should be delegated to the appropriate managers – in this case, the finance director and treasurer. A policy framework might be imposed. For example, the risk committee might establish a policy that all currency exposures above a certain amount should be hedged, and that the finance director or treasurer should have discretion about hedging exposures below a certain amount

Currency exposures, the nature of hedging methods used and the consequences of hedging or not hedging exposures, should be reported to management, including the risk management committee. The management risk committee should then include currency risk assessments in their reports to the audit committee and the board.

Each year, the board should satisfy itself that the system of internal controls, including the system for controlling currency risk, is satisfactory.

4 POOL PUBLISHING

(a) (i) Diversification can reduce risk. This is because the actual long-run average outcome from an event or series of events is likely to be close to the expected average outcome. For example, if a company invests in a large number of independent projects, each expected to earn a return of 10%, the actual return from any individual investment might be higher or lower than 10%, but the average return from the entire portfolio of investments is likely to be close to 10%.

The ability of an investor or company to reduce risk by diversifying investments and holding a varied portfolio of independent investments, can be demonstrated statistically. The standard deviation of returns from the portfolio (a measure of risk) will be lower for the portfolio as a whole than for individual investments within it.

However, certain conditions need to apply for diversification to be successful in reducing risks.

- The expected returns from each investment in a portfolio need to be independent. When the returns from two investments have positive correlation, this means that when one investment performs well ,the other will perform well, and when one performs badly, the other will also perform badly. To reduce risk by building up a portfolio, the correlation between returns from investments in the portfolio should not be strongly positive and ideally the correlation of returns should be negative.
- There is also an argument that management should diversify within areas of their own competence. In a business context, a company that seeks to diversify should have the management skills to manage the diversification successfully. For example, POOL Publishing might diversify successfully by publishing more books or acquiring more book rights through takeovers of other book publishing companies. However, it would be more risky to diversify into areas where management do not have demonstrable management skills and experience.

(ii) The diversification strategy of the board might be inappropriate for several reasons.

- The management of POOL Publishing might not have the skills or experience to take the company into completely different areas of business. There are no similarities between book publishing and operating internet cafes or a chain of restaurants. If management do not have the skills to manage new businesses, diversification will add to the business risk rather than reduce it.

- The same argument probably applies to the proposal to acquire the business of a magazine publisher. Magazine publishing is very different in character from book publishing.
- Even a proposal to acquire a book publishing company in another country could be risky, if POOL Publishing cannot rely on good local management to operate the business after an acquisition. However, in terms of management skills and experience, this acquisition prospect is possibly appropriate.
- There is also an argument that to a certain extent, shareholders can make their own decisions to diversify, and do not need companies to diversify on their behalf. For example, if a shareholder wants to invest in a book publisher, internet cafes and a restaurant business, he can buy shares in three different companies, each specialising in its own particular area of operations. Nothing is gained by the company making investments to create a similar portfolio, and it can be argued that the companies will perform better by concentrating on their core competences.
- If stock market investors believe that companies should concentrate on core competences, they are likely to 'punish' conglomerate companies that have a widely-diversified portfolio of investments by under-valuing their shares. In such a situation, the conglomerate can become a target for a takeover bid, with the bidder intending to make a profit by acquiring the conglomerate and 'spinning off' its separate businesses at their 'true' value in order to make a profit.

(b) (i) The expected value of sales is as follows:

Sales volume units	*Probability*	*Expected value* units
2,000	0.3	600
8,000	0.4	3,200
12,000	0.2	2,400
24,000	0.1	2,400
		8,600

The cost of printing 8,600 units would be $40,000 + (8,600 × $1.50) = $52,900.

The expected profit would be calculated as follows, assuming that actual sales will be exactly 2,000, 8,000, 12,000 or 24,000.

Sales demand units	*Sales revenue** $	*Costs* $	*Profit/ (loss)* $	*Probability*	*Expected value of profit/ (loss)* $
2,000	20,000	52,900	(32,900)	0.3	(9,870)
8,000	80,000	52,900	27,100	0.4	10,840
12,000	86,000	52,900	33,100	0.2	6,620
24,000	86,000	52,900	33,100	0.1	3,310
					10,900

*Sales revenue is restricted to the lower of sales demand and the quantity of units available.

Using expected values to estimate sales demand, and printing a quantity of books equal to the expected value, will give:

- expected value of demand = 8,600 units;
- expected value of profit = $10,900.

(ii) An alternative approach to the assessment would be to consider the expected profit or loss if the company decided to print (1) 8,000 copies (2) 12,000 copies or (3) 24,000 copies.

Print 8,000 copies

The cost of printing 8,000 units would be $40,000 + (8,000 × $1.50) = $52,000.

Sales demand	*Sales revenue**	*Costs*	*Profit/ (loss)*	*Probability*	*Expected value of profit/ (loss)*
units	$	$	$		$
2,000	20,000	52,000	(32,000)	0.3	(9,600)
8,000	80,000	52,000	28,000	0.4	10,200
12,000	80,000	52,000	28,000	0.2	5,600
24,000	80,000	52,000	28,000	0.1	2,800
					9,000

*Sales revenue is restricted to the lower of sales demand and the quantity of units available.

Print 12,000 copies

The cost of printing 12,000 units would be $40,000 + (12,000 × $1.50) = $58,000.

Sales demand	*Sales revenue**	*Costs*	*Profit/ (loss)*	*Probability*	*Expected value of profit/ (loss)*
units	$	$	$		$
2,000	20,000	58,000	(38,000)	0.3	(11,400)
8,000	80,000	58,000	22,000	0.4	8,800
12,000	120,000	58,000	62,000	0.2	12,400
24,000	120,000	58,000	62,000	0.1	6,200
					16,000

*Sales revenue is restricted to the lower of sales demand and the quantity of units available.

Print 24,000 copies

The cost of printing 24,000 units would be $40,000 + (24,000 × $1.50) = $76,000.

Sales demand	*Sales revenue**	*Costs*	*Profit/ (loss)*	*Probability*	*Expected value of profit/ (loss)*
units	$	$	$		$
2,000	20,000	76,000	(56,000)	0.3	(16,800)
8,000	80,000	76,000	4,000	0.4	1,600
12,000	120,000	76,000	44,000	0.2	8,800
24,000	240,000	76,000	164,000	0.1	16,400
					10,000

*Sales revenue is restricted to the lower of sales demand and the quantity of units available.

On the basis of the information available, it would appear that the expected value of profit will be increased by printing a quantity of books in excess of the expected value of sales. Assuming that print quantities could be 12,000 or 24,000 only, the expected profit would be maximised by printing 12,000 copies.

However, the risk would be greater of making a larger loss.

Adopting this approach to the assessment of probabilities, risk and returns would give management more useful information on which to base their decision.

(c) A significant risk in switching from one service provider for accounting services to another is the risk of loss or corruption to data during the change. ITW will be required to supply up-to-date and accurate files at the end of its contract, either to POOL or to the new service provider. During this handover process, records might be lost from files, or entire files might be corrupted. For example, ITW might hand over out-of-date files, missing some recent transactions. POOL needs to be able to check that all the information has been properly transferred.

One way of dealing with this problem might be to arrange for a short period during which both ITW and the new service provider are maintaining accounting records for POOL. An internal (or external) audit can then carry out a check on the files in the two systems, to ensure that they appear identical (e.g. with the same total number of records and same control totals).

There might be technological or software difficulties if the accounts are moved from ITW's computer system to the system of another provider, and there might be difficulties in getting the system to operate properly on the system of the new service provider. The solution to this problem is also to have a period of time during which the two systems are running in parallel, so that any technical problems can be identified and resolved.

There is also a risk of unauthorised retention of files. An individual within the ITW organisation might retain copies of the accounts files of POOL. This would create a risk of file data about customers getting into the possession of another organisation. Alternatively, the individual retaining the file copies might subsequently use the information they contain for fraudulent purposes. POOL needs to check, if possible, that there are no duplicate copies of files that have been retained within ITW without authorisation.

This risk is difficult to deal with. However, ITW should be asked to demonstrate that after the handover of the files, copies have not been retained in ITW's computer system. If ITW is an ethical organisation, it should be willing to comply with this request, and demonstrate that it no longer holds files for POOL.

There could be operational difficulties in changing from ITW to a new service provider, particularly if ITW is unwilling to be helpful. ITW might have no incentive to give assistance to another company that has taken their contract with POOL. Inevitably, operational problems will arise, and the new service provider might need to ask questions. Unless ITW is willing to provide assistance, operating difficulties might arise.

The efficiency and success of the change to the new service provider depends on the goodwill of ITW for a number of reasons, and POOL might wish to consider offering a bonus payment to ITW after the change has taken place, provided this has happened in a satisfactory way, and with the full co-operation and assistance of ITW's staff.

It has been assumed that the same system operated on behalf of POOL by ITW will be used by the new service provider. This is not necessarily the case, and it might be the intention of POOL to switch its accounting system to a different accounting system that is better able to handle the growing volume of transactions and data. If a new system is required, all the risks associated with new system design, development and implementation will arise.

(d) Accounting systems must be audited. Since ITW will be handing responsibility for the system to a new service provider, it would be appropriate to carry out an audit of the system before the change occurs. This will allow the auditors to satisfy themselves that the data transferred to the new service provider has been recorded accurately. The audit might be carried out by POOL's internal auditors, although the external auditors might wish to do some audit checks themselves.

CAATs are used to assist with the audit of computer systems, and it would be appropriate to use them for the audit of ITW's files.

(i) In view of the sensitivity of accounting files to corruption or fraud, the system will probably include embedded audit facilities that help the auditor to extract information for audit review.

(ii) The auditors might use audit interrogation software, that can be used to carry out substantive tests on transactions or account balances. For example, software can be used to identify transactions or balances of an unusual amount. The auditor can then check these, if necessary referring back to source documents for evidence of the validity of the transaction.

(iii) Audit software might also help to check for fraud, such as the existence of false suppliers (by checking for supplier records with the same address, or suppliers with the same address as the home address of an employee, or several suppliers all with the same address).

(iv) Audit software can be used to identify other unusual transactions that have occurred in the system, such as an unusually large number of transactions of a particular type within a short time period.

(v) The auditors might also use test data, that can be fed into the system to produce file data and output. The files and the output can be checked to ensure that the data has been processed correctly.

5 GHI GROUP (MAY 06 EXAM)

(a) The following risks are faced by the GHI Group:

Financial risks

(i) GHI is based in the UK, but organises holidays abroad. Its revenues will be in pounds sterling, but it will have to pay its suppliers of overseas accommodation and transport services in their local currencies. The group is therefore exposed to *currency risk* given the mismatch of currencies between revenues and costs. It will be possible to charge customers in local currency for services they buy while on holiday (e.g. excursions, wines and spirits at meals, etc), so some matching of revenues and costs is possible, but there will still be a large mismatch. The risk is that, if the pound depreciates against the foreign currencies, then more pounds will have to be paid to overseas suppliers, and the profitability of the holiday products may be undermined.

(ii) There will be a *cash flow risk* arising from the uncertainty about how many people will actually take the holiday that they originally book. The traditional pattern is for holidaymakers to pay a modest deposit when they book a holiday, with the balance payable (say) a month before the departure date. The company must contractually book a room in a hotel once the initial booking is made, and will be liable to pay the hotel, but in practice a proportion of holidaymakers will be unable to take up their holiday due to illness, family bereavement, etc. They may forfeit the deposit they have paid, but the company must pay for the hotel rooms it has booked, and will lose the profits they had hoped to gain from selling excursions, etc. This uncertainty about the actual number of customers who will turn up leads to the cash flow risk of the company.

Political risks

(i) The risk of terrorist acts in countries that are popular with UK holidaymakers continues to cast a shadow on the whole travel industry. Overseas holidays are often a discretionary purchase so, if a bomb goes off in Egypt or Turkey or New York, then some holidaymakers will avoid that destination and choose either to holiday in the UK or perhaps just to stay at home. It is difficult for a company such as GHI to predict when the next terrorist act will occur, but it is possible to buy insurance against the adverse effects that a major incident would cause the company.

(ii) GHI is planning to buy two new hotels in the Eastern Mediterranean. The question does not state the countries in which these purchases are to be made, but there will be a discrimination risk that the local government authorities may disapprove of foreign owners of local assets and may make things difficult for the company. A country such as Turkey may look negatively on a UK company if Turkey's application to join the EU is seen to be held up by UK opposition to its membership. If the hotels to be purchased are in the South of Cyprus, which is already an EU member, then the discrimination risk is probably lower.

Environmental risks

(i) An increasing number of people are using the internet to book 'self-managed' holidays directly, rather than visiting a travel agent. This development in technology has created the risk to GHI that customers will no longer visit its retail travel outlets, and will no longer buy its packaged products. GHI must react quickly by offering its products on the internet at a competitive price, otherwise it will get left behind as the market develops.

(ii) The growth in divorce rates and in people remaining single means that the traditional family 'bucket and spade' beach holiday with two parents and two children will become less of the norm. This social change means that GHI must offer products of interest to single people, older people and lone-parent families. The 'weekend break' trips to European cities are an example of products popular with the over 50s which will continue to grow in the future as the number of older people in society steadily increases.

Economic risks

(i) GHI has decided to purchase two new hotels in the Eastern Mediterranean. These will be overseas assets whose cost is denominated in an overseas currency, therefore their translated value in the group's balance sheet will fluctuate from year to year. This translation risk could mean that the balance sheet appears weaker if the pound strengthens against the relevant overseas currency, which could have implications for the cost of borrowing charged by future providers of debt finance.

(ii) GHI must decide on the currency in which it will pay its suppliers in overseas countries. Typically, anyone in the Americas or the Far East is happy to be paid in US dollars, while anyone in Europe or Africa can normally be paid in Euros. However, there is a currency selection risk in that, if GHI decides to pay Turkish suppliers in Euros while its competitors pay their similar suppliers in pounds, say, then GHI's relative competitive position will depend on the pound's performance against the Euro.

(b) The risk impact on each of GHI's financial statements is as follows:

Income statement

Purchasing its own overseas hotel properties will mean higher fixed costs and lower variable costs (i.e. higher operational gearing). This means that an increase in bookings will have a marked effect on the reported profit of the group, since any increase in the 'top line' of revenues will tend to flow through directly to the 'bottom line' of profit for the period. The corresponding risk is clearly that profits will be low if bookings are low, since the fixed costs of operating and financing the hotels must be paid regardless of the number of customers.

There will also be costs incurred in hedging the large foreign currency incomes and expenses that will arise.

Block booking rooms from local suppliers under the terms of the 2003–2005 contract has low fixed costs and higher variable costs, i.e. is a lower risk policy. GHI can cancel unwanted rooms without penalty at just one week's notice and will presumably be able to keep the deposits paid by customers who have to cancel at the last minute (although customers can claim this back from their travel insurance).

However, significant costs may be incurred in relocating customers who have been double-booked and in paying them compensation, although much of this cost may be recoverable from the overseas suppliers who had failed to come up with the rooms they had contracted to make available.

Balance sheet

Purchasing its own overseas hotel properties will lead to the hotels being shown in the group's assets, and the source of finance being shown in the group's equity or liabilities, depending on how the purchase is financed. There is then a risk that the asset value may decrease, either because the overseas currency may depreciate, or owing to impairment such as if the hotels gain a poor reputation. At the same time the source of finance must still be serviced, e.g. interest must be paid on loans taken out, regardless of the value of the assets that have been bought.

There is a further risk of expropriation of the hotels by a foreign government if relations between the UK and the foreign government turn sour. For example, if Turkey is refused membership of the EU, or if the hotels are situated in a politically sensitive area such as North Cyprus, then the risk of expropriation cannot be discounted.

A final risk arises from the probable lack of liquidity in the market for foreign hotels, should GHI decide that it wanted to sell them. There may be few willing buyers at the time, so GHI may have to sell at a loss if it ever wanted to sell the hotels in a hurry.

Block booking rooms from local suppliers has no effect on the assets and liabilities of GHI, so there is no risk impact. Over time, as profits are earned, the balance sheet will become stronger owing to the accumulated retained earnings, which should reduce the perceived risk exposure of the group.

Cash flow statement

Purchasing its own overseas hotel properties and then offering all-inclusive deals to customers (including all food and drinks) will require a larger up-front cash payment to buy the hotels, followed by significant regular payments in foreign currencies to buy all the goods and services to be supplied to the holidaymakers. Revenues will be earned in pounds sterling, as holidays are sold, and these should be a large amount per customer since GHI is attempting to sell a premium product.

The mismatch of currencies between pounds received and foreign currency paid out means that hedging costs will have to be incurred if currency risk is to be reduced.

Block booking rooms from local suppliers has a more predictable pattern of payments. A 20% deposit is payable by GHI in January (before the peak summer season begins, so at a time when cash flow might be weak), with the balance payable before the rooms are taken up. Since these are room-only deals, not all-inclusive holidays, the cash payments by GHI per customer will be smaller, with less risk therefore involved.

Summary

Purchasing its own overseas hotels will increase the financial risk of the group (particularly if the purchase is financed by new loans) and the operating risk of the group (since it is a new activity for the group). GHI will have carried out an investment appraisal before deciding to purchase the hotels, and it seems that the purchase passed the test of achieving a 10% hurdle rate before adjusting for risk, since the group has decided to proceed with the purchase.

Sales forecasts have been carried out which suggest that demand will grow in these resorts at 15% pa for the next five years, which sounds very encouraging. If these forecasts are reliable, then GHI would be justified in making a medium-term commitment to these resorts, buying the hotels, and offering the all-inclusive packages that it is planning.

(c) GHI has decided to move from offering traditional 'room-only' or 'bed and breakfast' holidays to offering 'all-inclusive' holidays where the customer pays a larger sum up-front but all food and drink, sports facilities, entertainments, and so on in the hotel are then free. The risk is that:

(i) customers may not be willing to pay the higher price; and

(ii) the costs of the additional items may exceed the incremental revenues, so that GHI is worse off after the decision.

The willingness of customers to pay more for a product depends on the elasticity of demand for the product. The demand for package holidays is price elastic, in the sense that higher prices will reduce demand, given the competitive nature of the market. GHI must therefore send a clear message in its marketing literature about the premium quality nature of the holidays it is offering. Services such as free magazines and drinks on aeroplanes are cheap to organise, but may differentiate GHI's offering from the competition.

The risk is that customers will compare the more expensive GHI holiday with a cheaper holiday offered by a competitor, and decide that the extras offered by GHI are not worth the premium price. GHI can combat this risk by describing long lists of facilities that are included in the price, e.g. use of the hotel gym, swimming pool, tennis courts, etc. In reality the likelihood of a customer using all these facilities is low, but they will impress the potential customer in demonstrating the added value in an all-inclusive holiday.

Keeping tight control of costs is also important. The risk is that customers and staff will not place any value on goods and services that are handed out for free in the all-inclusive environment. Customers might take several different desserts from a free buffet, eat the one that tastes best, and throw the others away. Portion control must be stressed to staff in their training: all portions of food and drink should be the minimum possible to dissuade customers from throwing large amounts away. A training and audit regime for hotel staff should be implemented to monitor and control all portions offered to customers.

A final method of monitoring the success of the all-inclusive packages is to ask customers to fill out questionnaires at the end of their holiday, asking for their feedback. After all, there is no point marketing a premium product that customers are not happy with. Their suggestions for improvements should be taken very seriously and fed back as inputs into the planning process for the future.

(d) The GHI Group comprises a number of subsidiaries, each operating as a separate company, for example:

- an airline;
- a chain of retail travel agents;
- different tour operators, each serving a particular segment of the market.

The group has now taken the strategic decision to buy two new hotels in the Eastern Mediterranean. Presumably these hotels will be presented in the balance sheet of the tour operator who will organise holidays to this resort, together with the associated finance.

In the GHI group, each company's performance is measured by its residual income (RI), i.e. the accounting profit less a notional charge for capital employed, calculated as a risk-adjusted interest rate applied to the capital employed in the division.

There will clearly be an impact in the tour operator purchasing the hotels when RI is calculated. The accounting profit would be hoped to rise, but the increased risk in the company described in earlier parts of this question will mean that a higher interest rate is used, and the amount of capital employed will certainly increase. The net effect on RI is therefore uncertain.

As far as other companies in the group are concerned, the success of the new hotels will have implications for their performance as well. The all-inclusive holiday will presumably include a flight with the company airline, and will be sold through the chain of retail travel agents. If a large number of customers book these holidays, this will have a favourable effect on other companies in the group. Head office management must be careful in setting transfer prices that one company in the group charges another company for services provided. For example, the tour operator must pay the airline for the flights that it uses for its customers. If this charge is too little, then the airline will be unhappy to take these passengers. If the charge is too great, the tour operator will seek an alternative airline to fly its customers. Thus transfer prices should be based on market prices as far as possible.

There are also capital allocation implications of the tour company buying the two hotels. This will necessarily reduce the funds that are available for capital investment in the other group companies. Head office must work hard to persuade the other group companies to submit proposals for possible capital investment, stressing that all investments that satisfy the 10% hurdle rate will be considered seriously.

(e) The role of the internal audit department is to provide assurance to senior management and the board of directors that business risks are being managed properly and that internal controls are operating as effectively as they were designed to. Thus, in the context of GHI's foreign property purchases, internal audit must first decide whether the controls over such property purchases are adequate, and secondly whether the controls have been carried out properly.

Relevant tasks for the internal audit department are as follows:

- Review the procedures by which potential sites are identified. This could mean checking that a minimum number of overseas property agents were consulted (say, a minimum of three agents in each country), and ensuring that the agents' advice is communicated to the relevant people at GHI.
- Checking that company procedures are followed in respect of negotiation of prices to be paid for each hotel.
- Checking that professional advice is sought and followed in respect of the appropriate method of financing the purchase price, e.g. bank loans, share issue, etc. The treasury department at GHI head office should receive this advice and give their opinion on it.
- Checking that the treasury department paid the appropriate amount of foreign currency to the hotels' builders on time, and that foreign currency risks have been hedged in accordance with group policy.
- Checking that health and safety regulations are fully complied with, before customers are allowed in. This should include fire drills and the servicing of boilers, given the public's sensitivity to faulty boilers following a well-publicised tragedy in Corfu at the end of 2006.
- Creating a rolling timetable within the internal audit department to test all the operating sections of the new hotels over the next few months. The new hotels will then be fully integrated into all the other group assets that internal audit inspects.

Tutorial note:

There are many other tasks that internal audit could carry out. The important thing here is to list out at least five items to reflect the five marks available.

---

6 BLU (NOV 06 EXAM)

(a) (i) The following risks face BLU in relation to its investment appraisal and approval process.

Investment appraisal is carried out using a discounted cash flow (DCF) calculation with a discount rate of 15%. This 15% rate has been in use for several years and appears to have been arbitrarily selected. The risk is that the actual cost of BLU's capital is materially different from 15%, so that projects with a negative real net present value might be being accepted and projects with a positive real net present value might be being rejected. This could have a negative effect on shareholder value.

There is a risk of conflict between the investment acceptance criterion and the company's strategic objective. Investments are accepted if they offer a positive NPV when discounted at 15%, while the stated strategic objective is to increase sales by 15% and earnings by 17.5% pa in the expectation that this will increase shareholder value. It would be possible to accept a project with a positive NPV but with low current sales potential, thus frustrating the stated strategic objective. In reality, the best way to increase shareholder value in an efficient market is to accept positive NPV projects, since the NPV should be passed on to the accumulated shareholder wealth as soon as the market learns of the project and is convinced of its prospects.

The above risk of conflict between objectives is compounded by the fact that senior management bonuses are contingent on annual increases in sales and in short-term projects. It would be better if such bonuses could be aligned with growth in shareholder value, perhaps by linking bonuses to a growth in the share price.

Investment approval currently depends on demonstrating a positive NPV. Where a number of positive NPV projects are competing for funds, the project with the highest NPV is selected. The risk therefore is that other positive NPV projects have been rejected, thus shareholder wealth is not as high as it could be. Research should be undertaken as to why the available capital funds are limited. If management have set themselves gearing ratios that they are unwilling to exceed, they should be asked to reconsider this policy as, although it might be avoiding some financial risk, it is costing the shareholders money in terms of profitable opportunities rejected.

(ii) The information system feeding the current investment appraisal process introduces a number of risks into the system.

The use of a five year strategic planning horizon has the advantage of simplicity, and the figures in the near future will be more determinable than those further into the future, but there is a risk of taking inappropriate decisions if all cash flows beyond year 5 are ignored. To take an extreme example, think of a nuclear power station. This has a large initial cost, then some decades of cash inflows, followed by a large cash outflow at the end of the power station's life when it is decommissioned. Ignoring this final outflow would seriously distort the appraisal of the investment's viability. BLU is unlikely to be thinking of investing in a nuclear power station, but the same principle holds firm. If an expensive overhaul of CNC equipment is requested after every six years, then ignoring cash flows beyond five years would give the wrong impression.

The Finance Department currently accept without question the forecasts of future demand that are prepared by the Market Research Department. They also accept the capacity information from the Production Department. There is the risk that their forecast figures will be inaccurate. Market Research produce their estimate from having asked the Sales Department how they think they will perform next year. Forecasts from sales departments are notoriously optimistic throughout businesses, so perhaps the Finance Department should compare previous years' forecasts with the actual figures that turned out in reality, to see if some adjustment factor needs to be applied to the forecasts that they have now been provided with.

Finally, there is a risk from the capital investment appraisal process being part of the annual budget cycle. A nimble business should be able to take advantage of opportunities quickly, to invest in possibilities as they arise. By waiting some months before approval is given to go ahead with a project, there is the risk that competitors will beat the company to market, or that the cost and revenue estimates are out-of-date by the time that the project finally goes ahead.

(b) An internal auditor carrying out an audit of the capital investment process at BLU should adopt a risk-based approach to planning the audit. Thus the audit procedures planned to be carried out should match the business risks identified in part (a) that are inherent in the current system.

In respect of the capital investment process, the audit plan should contain the following points:

- Assess whether 15% is a reasonable approximation to the company's cost of capital. BLU is listed on a stock market, so it should be fairly simple to derive a cost of equity as long as the share price is not too volatile. The cost of debt can be calculated quickly if the debt is also quoted, otherwise it may have to be estimated either from DCF principles or by comparison with similar debt instruments that are quoted.
- Discuss with senior management why capital funds are limited. If there is hard capital rationing (i.e. the reason for the limitation is external to the company and unavoidable), then perhaps projects should be chosen on the basis of their profitability index (NPV per £ required at the time of rationing) rather than on their absolute NPV. If there is soft capital rationing (i.e. the reason for the limitation is internal to the company, perhaps a self-imposed maximum gearing level) then management should reconsider the limit that has been placed.
- Find out from senior management how projects are managed once they have begun and whether there is a post-completion audit carried out after they have been completed. There are no details in the question in respect of these matters.

In respect of the information system feeding the capital investment process, the audit plan should contain the following points:

- Discuss with senior management whether a five year planning horizon is appropriate. What is the expected useful life for the machines, for example for depreciation purposes in the financial accounts? If it is five years with a nil residual value, then the policy of a five year horizon is acceptable. However, the sales income is continually increasing year-by-year in the forecast projected in the question, so there is no evidence that the equipment is becoming old and reaching the end of its life. It would seem appropriate for this type of equipment to have a planning horizon greater than five years.
- Compare the forecasts of sales produced by Market Research Department in previous years to the sales actually achieved, to gain an opinion on whether this year's forecast is likely to be accurate. Carry out a similar exercise for the cost information produced by the Production Department.

(c) The following internal controls should be introduced to improve BLU's capital investment process (using the five components of internal control identified in the COSO Framework and in International Standards on Auditing).

Control environment

The board of BLU should set the right 'tone' at the top of the company to ensure that integrity and ethical values are followed throughout the company. The current chasing of sales and short-term profits that is 'strongly promoted' as the strategic objective is inappropriate and should be replaced by a range of objectives that follow a balanced scorecard of measurements that are relevant to all the stockholders of the business.

Risk assessment

Once appropriate strategic objectives have been agreed, only then is it possible to identify and assess the risks that might frustrate those objectives from being achieved. This risk assessment can then be developed into the risk management system for managing the identified risks. For example, if BLU adopt as an objective that share price performance should be in the top quartile of its industry sector each year, then the risks that this will not be achieved can be addressed.

Control activities

These are the policies and procedures that ensure that the decisions and instructions of management are carried out. For example, an annual performance review should be carried out on each capital investment that is proceeded with. It is better to abandon an unsuccessful project at an early stage and cut one's losses rather than to struggle on and make continual losses year after year.

Information and communication

Managers need both internal and external information in order to make decisions properly. In the case of BLU, the Finance Department should assess the quality of the forecasts that it receives from the Market Research Department and Production Department before using this information in the DCF process, rather than just accepting it at face value.

Monitoring

The internal control system should be continually monitored. The role of the internal audit department should be strengthened at BLU so that all the audit procedures described in part (b) can be carried out on a timely basis.

7 Q FREEZE

(a) The current information technology system is centralised, and consists mainly of a variety of operational systems, for sales order entry, production control and distribution scheduling, within a stable operating environment.

Although there are some on-line facilities, there is batch processing of data and some stand-alone PCs, suggesting that users of the system are unable to access either up-to-date information or as much information as might be available within the organisation.

QF is proposing to move the bulk of its production capacity to producing the new range of foods, which means that many of the current information systems will become less important and will not be as heavily used.

The marketing team has identified several key success factors for the new strategy, and management will therefore need information about these factors in order to control operations and monitor the development of the strategy. Management will need readily-accessible and up-to-date information, and probably decision-making support, which the current IS/IT systems do not appear to provide on a large scale.

It therefore seems clear that the new business strategy needs to be supported by a new IS/IT strategy, and the success of the new business strategy will depend on the quality of the information provided to management by the new systems that will have to be developed.

(b) The IT strategy cannot be considered without also looking at the information systems required by management for the new business strategy. In addition to providing routine transaction processing and routine management control information, QF's managers will need information relating to:

- product innovation;
- product quality;
- range and choice of product;
- responsiveness to changing customer preferences;
- distribution, with an emphasis on flexibility and adaptiveness;
- pricing, with an emphasis on flexibility in pricing.

Information that might be helpful for product innovation will be both financial and non-financial. Financial information should relate to the costs of a new product and the probable price at which it can be sold. Non-financial information should relate to customer needs, market size, and the nature of any competitive advantage available to QF from the innovation. Much of this information will have to be obtained from sources outside the organisation (such as customer preferences, competitors' actions, etc) although information about costs might be obtained from internal as well as external sources.

Information about product quality and consumer preferences is not provided by QF's current IT systems, and a system for measuring quality – both the cost of providing the quality and the benefits it provides, and the actual quality standards achieved – will have to be devised. A system of reporting feedback from customers will be an important element of this system. Information about consumer preferences will have to be fed back into a strategic or tactical information system, used by management for making decisions about product range and choice.

The current distribution scheduling system appears to be designed for a stable and predictable operating environment. For the new products, QF will need to have a flexible distribution system, so that available inventories can be switched instantly to the customers who order them, and delivered within the agreed lead times to each customer. The distribution centre will therefore have to be on-line, with a facility for checking availability and location of inventory and entering orders for the delivery of products to customers.

A system to support flexible pricing policies needs to provide management with information about costs (possibly both variable and fixed costs), but also the prices currently being charged for similar products by competitors. Prices quoted to customers should be responsive to prices changes by rivals and competitive price levels in the market.

QF will probably need a major re-design of many of its information systems, with a greater emphasis on external information, and on-line access to up-to-date information. IT systems will need to be upgraded to handle these systems. The new systems will involve the use of remote terminals to central databases, and it its therefore unlikely that a centralised IT force will be appropriate – although an information centre might be useful.

In view of the amount of new system design required, and the need for on-line systems with access to external information sources, it is not certain that the existing systems development staff will have the skills and experience to design and develop the new systems themselves. The management of QF might therefore need to consider outsourcing the systems development work.

(c) **Total Quality Management (TQM)**

TQM is an approach that seeks to ensure that goods and services are delivered at the highest possible standard. The underlying principle is that the costs of preventing deficient quality are less than the costs of correcting poor quality. This denies the idea that improved quality can only be secured with greater expenditure, but adopts the approach that improved quality will reduce costs.

Quality related costs are concerned with both achieving quality and failure to achieve quality. Quality costs can categorised as:

Prevention costs – communicating the concept, training, establishing systems to deliver quality services

Appraisal costs – e.g. inspection and testing

Internal failure costs – wasted materials used in rejects, down time resulting from internal service quality failures, resources devoted to dealing with complaints

External failure costs – loss of goodwill and future business, compensation paid to customers and rectification costs

The TQM view is that, by getting it right first time and every time, the prevention and appraisal costs will be outweighed by the savings in failure costs, hence lower costs and improved quality are congruent goals. TQM requires everyone in the organisation to have identified customers, whether external or internal, so that a continuous service quality chain is maintained all the way through the organisation to the final customer.

Just In Time (JIT)

JIT is a manufacturing and supply chain process that is intended to reduce inventory levels and improve customer service by ensuring that customers receive their orders at the right time and in the right quantity. The system should facilitate a smooth workflow throughout the business and reduce waste. Goods are produced to meet customer needs directly, not for inventory.

Cost reductions should arise from:

- Lower raw material and finished goods inventory levels, therefore reduced holding costs:
- Reduced materials handling:
- Possibly, a reduction in the number of suppliers and lower administration and communication costs:
- Guaranteed quality of supplies reduces inspection and rectification costs.

Quality improvements should arise from:

- Fewer or even single sourcing of supplies strengthens the buyer–supplier relationship and is likely to improve the quality.
- The absence of customer inventories compels the supplier (if they want continued business) to guarantee the quality of the material that they deliver.
- The necessity to work regularly and closer with hauliers strengthens the relationship with them. The deliveries become high priority and more reliable.
- Customers are not faced with the traditional problems of having to wait until their suppliers inventories are replenished. The system is designed to respond to customers' needs rapidly.
- Direct focus on meeting an identified customers' need.

Value analysis

Value analysis is concerned with concentrating on activities that add value to the product/service as perceived by the customer. It examines business activities and questions why they are being undertaken and what contribution do they make. Value added activities includes designing products, producing output and developing customer relationships. Non-value added activities include returning goods, inventory holding checking on the quality of supplies received. Wherever possible eliminate the non-value added activities.

Value analysis commences with a focus on the customer – what do they want and what do they regard as significant in the buying decision. Value in a product comes from a mixture of function, appearance, longevity and disposal value, and customers are prepared to pay a price for the product that reflects the value they obtain. Value analysis is therefore concerned with identifying what customers regard as quality and then providing it. Effort and money should not be spent on what customers regard as unimportant. Value analysis is also relevant to the development of new products and new product improvements. For alternative designs, it is necessary to estimate costs and the value the product will provide, and to evaluate alternatives.

Activity Based Costing (ABC)

ABC is concerned with attributing/assigning costs to cost units on the basis of the service received from indirect activities. Activities vary within differing organisations, but might be public relations, recruitment, quality assurance, order processing and despatch, and so on. The organisation needs to identify cost drivers – the specific factor or factor for each activity that causes costs to occur, e.g. number of orders taken, telephone calls made, number of breakdowns or the number of visitors to an attraction.

ABC intends to avoid the arbitrary allocation of overheads to products/services by identifying a causal link between costs, activities and outputs. The increasing significance of overheads in the cost make up of output intensifies the need to improve the apportionment of them. Accountants can contribute towards providing better cost information to the value analysis referred to above. Product managers need to know what they are getting for their money – what is the real cost of quality? What are the cost driving activities that do not impact on quality? What activities that generate minimal costs have a significantly favourable impact on quality?

The **Balanced Scorecard** provides a framework for a business to achieve its strategic objectives include both financial and non-financial objectives. The approach claims that performance has four dimensions of which the Customer Perspective is one – how does the business appear to the customers and the internal perspective is another – what do we need to do to satisfy shareholders and customers, including the monitoring of unit costs. The scorecard is concerned with monitoring and measuring the critical variables that comprise the customer and internal perspective. The choice of variables for inclusion in the scorecard is significant because the scorecard report is a design for action. Inappropriate indicators will trigger damaging responses. For example, the organisation needs to monitor what factors customers regard as contributing to improved quality, not what the business thinks it should provide. The Balanced Scorecard attempts to improve the range and relationship between alternative performance measures, in the case under discussion, costs and quality.

(d) (i) A cybernetic system such as a thermostat is a mechanistic system where there is a specific required output for a given input. For example, if a thermostat is used to control the temperature of a room in a central heating system, the heat in the room is measured and compared with a target minimum temperature. If the actual room temperature falls below the target minimum, control action is automatically initiated to activate the central heating and bring the room temperature up to the required minimum. The thermostat acts as the controller of the system, that compares the actual and the target heat level, and initiates control action where the actual heat rises above or falls below the target.

Control systems in organisations are far more complex, and are by no means always mechanistic in character. The system itself is often a complex operation, requiring many different resources. Outputs from the system are varied and measured outputs are also varied.

If actual results differ significantly from the plan or target, control action might be taken. However, managers often have discretion about whether control action is required. Where control action is considered necessary, the control measures that are taken might differ, according to circumstances.

In an organisation, management apply systems of control in order to achieve certain stated goals or objectives. Typically, an organisation has one main objective, such as increasing shareholder wealth (expressed in terms of increasing the share price, or annual profits or annual dividends). Co-ordinating the efforts of all the individuals in the organisation in order to achieve this objective is difficult, for a number of reasons.

- The business environment in which an organisation operates is usually continually changing and often unpredictable in how it will change. Most external events are outside the control of the managers who run the business. The cybernetic system is essentially a closed system that operates independently of its environment, and is unaffected by factors outside the system itself. There is a predictable, controlled reaction to any changes in system operation. Organisations do not react with their environment in this way, but are open systems.
- As stated earlier, control in an organisation is rarely mechanistic. Control also takes place at several different levels in the management hierarchy. Control information from within the organisation should therefore be 'double loop feedback' (or 'multiple feedback') to each appropriate management level.
- Managers need to look ahead as well as backwards when deciding on control action. Feedforward is an essential part of an efficient control system. However, feedforward control is not a feature of a cybernetic control system.
- An organisation is a very complex system, with many different sub-systems and sub-sub-systems. The interdependence between sub-systems can make control difficult, because control action taken in one sub-system might have an unexpected and unwelcome consequence for an other part of the system. This interrelationship of sub-systems is difficult to model. In contrast, a cybernetic approach to systems analysis views the system as a unified whole, without any sub-systems (or with sub-systems that inter-react in predictable ways). This is not realistic.

It follows that for most aspects of control within an organisation, particularly controls that affect people, a cybernetic control model is inappropriate.

(ii) There are several requirements for control in an organisation, based on a cybernetic control model or something similar.

- **Objectives** – The system must have a measurable objective or target against which outputs from the system can be compared.
- **Outputs** – Outputs from the system must be measurable (and measured).
- **Predictive models** – There must be a clear cause-and-effect relationship, so that when outputs from the system vary from the objective, the causes can be identified and specific control measures will succeed in correcting the problem, in a predictable way.
- **Capability to take action** – The controller within the system (e.g. management) should have the capability to take control action, so that variations from the plan can be corrected by control measures.

8 ZZ BANK

(a) **To:** Chief executive, ZZ Bank

From: Internal auditor

Date:

Subject: Internal control weaknesses

Terms of reference

This report sets out the possible areas of weakness in an internal control system, that can result in a breakdown in control within an organisation such as ZZ Bank.

The report sets out the scope of the possible problems in fairly broad terms. It is recommended that as the next step in your investigation, you should assess in further detail the extent to which each of these possible control weaknesses might be contributing to the problems of the bank.

Introduction: types of internal control weakness

There are differing approaches to the analysis of internal control systems and their weakness. A widely-used approach is based on the framework provided by the Committee of Sponsoring Organisations in the US (the COSO Framework). This framework was used, for example, by the Turnbull Committee in formulating its guidelines for the assessment of an internal control system, for corporate governance purposes in the UK.

The framework identifies five elements of an internal control, where weaknesses can arise that result in control breakdown. These are:

1 A lack of proper direction from senior management, and a poor control culture within the organisation.

2 A failure to assess risks adequately.

3 The absence of effective internal controls.

4 Poor communication of control information.

5 Inadequate monitoring activities

A lack of proper direction from senior management

An internal control system must be given direction by the board of directors and senior management. The culture of control within an organisation is determined by the 'tone at the top'. If the directors of the organisation do not provide a suitable lead themselves, there is little chance that other employees will apply appropriate controls themselves. It might be argued that in ZZ Bank, there is a culture that encourages employees to take unjustified risks.

- Staff are rewarded on the basis of their performance in the previous year. Large cash bonuses are paid for successful performance. Cash bonus schemes of this sort send a signal that the bank wants its employees to make profits, without any consideration for the risks they might be taking.
- Managers might be rewarded for the performance achieved by their staff. This gives an incentive to managers to support the risks taken by their staff, particularly their trading staff, in the hope that they will be highly rewarded.

A failure to assess risks adequately

An organisation such as ZZ Bank ought to identify and assess the risks that it faces, and identify which risks could be significant. When risks have been identified and quantified, measures can be taken to deal with them in a cost-efficient way.

Unless an organisation has a system for assessing its risks, it will be unable to deal with them in a structured and purposeful way. Some risks will be ignored until an adverse event occurs. Other new risks might not be anticipated in time.

ZZ Bank should be assessing risks such as the risk of losing M and A clients due to a poor reputation, or risks from trading losses due to excessive un-hedged exposures.

The absence of effective internal controls

Within any organisation, there should be suitable internal controls to ensure that systems and operations work effectively and efficiently.

Without further investigation, it is not clear whether or not this is a problem for ZZ Bank. Key controls for the bank will include controls to ensure confidentiality of information during merger and acquisition negotiations, and controls to prevent insider dealing in shares of companies involved in M and A negotiations. Key internal controls over trading activities might include segregation of duties and proper supervision, to ensure that traders operate within their guidelines. There also have to be controls to ensure that profits on M and A activity or trading activities are not deliberately over-stated by staff, as a method of boosting their cash bonuses.

Poor communication of control information

For control to operate effectively, information must be fed back to management. Communications might be poor, partly because senior management do not always understand the nature of the operations performed by their staff! More significantly, staff might be reluctant to communicate problems to senior managers, because of the culture of 'success' within the bank.

Inadequate monitoring activities

The effectiveness and efficiency of controls has to be monitored. A failure to monitor controls increases the likelihood that breaches of controls will occur, for example due to senior managers deliberately over-riding controls that are in place.

Monitoring of controls should be performed by an independent group, and this is a function of the internal audit department.

The board of directors, or the audit committee, should certainly expect regular reports from the head of internal audit, and should:

- review the work of the internal audit teams;
- review the recommendations resulting from internal audit investigations and reports;
- monitor the extent to which internal audit recommendations are acted upon by the managers responsible for operations.

Conclusion

This report sets out the potential weaknesses in internal control in fairly general terms, but it is recommended that in pursuing your investigation further, you should consider all five aspects of control described in this report.

(b) Disaster recovery risk or business continuity risk in banking is the risk that in the event of a major disaster, the business of the bank will cease to operate. If a major commercial bank were to suffer a disaster, the entire banking system might be at risk.

The most significant disaster risk currently identified by banks is the threat of disaster from the effects of a terrorist attack.

In the event of a disaster, the main risks to business continuity would arise from:

(i) the risk that computer systems and communications systems would cease to function;

(ii) the risk of loss of data;

(iii) the risk that the employees of the bank will not be able to continue business operations in the circumstances surrounding the disaster event.

The bank should have as a major objective the requirement to keep its essential activities in operation immediately after the disaster. The bank should therefore have procedures to put into operation in the event of a disaster.

(i) As a measure to contain the risk to computer systems and communications systems, it would be appropriate to arrange for back-up facilities to be available in a different geographical location. The bank might decide that it should set up a duplicate computer system with its communications network. However, for many banks this would be a very expensive option. A more practical and cheaper arrangement would be to negotiate an agreement with another organisation, such as another bank, to move the key systems of ZZ Bank on to the other organisation's equipment. Back-up arrangements of this kind have been put in place by many banks.

(ii) The risk of losing data is difficult to avoid entirely. The computer systems of the bank should provide back-up copies of all data processed by its systems, which can be held on a file in a remote location. If data is lost at one location, the back-up copies can be used. However, at the time the disaster occurs, there will be some loss of data that will not be immediately discovered. Provided that the lost data does not prevent the bank's systems from continuing in operation, any such problems will have to be identified and rectified at some later time.

(iii) All employees of the bank should be given training in what they should do in the event of a disaster. The training should include periodic exercises (similar to a fire drill) in the bank's premises. Staff should have a mobile telephone number to contact, to inform the bank of where they are and that they are safe. Key personnel should also have instructions on where they should go to in the event of a disaster, to continue the bank's operations.

A business recovery committee should meet regularly to re-assess the risks, and consider whether the disaster recovery programme is still sufficient to respond to any foreseeable disaster. The committee might also arrange for 'stress tests', to assess what might be the effect on operations if various different disaster scenarios were to occur.

Managing disaster recovery risk should essentially follow the same structure as the management of any other risk: identify the risks, consider control measures and monitor the adequacy of the risk control measures, for example through testing.

(c) The risk classifications used within any organisation for risk management should be decided by the organisation's management. The classification of risks might therefore be decided by a senior risk management committee. This senior committee might then delegate responsibility for the review and monitoring of these risks to risk sub-committees for each risk classification.

A bank is similar to many other commercial businesses, but with the particular difference that since it operates in financial services and financial markets, many of its business risks are also financial risks.

An appropriate classification of the major risks for a bank might be as follows:

- Credit risk. Credit risk is the risk that the bank will suffer losses due to non-payment of debts by borrowers. The risk might apply to particular groups of borrowers (such as businesses in a particular industry) or to individual borrowers to which the bank has large credit exposures.
- Market risk. ZZ Bank operates in the financial markets (equities, bonds, derivatives and probably also foreign exchange). Risks arise in these markets from exposures to adverse price movements. Banks with large exposures could suffer large losses if a particular market price, interest rate or foreign exchange rate moves adversely.
- Liquidity and capital. Banks, like all other businesses, need adequate liquidity and capital. However, the liquidity risk is probably much higher for a bank than for other companies because it must have sufficient liquidity at all times to meet its liabilities (including demands for cash by its depositors). It must also have adequate capital to cover any losses that it makes, without putting the funds of depositors at risk.
- Strategic risks. Like all other businesses, banks face risks from the strategic decisions they make and the strategies they pursue. Strategic risk is a speculative type of risk, and the outcome from pursuing a particular strategy can be better than expected as well as worse than expected. Risks provide opportunities as well as threats. Strategic risks should be assessed by the board of directors and the senior executive management committee.
- Operational risks. Banks also face other risks in their day-to-day operations. These include risks from technology faults and breakdowns, the risk of losses through inefficiencies and excessive spending by employees, poor security arrangements, losses due to litigation in the courts. The risks of losses due to disasters can also be included in this general category of risks. The bank should establish an internal control system for the management of identifiable operational risks, as discussed earlier.

There might also be other particular risks that do not fall into any of these broad categories, such as the risk from new legislation or political actions by a government, or the broad issue of reputation risk for the bank and its potential consequences.

(d) A social and environmental report is a voluntary report produced by many companies. Such a report does not have a regulated structure or content, and companies will produce a report that addresses social and environmental issues specific to its own circumstances and business environment.

In broad terms, a report might include sections on:

(i) employees and the rights of worker;

(ii) the bank's relationships with the community or public;

(iii) environmental issues;

(iv) the bank's approach to dealing with customers and suppliers.

As a general principle, many investors believe that corporate social responsibility is a feature of good corporate governance, and expect companies in which they invest to deal in an ethical way with employees, customers, suppliers and the community at large. Some investment institutions also take the view that for most companies, there are also risks in the business environment (both opportunities and threats) that the company needs to recognise and exploit or manage.

In the case of a bank, major risks can arise from its lending policies. Banks can acquire a bad reputation if it is associated with lending to corrupt political regimes or companies with a bad reputation for environmental pollution or the abuse of human rights. (A bank might even exploit business opportunities for ethical lending and investment.)

Another feature of good corporate governance is communication between the company and its shareholders. A social and environmental report provides an additional method of improving these communications, and improving the strength of shareholder support for the company's policies and board of directors.

9 MAKERS

(a) The main problem facing the division is that the costs of the project are subject to risks that have been identified and measured, but the contract price will be fixed. In an ideal situation, the division would like to make a margin of 25% on attributable costs to cover overheads and make a profit. However, adding 25% to the worst-expected costs would simply result in failure to win the contract.

If the company would like to win the contract, it has to select a price that it thinks would be competitive, but which would not expose it to an excessive risk of low profits or even a loss on the contract.

The key problem is to find a satisfactory balance between risk and return in deciding on the price to quote.

Probabilities have been estimated for delay in starting the contract, site clearance difficulties and delays in completion. If these risks are independent of each other, a probability distribution of project costs can be determined, as follows.

SD = start delayed

SC = site clearance problems

CD = completion delay

Y = Yes

N = No

SD	*SC*	*CD*	*Probability*		*Cost* $m	*EV of cost* $m
Y	Y	Y	(0.2 × 0.1 × 0.2)	0.004	33.0	0.132
Y	Y	N	(0.2 × 0.1 × 0.8)	0.016	27.5	0.440
Y	N	Y	(0.2 × 0.9 × 0.2)	0.036	29.0	1.044
Y	N	N	(0.2 × 0.9 × 0.8)	0.144	23.5	3.384
N	N	N	(0.8 × 0.9 × 0.8)	0.576	22.0	12.672
N	N	Y	(0.8 × 0.9 × 0.2)	0.144	27.5	3.960
N	Y	N	(0.8 × 0.1 × 0.8)	0.064	26.0	1.664
N	Y	Y	(0.8 × 0.1 × 0.2)	0.016	31.5	0.504
						23.800

The Expected Value (EV) of the cost of the project is $23.8 million. The management might take the view that if they price all fixed price contracts on the basis of EV of cost plus 25%, actual profit margins should be equal to expected profit margins over the longer term, on all contracts. In this case, the price quoted might be $29.75 million (= $23.8 million + 25%).

Another approach might be to take the view that the company should expect the probability of achieving a 25% margin on direct costs to be no less than a target percentage amount, say 75%. In this example, there is at least a 75% probability that costs will not exceed \$26.0 million (0.576 = \$22 million, 0.144 = \$23.5 million, 0.064 = \$26.0 million). A price to achieve a 25% margin on this cost would be \$32.5 million (= \$26 million + 25%). This is still lower than the maximum expected cost.

This second approach is possibly preferable, because the company would have a clear policy of seeking to achieve the target return with a target probability. However, if the expected value of cost is higher, a price based on EV should probably be used instead.

Recommendation

Risk should be taken into consideration in deciding the price. A price based on the maximum expected cost plus 25% would be too high. A price in the region of \$29.75 million to \$32.5 million is probably reasonable, given the risk in the project. However, a risk-averse company might choose to quote a price at which it expects at least to cover all direct project costs: this would be the maximum expected cost of \$34.0 million.

(b) There are certain control measures that the division should take.

(i) Risk prevention. Certain risks should be prevented by negotiating protection for the company within the terms of the contract. Although the contract is a fixed-price contract, the customer should be required to agree to compensate Makers for costs arising as a consequence of failures by the customer. These would include delays to the project caused by the customer, including delays in obtaining any planning permissions and approvals and additional costs due to altering the specifications for the contract. It might also be possible to negotiate an agreement by the customer to add a payment for any variation in costs due to inflation during the construction period.

(ii) There should be a detailed budget for the project, and the managers responsible for each part of the construction work should agree to the budget and be held accountable for actual costs and performance.

(iii) There should be regular management accounting reports comparing actual costs to date with budgeted costs. Ideally, there should also be a revised project cost to completion in these reports, so that management are aware of the expected total costs or profitability of the project.

(iv) It would also be appropriate to identify key performance targets for the project. These should include dates for completion of each part of the contract. There might also be performance targets for the quality of work done, to reduce the risk that the customer will ask for some parts of the work to be re-done for failing to meet the contract requirements.

(v) Normal internal controls over expenditure should also apply. Spending on the contract should be properly authorised. The project manager should also be responsible for negotiating prices with sub-contractors, and keeping these within budgeted limits. Controls over material consumption will be monitored by technical staff and materials costs should be reported to management.

(vi) A large amount of work will be done by sub-contractors, and management controls need to be established to monitor the progress of the work that sub-contractors do. Progress in meeting target completion dates and contract specifications will be important.

(vii) Efficient control depends on having a reliable target and budget, taking measures to reduce the adverse effect of any identifiable risks, and communicating information about actual performance for monitoring and control purposes. Another essential requirement for control is therefore a reporting system that identifies expenditures and difficulties as soon as possible as they occur, and feeding back information to management.

(c) Credit risk is the risk of losses due to non-payment (or delays in payments) by the customer. Several measures might be taken to limit these risks.

(i) In negotiating the contract terms, the company might require the customer to make some payment in advance (to cover certain costs that will be made in advance, such as materials purchases), and then to make progress payments as each phase of the construction work is completed. The purpose of progress payments is both to reduce credit risk and also to require the customer to cover cash payments that the contractor is making.

(ii) If the customer has any connection to the government (for example, if it is a state-owned industry) the credit risk might be reduced if the government can be persuaded to provide a guarantee of payment.

(iii) For a major export contract, it might be possible to obtain export credit risk insurance, possibly through a government agency. Alternatively, credit risk insurance might be obtainable from an insurance underwriter. However, the company would have to pay a premium for the insurance.

(iv) Credit risk can be reduced though efficient administration. For example, the company should have procedures and policies for chasing customers for payment if a payment is due (or overdue).

Foreign exchange risk in this situation will arise from the fact that Makers will receive revenue from the contract in dollars, but will incur most of its expenditures in a different currency. If the dollar weakens in value over time against the customer's domestic currency, the costs of the project in dollars will increase, since Makers will need to buy the customer's currency with dollars to meet its payment obligations.

Short-term foreign exchange risks can be hedged with forward exchange contracts. However, the project would last for about three years, and it is doubtful whether forward contracts can be arranged for settlement so far in advance.

An alternative approach to obtaining some hedging against the currency exposure might be to arrange a three-year currency swap. The purpose of the swap would be to create receipts in the customer's currency from the swap, which can be used to meet the payments for the contract. In return, the company would make payments in dollars in the swap, and these could be paid for out of the dollar income from the project. The swap would fix the effective exchange rate for the three-year period, although the interest costs in each currency would need to be considered. The details of the swap and the payments schedule would, however, need to be negotiated with a bank.

(d) Kaizen is a management philosophy based on the principle that continuous improvements should be continually sought and obtained in operations. The improvements are generally small and cumulative over time. The philosophy is often associated with total quality management, and improvements apply to factors other than cost reduction – such as quality improvements.

Target costing sets a target level of cost for a product or operation, and then requires management to devise ways of achieving the target.

Within the doors and windows division, there would be an understandable purpose in target pricing for new products. Since competition in the market is intense, it is essential that new products should be priced at a level that customers will accept. New product development might therefore use target pricing by designing the new products in such a way that costs will be less than the price. Product designers might therefore usefully work with target costs.

In theory, target costing is consistent with continuous improvement, since one effect of continuous improvement should be lower costs. However, unless it has a clear purpose, target costing might have adverse consequences on employees (and management) by imposing targets that the employees do not accept. When target costs are applied to existing products, without acceptance by the employees concerned, it is unlikely that this would be consistent with a philosophy of continuous improvement, for which a key element is employee support and involvement.

10 RG

(a) (i) The MIS fails to provide information of the quality that management should expect.

- Reliability. Management information should be reliable, so that managers using the information to make decisions can be confident that they can rely on it to make decisions. The information for the business plan is almost certainly unreliable, because the cost estimates have not been based on historical costs and have been prepared by an individual who is probably unfamiliar with production operations.
- Relevance. Management information should be relevant to decisions that managers will make. RG's management information system does not appear to provide as much relevant information as management should require. For example, there appears to be no information to compare budgeted and actual costs; and there is no information to assist management with improving costs. On the other hand, 80% of the information produced relates to inventories and their cost; whereas it might be more relevant to provide information about the costs of holding inventories and the benefits of JIT purchasing and production.
- Comparability. Managers use information to make comparisons. Comparisons can help to identify strengths or weaknesses in performance, to assist to management with control measures for sustaining good performance or improving on poor performance. Although the MIS provides some comparative information about sales demand, there is no information on how costs have changed over time.
- Understandability. Information needs to be understandable. The poor presentation of the sales demand figures makes them more difficult to compare and understand.

An MIS should be capable of providing information to management at different levels of the business. The information system was designed to assist senior management with strategic control of the business. It should also be available to more junior management to assist with operational control and budgetary control.

(ii) The most obvious weakness of the MIS appears to be that is does not provide sufficient useful information to management. The following improvements might be appropriate.

- Provide a budgetary control system. The budget should include not only financial targets, but also non-financial targets. Actual performance should be compared regularly against the budget by means of control reports.
- Cost forecasts should be based on an analysis of historical figures. For established products, historical costs should provide a basis for estimating future costs.
- The company uses a large number of different inputs and has 35 products. Management need information about product profitability, and if there are raw material shortages, information about profitability in relation to the scarce resources. It is not clear what method of costing would be most appropriate for providing the information that management needs. A system based on marginal costing or throughput costing might be the most suitable.
- The MIS was introduced when the company was struggling to break even. It would therefore seem appropriate to provide information about contribution, break even sales and the margin of safety in the budget.
- The MIS is used to plan two years forward. Management should consider whether longer-term planning would be more appropriate.
- The current focus of the MIS on inventory reporting is surprising. Management should consider carefully what information is really needed with regard to inventory. It might be appropriate to consider whether a JIT approach to purchasing and production would be beneficial. If a JIT philosophy is adopted, management information would need to change. Management should then be much more concerned about throughput times in production, bottlenecks and supplier reliability.

The system operates on a computer network, and managers should be able to access information from their terminals. The MIS might be improved by making more information available on demand/on request.

(b) (i) The risk involved with publishing an annual price list in a foreign currency arises from the fact that the company is fixing its income per unit of sale in foreign currency but has not fixed the costs of sale.

If the foreign currency weakens in value against RG's currency, the products will become less profitable. RG will be exposed to the economic risk that its profit margins will fall as income (in domestic currency) also falls due to the currency depreciation.

In addition, there is the more general risk of price lists in any currency. If the prices are fixed for a stated period, such as one year, the seller is exposed to the risk of an increase in its costs, that will erode profit margins.

(ii) The most obvious risk from new competition is that the competitor will succeed in taking a share of the market, so that RG's own sales will fall.

The scale of the risk will depend on the competitive advantages that the new competitor might have (if any). If the Japanese company can produce glues and solvents at a lower cost, or at a higher quality for the same cost as RG's own products, RG could be faced with a large fall in sales.

There will also be a currency element to the risk. The Japanese supplier presumably incurs production costs in Japanese yen. RG currently manufactures in the UK. The cost competitiveness of the two companies will depend to some extent on changes in the exchange value of sterling and the yen over time.

(iii) There will be many operational and management risks associated with a relocation of 50% of production capacity to Spain. There will be a risk of disruption to output and sales whilst the relocation is taking place. The company will also have the added problem of controlling operations at two different locations instead of in a single location.

Presumably, output at the Spanish factory would be used for selling to markets in the eurozone. Costs at the Spanish factory need to be controlled, and to be the same as in the UK or even less. However, selling to the markets in the euro zone from a factory in the eurozone will remove the currency risks to which RG is currently exposed.

(c) The hedging strategy should be applied to the net receipts or payments in each currency. These are:

After 2 months:		€393,265	Payment
After 3 months:	(491,011 + 890,271 – 60,505 – 1,997,651)	€676,874	Payment
		Kr 8.6 million	Receipt

Forward market hedging

Using forward exchange contracts, the following payments and receipts could be fixed now:

- After 2 months: €393,265/€1.433 = £274,435 payment.
- After 3 months: €676,874/€1.431 = £473,008 payment.
- After 3 months: DKr8.6 million/10.83 = £794,090 receipt.

Money market hedging

For the euro payments after two months and three months, a hedge is created by buying euros now and putting them on deposit for two or three months, until the euros plus interest can be used to make the payments. The two-month investing rate for euros is 3.50% × 2/12 = 0.58333% and the three-month investing rate is 3.50% × 3/12 = 0.875%.

The quantity of euros to invest is therefore:

- For two months: €393,265/1.0058333 = €390,984. These can be purchased spot for £271,705 (€390,984/1.439).
- For three months: €676,874/1.00875 = €671,003. These can be purchased spot for £466,298 (€671,003/1.439).

Total cost now = £271,705 + £466,298 = £738,003.

For the kroner receipts in three months, a hedge is created by borrowing kroner now and converting them into sterling. The kroner borrowed plus interest will be 8.6 million kroner after three months. The three-month interest rate = 8.00% × 3/12 = 2%.

The quantity of kroner to borrow is therefore 8.6 million/1.02 = Kr8,431,372. These can be sold spot for £787,243 (8,431,372/10.71).

Futures market hedge

June contracts will be suitable for hedging the euro payment in two months' time. September contracts would be used to hedge the euro payment in three months.

- June payment (in two months): We need to buy euros to make the payment. The number of contracts required is 3.1 contracts (€393,265/€125,000) – say three contracts.
- July payment (in three months): We need to buy euros to make the payment. The number of contracts required is 5.4 contracts (€676,874/€125,000) – say five contracts.

For the hedged portion of the payments, the futures contracts fix the exchange rate at:

- For the payment in two months: 1/0.6964 = €1.436/£1.
- For the payment in three months, assuming zero basis risk: 1/0.6983 = €1.432/£1.

Conclusion

The different methods of hedging can be compared to establish which hedging methods might result in the lowest cost in sterling for the euro payments and the highest income in sterling from the kroner receipts.

(d) (i) Variation margin is required to maintain the margin at the same amount as the initial margin, £1,000 per contract.

	Day 1	*Day 2*	*Day 3*
Starting price	0.6916	0.6930	0.6944
Closing price	0.6930	0.6944	0.6940
Gain/(loss) per contract in ticks	(0.0014)	(0.0014)	0.0004
Euros per contract	125,000	125,000	125,000
Gain/(loss) per contract in £	(£175)	(£175)	£50

A loss means that the payment of a variation margin is required. A gain can be withdrawn in cash.

Tutorial note:

The futures were sold at 0.6916, and the closing price each day is the price at which futures must be bought to close out the contract. If the buying price is higher than the selling price, there is a loss on the overall position. For daily movements and the calculation of variation margin, an increase in the closing price increases the loss and a reduction in the closing price provides a profit.

(ii) The advantages of forward contracts for hedging foreign exchange risk are that:

- They are easy to arrange with a bank and require no administration between arranging and settlement of the contract.
- Provided that the future cash flows are certain as to amount and timing, forward contracts offer a perfect hedge.
- They are available for the exchange of all freely-traded currencies.
- No payments are required until the contract reaches settlement.

The disadvantages of forward contracts for hedging foreign exchange risk are that:

- The hedge ceases to be 100% if the amount of the cash flow changes.
- Unless a forward option contract is arranged, giving some flexibility on settlement date, a contract has to be re-negotiated if the required settlement date changes.
- It might be difficult to find the best exchange rates available from banks in the market, because each FX bank quotes its own prices.

The advantages of futures for hedging foreign exchange risk are that:

- There is flexibility in the settlement date, because futures positions can be closed at any time.
- There is a single market with a single price, and the current price fluctuates with demand and supply.
- The credit risk/default risk is minimal, because the contracts are guaranteed by the futures exchange itself as counterparty to each transaction.

The disadvantages of futures for hedging foreign exchange risk are that:

- A hedge is unlikely to be perfect, because contracts are in standard sizes.
- Dealing in futures requires an initial cash deposit (initial margin) and might require daily cash payments (variation margin).
- Margin requirements mean that futures involve some administrative time and effort. Margins might have to be paid in a foreign currency, such as US dollars.
- Futures are only available in limited pairs of currencies.

11 IDAN (MAY 05 EXAM)

Examiner's comments

This question is designed to test the candidates' ability to categorise risk, recommend appropriate controls in relation to such risks, recognise the function of internal audit and risk management and how hurdle rates may be used in the risk-return trade-off. The syllabus topics being tested are mainly B (Risk and Internal Control), C (ii, internal audit) and D (Financial Risk). The question meets the learning outcomes by providing a case study in the financial services industry which identifies trends and performance data. Candidates are expected to apply their understanding of risk management, internal control and internal audit to a financial services case.

Common errors that occurred May 05 exam:

The most common problem was the tendency to regurgitate material that may or may not have been directly relevant to the scenario. Questions are unlikely to reward lists of facts or points memorised from texts and candidates should concentrate on applying such material to the question as set.

Weaker answers also frequently lacked depth. For example, answers to part (c) frequently made no attempt to discuss the interaction between internal audit and risk management, choosing instead to discuss each in turn.

Many of the controls suggested in part (b) were either unrealistic or impractical. For example, it is unlikely that banks and their customers would find it cost-effective to require PIN numbers to be collected in person from branches rather than distributed by post.

Very few answers to part (d) derived any figures from the information available from the scenario. For example, a comparison of Return on Net Assets yields some interesting issues.

(a) **Main categories of risk**

Credit risk

Credit risk is the risk that a borrower may not be able to either make interest payments on a loan or repay the capital amount due at the termination of a loan agreement. Banks normally have a mixture of secured and unsecured loans. Secured loans by definition have some form of security against default. IDAN will be most exposed from unsecured loans from commercial or residential customers and needs to monitor repayments on these closely to identify credit risk.

Operational risk

Operational risk relates to the possibility of errors in transaction systems having a negative effect on income or profits. For example, IDAN has experienced a significant increase in online transactions. If customer payments are directed to incorrect payees as a result of faults in processing, then IDAN may be liable to reimburse those customers for the errors made.

Market risk

Market risk is the risk that a bank's earnings or capital will be adversely affected by changes in market prices. For example, IDAN may invest in equity trading either as a long term investment or for short term gain. If the value of equities falls, then expected capital repayments will also decrease and the bank will incur a loss.

Compliance risk

This is the risk that the bank will not comply with relevant legislation. This will be a complex area for IDAN as many different types of legislation affect the bank, e.g. Anti-Money Laundering through to Companies Act requirements. The bank also operates in 35 different countries so the legislation requirements in each country will also have to be adhered to. Failure to comply will result in financial penalties and additional reputation risk.

Business risk

Business risk relates to changes in the economic, political or competitive environment. For example, as customers prefer use of the Internet for banking purposes, IDAN must ensure that its website is continually updated and offers at least the same services as other banks. If this is not carried out, then the ease of switching banks on the Internet will mean that IDAN loses customers.

Reputation risk

Reputation risk arises from the adverse impact of other risks. For example, if IDAN is seen to be breaking Anti-Money Laundering regulations such as the FATF regulations on electronic funds transfer, then not only has the regulation been breached, but customers may not want to bank with IDAN due to the belief that IDAN is not keeping their money securely.

Advantages of risk categorisation in design of a risk management system

Advantages include:

Identification of risks

Forces a company to identify the risks that affect its business. The list is likely to be quite long, so placing similar risks into categories allows a common approach to risk management to take place.

Formal approach

Identifying and writing down risks also forces a formal approach to risk management. This can be contrasted with situations where companies take an ad hoc approach, with the result that risks are excluded from the analysis and not adequately guarded against.

Control systems

Placing risks into categories means that specific people can be designated as being in charge of each risk and appropriate control systems put in place to manage those risks. The impact of corporate governance regulations means it is important that companies do have appropriate internal control systems in place to manage risks.

Update

Having a risk management system in place means it is easy and cost-effective to add new risks into the system when they become apparent. Provision of existing systems means new systems do not have to be developed each time a new risk is identified.

(b) **Controls to reduce exposure to risks**

New European Union Law

The new law provides compliance risk to IDAN as well as reputation risk if the law is not followed correctly.

Controls to be implemented include:

- Ensure a list of non-resident accounts is available, with details of the jurisdiction of each account as one of its fields. Test details on list back to original details provided when account opened.
- Create and then test check withholding tax deduction program, ensuring that the tax due to each jurisdiction is separately identified.
- Test calculation of the total withholding tax due to each jurisdiction.
- Internal audit to test the setting up of the new program and the deduction systems.

Rises in interest rates

This is primarily a market risk as the cost of money will change. The actual controls required depend mainly on the bank's risk appetite to interest rate risk. Depending on this assessment, appropriate financial instruments will be chosen to manage the risk.

Controls that can be implemented include:

- Ensure that the Assets and Liabilities Committee is receiving up-to-date information regarding future interest rate changes.
- When interest rates change, ensure that interest rate sensitivity tables are updated to show the new rates on a currency by currency basis.
- Where loans made by the bank are linked to base rate, test check loan agreements to ensure that the rate of interest has been increased and that new interest rate repayment details are sent to the borrower.
- Ensure that revised figures for interest rate sensitivity are available following a rate rise and these are reviewed by the Assets and Liabilities Committee to ensure they are still within the bank's risk appetite.

Use of PIN numbers rather than signatures

There are various risks affected by this change including credit risk: credit card customer not paying, operational risk of debit card transactions being processed incorrectly and reputation risk if the change is not carried out effectively and efficiently.

Controls that can be implemented include:

- Inform customers of change. Ensure customer details are up-to-date and that mail merge programs produce letters for all customers. Check that customers will be informed of the change before PIN numbers are used. There is likely to be some overlap when both signatures and PIN will be accepted so timing may not be critical.
- Ensure appropriate security for the generation and sending out of new PIN numbers. This may include use of recorded delivery for PIN numbers or telephone verification prior to credit/debit cards being activated for PIN use.
- Where PIN numbers are forgotten or need to be changed, ensure security systems are in place to verify customers (e.g. use of telephone passwords or online identification numbers).
- Check that monitoring programs to identify unusual transactions and/or place holds on the use of credit/debit cards continue to work with the new PIN systems.

Use of internet and telephone banking

Risks associated with this trend include the operational risk of not being able to process transactions and reputation risk of web sites not offering the appropriate facilities for customers.

Controls that can be implemented include:

- Training for call centre staff to ensure that telephone queries are answered quickly and efficiently. This will help to minimise delays in answering calls and therefore decrease reputation risk of poor service being provided.
- Monitoring of the queue length for telephone calls and expansion of the call centre with additional staff based on trend analysis of calls being made.
- Stress testing of the operational systems of the bank (both via call centre staff and Internet transactions) to ensure that the bank's system can cope with the increased number of transactions.
- Personnel controls in place to ensure that new hires, especially in the Internet division, have integrity and will not amend Internet software inappropriately.
- Monitoring of IDAN's web site compared to competitors' to ensure that appropriate customer facilities are being offered. Where amendments are needed, an appropriate test plan is in place to check these prior to going live.

Claims of mis-selling

This is a compliance risk resulting from IDAN not following the banking codes of the jurisdictions it is offering banking services in. Most countries have specific banking codes regarding information that must be provided to customers regarding banking products that are being sold.

Controls that can be implemented include:

- Training of all staff involved in selling banking products so they are aware of what information needs to be provided.
- Use of checklists, either manual or computerised, which must be completed during each customer meeting, to ensure again that all necessary information has been provided.
- Compliance checks on promotional material (for bank loans etc.) to ensure that banking regulations are complied with.
- Ensuring any staff bonus schemes are not linked to the sale of specific financial products – but on good customer service and overall sales volumes achieved.

Anti-money laundering

This again is a compliance risk. The risk is that the bank does not obtain appropriate documentation for new customers or for specific transactions (e.g. electronic money transfers) linked to a customer's account. There is also associated reputation risk should IDAN break any specific anti-money laundering regulations.

Controls that can be implemented include:

- Training of all staff to ensure that anti-money laundering regulations are understood.
- On opening new customer accounts, use of checklists to ensure that all necessary documentation has been obtained and checked.
- Ongoing monitoring of transactions of customer accounts, especially large transactions or transactions with other jurisdictions, to ensure they are bona fide. Where transactions appear to be unusual, additional verification with the customer may be sought.
- Appointment of and training of a Money Laundering Reporting Officer (MLRO). Ensure that this person knows when to file suspicious transaction reports with the police.

(c) In a company, the internal audit department is primarily concerned with checking that the internal control systems are working correctly. Staff in the department will carry out tests on the control systems either by tracing documents through the system or by ensuring controls such as authorisation checks have been performed. They will then prepare internal audit reports, highlighting areas of weakness and proposing amendments to the control systems. To retain their independence, internal audit staff do not actually establish systems; they check what has already been established.

The risk management department provide a similar function in a company. Risk management is concerned with ensuring that risks facing the company are monitored and are subject to an appropriate risk management policy. The department will also advise the board on appropriate control processes to identify risks and determine the company's response to those risks. Part of the response process will be to recommend risk management policies and measure risks against target levels of risk – the targets being defined by the risk appetite of the company. Finally, the department will try and maintain a risk conscious culture so that new risks are identified as soon as possible.

The work of internal audit and risk management is similar in the following respects:

- Both departments will be reviewed by the external audit as part of their job of collecting evidence of the operation of control systems within a company.
- Both departments report to the audit committee, rather than the board, so that an impartial and independent committee can decide on appropriate action arising from those reports. In some situations the risk management department may report to a specialist risk management committee.
- Both departments tend to use a risk-based approach to their work, with more risky areas being reviewed on a more regular basis. They both ensure that risks within IDAN do not exceed the company's risk appetite.

The two departments tend to differ in that:

- Internal audit will review the work of the risk management department as part of the review of controls with a company.
- The risk management department design control systems; the internal audit checks those systems.
- Risk management review all risks in a company (e.g. financial through to reputation); Internal audit focus more on compliance risk.

(d) Analysis of the financial information provided in the question provides the following data:

	% assets employed 20Y0	% assets employed 20X0	Profits 20Y0	Profits 20X0
Corporate and investment banking	41%	41%	37%	36%
Personal financial services	24%	21%	26%	20%
Private banking	6%	6%	1%	1%
Commercial banking	29%	31%	36%	43%

Essentially, the two largest departments are corporate and investment banking and commercial banking. Both departments account for a significant proportion of the assets of IDAN, although commercial banking shows a higher return on profits compared to assets employed. Similarly, the personal financial services sector manages to return between 20% and 26% of total profits while employing 21% to 24% of total assets. Profits from private banking appear to be very low compared to assets employed (1% of profits for 6% of assets) although the question also notes that profits are influenced by a range of factors. It is possible that profits are low for the two years given rather than this indicating any long term weakness.

It is not clear whether managers are evaluated on total profit, percentage of total profit or total profit against budget, so actual performance is difficult to comment on. For example, the relatively low profits in private banking may be expected, and therefore the manager may still have met target for that division, even though it is the smallest. Changing the strategy to a different method of evaluation is feasible, although it is impossible to comment on the relative difference in bonus received as the current method of measuring performance is not sufficiently well stated.

One method of incorporating risk into the performance system would be useful to some form of return on assets actually employed in each division. The return on net assets can be calculated from the question information, and provides the following results:

	Return on net assets 20Y0	*Return on net assets* 20X0
Corporate and investment banking	22%	24%
Personal financial services	26%	26%
Private banking	5%	5%
Commercial banking	30%	38%

The table shows that return on assets is similar to the % of assets actually employed for private banking. However, corporate and investment banking show a relatively lower return which may indicate some inefficiencies in that department, or simply that it requires more assets. Also, the return on commercial banking is falling significantly, which may be indicative of a fundamental weakness in the department or that additional assets have been required to invest in future profits. In other words, the use of RONA by itself is also an insufficient measure against which to measure actual performance of managers.

Other methods of evaluation may be appropriate, although these are likely to involve some form of subjective judgement concerning the level of risk accepted, as well as attempting to determine whether or not that level of risk has been exceeded within a division. For example, the use of credit risk at a level of say 5% could be set for each division. However, this would fail to take into account the actual risk in each division. A different level of credit risk would therefore be required to be equitable, although this in itself a subjective judgement.

One method of evaluation may be to determine exactly what level of assets are required in each division, and to set a target profit for that level of assets. As assets are renewed and the RONA therefore changes as a result of this, the target profit can be adjusted to take account of that adjustment. If this is not done RONA will of course fall as more assets are added to the division, which is in itself a reason for non-investment. Allocating assets to a division simply because it is profitable does not guarantee more profit – assets should be allocated on a needs basis. Evaluating performance against adjusted asset values will hopefully be seen as equitable by the divisional managers.

12 VCF (NOV 05 EXAM)

Tutorial notes:

There appears to be significant control weaknesses in all areas of VCF. Remember to focus your answer on the control issues, noting any good control areas, but also stating the weaknesses identified. You may not have identified all the controls (or lack of controls) in your answer. However, given the imprecise wording of the question, control can be taken to apply to any area of VCF. Ensure therefore that you include a good range of points to show you have considered as many areas as possible.

(a) Evaluation of existing controls

Viktor – Chairman and CEO

Control of the board is maintained by splitting the roles of chairman and CEO. Viktor is currently the chairman and CEO of the VCF Company. Being in charge of the board and the company indicates that Viktor may have too much power and that there is a lack of control over his actions. Splitting the functions of chairman and CEO would provide appropriate control over Viktor.

Composition of the board

Control of the board is also maintained by having an appropriate mix of board members. The other board directors are appointed by Viktor and consist of Viktor's wife, a consultant and family friend. Given that two out of these three people are likely to follow Viktor's judgements without question, there is a further lack of control at the board level. Employing some non-executive directors will enable Viktor's decisions to be challenged effectively.

Board meetings – content

Overall control of VCF is also limited by lack of any formal board agenda. The agenda provides the framework for board meetings enabling directors to review the entire operations of a company, not simply focus on sales, as happens in VCF. Effective control involves setting and reviewing budgets, authorising R&D expenditure etc which does not appear to take place in VCF.

Board meetings – frequency

The board of VCF meets every three months. This is inadequate for control purposes as the situation in the company can change significantly over this period of time. Board meetings are normally expected every month.

Chain of command

Effective control is normally carried out within a company by directors delegating work to junior managers. However, in VCF, Viktor breaks the chain of command by by-passing area managers on a regular basis. This action queries how effective the area managers can be in implementing control when Viktor creates the impression that he does not trust those managers.

Performance measures

Control of a company is maintained by monitoring financial and non-financial performance measures. Viktor correctly uses some non-financial performance measures to try to maintain control of activities of VCF. However, the implication is that he does not make use of financial measures such as gross profit or comparison of expenditure under different budget headings. Precise monetary control can only be exercised using some financial indicators.

Control of staff

Control over staff appears to be exercised by the threat of dismissal if staff do not show sufficient commitment to VCF's objectives. Viktor's approach may well result in budget reports being 'massaged' to reflect what he would like to see, weakening any control system.

Also, dismissing employees because Viktor does not think they are sufficiently committed to company objectives indicates a lack of control in the Human Resources area. Viktor is likely to be breaching employment legislation, leaving VCF open to claims of unfair dismissal by staff.

Cost control

VCF does not use product costing. This control system would appear to be an appropriate control given the high value and low number of individual products produced. Production is also outsourced to a third party and the only control appears to be that cost of sales is 20%. There does not appear to be any check on the actual costs incurred by the outsourcing company, leaving VCF open to being charged high prices without its knowledge.

Research and development expenditure

R&D expenditure is not capitalised. This means that there is therefore a lack of financial control because development expenditure specifically is not matched with the income generated by that expenditure. VCF's financial statements may have material errors due to lack of application of appropriate International Accounting Standards.

Budget monitoring

Comparison of budget to actual expenditure is a normal method of controlling the activities of a company. Viktor's main method of budget monitoring appears to be using his own spreadsheet. While it is good to see that Viktor is monitoring the company in some way, the use of his spreadsheet indicates various control weaknesses including:

- Lack of focus on sales and expenditure; the spreadsheet only monitors cash flow.
- Lack of accuracy and completeness of input to the spreadsheet as Viktor maintains this personally outside of the normal budget monitoring systems of VCF.
- Potential lack of accuracy of output from the spreadsheet as inputs may not be complete and the integrity of the spreadsheet itself may not have been rigorously tested.

Exchange control risk

Exchange control risk is normally controlled by some form of hedging. In VCF, customers are invoiced in their own currency and VCF does not appear to hedge exchange risk. There is a lack of control in that exchange risk could be significant, but there is no information within VCF to determine this.

(b)

Tutorial notes:

It is unlikely that Viktor wants to amend his method of running the company and given his management style of dismissing employees you appear to run the risk of losing your job having written the report! However, the question does give areas to focus the report on. It is easier to make a mention of the control weaknesses as a method of justifying any improvements.

There is some overlap with Question 1, given that controls in that question also have an impact on the same areas identified for this question.

As with Question 1, our answer may be longer than you could write in an examination. Try to ensure that all three areas mentioned in the question are included in your answer, even if the number of points made is less.

Report

To:	Board of VCF
From:	Management Accountant
Subject:	Improvements to control systems
Date:	24 November 20X5

Introduction

This report has been written at the request of the Board to recommend improvements to systems in VCF in three specific areas. Specific examples are used from my knowledge of the company to show reasons why improvements are needed.

Corporate governance

Corporate governance relates to the way in which a company is organised and controlled, with specific emphasis on the Board. It is not clear in which specific country VCF is located, or which rules of corporate governance are most applicable. However, the UK framework is used as a basis for the following comments.

Board

Chairman and CEO

The roles of Chairman and CEO should be split to ensure that no one person can exercise too much power over the company and the board. Viktor is currently chairman and CEO.

Recommendation: On the assumption that Viktor were to continue running VCF (that is, being the CEO), then another individual (probably not from the current board) should be appointed as soon as possible to the position of Chairman.

Composition of board

A board should comprise a mix of executive and non-executive directors, with the role of non-executives being to monitor the executive directors ensuring that they focus their attention on the best interests of the company. At present, VCF does not appear to have any non-executive directors.

Recommendation: Appoint three non-executive directors as soon as possible.

Board appointments

Board members are normally appointed by a nominations committee comprising mainly non-executive directors. The committee must take into account the skills required on the board in making its appointments. In VCF, directors are appointed by Viktor. Although the consultant may provide some appropriate skills to the board, it is unclear why Viktor's wife and friend were appointed.

Recommendation: Establish a nominations committee. Review appointment of existing board members to ensure that their skills are appropriate to the company.

Board meetings

Board meetings should be held regularly and follow a formal agenda. This ensures that the activity of the company is monitored on a regular basis and that board members can adequately prepare for meetings. In VCF, board meetings appear to be informal and focused on sales, indicating that VCF is not adequately controlled.

Recommendation: Have regular monthly board meetings which follow an agenda circulated prior to the meeting. The agenda should cover the entire operations of VCF.

Risk management strategy

Patents

VCF has an aggressive strategy in always instituting legal action against infringement of patents. While this protects VCF's patents, it may be an expensive strategy where infringements are limited or in fact do not occur.

Recommendation: Attempt to ensure that the extent of the infringement is identified prior to instituting legal action. Contacting the other company first to discuss the situation may be a more cost effective option.

Exchange rate movements

VCF accepts exchange rate risk as historically exchange gains and losses have been roughly the same. However, this does not mean that the situation will continue. There is also the possibility that appropriate hedging controls would have minimised losses while maintaining the gains, resulting in an overall profit for VCF.

Recommendation: Appoint a financial accountant. Part of the accountant's job description will be to review exchange risk on a contract-by-contract basis and take appropriate hedging actions.

Recession

Viktor's focus on controlling costs does not appear to allow for any significant forward budgeting activities. This means that VCF may be unprepared for any changes in world demand for its products.

Recommendation: The accountant should produce a five-year budget, taking into account changes in worldwide demand, both in general terms and in the computer numeric control area, to ensure that VCF focuses production strategy on expected demand.

R&D investment

Within VCF, there appears to be a lack of control of the R&D function (e.g. lack of reporting to the board) which may explain part of the concern that technological leadership is not maintained. Simply allocating 15% of sales revenue to R&D may be an inappropriate method of control if results are not actually monitored.

Recommendation: Provide a monthly report to the board on the progress of R&D projects and actual expenditure during the year compared to budget.

Control of costs

Although budgets appear to be produced within VCF, cost control is focused on an independent spreadsheet maintained by Viktor. This appears to be inappropriate as no monitoring is carried out against budget and it is not certain that the spreadsheet includes details of all costs incurred, as it is separate from the main accounting systems in VCF.

Recommendation: The accountant should produce a report for the board each month showing budget and actual expenditure, clearly identifying reasons for significant variances from budget.

Internal controls

Little information is provided concerning the actual internal control system in VCF. Key high-level internal controls recommended in a company such as VCF are outlined below.

Expenditure

- Board to produce and authorise an annual expenditure budget.
- Monthly reports produced for the board explaining significant variances from budget expenditure.
- Budget amounts delegated to area managers with authority to spend and accountability for over-expenditure. Recommendation that Viktor does not override the decisions of area managers.
- For individual contracts, budget amount agreed with outsourcing company prior to manufacture commencing. Actual invoice compared to budget confirming amounts agree.
- R&D expenditure. All amounts over a given limit e.g. $1,000, to be authorised by R&D controller. Invoices received reviewed by R&D controller to ensure properly incurred on R&D projects within VCF.

Income

- Contracts reviewed monthly for progress payments due – invoices raised for each customer in accordance with contract conditions.
- Receivables ledger maintained with list of outstanding balances being reviewed regularly. Slow paying customers identified and monitored to ensure payments are received in a timely fashion.
- At the end of each contract, review total amounts invoiced ensuring that they agree to the total contract amount.

(c)

Tutorial notes:

The requirement word *identify* is very low level, so as long as you recognise the risks and include them in a list, this satisfies the question requirement.

For the second part of the question *recommend the methods* implies you must be selective and only list methods that VCF can use.

Overall, for 10 marks you will find this section extremely time-pressured, hence our attempt to manage time in the answer using a bullet point format.

VCF invoices customers in the customer's own currency.

Exchange rate risks faced by VCF include:

- Transaction risk – the effect of changes in nominal exchange rates on VCF's contractual cash flows in foreign currencies.
- Economic risk – the degree to which VCF's future case flows can be influenced by exchange rate fluctuations.
- Translation risk – the extent to which the balance sheet of VCF is affected by translating foreign currencies into its home currency. This risk only affects VCF at the balance sheet date.
- Political risk – the unwanted consequences of political activities which have a detrimental effect on VCF.

The methods that can be used to manage each risk include:

Transaction risk

- Invoice customers in the home currency of VCF. This does not avoid the risk, but places this on the customer rather than being borne by VCF.
- Leading and lagging – asking for payment from customers more quickly or slowly than standard credit terms depending on expected movements in the exchange rate.
- Use of forward exchange contracts to purchase the amount of currency owed by the debtor now at a definite rate of exchange.
- Use of money market hedge.
- Taking out 'options'.

The easiest option is for VCF to invoice in its home currency as this transfers the risk to the customer and relieves VCF from the expense of setting up any form of forward exchange contract.

Economic risk

Exchange rates in countries can be influenced by many economic factors. There is nothing that VCF can do to affect this risk – however, it can be mitigated by invoicing customers in the VCF's home currency. Again this gives certainty over the funds to be received, with the customer bearing the risk of any exchange rate fluctuations.

Translation risk

Most of the risk can be managed by comparing the actual funds received from debtors with amounts payable at the balance sheet date. Any material fluctuations can be accounted for prior to publication of the financial statements. There will be some residual risk of balances unpaid which VCF may choose to manage by simply accepting the risk.

Political risk

VCF needs to monitor the political situation in different countries and may choose not to trade with customers where there is increased risk of non-payment due to political factors, e.g. imposition of exchange control regulations.

Section 4

ANSWERS TO SECTION-B TYPE QUESTIONS

MANAGEMENT CONTROL SYSTEMS

13 SMILE TRAINING

To: CEO, Smile Training

From: Management Accountant

Date:

Subject: **Organisation controls and training quality**

Introduction

I have been asked to set out the features of an organisational and management control system that should help to ensure high-quality training within Smile Training. My recommendations, and reasons for those recommendations, are set out below.

The key issue

The key issue facing Smile Training appears to be the need to achieve a consistently high standard of training. The risks to this objective come largely from the abilities, behaviour and attitudes of some of the trainers. Improving and sustaining training performance should be achievable through the application of organisation and management controls, discipline and incentives, in a suitable balance or mix.

Trainers need to understand clearly what is expected of them, and there should be controls for recognising when they fail to achieve the required standards and for dealing with the problem. At the same time, trainers should be given incentives to perform well, so that they are motivated to deliver high-quality and successful training programmes.

Poor trainers

Some individuals are naturally better at training than others. The current recruitment and selection process for trainers should seek to ensure that individuals will be employed only if they appear to have the potential to perform well. However, mistakes can be made in the selection process, and individuals might be employed as trainers when they are not well-suited to the job.

My recommendation is that when trainers are initially employed, they should be given a probationary period of employment. If the individual does not perform to a satisfactory standard during the probationary period, the contract of employment can be terminated.

Working for other organisations

The practice of working for other organisations is clearly undesirable and should not be permitted. Unfortunately, such practices appear to be common, suggesting that they are permitted by the trainers' contracts of employment.

My recommendation is that when new trainers are recruited to the company, there should be a term in the contract prohibiting them from working for any other organisation whilst they are a employee of Smile Training, except with the express permission of their manager. Basic salaries paid to trainers should be adjusted if necessary in recognition of this restriction.

Policies and procedures

Trainers should be required to operate in accordance with policies and procedures that help to ensure high-quality training. A variety of measures might be appropriate. Some are suggested below, but others should also be applied.

(1) There is a problem with trainers occasionally failing to turn up for a training course, and later claiming to have been ill. The problems that arise due to non-attendance might be reduced by installing an emergency 'hot line' at head office, and implementing a procedure that all trainers must contact head office on this line as soon as they are aware that they will not be able to run a course, or might be late in arriving at the course. This should give head office some time to arrange emergency cover.

(2) There should be regular 'refresher' training programmes for the trainers, to help them to develop their training skills.

(3) Training standards could be brought to a similar standard if all trainers are required to use a common set of course notes and displays for courses on the same subject. All trainers should then be required to use the notes and displays, to deliver courses of a consistent content.

Performance appraisal and feedback

There should be a system of performance appraisal for trainers within Smile Training. Management need to be kept regularly informed about how well or badly trainers are performing, so that they can take control measures when appropriate. Individual trainers should also be given regular feedback on their performance, so that they are aware of any strengths or weaknesses in their work. There should also be a formal system of performance review, possibly carried out annually, in which trainers discuss their performance throughout the period with their manager, and consider measures for development and improvement in the future.

Performance and appraisal feedback could be based on questionnaires that students are asked to complete at the end of each course. In addition, since the training programmes lead to examinations, performance can be monitored by the examination pass rates of the students.

Reporting structures

Trainers should report to a line manager. It is possible that at the moment all trainers report directly to you as CEO. If so, there is a risk that management control is insufficient due to a shortage of management time. I recommend that the management reporting structure should be reviewed, to make sure that each trainer has clear lines of reporting to a manager and is accountable to that manager for his or her work and performance.

Discipline and reward

Encouraging good performance from employees often requires a suitable balance between discipline and incentive. Appropriate disciplinary action should be taken when a trainer performs badly in the training room, or is in breach of his or her employment contract or fails to comply with established policy or procedures.

At the same time, trainers should be given an incentive to perform well. The most appropriate form of incentive might well be a cash bonus arrangement of a share option or share award scheme. I recommend that if such a scheme does not already exist, an investigation should be undertaken with a view to designing and introducing a scheme in the near future. If an incentive scheme does exist, I recommend that an investigation should be carried out into how successful or otherwise it has been, with a view to recommending improvements if necessary.

Please contact me again if you require any additional information.

Management Accountant

14 WAL

(a) The current management accounting system is designed to provide control information for management, in the form of cost variances and sales price and sales volume variances.

Some of this information is probably very useful for controlling efficiency and costs. However, the system has operated for many years, and there are some aspects of information provision that might no longer be appropriate.

(i) WAL operates in a market where there is 'severe competition'. In such a market, it is by no means clear that a cost-plus pricing system using standard procedures is suitable. If standard cost plus pricing is unsuitable, the sales price variances might have no practical significance.

(ii) WAL is only a small engineering company and the costing system might be too elaborate for a small company. It is not clear, for example, what value is obtained from a full absorption costing system. Since budgeted fixed costs for each month are calculated as one-twelfth of the annual budget, and cost variances will be calculated by comparing budget against actual costs, monthly fixed production overhead expenditure variances might have very little meaning.

(iii) The previous managing director was proud of the punctuality of the management control reports and their comprehensiveness. This also suggests that the information system might be using too many resources and incurring too much cost, compared with the benefits that it provides.

(iv) The control reporting system does not report on issues that might be of operational significance, such as the proportion of key resources not utilised each month and under-capacity, and the contribution that is being earned per unit of scarce resources.

(v) The current system has not been designed to provide forward-looking information for decision-making, and it ignores information needed to manage the strategic aspects of the company.

(b) WAL operates in a very competitive environment, but is profitable. The directors believe that they could increase profits by increasing capacity and taking on larger-scale work. Switching from small-scale to large-scale production could be a high-risk investment, because it is not clear that WAL would be able to fill any additional capacity it creates, nor whether it has the engineering skills to provide high-quality work, nor whether it could carry out large-scale jobs at a sufficient profit to obtain a good return on investment.

WAL needs strategic information to help the directors to assess business strategy better, and to evaluate any proposed investment thoroughly.

As a matter of some urgency, WAL's management accounting system should provide information to senior management about:

- the amount of business that is turned down because of inadequate facilities. Details should be recorded of the orders that are rejected;
- the profitability of current small-scale work. Relevant information about the profit margin on the different products, jobs and customers. This will assist the managers to make correct decisions about accepting or rejecting work and pricing jobs. Information should also be obtained and reported about competitors' pricing policies. It is also important to know about the profit generated by each group of customers. It is essential to know the reason why customers prefer to buy from WAL and what makes the company's technology and skills unique in small-scale engineering.

An information system should be designed to assist WAL's managers to obtain more information about the environment within which it operates and in particular the potential customers and competitors, and also suppliers (and availability of raw materials and skilled labour).

Forecasts of future market trends and possible developments in technology of products and production methods would also be helpful.

A better understanding of the market, profit margins and competition should help senior management to assess the costs and benefits, and the risks, of expanding production capacity and moving into a new area of the market (large-scale engineering).

15 CDE (MAY 06 EXAM)

(a) (i) The following types of information system are available to manufacturing firms like CDE:

A **transaction processing system** (TPS) serves the operational level of the organisation. The system records all of the daily routine transactions that take place within the organisation, relating to each particular aspect of operational activities.

Data from the TPS is fed into a **management information system** (MIS). An MIS takes the bulk of data from the TPS and develops it into something useful to management in support of its decision-making responsibility. The MIS is usually computer-based, making use of spreadsheets where 'what if?' analysis can be carried out.

An **enterprise resource planning** (ERP) system is a sophisticated MIS system that covers the whole range of the organisation's activities. It promises the 'seamless integration of all the information flowing through the company'. ERP can be thought of as a development of the MRP II system used currently by CDE. A data warehouse is maintained of inputs from the TPS and MIS systems, from which any required customised report can be produced.

A **strategic enterprise management** (SEM) system assists management in making high-level strategic decisions. Tools such as activity-based management (ABM) and the balanced scorecard are applied to the data in the data warehouse to enable the strategic goals of the organisation to be worked towards.

An **executive information system** (EIS) or **executive support system** (ESS) gives management access to both internal and external data. Managers can access information to monitor the operations of the organisation and to scan general business conditions. The data for an EIS is online and updated in real time to ensure its integrity for decision making at a senior management level.

(ii) CDE is a substantially sized company, listed on the stock exchange, and operating in a highly competitive and fast-moving business. It currently uses an MRP II system to control production scheduling and labour and machine utilisation. This is satisfactory as far as controlling day-to-day operational requirements, but there is an absence of information being collected and presented to management for strategic and decision support purposes. I recommend that CDE moves towards establishing an EIS system. This will enable managers to integrate the data from the current MRP II system with the known data about customer requirements and available suppliers. Then managers will be able to see an overview of the business as a whole, and can drill down if they wish to see more detail on the contents of any particular figure.

(b) (i) The current management accounting system provides:

- a detailed annual budgeting exercise;
- standard costing for labour and materials;
- production overhead recovery on the basis of machine hours.

Labour and material costs are analysed from operator and machine timesheets, and variances from standard costs are calculated and investigated.

CDE is therefore carrying out traditional old-fashioned management accounting, whose relevance can be questioned in a fast-moving business environment such as the manufacture of automotive components.

An annual budget is currently drawn up at the beginning of each year and then used for feedforward (planning) and feedback (control) purposes. However, with an uncertain sales mix and in a competitive sales environment, it will be very difficult to draw up an accurate budget. The objective of accuracy may be frustrated, anyway, by managers submitting sales targets that are very low and easy to achieve so that they will not be under any pressure to achieve the budgeted amounts.

Overhead allocation will be difficult to achieve accurately when so many different components are being offered for sale, in both large and small batches. Allocating such overhead on the basis of machine hours is a convenient, but essentially arbitrary, method.

Standard costing is currently carried out for labour and for materials. A standard cost card will be drawn up for each product, suggesting the 'standard' amount of cost of labour and materials that is appropriate. Variances are then calculated between actual amounts and standard amounts. Such traditional standard costing is appropriate in a mass production scenario where competitive advantage is sought by obtaining a low unit cost of production by producing very large production runs. It is much less appropriate in a JIT environment such as at CDE.

In conclusion, the current management accounting system is not altogether relevant to the JIT operations of CDE in the competitive environment in which it operates.

(ii) The management accounting system should be improved by:

- introducing rolling budgets rather than fixed budgets;
- replacing the current detailed standard costing system with a 'lean' management accounting system focused on eliminating waste rather than on building up inventories to reduce the unit cost of production;
- moving to an ABC method of overhead allocation rather than recovery on the basis of machine hours worked. This should enable accurate costing and pricing decisions to be taken, which is essential in the price sensitive market in which CDE operates.

CDE currently operates a management accounting system dominated by the costings of its MRP II system. As described in part (a), the move to an EIS system should enable a more holistic view of decision taking by management, concentrating on adding value and satisfying customers rather than on the pursuit of accounting-based cost control.

16 MOVE

(a) As a guiding principle, the management accounting system should identify the responsibility and control centres within the organisation, and ensure that control information is provided to (and is continually available to) the managers of those responsibility centres.

It is not clear from the question whether decision-making is centralised at head office, or whether most decisions are delegated to management at a divisional level. The management structure of the organisation should affect the structure of the management accounting system. Another principle of a management accounting system is that it should be based on the decision-making structure. This is because management accounting information is a major source of information to assist management with decision-making, and it is appropriate that the information system should be under the control of the managers who use the information most for making decisions.

A factor in deciding whether to operate with one management accounting system or two separate systems is whether the two divisions share much information, or whether their information needs are largely different. If they do not share common information, it is easier to decentralise the information systems and operate them separately. However, if the management accounting system is divided into two parts, there must be a supplementary system that enables management at head office to extract information from both systems, to provide control reports at a company level.

Since the management accounting information of each division has to be consolidated for reporting at head office level, the file and database structures of each division will have to be similar.

Finally, if MOVE's directors are contemplating a de-merger of the company, or selling one of its divisions, there is a strong argument for separating the information systems, so that a de-merger or sell-off would be administratively easier to accomplish.

(b) In a bonus incentive scheme individuals who will benefit from the scheme should be motivated to achieve or exceed performance targets on which their bonuses will be calculated. However, managers will almost certainly focus on the bonus performance targets to the exclusion of other considerations.

Unless the performance targets on which the bonus scheme are carefully devised, there is a risk of unexpected behavioural consequences, with managers making decisions that were not intended when the scheme was devised, and that might be damaging to the business. An example is the use of annual profit targets for a bonus scheme, particularly when sales growth is not strong and opportunities for improving profits through higher sales are limited. When a business operation's costs are largely fixed costs, management will often seek to increase profits by reducing discretionary 'fixed cost' spending. With train and bus services, the risk might be a decision to cut back spending on repairs and maintenance, or the cleaning of trains and carriages. Cutting expenditure in certain areas will improve profits in the short-term, but could have adverse longer-term consequences through the reduction in quality and public perception of the service.

Another behavioural problem might be the use of the punctuality target for the railway services. If the division's managers are rewarded for achieving a target for the percentage of services operated that arrive on time, there might be a temptation to cancel services where delays have become inevitable. Cancelling services means that the service does not operate, and so will not affect the punctuality statistics.

(c) The current management accounting system appears to identify the costs of operating each bus service or railway service, and the profitability of each service. From the information available, it appears that many costs are related to the provision of services. Costs such as track rental charges, bus station rental charges and repairs and maintenance costs would appear to be related to service provision. If this is the case, the current focus on service profitability is probably appropriate, because providing train and bus services are the major activities driving overhead costs.

There may be other activities which the Finance Director believes is a driver of overhead costs, such as ticket sales. However, it is not clear what these are, and the Finance Director should be asked to state more specifically how an ABC system would be of benefit in the case of MOVE.

(d) When many costs are fixed, revenue maximisation becomes a key aspect of performance. The Marketing Director is almost certainly correct in expressing the view that control reports should give emphasis to revenues.

However, the view of the Marketing Director that control reports should focus on revenues to the exclusion of costs may be incorrect. There are two reasons for this.

(i) Some costs are variable and others are directly attributable to particular rail or bus services. For example, fuel costs are a variable cost of bus services. The cost of drivers is a directly attributable cost of both bus and rail services. Performance reporting should provide management information about the contribution from services, and the contribution after deducting directly attributable costs. This will provide more information than just revenue about the profitability and viability of each service.

(ii) Management need to know what their costs are and whether revenues are sufficient to cover costs. The company relies on subsidies, which means that operating costs exceed revenues before subsidies. Senior management need to be aware of the size of this shortfall, which means that reporting costs is essential, at least at a senior management reporting level.

17 SPECIFIC PERFORMANCE MEASURES

(a) (i) **Over-emphasis on the short-term**

In many organisations, the performance of managers is assessed on the basis of short-term performance measures, particularly financial measures such as profits or growth in profits or cost reduction.

Although short term performance is important, it should not be over-emphasised, because focus on the short term leads to the neglect of longer term objectives. For example, when performance is measured by achieving target cost reductions or improving cash flows, a manager might seek to achieve these by avoiding or deferring spending on discretionary items such as research and development expenditure or capital investment. These cuts might have no effect in the short term, but over the longer term the organisation might suffer through lack of new products and under-investment in operating assets. Even when there are short-term constraints on spending, a balanced view needs to be taken of short-term and long-term necessities.

(ii) **Over-emphasis on the achievement of specific measures**

Performance measurement might focus on one or a small number of key target measures, and performance is then judged according to whether the target has been achieved or exceeded. Clearly, this will encourage managers to act in such a way as to achieve those specific performance targets. There are several problems with this approach:

(1) It might be inappropriate to focus on just a small number of performance measures, given the need to ensure that short-term and long-term performance is satisfactory.

(2) The performance measures selected might be inappropriate. For example a production manager might be given a target for machine output efficiency, measured as the ratio of output achieved (in standard hours of work) to total operating hours. Efforts to improve this measure from (say) 85% to 90% may focus on improving machine speed to increase the throughput rates. However, faster throughput might affect quality adversely, and the production department might be working at below 100% capacity, so that the faster throughout rates have no effect on total output.

(3) The manager accountable for the performance might make decisions that are harmful to other aspects of performance in order to improve the key performance measure. For example, a manager of a hospital who is given a key target to reduce waiting times in Accident and Emergency (A and E) might try to meet the target by switching staff from other departments into A and E.

(iii) **Over-simplification of the meaning of specific measures**

When performance measures are over-simplified, there is a risk that they will be misunderstood, and actual achievements misinterpreted. This could result in a failure to recognise the complexity of the situation. For example, if actual sales are less than budgeted sales, this might be interpreted as poor sales performance. However, the budget might be optimistic, and actual sales might be significantly higher than the comparable period in the previous year.

In a non-accounting context, measures in education of students' performance in examinations might suggest significant improvements in education standards because pass rates are higher and grades are better. However, the improvements might be due to easier examinations or a more generous marking scheme.

(iv) **Deliberate distortion**

The deliberate distortion of a performance measure might occur for two reasons. Performance might be deliberately under-stated in the current period, in order to avoid higher targets being set for a future period. This might be particularly beneficial to the manager concerned when he or she has just replaced an outgoing executive, who can be 'blamed' for the bad performance. Alternatively, performance might be deliberately distorted to make it seem better than it really is, when the manager concerned is rewarded for the achievement of a performance target.

(b) The following actions could be implemented in order to overcome problems in the operation of a performance measurement system.

- In selecting measures of performance, management should give appropriate consideration to all aspects of the organisation's objectives, both short-term and long-term. An attempt should be made to identify performance measures that will reflect progress towards longer-term objectives, and these should be given suitable emphasis.
- The performance measurement system could identify a range of different performance targets, qualitative as well as quantitative, and both financial and non-financial. A system of measuring performance against a range of key performance indicators could then be used.
- Actions to discourage the oversimplification of the meaning of specific performance measures must be initiated by senior management. A control system should recognise that measured performance gives some indications about whether results are satisfactory, but managers should be encouraged to investigate the reasons for good or poor performance, and not to take simple measurements at face value. In practice, this cannot be achieved unless a realistic approach to performance measurement and control comes from top management. In other words, the 'control environment' must be suitable.
- The performance measurement systems should be audited by the internal auditors, to confirm that reported results are accurate and deliberate distortions have not occurred.

(c) A control system needs to be designed according to the structure of the organisation, and the degree of centralisation or decentralisation in decision-making authority. Control reports must be sent to the relevant decision-maker. In a centralised organisation, it is inappropriate to provide detailed performance reports to local managers, since these managers would not be in a position to react to the information they are provided with.

The structure of authority within an organisation can also vary according to seniority and the chain of authority. A management accounting control system should recognise the information requirements of management at each level in the management hierarchy, and provide control reports that are appropriate to each level. The principle of reporting relevant information to the managers responsible should apply at all management levels.

The design and structuring of a management accounting control system should also recognise the nature of the information required, and the regularity or frequency of reporting. Information provided to management needs to be relevant, reliable and understandable, and provided in a timely manner.

A control system should also be flexible, and capable of developing and changing in response to changes in operating conditions and changes in management requirements for information.

18 JKL

(a) **MEMO**

To: CEO, JKL

From: Management Accountant

Date:

Subject: **The value of a management accounting system**

This report explains why a management accounting function will continue to be needed when a new computer system is introduced.

The new computer system should be designed in a way that reduces the need for paperwork by providing for the automatic input of data into the system. JKL should be trying to achieve labour-saving efficiencies with the new system, and avoiding the requirement for a cost accounting function is a valid objective.

You also argue that the new system can produce standard control and performance reports, and that line managers can extract information from the system on demand. As a result, the need for a management accounting function is reduced. It is certainly a desirable objective that line management should be financially aware, and they should be able to extract key information on demand from the system, without the need for assistance from a management accounting.

However, I would argue that JKL needs the support of a management accounting function, for a variety of reasons.

(1) It is important to provide management with information. Management accountants are able to assess the information needs of managers and consider how that information can be obtained and provided, to a sufficient quality standard. Although line managers should know how to extract information from a computer system and use it, management accountants have the skills to continually review information requirements and ensure that the information is provided.

(2) The management accountants should be responsible for the quality of the information available on the system. They can audit the information that is being input by system users, and investigate any suspected cases of errors or omissions in the input data. It might help to think of a management accountant as a protector of the integrity of the information system and control system that uses it.

(3) Management accountants can assist managers with 'one-off' information requirements, such as the provision of information to support strategic decision-making and investment decisions. The information required for decisions of this kind, unlike standard control information, will not be readily available on the system. Management accountants might therefore act as advisers to management in such matters.

(4) There is an increasing awareness of risk. Management accountants should be able to provide guidance to managers on risk matters. They should be able to provide an analysis of the risk in particular business decisions, given uncertainty about the future. They should also be able to provide advice about risks in the internal control system, including risk arising from inadequacy in the information provided.

In summary, the role of the management accountant is to provide information to managers. Computer systems make it easier for managers to extract information themselves, but information systems also provide an opportunity for obtaining and analysing data in different ways and extracting it from different sources. As information systems grow in size and sophistication, the role of the management accountant is to help ensure that the full potential of these systems is exploited.

(b) Quality, in the context of management accounting, refers primarily to the quality of the information provided by the management accounting system. The quality of information relates largely to its relevance, reliability and understandability. Information needs to be provided in a timely way, so that it can be used for decision-making and is not too late to be of use. It needs to be sufficiently accurate for its purpose, so that a manager can have confidence in it for making decisions.

When information is of a poor quality, there is an increased risk that:

(i) managers will take 'wrong decisions' that they would not have taken if the information had been better, or more accurate;

(ii) managers will not use it at all to make decisions, so that the decisions they take without the information are worse than they would have been if reliable information had been available;

(iii) managers do not take decisions that they should have done, such as correcting adverse operating results, because they were unaware of the problem due to an absence of control information.

Quality costs can be categorised into two types:

(i) The costs of providing quality information. These are 'prevention costs' in the sense that incurring costs to improve information quality will reduce the risks of bad management decisions.

(ii) The costs of poor management decisions. These are 'failure costs' that arise due to the lack of sufficient quality.

It might be argued that there is an optimum balance between incurring costs to provide better quality information and the risk of losses from making bad decisions as a consequence of poor-quality information. However, another argument is that an organisation should continually seek to improve the quality of its information systems, because better-quality information is a key competitive advantage that will help an organisation to achieve its strategic objectives over the longer term.

19 SUNDOWN SUPERMARKETS

The management accounting system should provide control information to management in the form of regular reports, and managers should also be able to access information on demand. Information should be obtained from both internal and external sources. The key source of external information is other supermarkets, and in particular their prices and product ranges, together with market research for the industry as a whole, including market share information. Control reports should also be available at all levels of management, in a form and at a level of detail suitable for their specific requirements.

Although management should be provided with a range of control information, the system should identify key performance targets, and provide regular information to management about actual performance compared with the target. Key performance measures for the stores operations might be the number of customers buying goods (compared with a target, or a comparable earlier month) and the average spend per customer. Distribution management should be made aware of the proportion of items in stores for which there has been zero inventory on occasions. The marketing department needs to be made aware of the effect on sales of special promotions, such as discount offers. The buying department should be informed about actual prices. Senior management need access to all these indicators, plus market share data, and a comparison of Sundown's prices for a variety of items compared with the prices of rival supermarkets.

There should be regular control reports based on a system of budgetary control, with actual costs and revenues compared with budget.

Control information should be provided though regular benchmarking reports. The performance of individual stores and individual warehouses can be compared with each other, in a variety of ways, and control information should be fed back to the stores managers and warehouse managers. For senior management, the stores and warehouse statistics might be analysed to identify any significant correlation between factors, such as the correlation between out-of-stock events and total store sales, or out-of-stock events and the growth or decline in customer numbers.

For senior management, benchmarking information should include comparisons of Sundown Supermarkets with rival supermarket operators. A key comparison, as indicated earlier, would be the price of a variety of similar products in each supermarket. The CEO is aiming to cut prices to become more competitive, and pricing information will therefore be critical.

It might be difficult to provide a control reporting system that allows management to monitor the 'experience' of customers in stores. However, if this is considered a factor of some importance, information should be provided regularly to management. One possible approach would be to conduct 'audits' in individual stores, with the auditors or investigators being asked to check on factors such as waiting times at the check-out desks, the availability of shopping trolleys and assistance. Audits can also confirm that the actual non-availability of items on shelves is consistent with the information provided by inventory records.

It will also be difficult for a management accounting system to provide data on the actual or perceived quality of the goods sold by Sundown Supermarkets, compared with rival supermarkets. For example, it is difficult to compare the quality of fresh food, meat and fish, and the quality of many products sold under the brand name of the supermarket. Perceptions of quality, and the general 'brand image' and reputation of Sundown, are items of information for market research to provide.

The significance of short-term performance requirements must not be under-estimated, and the routine control reports to management should include information about sales, cost of sales, gross margin, other costs and net operating profit margin. The reports should help management to identify aspects of performance that appear exceptionally good or weak, and should provide costs for matters that could be operationally significant. These might include not just information about revenue, sale per customer, and gross and net profit margins, but also aspects of controllable cost such as the cost of unsold inventory written off, and costs of overtime or part-time labour costs in stores.

Sundown's problems are both short-term and long-term. A management accounting system can provide control information for both the long term (strategic management control) and the short term.

20 TRADITIONAL MANAGEMENT ACCOUNTING

(a) The **traditional management accounting** approach to performance measurement is based on budgeting, budgetary control and standard costing. Performance is reported as variances between actual and budget or standard. Overheads are generally associated with direct labour, and where absorption costing is used, production overheads are often absorbed on a direct labour hour basis. The budgets are normally prepared annually and the standards are applied to all products of a particular type.

Greater flexibility, a readiness to meet customer requirements and smaller batches means that manufacturers provide a wider range of products or 'jobs' to meet specific customers requirements. Consequently, product costs are much more varied and it becomes difficult (or impossible) to use standard costs. If standard costs were used to calculate variances, the cause of favourable or adverse variances would often be due to differences in customer specifications, and not to any controllable cost factor.

In a modern manufacturing environment, efficiency is determined by machinery rather than direct labour. As a result, traditional labour and production overhead efficiency variances are of limited significance. Much more significantly, a different approach to measuring costs is required, that recognises the predominant importance of the machines and machine-driven processes.

The emphasis on continuous improvement and quality is incompatible with traditional management accounting, which is based on the view that costs should be minimised, and additional costs should be justified by the short-term benefits obtained. Management information systems now need to recognise the quality aspects of performance. A reporting system might have target and actual standards for quality, and continuous improvement might be measured over time against key quality performance indicators.

Taking all these factors into consideration, I would support the view that traditional management accounting measures may be inappropriate in a modern manufacturing environment.

(b) Management accountants might need to adapt the services they provide in a number of different ways.

(i) Although the overall objective of a manufacturing company should be profitability (or a similar financial objective), it is important to recognise that control information and performance data must focus on non-financial as well as financial data. The need for flexibility might be monitored by performance targets such as the percentage of orders turned away or the time taken to process and satisfy an order. A suitable performance measure might also be devised for measuring success in meeting customer requirements. With smaller batch sizes, an important management control measure might be the average down-time or set-up time between batches. Alternatively, management reports might shown the number and severity of production bottlenecks during a period. As suggested earlier, it will also be important to establish quality targets, and measure actual quality performance against these targets, perhaps using **statistical quality control charts**. A management accounting system should therefore be capable of providing performance reports based on multiple performance measures, and a **balanced scorecard approach** might be appropriate.

(ii) The emphasis in a modern manufacturing environment is with throughput of production and meeting customer orders quickly. Many production costs, including direct labour costs, can be regarded as fixed (at least in the short term), and it might therefore be appropriate to report profitability using a **throughput accounting** approach.

(iii) **Activity based costing** might be used to provide a better analysis of overhead costs. With ABC, costs are attributed to activities rather than production departments, and one or more 'cost drivers' are identified for each activity. In the short run, overhead costs are charged to activities, and then absorbed into product costs on the basis of activity levels for each product. In the longer term, overhead costs attributable to activities might be controllable through improved management of those activities.

(iv) A feature of the modern manufacturing environment is improvement in manufacturing methods and systems. If improvements are a key target for management, the management information system must be capable of providing information to management that assists with achieving improvements. For example, management accounting systems might need to be adapted for reporting within a **just-in-time production environment**.

RISK AND INTERNAL CONTROL

21 DOCTORS' PRACTICE (NOV 05 EXAM)

Tutorial notes:

Part (a) implies that the risks require little explanation, the requirement word is *identify*, which is a low level requirement. Your answer therefore needs to mention the main types of risk and then provide a brief example from the scenario. The second part of the question how the CIMA model can be used – the best approach appears to be to mention the main elements of the model and apply these to the situation in the scenario where possible.

Part (b) is relatively straightforward; ensure that risk appetite is explained and then provide reasons for choosing individuals in the partnership who will define the risk appetite there.

Part (c) is difficult to 'get into' initially. So, define the terms first and this may help identify that risk management is a system, and therefore the internal auditor can be involved in monitoring that system.

(a) **Business risk**

Business risk relates to the activities carried out within an organisation, including business interruption, errors or omissions by employees, loss of key staff, etc. In the context of the doctors' practice, business risks include:

- Loss of key staff; with only eight staff, one or two partners leaving may mean the surgery will have insufficient staff to operate.
- Lack of drugs for the new surgery due to loss of suppliers or delays in supply.
- Blood and samples being lost in transfer to the local hospital prior to testing.

Financial risk

Financial risk relates to the financial operation of the business, including credit risk through to interest rate and cash flow risk. In the context of the doctors' practice, financial risks include:

- Insufficient cash resources to pay for the new surgery.
- Practice income not increasing by the estimated 20% leading to cash flow problems after the surgery is operational.
- Increasing interest rates on loans taken out to pay for the surgery which are unforeseen or not sufficiently well hedged.

Environmental risk

Environmental risk relates to changes in the political, economic, social and financial environment within which the company operates. In the context of the doctors' practice, environmental risks include:

- Changes in legislation making the operation of a local surgery illegal – all surgery to be carried out in local hospitals.
- Other doctors' practices opening their own surgeries, taking customers away from this practice.
- Outbreaks of new diseases (e.g. bird flu) which the surgery has insufficient inventories of drugs to treat.

Reputation risk

Reputation risk is caused by the organisation failing to address some other risk. In the context of the doctors' practice, this could be a result of:

- The surgery providing poor or ineffective treatment due to lack of staff training.
- Doctors giving incorrect advice because blood samples were not tested correctly or results were mixed up between different patients.
- Drugs becoming contaminated due to poor storage conditions.

All of these points would affect the reputation of the practice, causing patients to move to other surgeries.

CIMA's risk management cycle might be used to understand and control risks because it:

- Recommends establishing a risk management group to set goal for risk management.
- Notes the need to identify risks before they occur.
- Ensures that risks are understood and the scale of risk identified so risks can be ordered in priority potential significance.
- Recommends that a risk response strategy is developed.
- Recommends that responsibilities are allocated to ensure that the risk response strategy is implemented.
- Ensures that controls over risks are monitored and updated as required.
- Checks that the whole risk management strategy is reviewed and updated on a regular basis.

(b) Risk appetite refers to the amount of risk that an organisation is prepared to accept in the pursuit of value. It will be formulated as part of an organisation's overall strategy as risk appetite has an effect on the growth of the organisation and the return expected from different projects. For example, higher levels of growth or increased returns will normally result in additional risk – whether the organisation is willing to accept that risk has to be discussed as strategy and projects are considered.

Risk appetite is not necessary discussed explicitly; however, it will be inherent in any discussion of company strategy, as noted above. For example, a board may ensure that a company has a suitable mix of projects, some with high risk but others with low risk, to ensure that risk is managed appropriately.

Within the doctors' practice, the risk appetite is likely to be decided by the six partners. These people run the practice and, in a partnership situation, they will take the risk of investing their money as well as sharing the rewards from the running of the partnership. As projects like the new surgery increase risk to the practice, the partners must understand and evaluate that risk prior to undertaking the project. If the project is considered too be too risky – that is it, exceeds the risk appetite of the partners, then it will not be undertaken.

(c) Systems based internal auditing focuses on reviewing systems in place which mitigate risk within an organisation. The internal auditor will determine what risks could occur within the organisation, and then ensure that appropriate controls have been implemented to limit the occurrence of those risks.

Risk management procedures relate to the system of identifying risks through to reporting on risks. So, given that there is a system involved in risk management, then the internal auditor can provide an effective check to ensure that an appropriate risk management process is in place within an organisation.

Specifically, the internal auditor can assist by reviewing the risk management process in three areas:

Risk assessment. This is the analysis and evaluation of risk by identifying specific risks within an organisation and then deciding on the treatment of each risk. The internal auditor can ensure that appropriate systems are in place to identify risks and that the proposed treatment of each risk is acceptable.

Risk reporting. This relates to the regular reporting of risks to the board and other stakeholders within an organisation. The internal auditor can review reports for completeness as well (as ensuring that they accurately reflect the risks identified in the organisation and any situations where risks have crystallised) and the responses taken.

Risk treatment. This is the process of selecting and implementing specific measures to modify individual risks. Specific measures will include risk avoidance, transfer or mitigation. Again, the internal auditor can ensure that the risk model used (likelihood of risk compared to financial effect on the company, for example) is appropriate and that the responses proposed are appropriate to the organisation.

22 QUANTIFYING RISK EXPOSURES

The expected value of irrecoverable debts can be calculated as follows:

% of sales	*Probability*	*Expected value*
%		%
0.5	0.2	0.1
2.0	0.5	1.0
3.0	0.2	0.6
6.0	0.1	0.6
		2.3

If this expected value is regularly reviewed, and updated where appropriate, it should be a reliable estimate of the long-run average of irrecoverable debts. The provision made each month should therefore be equal in the long run to actual irrecoverable debts written off.

The Finance Director is therefore correct in stating that expected value is a satisfactory method of providing for irrecoverable debts, because it is a long-run average for monthly amounts.

The Chairman of the Risk Committee, however, has a different concern. He (or she) is not concerned about accuracy of measurement, but with management of credit risk. Using expected values is not a particularly effective method of assessing or monitoring the credit risk.

To assess the credit risk, management should consider whether the risk is acceptable or whether the risk exposure is excessive. To make this assessment, it would be useful to have credit risk information for the industry as a whole, but this might not be available. Management should also assess the possible consequences of the risk. In particular, it would be useful to assess what would be the impact on monthly profits of irrecoverable debts of 6%, for which there is a 10% probability of occurrence.

Risk should also be monitored. One way of doing this is to check on changes in the risk over time. Although the bad debt probabilities are reviewed regularly, it appears that they have not been monitored sufficiently, in spite of the concern that management has expressed. Annual sales have been increasing at a rapid rate in recent years, and irrecoverable debts may also increase as a result of this. Management should assess whether the increase in irrecoverable debts is an inevitable consequence of sales growth, or whether credit controls are too weak.

It is also important to assess the overall effect of marginal sales on profits. A point might be reached where the additional cash income from higher sales, after allowing for irrecoverable debts, is less than the extra cash expenditures incurred in making the sales.

There are several approaches to strengthening credit risk assessment.

(i) Staff involved in credit risk assessment should be encouraged to recognise the importance of the assessments they make. They should be given full support from senior management (creating a suitable control environment) and should be given suitable training in assessment procedures and policies.

(ii) There is an increasing risk of irrecoverable debts. The managers responsible for credit risk assessment, or the internal audit team, should be asked to carry out an investigation into bad debt levels and why they are increasing. The investigation should look in particular for identifiable weaknesses in the current system and for ways of strengthening credit risk controls. For example, if the company does not use credit reference agencies for checking the credit status of new customers, they should perhaps consider asking for an on-line credit status report from an agency before making a decision about giving credit to a new applicant.

(iii) Credit risk should be measured not only to establish the monthly provision for irrecoverable debts, but also as a means of assessing and monitoring the risk. This assessment should be continuing and changes in irrecoverable debts should be monitored over time. A simple but useful management control report might show the growth in sales over a period, and the growth in costs including irrecoverable debts, to establish the marginal profit (or loss) from gaining higher sales on current credit terms.

23 LANDMASS PLC

(a) Risks should be categorised by companies according to the circumstances in which the company operates and according to how it perceives its risks.

(i) A distinction might be made between business risks and governance risks. Business risks relate to the risks of failing to achieve objectives in business operations. Governance risks would relate to the risks of failing to comply with best practice in corporate governance, a failure of internal controls, or a failure to comply with legislation or regulations.

(ii) Broad categories of risk should be divided into sub-categories: for example, business risks might be categorised into strategy risks, competition risks and environmental risks (political risks, legislation risks, economic risks, technology risks, and so on).

(iii) If a company consists of several independent investment centres, each investment centre might be responsible for its own risk classification and risk management.

(iv) There might be established classifications of risk within a particular industry. For example, in banking, risks are classified for risk assessment and capital management purposes into credit risk, traded market risk, operational risk and other risks.

In most situations, however, companies should carry out regular assessments of the risks that they face, using risk categories that seem appropriate to their individual circumstances.

(b) When Landmass plc becomes a listed company in the UK, it will be expected to comply with the corporate governance guidelines in the Combined Code. The board of directors will be required to carry out an annual review of the system of internal control and risk management, and report to the shareholders that they have done so.

In order to do this, a formal system of risk management should be put in place. An appropriate approach would be to establish one or more risk management committees. The risk management committee(s) should be responsible for the supervision of risk management within the company. The role of a risk management committee might be to:

- identify and assess risks regularly, and provide information to the board of directors and executive management;
- formulate risk management policies, for submission to the board of directors for approval;
- communicate with executive management, to ensure that risks are taken into consideration in decision-making.

Since many of the specific business risks and internal control risks will differ for each of the three business areas of Landmass plc, it might be appropriate to establish risk committees at a divisional level. However, other risks might apply to the group as a whole (for example, risks arising from changes in the value of land, or changes in legislation relating to property rights) and it might therefore be appropriate to have a risk committee at group level, to consider broader strategic risks facing the company.

The management of risk, and the implementation of risk controls, is the responsibility of the management who make decisions for the company. This responsibility might remain at board level (for example, in assessing strategic risk, or making decisions about acquisitions or major capital investments), or might be delegated to senior management.

A risk management committee should assess business risks and strategic risks, but there will also be a requirement to assess the system of internal control in the company. In the UK, guidelines for the review of internal control systems were provided in the Turnbull guidelines, which were based on the review structure proposed by COSO. It is recommended that the management and review of internal control should be based on five elements:

- creating a suitable control culture and risk management environment within the organisation;

- the regular review of risks, including procedures for identifying, assessing and prioritising risks;
- selecting suitable internal controls to contain or prevent the risks;
- communicating information about risks and risk controls throughout the organisation to the individuals affected by them;
- monitoring the effectiveness of controls, with a view to rectifying weaknesses in control that might be discovered.

This continual review of internal control could be made a responsibility of the risk management committee(s).

The board of directors should assess the adequacy of internal control and risk management systems each year. In addition, the company might be required to publish an operating and financial review (OFR) each year in which the significant risks facing the company are explained to the shareholders, together with information on how the company is managing these risks. The board of directors should therefore also consider a system for reporting on risks, based on the information provided by its risk committee(s).

It might also be appropriate to consider the role of an internal audit department within a risk management system. If a company has an internal audit department, the audit staff can provide a means of monitoring risks and controls, and reporting their findings to operational managers, possibly the finance director (or the person to whom the internal audit department reports) and the risk committee(s).

24 DRUM

Parts (a) and (b) of the question are dealt with together, for each of the four items in the question.

(1) The risk with the purchase of shares by the company in STK arises from the nature of the continuing relationship between the companies. Presumably the initial purchase was approved using proper procedures and has been properly disclosed. The risk, however, could be that the chairman might have a conflict of interest between his responsibilities as chairman of DRUM and his interest in STK as CEO and major shareholder.

It would seem appropriate that the situation should be kept under review, to establish the nature of the continuing business relationship between DRUM and STK, and if this relationship seems inappropriate, the matter should be flagged for urgent attention by the board. Clearly, any such monitoring will need the approval of senior management. If senior management refuse to agree to the situation being monitored, an ethical issue will arise. At this stage, however, the problem has not yet reached a stage where an ethical issue does exist.

It is also likely that the external auditors have this matter under review, and might be a matter for discussion with them.

(2) The risk in this case is that development costs are already over budget, and there is presumably a possibility that the project is no longer expected to provide returns in excess of the costs that are being incurred. It might therefore be appropriate to carry out an investigation in to the project and its costs: there might be problems of management control or cost control that an investigation would reveal. An investigation might be conducted immediately if the issue is considered serious: alternatively, a post-audit of the project might be carried out when the project has been completed and implemented.

If the development project is still incomplete at the end of the current financial year, there is a possibility that the valuation of the development costs in the balance sheet will have to be reviewed, and some impairment might have to be recognised as an expense in the income statement for the current year. This is a matter that the external auditors will no doubt consider and discuss with management. It might be appropriate to re-assess the expected future costs and benefits of the project, with a view to making an end-of-year assessment of the asset value.

(3) The risk with a cash bonus scheme based on current year profits is that senior management, who will benefit from any increase in profits, might take measures to ensure that profits do rise. They might defer expenditures to the next financial year, and might make judgements on valuations designed to improve the current year profit performance.

It might appear that a corporate governance issue will arise here, because it might be questioned whether the board of directors or the remuneration committee has acted properly in agreeing to this bonus scheme.

The problem is probably one that the external auditors are better placed to review. All valuations that are subject to management estimate, such as irrecoverable debts and the allowance for receivables, inventory obsolescence, and valuations of development costs as intangible assets will all require careful scrutiny, to ensure that profits are not being 'manipulated' to improve the senior management bonuses.

(4) The risk in this case is that the gearing ratio will soon exceed 30%, and DRUM will be in breach of its bank loan covenant. This will give the bank the right to call in the loan immediately, or to insist on more restrictive measures to protect its interests. As a matter of some urgency, the expected future change in the gearing level should be estimated. If there is a risk that the ratio will exceed 30%, the reasons for the increase should be established. If the problem is controllable, suitable control measures should be recommended. If the problem is unavoidable, discussions should take place with the bank as a matter of some urgency, with a view to finding a longer-term solution.

The risk in this situation could be very serious, and the matter should be investigated by the management responsible and should therefore not require an internal audit investigation. If measures have not already been taken to investigate this problem, the matter should be brought to the attention of the board, possibly initially by means of a report to the finance director.

25 EXPORT-LED GROWTH

(a) Credit risks can be higher with export sales than with domestic sales, for several reasons.

(i) It might be more difficult to obtain information about customers in other countries in order to check their credit status. Information should be easier to obtain from European countries, where the services of a credit reference agency can be used, than from developing countries. When credit information is not available, decisions about granting credit are likely to involve an acceptance of greater-than-usual risk.

(ii) When customers are in countries where economic conditions are difficult, perhaps in developing countries, customers might have financial difficulties. They would therefore be higher credit risks.

(iii) There can be problems with late payment, when goods are delayed in shipment. Customers are usually reluctant to pay for goods until they have been delivered or at least are in transit. Delays in shipment are therefore likely to result in delays in payment.

(iv) Many customers need to be 'chased' for payment. It is easier to chase customers in the same country than it is to chase customers in other countries, due to difficulties with language and time differences.

(v) When a customer refuses to pay, there could be problems with taking legal action. If a customer is in another country, the difficulties will include a lack of knowledge of the local legislative system.

(b) Since credit risks can be higher with export sales, it is important to take measures to restrict the risk and keep it within acceptable limits.

RED might consider the following options:

(i) For sales to countries where credit reference agencies operate, the services of a credit reference agency might be used to obtain information on the credit status of potential customers. In developing countries, the trade section of the embassy might be able to provide assistance in obtaining information about credit conditions in the country.

(ii) The company should develop clear policies and procedures on granting credit and collecting payments. The staff involved in granting credit and in chasing customers for payment should be given training in how to apply these policies and procedures. The policies and procedures, and the internal controls that are applied to credit checking and debt collection, should be reviewed and re-assessed regularly, and adjusted where weaknesses are identified.

(iii) It might be possible to agree to a secure method of settlement of debts for exports to developing countries. With export trade to many countries, documentary credits are a commonly-used method of payment. The exporter is required to deliver a specified set of documents to a bank representing the importer: these documents typically include shipping documents, insurance documents, an invoice and a letter of credit. If the documents are all in order, the buyer agrees to make the payment, usually by means of a term bill of exchange drawn on the buyer's bank that gives the buyer a suitable period of credit. The bill of exchange, since it is a bank bill (and which might be confirmed by a second bank in the exporter's country), should be a fairly low credit risk. It is a promise by the bank to make the payment on the due date. If the exporter needs earlier payment, the bill can be discounted.

(iv) Letters of credit are much less common for sales to countries with an advanced economy. For sales to customers in Western Europe, RED might be required to give credit on normal trade terms. The credit risk might be reduced if RED used the services of an export factor. The factor would undertake to collect debts on behalf of RED. If the service is a without-recourse factoring service, the factor would also make the credit checks on the customer, and would effectively insure RED against the credit risk.

(v) RED might consider the possibility of export credit insurance, although the premiums can be expensive.

(c) There are significant business risks in an export-led sales growth strategy.

(i) Due to cultural differences, customers in other countries might have different needs and requirements from the products they buy. RED would therefore need to consider whether its products need to be adapted and altered to meet country-specific needs.

(ii) Similarly, due to cultural differences there could be difficulties in adapting to the business practices of the targeted countries.

(iii) Other business risks include the potential difficulties in building up good relationships with customers in distant countries. It might be necessary to negotiate agreements with a local agent or 'partner' for the storage and distribution of products locally. These will need to be managed carefully, and operational difficulties are likely to arise.

(iv) Inevitably, there will be risks of loss or damage to goods during shipment, but it is standard business practice to insure the goods against loss and damage (with either the seller or the buyer paying the insurance cost).

(v) If RED agrees to invoice customers in their domestic currency, or in another foreign currency (such as US dollars or euros) foreign exchange risk would arise on transactions. However, these risks could be hedged using forward foreign exchange contracts.

(vi) In some developing countries, there might possibly be political risks. A government might take action, for example, to restrict foreign currency payments by residents to foreign suppliers.

(vii) A developing country might experience severe economic difficulties for a time: this has been the experience in the past, for example, of several countries in South and Central America. For a company exporting to such countries, there will be a risk that an economic downturn could disrupt export sales.

26 REGIONAL POLICE FORCE

(a) There are several significant risks to the achievement of the corporate objectives of the regional police force.

- The police force has several different stated objectives, which means that there will have to be some prioritisation of objectives, given limited resources to carry out the police work. For example, how should decisions be taken about allocating resources to tasks that reduce crime and those that promote community safety (such as road traffic safety or anti-terrorist measures).
- The objective of reducing crime and disorder is a very broad one, given that there are many different types of crime and lawlessness. Priorities will have to be assigned to the reduction in different types of crime, and efforts to deal with some types of crime will not receive adequate police resources.
- There might also be a temptation for the police force to divert resources away from 'normal' police work to money-earning activities such as policing football matches. There is a risk that money-earning activities will divert too many resources away from normal police work, and the amounts of money earned will be insufficient.
- Since the police force is a public body, there is a high risk of political interference. Political decisions are taken about specific priorities for dealing with crime, setting targets for achievement, and allocating money from taxation. Political decisions might increase or decrease the funds available to the police.
- There might be some conflict between the objectives of the police force. For example, if tough police measures are taken to reduce rates of crime or to deal with public disorder, public confidence in the police force might be adversely affected if the police tactics are too aggressive. Excessive violence in dealing with political demonstrations is a particular source of risk to public confidence.

- Risks to the achievement of the corporate objectives might also arise from a lack of public support. The police force are accountable to the general public as well as to politicians, and success in dealing with crime and improving community safety depends heavily on public support for the police – for example in reporting crimes and being willing to give evidence in criminal trials.

(b) The risks in a regional structure for the police force are as follows.

- The regional management will want to set its own targets for the achievement of corporate objectives, but these might conflict with national targets set by government.
- A regional police authority might formulate its own strategies for dealing with crime that are different from the strategies adopted by other regional authorities. As a result, different crimes might be dealt with in completely different ways in different regions. The resulting lack of consistency in policing around the country could have an adverse effect on public opinion and public confidence in the police force.
- Crime is not restricted to regional boundaries, and regional forces rely on co-operation from other regional forces to carry out their work. Operational difficulties might arise that reduce the efficiency and effectiveness of inter-regional co-operation.
- Some crimes are of such potential importance, and operate on a national or international basis, that they need to be dealt with on a national or international basis, and not at regional level. Without national and international structures and organisation, much police work would be ineffective.
- Information will have to be shared between regions. There might be some risk that information held in one region might not be properly accessible to another region.

(c) In broad terms, the internal controls that should apply within a police force are similar to the internal controls that should operate in any large organisation. The aim of internal controls should be to ensure that the policies of the organisation are properly applied and that operations are conducted efficiently and effectively.

- There must be procedural controls, to ensure that activities are carried out in accordance with policy and legal requirements. Police work is subject to extensive procedural controls.
- There should be adequate management and supervisory controls. Supervisors should monitor the work of their subordinates, and should be accountable to their own superiors for the actions of the individuals in their charge.
- There should be controls over recruitment and training (personnel controls), to ensure that appropriate individuals are employed and that these individuals are given sufficient training to do their work properly.
- Organisational controls should ensure that there is sufficient accountability for police work that is carried out. Although there will be accountability through normal reporting lines in the organisational hierarchy, the work of a police force should also be subject to external assessment, for example from public or political bodies.
- There must be procedures for the authorisation and approval of police activity, including the commitment of expenditure to activities. Decisions to commit resources and spending to various activities should be taken at an appropriate level within the management hierarchy.

27 FRANCHISING AGREEMENTS (PILOT PAPER)

(a) *Assumption*

It is assumed that when there is a loan default, ZX will lose all the money it has lent to the franchisee, including money provided for the property loan. In reality, ZX might expect to recover some of this money, particularly of the property loan is secured.

	€
Franchise loans (25 franchisees × 80% × €100,000)	2,000,000
Property loan facility	4,800,000
	6,800,000
Number of franchisees who borrow (25 franchisees × 80%)	20
Average loan per borrower	€340,000
Total annual interest cost of loan finance (at 10%)	680,000
Total annual interest income from loan finance (at 7%)	476,000
Interest income from each borrower (20 borrowers)	23,800
Planned sales revenue	26,000,000
Expected sales commission (planned): 1%	260,000
Net margin on goods supplied (planned): 12%	3,120,000
Total planned income for the year, excluding interest income	3,380,000

Sales	*10% below*	*20% below*	*As plan*	*As plan*
Loan defaults	2	4	0	1
Non-defaulting borrowers	18	16	20	19
	€000	€000	€000	€000
Income excluding interest:			3,380	3,380
90% × €3,380,000	3,042			
80% × €3,380,000		2,704		
Interest income: €23,800 per borrower	428	381	476	452
Total income	3,470	3,085	3,856	3,832
Interest cost of finance	680	680	680	680
Loans written off (at €340,000 each)	680	1,360	0	340
	1,360	2,040	680	1,020
Profit for the first year	2,110	1,045	3,176	2,812
Probability	0.1	0.3	0.4	0.2
Expected value	211 +	314 +	1,270 +	562

Expected value of profit in the first year = €2,357,000

The current exchange rate = €1.3939/£1.

The euro is expected to strengthen over the next 12 months by 5% to €1.3242 (€1.3939 × 95%).

The average exchange rate for the year is therefore expected to be €1.3591/£1.

The **sterling value of the expected profits** is therefore expected to be €2,357,000/€1.3591 = £1,734,235, say **£1,734,000**.

The **amount of finance required** = €6.8 million + £3.65 million working capital.

At the current exchange rate, the total investment in sterling = (€6.8 million/€1.3939) +£3.65 million = **£8.528 million**.

The annualised return in the first year would be £1,734,000/£8,528,000 = 20.3%.

This exceeds the minimum acceptable return, and on this basis, the investment would meet the Treasury's minimum requirements.

(b) ZX faces a number of risks, both financial and non-financial in nature, in seeking to expand into Europe through franchising.

- The financial risks are mainly the credit risk and the currency risk.
- The credit risk arises from the possibility that several franchisees will default, and ZX will lose all the money that it lent. If four franchises were to default and sales were 20% below plan, the expected profit in the first year would be just £769,000 (€1,045,000/€1.3591), and the return on investment would be just 9%, below the Treasury's minimum acceptable level of 15%. This possibility has been assessed as having a 0.30 probability.
- The currency risk arises from the fact that the costs of ZX are in sterling, but revenue would be in euros. A 5% strengthening of the euro has been included in the estimates. If the euro did not strengthen in value, and if the euro weakened rather than strengthened, the return for ZX would be significantly lower.
- ZX is exposing itself to a significant strategic risk in trying to expand into five different countries, with five franchisees in each country. This is possibly an over-ambitious strategy, and ZX might have difficulty in finding 25 different franchisees that meet its standards or expectations.
- By investing heavily in foreign expansion, there might also be the risk that ZX management will not give the UK operations sufficient attention, and performance in the UK might suffer as a consequence.
- ZX will also have significant problems of control. The franchisees will be expected to meet the standards required by ZX, but the standards achieved by some of the franchisees might fall below expectation. If there are operational weaknesses in any franchise, these might be difficult to control from the UK.

(c) There are three types of financial risk that arise from a UK entity granting euro-denominated loans to franchisees in the eurozone countries.

(1) **Credit risk**. Credit risk in this situation is the risk of non-payment of interest and non-repayment of loan principal. The probability of at least one franchisee defaulting appears to be quite high. The credit risk can be minimised by carrying out a thorough credit check on potential franchisees before agreeing to lend money. Credit information might be obtained from credit vetting agencies, supported by a bank reference and supplier references. The franchisee might also be able to provide financial statements for analysis. However, credit checking of potential franchisees in other countries is likely to be difficult, and the credit risk exposure could be a matter of concern.

ZX management might try to manage the risk by monitoring the loans closely after they have been granted. Any overdue interest payments should be pursued vigorously. In addition, it should be possible to take some security on the property loans. (The nature of the security is likely to vary between the different countries.)

(2) **Currency risk**. A currency risk exposure could arise from lending in euros. For ZX, the euro-denominated loans would be assets, and the risk is therefore that the value of these loans in sterling would fall. This will happen if the euro falls in value against sterling. In the short term, the euro is expected to strengthen in value; therefore ZX would be expected to benefit from having euro-denominated loans to franchisees.

However, the risk of a fall in the value of the euro can be hedged by borrowing in euros to provide the loans to franchisees. ZX would then have matching assets and liabilities in euros, and most of the currency exposure would be hedged. Some currency exposures would remain, because the interest cost of borrowing by ZX will not match the interest income from its lending to franchisees. Some transaction exposures will therefore arise on the interest payments.

(3) **Interest rate risk**. Interest rate risk will arise if ZX borrows at a floating rate of interest but lends at a fixed rate. The exposure would be to an increase in interest rates that make the cost of borrowing more expensive, without affecting the interest income. Alternatively, if the loans to the franchisees are at a floating rate but ZX borrows funds at a fixed rate, the exposure is to a fall in interest rates that reduces interest income but leaves interest costs unchanged.

This risk can be avoided by either borrowing and lending at a fixed rate, or borrowing and lending at a floating rate. Any movements in the general level of interest rates would then affect income and expenses by approximately the same amount.

28 POLITICAL RISK

(a) Political risk is the risk to a business from events that might occur or situations that might arise due to political conditions and developments in a particular country. Political risk could have a direct impact on a business, such as the risk of nationalisation of foreign-owned assets, risks of government decisions to raise taxation or restrict payments by businesses to foreign shareholders, and risks of changes in the law, such as the employment laws. Political risk can also be indirect, because of the effect of government policies on the economy, interest rates and exchange rates.

It has been a generally-accepted view that political risk is greater in countries with developing economies. However, there is some political risk from investing in any country, even countries with advanced economies and stable political systems.

(b) (i) The consultant has suggested a method of measuring political risk in a country, and has provided data for the three countries in Africa. Allowing for the double measurement of the economic growth and political stability factors, the political risk scores are:

Country 1	29 points
Country 2	24 points
Country 3	28 points

However, there is no information about:

(1) how the scores for each factor have been given, and so what they mean or how reliable they are;

(2) how the eight factors were selected, and why other factors such as legal and regulatory risk, and banking and financial systems, have not been included;

(3) why two of the factors have double weighting; or

(4) why a minimum score of 30 points is considered a maximum acceptable political risk.

(ii) An investment decision should be based on an assessment of both the expected return and the potential risks. The consultant's decision rule is based on an assessment of political risk only, without regard to the potential returns. This is inappropriate.

(iii) A significant element of risk will be the risk that returns from the investment will be less than the estimates, regardless of political factors, and these must not be overlooked in any investment decision.

The consultant is giving a recommendation that is not acceptable, partly because it ignores the basic principles of investment analysis and partly because the risk assessment model might be very unreliable. However, the underlying problem, that political risk should be assessed whenever an investment decision is made by an international company, is a valid one.

(c) If Beela decides to invest in Africa, the risks should be monitored continually. The significant risks, including aspects of political risk, should be identified before an investment is made. The risks should also be reviewed and re-assessed regularly, so that suitable measures might be taken as soon as new risks emerge, or some risks become more (or less) material.

(i) Beela should establish business relationships with local businesses. This might be done through partnerships with a local business (and this might be a legal requirement for investment by a foreign company). Alternatively, business relationships might be established with local suppliers for key raw materials. Local partners or suppliers will help Beela to learn local business customs and practices, and their advice and help should help to reduce the risks from nationalism and anti-foreign sentiment in the country.

Beela should also benefit from setting up a local operation, headed by a local manager. Having a local presence should also help to reduce risks from nationalist attitudes.

(ii) If possible, Beela should attempt to borrow capital in the local currency, so that the profits from its business operations can be used to pay interest and repay loan principal, without any risks from currency convertibility or restrictions on payments out of the country.

(iii) If Beela's investment is substantial, it would be advisable to develop contacts with the government, to explain its plans for continued investment. It might also be possible to gain government funding for some of the investment, and it might be appropriate to invite a government representative to join the board of directors of the local subsidiary. Winning support from the government should reduce the risks of hostile or unhelpful political measures, such as the refusal by government of planning permission for new developments.

(iv) Where the political risk is high, Beela might take other measures to protect its position. One measure might be to set up only a part of the operation in the country and maintain some operations outside the country. If Beela does not set up a complete operation in the country, the incentive for the government to nationalise the business will be reduced.

Alternatively, Beela might look for a joint venture partner to share the investment risk.

(d) Companies engaged in foreign trade are likely to face enhanced commercial risks, although these will vary according to the country concerned. The most significant additional commercial risk is likely to be a higher credit risk, because if a customer in another country refuses to pay, or is late with payment, it is more difficult to take measures to collect payment. This type of credit risk might be managed by:

(i) careful credit screening of potential foreign customers, possibly with the assistance of the commercial section of the local embassy or consulate;

(ii) agreeing a low-risk method of settlement of the amount payable by the customer. The highest risk arises when payment terms are on open account, and the customer is given credit terms for payment. A lower risk option would be to arrange settlement through a letter of credit arrangement, and payment by bill of exchange or promissory note;

(iii) subject to cost it might be appropriate to arrange export credit insurance against the risk of non-payment.

When goods have to be shipped to another country, there will be higher risks of loss in transit, due to damage, theft or loss. The risk from this type of loss can usually be reduced through insurance.

There could be a major business risk from the fact that the products manufactured by a company that are widely popular in some countries might be unpopular in other countries, unless they are adapted to local tastes and customs. This type of risk should be managed by careful investigation of the local markets and testing of products in those markets before a major investment or product launch takes place.

Risks could also arise due to a lack of knowledge of local regulations and customs. Depending on the extent of the international business, a company should try to obtain information about local laws before making a large commitment of finance or other assets.

29 ROLES AND RELEVANCE

(a) It is generally regarded as best practice in corporate governance that the roles of chairman of the board and chief executive officer should be held by different individuals. The chairman of the board has the responsibility for managing the board of directors, and ensuring that the board functions effectively. The Chief Executive Officer (CEO) is head of the executive management team, and all executive management, including the executive directors, are accountable to the CEO.

Best practice in corporate governance is therefore for the chairman to control the board and the CEO to control the company. However, if the same individual combines these two roles, there would be a high risk of the company being dominated by one individual.

The scale of this risk, and the potential consequences for the company, are possibly difficult to assess. However, there have been reported cases of companies coming under the control of an over-powerful chairman/CEO, with harmful consequences for shareholders.

In the UK, the Combined Code also recommends that the chairman of the board should not be a former CEO, because this would create a risk that the new CEO would be subject to the chairman's influence on executive matters, and that the chairman would try to persuade the new CEO to run the company in the same way as the chairman did in the past.

(b) A Non-Executive Director (NED) has several roles.

(i) NEDs are expected to bring a variety of skills and experience to the board of directors from outside the company to complement the experience and skills of the executive directors. They should therefore bring greater balance and a broader outlook to the discussions of the board. In general terms, the NEDs should help to prevent the domination of the board by a single individual chairman or CEO.

(ii) They should contribute to the decisions of the board of directors. The board should reserve certain decisions to itself, and should not delegate the decision-making authority to only executive management. NEDs should contribute fully to the decision-making processes of the board, for example making decisions about the company's strategy.

(iii) NEDs also perform a policing and monitoring role. Under the leadership of the senior independent director, NEDs in UK listed companies are expected to monitor the performance of the chairman. The NEDs are also expected to meet at least once each year, with no executive directors present.

(iv) The audit committee, consisting entirely of independent NEDs, is required to monitor the integrity of the financial statements and the independence of the external auditors.

(v) The remuneration committee, also consisting entirely of independent NEDs, is responsible for negotiating the remuneration of their executive director colleagues.

(vi) Independent NEDs should make up a majority of the members of the nominations committee, which is responsible for recommending board appointments to the main board.

(vii) There should be a senior independent director, whose functions include acting as an alternative channel of communication for the shareholders in the event that their communications with the chairman are ineffective and unsatisfactory.

(viii) Some NEDs are not independent, and represent the interests of a major shareholder. These NEDs are therefore expected to express the views of the major shareholder at board meetings. However, all directors are expected to carry out their fiduciary duties, and consider the interests of the company when expressing their views.

In their role as contributors to decision-making about the company's strategy, NEDs work together with their executive director colleagues. All directors, executive and NED, have fiduciary duties to the company and a duty of skill and care. All directors are in principle equally liable for the consequences of decisions taken by the board.

However, in their roles on the audit committee and the remunerations committee, and in their role as monitor of the chairman's performance, and in the potential role of the senior independent director as a channel for shareholders to express complaints, NEDs act as a policeman or monitor of the executive management and the chairman.

These two broad roles of colleague and policeman might be difficult to reconcile, and this can create a tension for the NEDs in carrying out their responsibilities.

(c) There is a risk that the directors of a company will run the company in their own personal interests, without sufficient regard to the interests of the shareholders.

It is generally accepted that executive directors will respond to incentives in their remuneration package to improve the company's performance. In theory, a remuneration package should therefore be structured in such a way that directors are suitably rewarded for company performance that benefits shareholders. With a well-structured package, there should be shared interests of shareholders and directors in improving performance in both the long-term and short-term.

On the other hand there is a risk that the remuneration package of an executive director will provide an incentive to the director to achieve performance targets that are not in the company's best interests.

The principles that should be applied by a remuneration committee in negotiating a remuneration package for an executive director are as follows:

(i) The remuneration package should consist of a combination of basic salary and incentive payments. A good basic salary is considered necessary to attract individuals of a suitable calibre.

(ii) The proportion of a remuneration package that is basic salary and the proportion that consists of incentives and rewards is a matter for negotiation, but the incentives element should be significant.

(iii) There should be a combination of long-term and short-term incentives. Executive directors should be rewarded for achieving performance levels that benefit the company both in the long-term and the short term. It is usual to reward directors with cash bonuses for achieving annual performance targets, and with shares or share options that reward the director over time for growth in the company's share price.

(iv) The remuneration package will probably also contain a pension element, with the company making contributions into a personal pension scheme for the director, or guaranteeing a minimum pension on retirement. An attractive pension package is often regarded as a necessary feature of remuneration to attract suitable talent, but it can also be a means of persuading a talented executive to remain with the company.

(v) The remuneration committee should also consider the possibility that the executive director will perform badly, and might be asked to resign from the company. In these circumstances, there is a risk that the 'dismissed' director will receive a high payment on leaving the company, in settlement of the company's contractual obligations. Such settlements, if excessive, might be criticised as 'rewards for failure' and damage the company's reputation with investors. The remuneration committee should therefore negotiate terms with a director that seek to limit any such payments in the event of dismissal: for example, the director should have a right in his or her contract to a notice period not exceeding one year (or even less) – as recommended in most cases by the UK Combined Code. In addition, the remuneration committee should seek to negotiate terms such as the payment in lieu of notice to be made in instalments over a one-year period, and to be forfeited if the individual finds similar new employment with another company during the notice period.

The NEDs on the remuneration committee are faced with the problem that they are not remuneration experts, and many remuneration committees in the UK hire the services of external remuneration consultants. The committee should be aware, however, that remuneration consultants might recommend comparatively high remuneration packages with complex conditions and terms. A principle for the committee should therefore be to consider the advice of remuneration consultants, but to make decisions on remuneration that appear to be in the company's best interests – which might be something different.

30 CORPORATE GOVERNANCE (NOV 05 EXAM)

Tutorial notes:

In part (b) the CIMA study guide relates to the principles of corporate governance – there is no method of underpinning corporate governance regulations. The question has therefore to be taken as actually asking for a summary of the key points of each part of the Combined Code. This does make this section extremely time pressured as it is not clear how many points are needed to obtain the marks on offer.

Overall, this is a factual question – if you know the material you can score high marks, otherwise it is a question to avoid as there is no scenario or other hints as to the content required in your answer.

(a) Key reasons for the emergence of corporate governance regulations include:

- Concern in the ways in which organisations are run, with particular focus on corporate scandals such as Maxwell (UK), Holtzman (Germany), Enron (USA) and OneTel (Australia).
- The need to provide some form of enforcement mechanism to try to stop company failures such as those noted above, occurring again in the future.
- The desire of many institutional investors to become more involved with the companies in which they have invested.
- The need for stability and security in the equities markets as investment from areas such as pension schemes expands. Private individuals as well as corporate investors are looking for similar stability in equities as in, say, government stocks to protect their investments and eventually their financial security in old age.
- The need to raise the standard of corporate reporting, particularly when auditors appear to 'miss' important control failures or window dressing of financial statements.

(b) The main principles of corporate governance in the Combined Code are:

- Directors
- Remuneration of directors
- Accountability and audit
- Relations with shareholders
- Institutional shareholders
- Disclosure.

Core principles underpin each of these areas.

Directors

A company should be led by an effective board which is also responsible for the success of the company.

To limit the power of any one individual, there should be a division of responsibilities between the person running the board (the chair) and the person running the company (the CEO). One person should not therefore hold both posts at the same time.

To ensure that the board focuses attention on the best interests of the company, and no group of directors can exert too much power, the board should comprise of a mix of executive and non-executive directors.

So shareholders and other interested parties have confidence in the abilities of board members, the appointment procedure for directors should be transparent.

To ensure that directors can carry out decision making effectively, they should be provided with information in a timely manner.

To check that the board is working effectively and efficiently, an annual evaluation should take place of the performance of the board against agreed standards and targets.

To ensure that board members do not become too blinkered in their decision making, new board members should be introduced on a regular basis to question the decisions and philosophy of the board.

Remuneration

To attract directors with the necessary skills, remuneration levels should be adequate but not excessive compared to other companies. Some elements of the reward systems should also be linked to company performance so as not to reward 'failure'.

The way in which remuneration is decided should be transparent so that third parties can see clearly how much remuneration each director is receiving.

Accountability and audit

So investors and other interested parties can check on how their investment is being managed, the directors are charged with presenting an understandable assessment of the company's financial position.

Similarly, the board has to maintain a sound system of internal control to protect the assets of the company and therefore the investment of the shareholders.

To provide confidence in the financial statements, the method of preparation of those statements should be transparent and understandable.

Relations with shareholders

Shareholders, particularly institutional shareholders, require input into how their investment in the company is being managed; the board has the responsibility of ensuring that this input is received.

Additional input should also be obtained from investors at the Annual General Meeting.

Institutional investors

Institutional investors are recommended to use their votes carefully. They should also ensure that the objectives of the company fit their objectives (e.g. perhaps regarding ethical trading) to ensure there is no conflict of interest between their objectives and the company.

Disclosure

The core principle here relates to the information which should be provided in the annual report. In overview, the report should provide investors with all the information that they need to confirm that the directors are managing their company effectively without any conflicts of interest. The reports will therefore information such as:

- a statement of how the board operates;
- details of all board members;
- details of board sub-committees and their work (e.g. remuneration and audit committees);
- details of remuneration;
- how the board conducts its activities.

(c) According to the Combined Code, the board of a company should establish an audit committee of at least three or, in the case of smaller companies, two members who should all be independent non-executive directors. The board should satisfy itself that at least one member of the audit committee has recent and relevant financial experience.

The audit committee is therefore a formal sub-committee of the board of a company. Its main role is to assist the board in fulfilling its stewardship responsibilities by reviewing the system of internal control, the external audit process, the work of internal audit and the financial information that is provided to shareholders. The overall role is therefore supporting the board by providing an independent check on the process of production and review of financial information in the company.

At a more detailed level, specific responsibilities of the audit committee include:

- Checking the integrity of the company's financial statements. The committee will review the judgements made by the board in preparing the financial statements, ensuring these are appropriate to the company. The committee will also check stock exchange announcements to confirm those announcements accurately reflect the situation of the company.
- Reviewing the company's internal control and risk management systems (unless the latter is undertaken by a separate risk management committee). The committee will ensure that the directors establish suitable systems of internal control including internal audit. Reports from internal audit will also be received by the committee which will then ensure that appropriate action is taken on those reports.
- Reviewing the work of the external auditor, with specific responsibility to recommend to the board the re-appointment of existing auditors, or their removal and appointment of a different firm. Making this decision helps maintain the external auditor's independence from the board of directors, improving the effectiveness of the external audit function. The audit committee will also recommend the remuneration level of the external auditor.
- Producing and implementing a policy regarding the provision of non-audit services to be provided by the external auditor (where specific country legislation or corporate governance guidance allows this). Again, this process helps to protect the independence of the external auditor while demonstrating that the company itself does not automatically appoint the same external audit firm to provide all financial services.

- Finally, the audit committee has the responsibility of reporting to the board regarding matters such as recommending amendments to internal control systems. The committee may also be available to receive confidential reports from staff regarding financial irregularities in the company.

31 GOVERNANCE (PILOT PAPER)

(a) **Report**

To: Chief Executive

From: Head of Internal Audit

Date

Corporate governance for UK listed companies

Terms of reference

This report provides key information on certain aspects of good corporate governance for UK listed companies. The contents of this report describe principles and provisions of the UK Combined Code on Corporate Governance.

The Combined Code is a voluntary system of corporate governance, in contrast to the legislative approach taken in the US with the Sarbanes-Oxley Act. UK listed companies are expected to comply with the provisions of the Code, and the UK Listing Rules require companies to comply with the provisions of the Code or explain their non-compliance.

Role and responsibilities of the board of directors

The Code states that every company should have an effective board that provides entrepreneurial leadership for the company within a framework of prudent and effective controls that enables risk to be assessed and managed.

More specifically, the board is responsible for:

- setting the company's strategic aims;
- making sure that there are sufficient human and financial resources in place to enable the company to achieve its objectives;
- reviewing the performance of executive management;
- setting the company's values and standards (an essential element of a sound system of internal control); and
- ensuring that the company's obligations to shareholders and others are met.

The Code also specifies certain responsibilities of the board with regard to financial reporting.

- In the annual report and accounts, the board should present a balanced and understandable assessment of the company's position and prospects.
- The board should maintain a sound system of internal control, to safeguard shareholders' investment and the company's assets. The board should therefore carry out a review, at least once each year, of effectiveness of the company's system of internal controls (financial, operating and compliance controls, and risk management systems) and report to the shareholders that they have done so.

(b) The Combined Code requires that the board of a listed company should establish an audit committee, which in large companies should consist of at least three members, all independent non-executive directors and one of whom has recent and relevant experience.

The main role and responsibilities of the audit committee should be to:

- monitor the integrity of the financial statements of the company, including the interim financial statements and preliminary announcements, as well as the main annual financial statements;
- review the company's internal financial control system;
- unless the task is the responsibility of the board as a whole or a separate committee of the board, review the company's risk management systems generally (operational controls, compliance controls and risk management system);
- monitor and review the effectiveness of the company's internal audit function. Where the company does not have an internal audit function, the committee should consider each year the need for such a function and make a recommendation to the board;
- oversee the company's relations with the external auditors;
- make recommendations to the board with regard to the appointment of the external auditors, and following the appointment of the external auditors by the shareholders at the annual general meeting, approve the remuneration and terms of engagement of the external auditors;
- monitor and review the independence, objectivity and effectiveness of the external auditors;
- develop and implement a policy on the engagement of the external auditors to supply non-audit services;
- review arrangements by which staff can, in confidence, raise matters of concern about possible improprieties ('whistleblowing' procedures).

Where the monitoring and review activities of the audit committee indicate matters of concern or suggest scope for improvement, the committee should report to the board on the action it considers necessary to deal with the problem or make the improvements.

(c) A Schedule attached to the Combined Code sets out the requirements for the disclosure of corporate governance arrangements. The annual report should record:

- a statement of how the board operates, including a high level statement of what types of decision are taken by the board and what is delegated to management;
- the names of the chairman, deputy chairman (if there is one), chief executive, the senior independent director and the chairmen of the nomination, audit and remuneration committees;
- the number of meetings of the board and the three committees mentioned above, and the attendance record of individual directors at those meetings;
- the names of the non-executive directors that the board considers to be independent;
- the other significant commitments of the chairman of the board (and any changes to these during the year);
- how performance evaluation of the board, its committees and individual directors has been conducted;

- the steps the board has taken to ensure that individual board members develop an understanding of the views of the shareholders.

The annual report should also include:

- a separate section describing the work of the nomination committee;
- a description of the work of the remuneration committee, as required under the Directors' Remuneration Report Regulations 2002 (included in the Companies Act 1985);
- an explanation from the directors of their responsibility for preparing the accounts and a statement from the external auditors of their responsibilities;
- a statement from the directors that the business is a going concern;
- a separate section describing the work of the audit committee in discharging its responsibilities;
- where there is no internal audit function, the reasons for not having one;
- an explanation of how, if the external auditors do non-audit work, auditor independence is safeguarded;
- where the board has not accepted the recommendations of the audit committee on the appointment, re-appointment or removal of the external auditors, a statement from the audit committee of the reasons for its views and the reasons why the board has taken a different view.

32 LMN (MAY 06 EXAM)

(a) **The purposes of risk management**

Risk management is concerned with:

- identifying the risks facing an organisation;
- assessing each risk in terms of its likelihood and its consequences;
- responding to each risk, taking into account the organisation's risk appetite;
- establishing a system of controls to monitor the management of risks over time.

For an organisation like LMN, the purposes of a risk management system are therefore:

- to ensure that exposure to severe risk is avoided or minimised;
- to avoid unnecessary risks;
- to ensure that measures are taken to monitor the risks that will be accepted;
- to ensure that a satisfactory balance is achieved between exposures to risk and expected returns.

One of the components of a risk management system is an effective system of internal controls.

The importance of risk management

An organisation like LMN will have identified its objectives, particularly in terms of providing low-cost housing for people on low incomes. There will be risks that can block the achievement of these objectives, such as being unable to secure sufficient housing stock to meet the needs of its potential clients. Risk management is concerned with responding to the threats that objectives may not be achieved, so it goes to the heart of the organisation's purpose.

Although LMN has identified more than 200 individual risks, it is important that attention is concentrated on the most serious risks, particularly any that are judged to have a high likelihood of occurring and a high impact if they do occur.

The relationship of risk management with the internal control system

The internal control system comprises the control environment and control procedures. It includes all the policies and procedures (internal controls) adopted by the organisation to assist in achieving its objective of ensuring, as far as practicable:

- the orderly and efficient conduct of the business, including adherence to internal policies;
- the safeguarding of assets;
- the prevention and detection of fraud and error;
- the accuracy and completeness of the accounting records; and
- the timely preparation of reliable financial information.

Risk management is therefore a necessary precursor to setting up an internal control system. Risk management should identify the most important risks facing the organisation; internal controls will then be put in place to ensure that serious adverse events are not allowed to occur, as far as practicable.

LMN has already identified the major risks that it faces. Internal controls can now be set up to cover:

- capacity management of available housing stock;
- proper investment appraisal techniques to justify the investment in additional properties;
- checks that all the requirements of the regulator are being complied with;
- effective cost control and chasing of outstanding receivable balances; and
- management of vacant properties.

(b) The UK Combined Code on Corporate Governance identifies the appropriate responsibilities of an audit committee, following Sir Robert Smith's research into this topic (the Smith Guidance). These responsibilities include 'to review the company's internal financial controls and, unless expressly addressed by a separate board risk committee …, to review the company's internal control and risk management systems'.

Whenever management has itself carried out a management review of controls, then the audit committee will be interested in looking at this review when it carries out its own review as required by the Code.

The Turnbull Guidance on internal control (also now incorporated into the Combined Code) states clearly that the board of directors is ultimately responsible for a company's system of internal control. At least annually the board should conduct a review of the effectiveness of the internal control system and should report to shareholders that it has done so.

The audit committee is not responsible for the effectiveness of internal controls, but it must review the controls in force. It will discharge this responsibility partly by reviewing management's review of effectiveness, but also by any other procedures that it believes are appropriate in the circumstances. For example, it may wish to read the internal control memorandum (letter of weaknesses) sent to the company by the external auditors in which weaknesses in control that came to light during the course of the external audit are communicated to the board of directors.

(c) (i) The UK Combined Code on Corporate Governance has a main principle that the board of directors should maintain a sound system of internal control to safeguard shareholders' investment and the company's assets. As a supporting provision the board is recommended, at least annually, to conduct a review of the effectiveness of the group's system of internal controls and should report to shareholders that it has done so. The review should cover all material controls, including financial, operational and compliance controls and risk management systems.

The wording of the Combined Code is clearly written to be relevant to listed companies, but the principles of best practice in corporate governance that it sets out can also be applied to other sorts of organisation. LMN is a charity but is constituted as a company and it has a board of directors and an audit committee. The board is ultimately responsible for the internal controls at LMN, although it can delegate day-to-day responsibility to the audit committee if it chooses.

The important point, as introduced in part (a) of this question, is that the internal controls at the charity should tie in with the risks identified and set out in the risk register. In the scenario given, the board of LMN is made up of volunteers, so it is unrealistic to expect them to carry out a review of controls themselves. It is assumed that the board in this instance has delegated the duty to review the controls to the audit committee. The audit committee should communicate its findings from these reviews on a regular basis to the board, so that the board is kept fully aware of the extent to which the most serious risks are being controlled.

(ii) The Combined Code requires the board to report to the shareholders each year that it has conducted a review of the effectiveness of internal controls. This is discharged in practice by inserting a sentence to that effect in the company's Annual Report and Accounts.

The Turnbull Guidance requires that, in the narrative statement of how the company has applied the Code's principle in respect of maintenance of a sound system of internal control, the following should be disclosed as a minimum:

- that there is an ongoing process for identifying, evaluating and managing the significant risks faced by the company;
- that it has been in place for the year under review and up to the date of approval of the Annual Report;
- that it is regularly reviewed by the board; and
- that it accords with the guidance in the Turnbull Report.

LMN will produce an Annual Report containing the year's financial statements and will make this available to every shareholder (by sending it to them) and to the wider stakeholder community (by sending copies to representatives of each stakeholder group, and by publishing it on the charity's website).

It is now common practice for there to be a separate section of the Annual Report dealing with corporate governance matters. This should include all the disclosures described above that are required by the Turnbull Guidance to be contained in the board's statement on internal control.

33 BJP (MAY 05 EXAM)

Examiner's comments

This question is designed to test the candidates' ability to make recommendations in relation to internal controls, understand the costs and benefits of internal control and show how analytical review can be used in internal audit. The syllabus topics being tested are mainly C (Review and Audit of Control Systems) and B (Internal Control Systems). The question meets the learning outcomes by providing a scenario of an organisation that appears to have little control over sales representative expenses. Candidates are expected to apply their understanding of risks, internal controls and internal audit to the scenario.

Common errors that occurred May 05 exam:

Answers to part (a) were generally weak because many candidates concentrated on sales representatives' expenses and missed the wider issues associated with the freedom granted to the sales representatives.

In part (b) few candidates appeared to know what a control environment was, often attempting to repeat a definition and being unable to add anything else to their answer.

(a) **Risks resulting from lack of control over sales representatives**

Risks fall into two main categories:

Expenditure

Sales representatives incurring costs that are either unauthorised or unnecessary. Sales representatives can incur expenses for which there does not appear to be any specific budget and the question does not mention any specific monitoring or control system by managers. Representatives could, therefore, spend potentially excessive amounts entertaining new or existing customers, such expenditure normally being "unauthorised" if budgetary control was being maintained. Similarly, expenses could be incurred for private use e.g. use of the company paid for mobile telephone or company car.

Risks in this situation include fraud risk, where the representative is effectively using company money for inappropriate purposes and business risk where value for money is not being obtained from the expenditure.

Time

Sales representatives may not spend all of the time they are paid for by the company on actual company business. Although a list of customers visited is submitted on a weekly basis, this does not mean the visits actually took all day or indeed that the visits actually took place. Representatives could therefore be using company time more effectively.

Risks in this situation for BJP are mainly financial – BJP is paying representatives but not obtaining appropriate financial return for that expenditure.

Controls

An appropriate mix of financial and non-financial controls is required to rectify the situation.

Controls over expenses

- A budget should be set for a normal level of expenses based on the size of the sales representatives' geographical sales area and expected number of customer visits each day.
- The representative should submit expense claims on a monthly basis, which are authorised by the manager. Any unusual claims to be queried with the representative.
- All claims to be accompanied by receipts showing clearly why the expense was incurred and where appropriate the customer to which the receipt relates to.
- The manager should compare budget with actual expenses and again query any over-expenditure with the representative.
- Representatives to sign a contract with the company which clearly specifies what business expenses can be incurred using BJP's mobile and company car as well as the level of entertaining that is expected.
- BJP to be invoiced directly for expenses (e.g. by use of company charge card for petrol) rather than sales representatives to submit claims.
- Comparison of expenses between the different representatives to check that expenditure levels are appropriate.
- Annual review made of all expenses by BJP's internal audit department.

Control over time

- Representatives to sign a contract of employment which clearly states the hours to be worked.
- Outline budget for number of visits to new and existing customers to be agreed weekly in advance with manager at head office.
- Representatives to keep a list of customers visited, noting reasons for differences between this list and the budgeted list.
- The manager, or other person independent of the representative, to contact a selection of customers following a visit by the representative to determine that the visit actually took place.
- Comparing number of sales visits made between different representatives to ensure that number of visits are comparable.

(b) **Internal control system**

An internal control system is the whole system of controls, financial or otherwise, that are established by the management in order to carry on the business of an enterprise in an orderly and efficient manner, ensure adherence to management policies, safeguard the assets and secure as far as possible the completeness and accuracy of the records. The system therefore includes specific controls and procedures that are implemented by management and which employees are required to follow.

Control environment

The control environment is the system within which the internal control system operates. The environment therefore includes the overall ethics and culture of the organisation, which management should attempt to direct. The environment is effectively set by the philosophy of management, the management style, the way in which authority is delegated, the way in which staff are organised and developed and finally by the commitment of the board of directors.

Without an appropriate control environment, the internal control system will not be able to operate. For example, if the philosophy of management is not to set clear policies or not bother to review the work of junior managers, then those managers will not bother to follow the control systems. Good internal controls therefore need a good control environment.

Cost, benefits and limitations of internal controls

The actual cost of internal controls is difficult to determine because it is difficult to split costs between the policies and procedures that an organisation needs for basic record keeping and the additional costs for the internal control system. For example, some basic record keeping controls such as balancing control accounts can also be determined as part of the internal control system.

However, costs will include:

- time of managers to monitor and maintain the internal control systems;
- time of designing the internal control systems;
- opportunity costs of applying internal controls compared to carrying out income generating activities.

Similarly, the benefits of internal controls are difficult to determine partly because benefits are intangible and partly because it is unclear what costs would have been incurred had the control system not been operating (e.g. in terms of fraud, lost production, etc).

Estimates of benefits can be obtained by:

- comparing efficiency of operations before and after internal controls were implemented;
- comparing levels of waste, fraud etc. again prior to and after internal controls were implemented.

Both these estimates will be obtained by comparing activities of sales representatives before and after the introduction of control systems.

(c) Analytical review is the examination of ratios, trends and changes in balances from one period to the next, undertaken in order to obtain a broad understanding of the financial position and results of operations and to identify any items requiring further investigation.

Within BJP, analytical review can be used as follows:

- Comparison of total expenditure and individual items of expenditure such as motor vehicle costs between different representatives to ensure overall amounts being claimed are reasonable.
- Trend analysis of representative's expenditure compared to sales income generated.
- Comparison of expenses compared to budget, with explanations being sought for large or unusual variances.
- Review of customers gained and lost by each representative, with explanations sought, again, for unusual differences.

34 COMPANY A AND B (NOV 06 EXAM)

(a) The question describes the functional structure of each company.

Company A

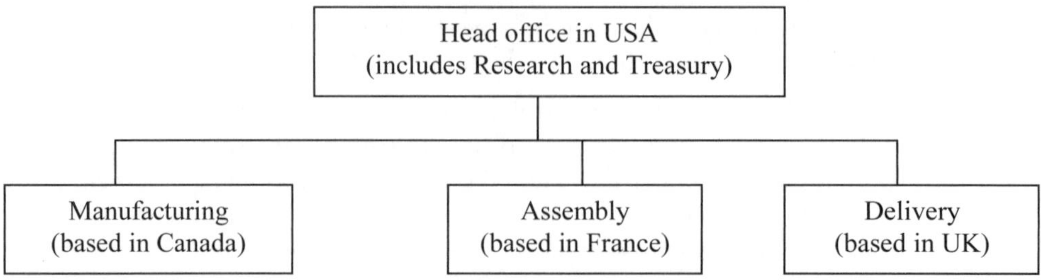

Company B

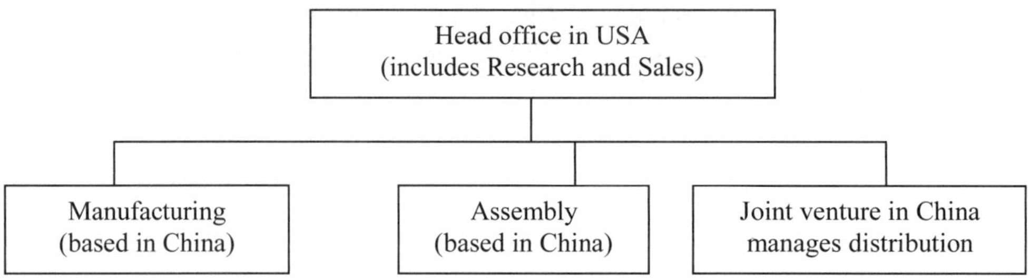

The following points can be made about how company structure, market types and location can impact on the risk profile of a company.

Company structure

Company structure refers to the way in which a group of companies is arranged by the parent company directors. Traditionally, the discussion was between 'tall' and 'flat' structures. Tall groups had numerous levels of subsidiaries and sub-subsidiaries, whereas flat groups had a small number of hierarchical levels – perhaps just the parent company with direct holdings in all the operating subsidiaries.

Tall structures are now out of favour, since there is a great risk of remoteness of top management from those who do the actual work at the bottom end of the organisation. There are often serious communication problems up the hierarchy, so that information is distorted or blocked as it travels up or down the structure.

Both Company A and Company B have chosen a flat structure for their group, with a parent company carrying out some functions and subsidiaries carrying out others. There is a risk of lack of competitiveness since duties may have to be duplicated in the companies across the group (e.g. Company B requires each company to have its own treasury operations), but each subsidiary should be able to become specialised in the function on which it concentrates.

Market types

Company A has a higher proportion of business-to-business (B2B) sales rather than a business-to-consumer (B2C) sales. 40% of its sales comes from two key European business customers. Company B has a higher proportion of B2C sales than B2B sales. Many B2C sales are made via the internet from the US. One Canadian company takes 15% of Company B's sales, but no other company takes more than 1%.

The risk to Company A is that it relies so heavily on two (European) customers. If the dollar strengthened substantially, for example, then Company A's products might become so expensive in Europe that these two customers would stop buying from Company A, thus losing 40% of sales revenue at once. A further risk to Company A arises from it concentrating on B2B sales which will take a longer credit period than B2C, resulting in the risk of poor liquidity.

The risk to Company B is a technological one. If its computers go down, then it cannot make any sales. There have been examples of workmen drilling through internet cables by mistake which have cut off some companies from the internet for days. The effect of such an accident on Company B would be severe.

Location

Company A's products are manufactured in Canada, but assembly and delivery are organised from Europe, to be close to the company's two key customers. There are several risks arising from this location structure. First, there will be currency risks arising between the US dollar as the presentation currency and the Canadian dollar, euro and pound sterling as operating currencies. Secondly, there will b e the risk of cultural clashes between English-speaking countries and French-speaking countries. Finally there is the risk of being undercut in terms of price by competitors who can manufacture their products in lower-wage countries (e.g. in Eastern Europe) who do not have to pay to transport the manufactured components half-way across the world to be assembled.

Company B has gone for the low-cost manufacturing route. The products are manufactured and assembled in China. There is some political risk of operating in China that the government may become anti-business, but for now the Chinese government is welcoming towards inwards investment. However, the assembled goods are mainly sold in America so have to be transported a long distance and there is a risk that transport costs will rise rapidly as oil supplies across the world begin to run out.

(b) Company A has fully centralised its treasury operations in its head office in the US. There is a risk of lack of motivation towards managing cash in the subsidiaries, since any cash that is received is swept up to head office to be managed from the group's perspective. There is also the risk that, should head office commit some error in their treasury operations, the financial health of the whole group could be placed in jeopardy.

Company B has decentralised its treasury operations to each company, where they are run as cost centres. There is the risk that one company might pay large overdraft interest costs, while another has cash balances in hand earning low interest rates. This is inefficient from the group's perspective. There is also the risk of not generating the profits for the group that would be earned if the group funds were actively managed by a treasury operation seeking profits rather than individual executives just seeking to minimise costs.

(c) Company B could implement the following controls.

A *financial* control would be regular budgets drawn up for each of the components of the business: sales revenues, research costs, manufacturing costs, assembly costs and distribution costs. Such budgets would be useful as a feedforward planning tool to ensure that management is steering the business towards achieving the corporate objectives, for confirming that each component of the business has a plan that ties in with the rest of the business, and also as a feedback tool at the end of the budget period to assess the company's performance.

A *non-financial quantitative* control would be the monitoring of a balanced scorecard of performance measures for the company. What proportion of products are new products introduced during the year? What proportion of research costs were spent on projects that were abandoned before coming to market? By monitoring a balanced scorecard, management can be confident that it is considering the interests of all stakeholders of the business in the longer term, rather than just concentrating on short-term financial performance.

A *non-financial qualitative* control would be the security of the IT infrastructure that receives the internet orders at the US sales department in the head office. Since it is of such importance to Company B that its computers can operate 24 hours a day, seven days a week, the company should have formal controls over the physical access to its computers and program access for its IT staff.

REVIEW AND AUDIT OF CONTROL SYSTEMS

35 REVIEW OF INTERNAL CONTROL

(a) **Answer to question 1**

On the assumption that Gash is a UK listed company, the annual review of internal control should apply to the entire system of internal control, not just to internal control for financial reporting. The internal control subject to review will therefore be all operations/management systems and the efficiency and effectiveness of systems and operations; financial controls and compliance controls (= controls to ensure that the company complies with relevant laws and regulations).

In other countries, notably the US, the annual review of internal control required by corporate governance law is restricted to financial controls and financial reporting.

Answer to question 2

(i) Senior management are responsible for implementing the internal control system. They should provide the culture or control environment for the organisation, giving a lead to all other employees. They are also responsible for establishing the systems for identifying and assessing risks, for deciding and implementing the internal controls for managing the risks, and for establishing a system for control reporting and a system for monitoring the effectiveness of controls. All these are executive tasks and are therefore the responsibility of executive managers.

The executive management is also accountable to the board of directors for their management of the internal control system.

(ii) According to the Combined Code in the UK, the audit committee should have the task of reviewing the effectiveness of the system of financial controls annually. In addition, unless a separate committee of independent non-executive directors is given the task, the audit committee should also review the effectiveness of the entire system of internal control for the company (operational and compliance controls as well as the financial controls) and the risk management system. The purpose of this review should be to check that the control system appears to be functioning adequately, or to identify any weaknesses in the system (which should then be discussed with the executive managers and possibly the external auditors). The audit committee should report its findings to the board of directors.

(iii) The board of directors is required by the Combined Code in the UK to report to the shareholders (in the annual report) that they have reviewed the effectiveness of the system of internal control.

The UK Combined Code does not require the board of directors to **evaluate** the effectiveness of controls, and the Turnbull Guidelines do not make this requirement either. The board is simply required to inform shareholders that they have made the review, but without giving their assessment.

(b) If the audit committee is responsible for the review of controls, it is important to remember that the committee consists of non-executive directors, and the time the committee members have available is therefore restricted. The review should be carried out in a way that makes the most effective use of the committee's time.

The review should be structured, and should consider the important elements of the control systems. A useful framework might be the COSO framework for internal control, which states that an internal control system has five elements:

(i) a suitable control environment and control culture;

(ii) a system of risk identification and assessment;

(iii) devising and applying suitable internal controls;

(iv) communicating and providing control information (and other relevant information);

(v) carrying out reviews of the control system and the controls.

An effective internal control system must function in each of these five areas. A review should therefore consider all five areas.

The most efficient method of carrying out the review is probably to study documents and hold meetings with key members of the management team, including the chief executive, finance director, chairman of the risk management committee and head of internal audit. Key documents would include minutes of the risk committee meetings, reports by the internal audit team and recommendations for improving controls provided by the external auditors (as part of the annual audit).

The control environment and culture can possibly be reviewed simply by discussing controls with senior management, and assessing the opinions and views that they express.

The system of risk identification can be reviewed by discussing risk assessment with the manager responsible (for example, the chairman of the risk committee) and by reading reports of the risk committee meetings. Any issues that arise from reading these reports can be discussed with the relevant executive manager.

The committee members need to understand the key risks that have been identified by management, in operational, financial and compliance areas. They then need to establish whether the system of devising and implementing controls is effective. To carry out this review, it might be useful to discuss controls with the finance director (financial controls) and the head of internal audit (all controls). If there are internal audit reports recommending improvements in controls, the committee should establish whether the recommendations have been implemented (and if not, why not).

The effectiveness of communicating relevant information might be reviewed by discussing with the CEO how managers are expected to respond to control reports, and how control reports are used. It might also be appropriate to identify any new regulations introduced during the year, to find out how quickly the information about the regulations and procedures to comply with the regulations was distributed to staff.

The effectiveness of monitoring controls should be discussed with senior management. Recommendations of the external auditors and the effectiveness of internal audit should be discussed.

Since senior executive managers are accountable to the board of directors for the system of internal control, it would also be appropriate to require the CEO to make presentations to the board, or prepare occasional board reports, that provide a review of the control system from the viewpoint of the management.

(c) The potential ethical problem for the internal auditors is that in carrying out their audit work, they might conclude that the finance director is at fault, for example for failing to apply sufficiently strong controls or for failing to communicate control information. From a professional point of view, the internal auditor would be required to criticise his or her boss. From a personal and career perspective, an auditor might not want to make any such criticism.

The CIMA Ethical Guidelines apply to all CIMA members, who might include not only the internal auditors, but also the finance director.

The fundamental principles could be helpful because if they are applied, they should help to remove personal animosities from the situation, that can affect the judgement of individuals.

The principles include the requirement for accountants to conduct themselves with integrity and objectivity. They should also apply professional and technical standards in their work. If these principles are applied, the internal auditor should be able to discuss any weaknesses in the control system with the manager responsible, even if this individual is his or her boss. By acting in an open and honest manner, without any personal bias being shown, and by taking an objective view of the situation, the auditor should try to establish a platform for a professional discussion of the audit findings. Where relevant, if professional and technical standards are applied, the auditor can demonstrate the objectivity and rationality of his approach.

If the finance director is a CIMA member, the Ethical Guidelines require him or her to act in a similar manner. Problems presented by the internal auditors should be considered objectively, without feeling a need to deny responsibility and escape blame.

The Ethical Guidelines can also help in this type of situation because they provide an external guide to professional conduct that both parties can refer to and recognise.

36 HIJ (MAY 06 EXAM)

(a) Three categories of management controls would be appropriate for the Principal of HIJ to have in place:

- financial controls;
- non-financial but quantitative controls;
- qualitative controls.

Financial controls are intended to help the organisation achieve its financial objectives, to safeguard assets, and to ensure the accuracy of the accounting records and the timely preparation of reliable financial information.

Examples would include:

- *Budgets for both income and expenses.* The Principal is constantly on the look-out for new clients, so the budgeted income should include a realistic estimate of income from new clients gained during the period. We are told that the Principal currently carries out strict cost control, so he should already be drawing up budgets for the company's expenses e.g. salaries, travel costs to the clients, marketing costs, IT costs (including the specialist accounting software that HIJ uses) and training costs to keep the employees technically up-to-date.
- *Budget variance analysis.* At the end of regular budget periods (e.g. quarterly) the Principal should compare the actual figures for income and expenses with the budgeted figures and take any action that is necessary from the variances identified.
- *Cash flow forecasts* should be drawn up regularly by the Principal to ensure that the company will have sufficient cash to pay its liabilities as they fall due. HIJ is a new company, so cash management is particularly important until the company has achieved a critical mass of clients who will pay their monthly fees to the company. Any cash deficits that are forecast can be managed in advance, either by delaying items of expenditure, or by raising new forms of finance, e.g. a bank overdraft.
- *Capital investment appraisal.* Any planned new large items of capital expenditure should be subjected to a formal appraisal exercise to determine whether their acquisition is worthwhile.
- *Receivables management.* The clients are billed monthly for the ongoing service provided, with each invoice perhaps offering 30 days' credit. The Principal must watch out for clients who are not paying their invoices on time, since this will have a negative impact on the company's cash flow position.

Quantitative non-financial controls should be set in place to complement the financial controls. The best approach would be along the lines of the balanced scorecard, looking at the customer perspective, internal business perspective and innovation and learning perspective to go hand in had with the financial perspective already discussed.

A *customer measure* would be the proportion of customers who renew their subscriptions each year. An *internal business measure* would be the ratio of chargeable to non-chargeable time achieved by each employee. An *innovation and learning measure* would be the number of hours training carried out by each employee. By monitoring the trend of each of these measures, the Principal can keep control of the business.

Qualitative controls are particularly important for the human resources aspects of the business. How are professional and support staff recruited? How is their progress monitored? Do they all report personally to the Principal, or is there some intermediate management structure? In a business offering professional services, the morale and commitment of all employees is a key driver of business success.

(b) There are various possible types of audit that could be considered to decide if they are appropriate:

- statutory audit carried out by an external audit firm
- internal audit assignments:
  - compliance audit
  - value of money audit

  - post-completion audit after a project is completed
  - management audit
- other audit assignments
  - environmental audit
  - health and safety audit.

The purpose of any audit is to examine the procedures and transactions of an entity in order to reach some conclusion about the entity. For example, the purpose of an external audit is to give an independent opinion on whether the published financial statements give a true and fair view. Consider now which types of audit are appropriate for HIJ.

In most countries (including the UK), it is only large companies and publicly quoted companies that are required by law to undergo an annual statutory audit. HIJ appears to be a small private company, therefore there is no legal obligation to appoint external auditors. However, the Principal may decide voluntarily to appoint external auditors in order to improve the reliability of the published financial statements. For example, if he were thinking of approaching his bank for a company loan, the bank would be more likely to approve the loan application if audited financial statements could be produced showing that the financial position of the company was sound. It is a matter for the Principal to weigh up the costs and benefits and to make a decision as to what is best.

Establishing an internal audit function is not mandatory in the case of a small private company such as HIJ. The Combined Code tacitly recommends that a listed company should have internal auditors, but again there is no absolute compulsion. It is up to the Principal to decide whether the costs of internal auditors would exceed or be less than the benefits derived.

A compliance audit looks at whether the company is complying with all applicable laws and regulations, e.g. that all software used is properly licensed and not pirate copies bought without a licence. A VFM audit examines whether a particular operation is being carried out economically, effectively and efficiently (the 3 Es). A post-completion audit considers whether, in hindsight, a capital project has been a success. A management audit looks at the corporate structure and the effectiveness of managers in achieving the company's objectives.

The Principal of HIJ has three possible options in the provision of internal audit services:

- he can decide that no internal audit work is necessary;
- he can decide that, as he is a qualified accountant, he can carry out the necessary work himself;
- he can buy in internal audit staff, either employing them within the company or paying an external contractor.

Since HIJ is currently a small company, the middle option is probably the most appropriate. The Principal can carry out all necessary internal audit work by himself, for now.

Other possible types of audit, such as environmental audit, do not seem to be a priority, since the company's operations have no substantial impact on carbon emissions, etc. If the Principal wanted advice in a particular area, he could pay for an external specialist to give him the advice that he wants, rather than pay for a formal audit to be carried out.

(c) **Costs of a system of internal controls**

There will be establishment costs associated with designing the controls in the first place and setting them up. Then there will be regular ongoing costs associated with maintaining and improving the controls. These costs will be both cash costs and also opportunity costs, e.g. of the Principal's time when he could be out looking for new business or generating chargeable hours on existing clients.

The controls identified in part (a) will all have costs associated with them. It is up to the Principal to decide which controls have benefits in excess of their costs so that they should be implemented. For many controls, e.g. making back-ups of work-in-progress for clients, which are stored at a remote fire-proof location, there is no practical choice. The control has to be implemented, since the consequences of not having a back-up file would be unthinkable if an employee's main computer failed. Other controls can be regarded as discretionary costs that the Principal must make a judgement about.

Benefits of a system of internal controls

Internal controls are established to help the business to be run in an orderly and efficient manner. Without controls, the business would suffer losses that can be avoided if the controls are operating satisfactorily.

To use again the example of taking back-up copies of computer files of current work-in-progress engagements, the risk is that all the work would be lost if the main computer failed or was stolen and there was no back-up. This would upset the client hugely and it is likely that they would seek to end their relationship with HIJ.

The controls assist in avoiding the loss of clients, but also the loss of money (e.g. in strict control of costs and chasing of overdue debts) and the loss of goodwill (if HIJ starts to gain a poor reputation in the market).

37 CARPETS AND FLOOR COVERINGS

(a) A value for money audit is an audit of economy, efficiency and effectiveness (the '3Es'). The audit investigates an aspect of operations, such as the work done in a particular department, or the work carried out to perform a particular activity (in more than one department). The aim of the audit is to establish the objective or objectives of the operations, and consider:

(i) whether the objectives are being successfully achieved, and if not what the reasons might be;

(ii) whether the operations are being performed in a cost-efficient manner, or whether there is unnecessary and wasteful spending on items of expense;

(iii) whether operations are being performed efficiently.

A Value For Money (VFM) audit of the accounts department might therefore look at issues such as:

(i) staffing levels in the department, and whether these are too high (resulting in low productivity);

(ii) whether customers pay on time, or whether the debt collection staff give customers too much time to pay, and whether bad debt levels are high. (Poor debt collection procedures and high irrecoverable debts would indicate a lack of effectiveness);

(iii) whether the department has spent too much on its computer equipment (resulting in poor economy).

A VFM audit might also investigate part of the accounts department that are not subject to an 'accounting audit', such as the management accounts and the capital expenditure appraisal procedures. For example, a VFM audit might assess the value that is provided by the current management accounting control system (in terms of what it achieves, and whether it does its work efficiently and economically), and whether the benefits justify the costs incurred.

In contrast, an audit of the accounting system would be concerned with the reliability of the accounting records and whether the assets of the company are being properly safeguarded. The audits will therefore consider the reliability of internal controls, and whether the auditors can rely on the effectiveness of those controls. The focus is therefore entirely different. An audit of the accounts is not particularly concerned with efficiency or economy.

(b) An audit needs to be conducted against a clear set of standards or targets. Since the company intends to publish an annual Social and Environmental Report, it has to decide the criteria against which its performance and policies should be measured.

The key issues should be established. The board of directors should have some idea of what these issues are, but guidance can be obtained if necessary from the company's shareholders, or from external agencies that have been established to assist companies to prepare Social and Environmental Reports (or Sustainability Reports). These sources include the UN's Global Research Initiative sustainability reporting guidelines.

The aspects of social and environmental and responsibility that might need to be covered by the report – and audited – include environmental issues (pollution, waste, sustainable supplies of raw materials) and work-related issues (human rights, working conditions, pay, employee education, avoiding discrimination at work, and so on).

A social and environmental audit should be planned within the framework of the company's policies for social and environmental matters and targets for achievement. An audit can then assess whether the policies are being applied and whether progress is being made towards the stated targets (which could be either quantitative or qualitative targets).

From the information available, two social and environmental risks are apparent. It is not clear how serious they are, but if they could affect the short-term or long-term value of the company, they should be disclosed in the Social and Environmental Report. (In the UK, listed companies may be required in the future to disclose significant risks, including risks relating to social and environmental issues, in their annual Operating and Financial Review.) The two issues that seem apparent are:

(i) Environmental issues relating to the disposal of old carpets and floor covering. BK currently burns some old materials and disposes of the rest using methods that are not stated. There is an immediate risk that BK is in breach of the law by burning the materials (air pollution and possibly other pollution) and might also be in breach of the laws on disposals of materials. Checking on compliance with the laws should be an element of a social and environmental audit. The company might also be affected by further legal restrictions on disposals (and recycling) of used items.

(ii) There are also human rights issues in connection with the possible use of child labour or slave labour by suppliers. Although BK is not directly responsible for the labour policies of its suppliers, a socially responsible policy would be to influence suppliers to adopt different labour policies or switch to different suppliers. If BK is using suppliers who use child labour or slave labour, there will be a risk to the company's reputation. This could have an impact on sales of the company's services.

(c) From the information available about the dispute, it is not clear whether or not the internal auditor acted ethically.

(i) The CIMA Ethical Guidelines state that an accountant should act with integrity, and should be honest and straightforward in carrying out his or her work. There is a suggestion that this might not have been the case. The executive director accused the auditor of being 'deceitful'. It would also appear that the auditor did not discuss his findings or his concerns with the director or anyone else in the department subject to audit. This would have been inappropriate behaviour, because it would have lacked integrity. An internal auditor is required to look for weaknesses in systems, management and controls, but should discuss issues with the individuals concerned and be straightforward in doing so.

(ii) The Ethical Guidelines also require an accountant to act with objectivity, and to be intellectually honest and fair. It is not clear whether the auditor acted in this way, or whether perhaps a personal dislike of the director might have affected his opinions and biased his judgements.

(iii) The Ethical Guidelines require an accountant to show professional competence and due care in his work. The director has accused the auditor of not being qualified for the work. Without further information, this cannot be assessed any further.

It is also possible that the internal auditor was subjected to strong pressure from the director and others in the department to give a favourable audit report, when a more critical report would be appropriate. If this was the situation and the auditor was under pressure from the director, he would have been the victim of an ethical conflict of interest. The CIMA Guidelines recommend that in such circumstances, the accountant should report the problem to his superior. However, since the target of the auditor's criticism was a director of the company, it is quite possible that his superior also felt a conflict of interest and inability to stand up to such a senior person.

When an accountant is unable to resolve a conflict of interest by referring the problem to a superior (or the superior's boss), the CIMA Guidelines state that there may be no alternative to resignation. It is possible that this is what happened in this particular case.

In conclusion, from the limited information available, it is not clear who was 'at fault', the director or the accountant (or both of them). However, with more information, it would be possible to judge the matter by reference to the CIMA Ethical Guidelines.

38 ROXY HOTELS

(a) In order to achieve their objectives, organisations must manage both their business risks and their governance risks. Governance risks are managed by the system of internal control.

The internal control system has an important role in the management of risks that are significant to the fulfilment of an organisation's business objectives. A sound system of control contributes to safeguarding the organisation's assets, helps to improve the efficiency and effectiveness of operations and helps with compliance with laws and regulations.

Effective financial controls, including the proper maintenance of accounting records, are an important element in internal control because they help to make sure that the organisation is not exposed to excessive financial risks. They also help to ensure that financial information is reliable and with the prevention and detection of fraud.

Where an organisation has an internal audit function, the role of internal audit is to provide a check on the internal control system, to ensure that it is operating effectively and efficiently. Weaknesses in the control system should be identified, and recommendations made for improving the system. By monitoring the internal control system, internal audit therefore contributes to the achievement of an organisation's objectives.

(b) An internal audit department might carry out a variety of activities.

(i) It carries out checks on internal controls, to ensure that the controls are functioning effectively. In particular, it carries out checks on financial controls, such as checks on the accuracy of balances and recorded transactions in the accounting system. The work done by the internal audit department in this area might be relied on by the external auditors, for the purpose of the external audit.

(ii) It carries out checks on systems, to make sure that the system is operating efficiently and effectively.

(iii) It might carry out special investigations, for example where fraud is suspected or alleged.

(iv) It might carry out compliance checks, to ensure that laws and regulations are being properly complied with.

(v) It mighty conduct value for money (VFM) audits, which are investigations into the efficiency, effectiveness and economy (cost efficiency) of a department or operation.

(vi) In some organisations, the internal audit department might assist with risk identification and assessment procedures, as a part of the system of risk management.

(c) (i) An audit might be carried out into the system of hotel room bookings, to ensure that bookings received are properly recorded in the system, that customers do stay for the period of time that has been booked, that they are correctly invoiced and that the invoices are fully paid. This could involve a detailed check of a sample of bookings logged on the system.

(ii) Similarly, checks could be carried out on the system of booking conference rooms and paying for them. In this system, customers are likely to be invoiced and given credit terms for payment. Checks could ensure that receivables are properly collected and recorded in the accounts.

(iii) A check might be carried out into inventory and purchases, to ensure that items such as food are properly requisitioned from established suppliers, correctly delivered and paid for.

(iv) Checks could be carried out on the expenditure authorisation system. One set of checks could be made to ensure that when expenditure is authorised, the item is actually purchased. Another set of checks could be to look at a sample of assets, to make sure that their purchase was properly authorised.

(v) Checks could be carried out on the payroll system, to make sure that the employees on the payroll actually exist (or did exist), that overtime has been properly authorised and recorded, and that payroll procedures have been performed correctly.

(vi) Checks might be carried out on the takings of the restaurants and bars, to make sure that actual receipts banked matches the amounts on the till rolls of the bars and the billing system of the restaurants.

(d) The internal audit department might also carry out investigations into the efficiency and effectiveness of systems and operational performance.

(i) A review of room occupancy rates could be carried out, and comparisons made between the 40 hotels. This might indicate hotels that are performing significantly below average or expectation. Remedial action could then be taken to improve performance.

(ii) A review could be carried out into the system of budgeting and cash flow forecasting, to make sure that management are making proper use of historical data when making future plans and forecasts. This will have the benefit of ensuring that budgets are as accurate as possible and provide an appropriate monitoring tool for each hotel in the group.

(iii) An investigation might be carried out into operational efficiency in the restaurants and bars of the hotels, for example by carrying out a review of the average spend per guest per day in each hotel, and then making comparisons. The review may highlight hotels where guests are not using hotel facilities as much as expected. Reasons for this, e.g. good restaurants in close proximity to the hotel, can be identified and where possible remedial action taken.

(iv) A check could be made into the security of the computer system, to ensure that the system successfully prevents unauthorised access. Security is an important concern, especially as personal data will be stored on the computer systems, and Roxy Hotels will be required to comply with appropriate data protection legislation.

Note: Answers could suggest other system or operational performance checks, such as a review of the efficiency of the central booking system.

39 SPQ (NOV 05 EXAM)

Tutorial notes:

This question provides a mix between theory (parts (a), (c) and part of (d)), and some application. The information on the computer system is not complete, so some speculation is needed in part (b) while much is made of the ethical issue for part (d). Be careful to allocate time in accordance with the mark allocation, and do not get carried away in explaining ethics in part (d).

(a) Regarding internal control, internal auditors will review the system of internal control within an organisation. They will test the effectiveness of the controls as an independent third party and then provide a report on their work. Internal auditors do not establish the operational controls they test as this would impair the independence of their review.

Regarding risk management, internal auditors will again review the system for identifying and responding to risks in an organisation. They will focus on high risk areas specifically, and, where controls are found to be weak, they will again prepare an appropriate report, making recommendations for control improvements.

To be clear, internal auditors are specialists in risk management and internal controls – but those risks are managed by individual line managers. Internal auditors ensure that risks have been identified, analysed and managed, giving advice on appropriate controls when asked.

Internal auditors may also advise the board of various internal controls and risk management, including areas such as:

- how to identify risks;
- how to establish a culture to manage risks within an organization;
- reporting on how effective management are at managing risk in the organization; and
- ensuring that appropriate legislation has been complied with.

(b) *Risk: hacking and fraudulent access to computer systems*

SPQ's computer systems appear to have been accessed by unauthorised third parties with the aim of obtaining goods without paying for them. It is not clear how access occurred, although it is possible that other systems are also vulnerable.

Control recommendations

- Monitor access requests from 'customers' to identify where multiple requests are made from the same computer. Where this occurs, check transactions to ensure that they do not 'disappear'.
- Review firewall controls to ensure these are effective.
- Monitor system access from internal sources, using a control log, to identify whether staff in the IT department are placing fraudulent orders.

Risk: non-payment of deliveries

It appears that deliveries of goods have been made without the customer being invoiced for the goods or cash being received. The risk is that sales in SPQ are understated.

Control recommendation

Only despatch goods where payment has been received in full. This may require amendment to computer programs to ensure that this control is active.

Risk: transactions deleted from customer database

It is possible that the customer database is not complete given that transactions appear to have been deleted after delivery of goods. The risk is therefore that SPQ's accounting records are not being maintained correctly.

Control recommendations

Check the integrity of the details in the database using run-to-run totals or similar methods of reconciling transactions on a daily basis.

Monitor access to the database ensuring that all internal amendments are routed through the Database administrator. Control logs can again be used for this purpose.

Risk: ineffective internal audit reports

There is a risk that internal audit reports do not identify the extent of risks identified in SPQ as managers are requesting that the report is modified. There is also the risk that the audit reports may not be actioned anyway as the internal auditor reports to the CEO rather than to a person independent of the operational running of the company.

Control recommendation

The internal auditor should report to an independent person, such as the Chair of the Audit Committee. The latter will be able to ensure that all internal audit reports are actioned appropriately.

(c) *Issues to be considered in planning an audit of activities*

Previous internal audit reports. These will identify the results of previous audits for each activity and therefore indicate the extent of work expected for the next audit.

Changes made to the system. Where significant changes have been made then the audit will take longer as amendments will have to be documented and tested. The level of testing will also increase as less reliance can be placed on the results of previous audits.

Review of the work carried out by external auditors. Where external auditors have audited a system and found no errors, then the internal audit department can take some confidence from these results and decrease the extent of its testing.

Discussion with local managers. This will help identify any concerns with the system and therefore affect the extent of work undertaken by the internal auditor.

Obtain information on known risks. In SPQ, the internal audit department was directed to audit the system by the Chief Accountant, who may have realised the risk of error. Identifying known risks will help internal audit focus work on those areas to determine the extent of risk and errors.

Confirm the audit objectives. Audit work should always be carried out with specific objectives in mind.

(d) *Integrity*

The internal auditor should be straightforward and honest. He should not supply any information which is known to be misleading, false or deceptive. This means that the internal auditor should not give in to pressure to amend the report unless factual errors are identified in it.

Objectivity

This is a combination of impartiality, intellectual honesty and freedom from conflicts of interest. It means that the internal auditor should not allow the influence of others to override his decisions. Again this means that the report should not be amended, simply because managers suggest it will be unpopular.

Professional competence and duty of care

As a new appointee, the internal auditor will have confirmed that he has the appropriate skills and knowledge to perform his job and therefore that reporting will be carried out with reasonable skill and diligence. To amend the report would suggest that reasonable skill and care will not have been used, as the report would be inaccurate.

Professional behaviour

The internal auditor has to act in a manner which is consistent with the good reputation of the Institute. To amend a report would effectively involve being conservative with the truth, which a CIMA member should avoid.

Resolution of ethical conflict

Ethical conflicts should be resolved by:

- following the organisation's grievance procedures;
- discussing the matter with a superior (unless that person is involved with the ethical situation), and then subsequent levels of management;
- where necessary, discussing it with the member's professional body;
- where the conflict has not been resolved, the member may have to consider resignation.

40 BRIDGEFORD PRODUCTS

(a) There are several reasons why internal auditors should plan their audit work.

(i) It is important to ensure that the audit work is effective. Greater emphasis should be given to the audit of high-risk operations and activities. To ensure that the limited resources of the audit team are used effectively, an audit plan should be prepared for a future period, and updated on a rolling basis.

(ii) An audit plan will help senior management, and particularly the manager to whom the head of internal audit reports, to give their formal approval to audit activity for a given period.

(iii) The benefits from internal audit work should justify the costs of providing it. Planning audit work should help management to assess whether internal audit will provide value for money.

(iv) The performance of the internal audit department can be more easily monitored, by comparing actual work done with the plan, and actual costs with budget.

(v) An audit plan will help management to make sure that sufficient resources are provided to the internal audit department to enable it to carry out its work.

(b) (i) The management accounts show that annual sales in 20X4 are much higher than in the previous year, but the profit before tax has fallen by about one half. This might suggest that the company has reduced profit margins substantially in order to boost sales. As internal auditor, I would want to find out from the management responsible why profit margins have fallen and whether the trend is getting worse.

(ii) As internal auditor, I would want to obtain assurance that the computerised inventory control system records inventory movements and inventory quantities accurately. If it is proposed to rely on the computer records for the end-of-year inventory count, the system must be reliable – otherwise the external auditors will not be satisfied. I would propose an audit of the inventory system, which includes a comparison of the inventory balances on the computer system with the balances obtained from a physical inventory count.

(iii) There may be a substantial risk for the company from unreliable products. In addition to the cost of legal claims and disputes with customers, there are risks to the company's reputation and the possibility of falling sales demand in the future. An investigation into the problem will help to establish the scale of the risk, and recommendations could be made, as appropriate, for improving systems and controls.

(iv) Although the change in credit policy is a policy issue for senior management, it would be appropriate to investigate the effects the new policy is having. Receivables were not being collected on time before the change, but the receivables age is now 4.1 months when it should be three months at most. There is also a risk that the easier credit terms will attract less creditworthy customers, and the irrecoverable debts risk will increase. An investigation might establish the costs and benefits of the new policy.

(v) It is not clear why the purchasing manager was dismissed, and it is conceivable that mismanagement or fraud was an issue. There might be a risk that during the period before the new purchasing manager takes up her position, purchasing activities might not be performed according to established procedures and controls might not be applied as effectively as they should be. It might therefore be appropriate to carry out an audit of purchasing activities, covering purchasing transactions in this period.

41 GRAPE

(a) A satisfactory explanation of each of the changes would be:

- The increase in days sales in accounts receivable ('days sales outstanding'): an increase in normal credit terms, for example from 30 days to 60 days. (Alternatively: the inclusion in the closing receivables in the current year of one very large amount outstanding from a reliable customer with good credit quality, such as a government department.)
- The reduction in inventory turnover, which means a slower average inventory turnover period: the company might have deliberately increased inventory levels in anticipation of a new sales campaign. (Alternatively: higher inventories due to a deliberate policy of buying in larger quantities of key materials that are currently in short supply.)
- The lower ratio of depreciation to costs: there might have been a re-assessment of economic lives of plant and machinery items, with expected economic lives becoming longer.
- Higher repairs and maintenance as a percentage of sales: a decision by management in the current year to carry out an unusually large number of maintenance overhauls of plant and equipment.

(b) The main concern of the external auditor will be that the change in the ratio is due to a mis-statement of a figure in the financial statements. For example, a large increase in the days sales in accounts receivable could be due to an over-statement of receivables in the balance sheet. Similarly, the fall in the ratio of depreciation to plant and machinery cost could be due either to an under-statement of the depreciation charge or an over-statement of plant and machinery at cost.

The external auditor will therefore need to carry out checks to substantiate the figures that might have been mis-stated.

Although the internal auditor would also be interested in control failures leading to a mis-statement of figures in the accounts, he should also be interested in the reasons for any changes in the ratios that might indicate inefficiencies in systems.

For example, a slower average payment period for trade receivables might indicate inefficiencies in debt collection procedures, and slower inventory turnover might indicate inefficient inventory management. Similarly, a higher ratio of repairs and maintenance costs to sales could indicate problems with ageing equipment and, indirectly, quality control problems in production.

An internal audit programme might therefore be planned that includes investigations into these areas, with reports and recommendations prepared for the line management.

(c) If these changes in the ratios are significant and cannot be readily explained by the managers responsible for operations, there could be serious weaknesses in the management accounting control system.

- Control reports should provide management with key performance indicators. The control reports prepared for management might be failing to reveal the decline in operating efficiency, perhaps because the ratios have not been regarded as key performance indicators. The information provided to management might have indicated that performance was satisfactory.
- Control reports to management might contain too much detail. There is a risk that when control reports provide excessive detail, users of the reports are not always able to distinguish what is important from what is of little relevance. An effective control reporting system might therefore provide feedback on the basis of exception reporting, and drawing management attention to key ratios and variances.
- The control reports might be presented to managers who are not responsible for control and performance, whereas the managers responsible might not be receiving the reports at all, or might not be receiving them in good time.

42 AL & CO. (MAY 05 EXAM)

Examiner's comments

This question seeks to test the candidates' ability to identify shortcomings in internal controls systems, and the parties responsible for fraud management and detection. By placing the question in the context of a small sized business, the need for fraud control across all types and sizes of business is emphasised.

The syllabus topics being tested range across both B (Risk and Internal Control) and C (Review and Audit of Control Systems). Candidates are expected to recognise that control of directors is central to fraud management and to identify mechanisms for improving internal controls, as well as understand the limited role of the external auditors in relation to fraud detection. The design of a fraud response plan forms the final part of the question.

Common errors that occurred May 05 exam:

Answers frequently identified weaknesses, but failed to suggest satisfactory controls. An unrealistic burden was placed on the internal audit department.

The discussion of the concerns raised by the variable overhead was frequently written only from an internal audit perspective rather than the external audit and internal control aspects as required by the question.

Discussion of the limits of the ability of the external auditor to detect fraud and of the fraud response plan was generally superficial, with many candidates demonstrating very poor knowledge of fraud response plans.

Report to the Directors of AL & Co.
Internal control systems within AL & Co.

May 20X0

Introduction

This report has been written following the external audit of the accounts for the year ended XX XX 20X0. As your accountant, there are various matters which need to be brought to your attention and which require action prior to the audit for the year being completed.

(a) **Inadequacies in internal control systems and recommendations for improvement**

Overview

The system of internal control with AL & Co is limited, with many controls being informal or simply non-existent. There remains the possibility of collusion and fraud due to the lack of a clearly defined internal control system. As directors, you do have responsibility for implementing an appropriate control system. This section of the report identifies control weaknesses and makes recommendations for improvement.

Lack of checking

As directors, you have responsibilities for different sections of the business of AL & Co. The work of each director is not checked due to your inherent trust. While trust is essential in a business context, lack of checking does not remove the possibility of unintentional error. Some form of cross checking and verification is therefore recommended to ensure that the business of AL & Co overall does not suffer from errors.

Job costing

Only the cost of materials are charged to individual jobs – with other costs being collected and charged as a lump sum prior to net profit. This means that the profitability of individual jobs cannot be determined.

Charging all costs to specific jobs will help to determine the actual profitability of individual jobs. Reasons for poor profitability can then be determined and measures taken to ensure that specific types of jobs where profit is lower or even negative, are charged at an appropriate fee.

Time variances

Similarly, actual time to complete specific jobs is not monitored. This can lead to hidden cost overruns where time exceeds budget. Monitoring time will help identify difficult types of jobs, or contractors who consistently do not meet budget. Action can then be taken to remove those contracts where necessary.

Job costing

It is not clear how the two employees determine the labour and material costs for each job. Errors in estimation may result in contracts being over or under priced.

Production of a formal job costing sheet detailing all costs to be incurred would help provide more accurate budgets. Director Y should continue to review and sign each costing as a control over the accuracy of the job cost.

Payments

Payments are due on completion of work done. Given that some contracts last for a number of months then this places unnecessary burden on AL & Co to fund work-in-progress. Controls should be implemented for the contract to request stage payments where jobs exceed say two months, to decrease the financial burden on AL & Co.

New suppliers

New suppliers are recommended by director Y. It is not clear how these suppliers are recommended. For large items of expenditure, competitive quotes should be obtained rather than accepting verbal recommendations. This will ensure AL & Co receive value for money as well as removing the potential for fraud or personal relationships to affect the procurement process.

Management accounts

No management accounts are produced. This means that overall management control is weak as the directors have no ongoing picture of how AL & Co is performing throughout the year. Production of regular management accounts would help highlight, for example, changes to expected gross profit, allowing investigation to be made on a timely basis rather than waiting for production of year end accounts.

(b) **Rise in variable overheads**

The rise in variable overheads is concerning from two perspectives.

External audit perspective

External auditors form an opinion on whether the financial statements show a true and fair view. This means they will seek explanations for any unusual items, areas of expenditure etc. so they can form their opinion. The fact that variable overheads have increased and that appropriate audit evidence cannot be obtained to verify these expenses will be a cause for concern. External auditors will normally expect to contact third parties to ensure that there are no unrecorded liabilities; the non-return of telephone calls and potentially letters is therefore not acceptable. Similarly, external auditors will need to ensure that expenditure is bona fide to the business. As it is difficult to determine why these expenses have been incurred, then the issue of legitimate business expense is raised. At the extreme there is the possibility of reporting under the Proceeds of Crime Act of 2002 that the business may have been involved in fraud or money laundering. While an extreme situation, the external auditors as professionals have no choice but to follow these reporting requirements if necessary.

Internal control perspective

The lack of apparent reason for incurring the additional overhead expenses also appears to be a weakness in the internal control systems. As one director is effectively ordering these items, then the second director should sign the purchase invoice to show these are legitimate business expenditure.

(c) **Auditor's responsibility to detect fraud**

International Standard on Auditing 240 requires auditors to *perform procedures to obtain information that is used to identify the risks of material misstatement due to fraud.* In other words, the auditor is attempting to identify material fraud, rather than all instances of fraud. The auditor may fail to detect some frauds, particularly if the fraud is immaterial. This means that detection of fraud is primarily the responsibility of the directors.

However, under the 2002 Act, even immaterial fraud must be reported to the appropriate authorities. So even if the overstatement of overhead expenses is immaterial, and so does not affect the true and fair view given by the financial statements, the auditor will still be required to report this to the relevant authorities.

Fraud response plan

One method of resolving the issue of overhead expenses is to devise a fraud response plan. While this may appear to be excessive for a small business, the overall procedures within the plan should be useful.

Sections of the plan will include information on:

- the person to lead the investigation – ensuring they have appropriate experience;
- how the investigation will be carried out;
- identification of systems to remove the risk of fraud in the future;
- methods of obtaining evidence and dealing with suspects;
- how or when to involve the police.

I suggest we convene a meeting as soon as possible to discuss the situation and agree the evidence to be presented to the auditors. Hopefully, the matter can be resolved quickly and with minimum disruption to the company.

43 INTERNAL CONTROLS (NOV 06 EXAM)

REPORT

To: The Board of Directors

From: AN Accountant

Date: X-X-XX

Subject: The effectiveness of internal controls

Introduction

The report considers:

- your responsibilities in relation to ensuring the effectiveness of internal controls;
- methods that can be used to assess the effectiveness of controls;
- reporting the results of internal control reviews to the stock market.

The board's responsibilities

Best practice in corporate governance matters is set out in statements such as the UK Combined Code on Corporate Governance. You are the directors of a stock market listed company, so your company falls within the scope of the Combined Code.

Main Principle C2 of the Combined Code states that the board should maintain a sound system of internal control to safeguard shareholders' investment and the company's assets. This is backed up by a Provision stating that the board should, at least annually, conduct a review of the effectiveness of the group's system of internal controls and should report to shareholders that it has done so. The review should cover all material controls, including financial, operational and compliance controls and risk management systems.

Further guidance on the board's responsibilities is given in the Turnbull Report on Internal Control. In deciding what is a sound system of internal control, the board should consider the following matters:

- the nature and extent of the risks facing the company;
- the extent and categories of risk which it regards as acceptable for the company to bear;
- the likelihood of the risks concerned materialising;

- the company's ability to reduce the incidence and impact of risks that do materialise;
- the costs of operating particular controls relative to the expected benefit obtained.

By considering these matters in the particular circumstances of the company, you as a board should be able to set appropriate policies with regard to internal control. It is then management's job to implement the board policies that you have established.

However, the board's responsibility goes further than just ensuring that a sound internal control system is set up properly. The Code Principle states your responsibility as to *maintain* a sound system. Therefore, there must be effective monitoring of the system on a continuous basis, both by embedding monitoring processes within the system and by your receiving and reviewing regular reports on internal control.

Should the board become aware at any time of a significant weakness in internal control, you should determine the facts of the situation and reassess the effectiveness of management's ongoing processes for operating the internal control system.

Assessing the effectiveness of internal controls

The board must regularly review management's reports to it on internal control and must discuss these matters with management. Furthermore, the board must carry out its own annual assessment as required by the Combined Code. The Turnbull Report again gives useful guidance on matters that the board should consider when discharging these responsibilities:

- Risk assessment
  - Are all significant risks identified and assessed on an ongoing basis?
  - Is there a clear understanding of what risks are acceptable?
- Control environment and control activities
  - Does senior management demonstrate a commitment to competence and integrity and foster a climate of trust within the company?
  - Does the company communicate to its employees what is expected of them and the scope of their freedom to act?
- Information and communication
  - Do management and the board receive timely reports on progress towards business objectives and the related risks?
  - Are there established channels of communication for individuals to report (in confidence) suspected improprieties?
- Monitoring
  - Are there ongoing processes embedded within the company's business operations that monitor the effective application of the policies and processes related to internal control and risk management?
  - Are there procedures to ensure that appropriate action is taken in response to changes in risk and control assessments?

Examples of specific methods that can be used by the board to address these questions would be control self-assessment questionnaires, regular confirmation by personnel that they are familiar with and have complied with the company's policies and codes of conduct, internal audit reviews or other management reviews.

Reporting the results of internal control reviews to the stock market

The Listing Rules of the London Stock Exchange require that listed companies must disclose in their Annual Report *how* it has applied the principles of the Combined Code and *whether* it has complied with the provisions of the Code (if not, then it must explain its non-compliance of any particular provisions). In practice, most listed companies do comply with all the provisions of the Code, so the Annual Report contains a narrative statement of how it has applied Principle C2 and a factual statement that the board has conducted a review of the effectiveness of the system of internal controls.

Once again, the Turnbull Report offers guidance on what should be contained in the board's statement on internal control. It its narrative statement, the board should disclose:

- that there is an ongoing process for identifying, evaluating and managing the significant risks faced by the company;
- that it has been in place for the year under review and up to the date of approval of the annual report;
- that it is regularly reviewed; and
- that it accords with the Turnbull Guidance.

In relation to the provision of the Code relating to internal control, the board should summarise the process it has applied in reviewing the effectiveness of the system of internal control, including how it has dealt with any significant problems disclosed elsewhere in the Annual Report.

I hope that this report has been helpful to you in this matter. Please contact me again if I can be of any further help to you in the future.

MANAGEMENT OF FINANCIAL RISK

44 LIABILITIES (PILOT PAPER)

(a) (i) From the information provided, it would appear that the main financial risks facing the group are interest rate risk and currency risk.

Interest rate risk is the risk that interest costs will be comparatively higher (or interest revenue comparatively lower) due to an adverse movement in interest rates. The group's interest-bearing liabilities are 23% fixed rate (33/143). The weighted average interest rate on the fixed rate liabilities is 7.25%, whereas interest rates are currently around 5%. This indicates that interest rates have fallen since the fixed rate borrowings were created, and the group is now paying more in interest than it would have had to if all its borrowings had been at a floating rate.

The UK group is also exposed to currency risk. This arises from the fact that organisations trade across international borders and in different currency areas. As a result, some organisations buy goods and services, or sell goods and services, in foreign currencies. In addition, some organisations borrow, lend or invest in foreign currencies. Currency risk arises from the effect of changes in an exchange rate on the value, in domestic currency, of receipts, payments, assets or liabilities in foreign currency.

In this example, currency risk arises from the existence of foreign currency liabilities and, presumably, foreign subsidiaries.

(ii) It is not possible to quantify the transaction risk exactly, because there is insufficient information to quantify the transaction risk relating to interest payments on the foreign currency liabilities.

However, the group has US dollar liabilities of £41 million and liabilities in euros of £4 million (£ equivalent amounts). At some time in the future, these liabilities must be paid back to the lender, and these repayments of principal give rise to a transaction exposure.

If the £ were to depreciate by 10%, the amount repayable would increase by 11.1111% [100/(100 – 10)]. The total liabilities, in £ terms, would therefore increase from £45 million to £50 million. The higher payments due to the adverse currency movement would be £5 million.

Tutorial note:

If you get confused by the mathematics, try a simple example. If the exchange rate is £1 = US$2 and sterling falls in value by 10%, the new exchange rate will be £1 = $1.80. A liability of $3,600 that was originally going to cost £1,800 in sterling to settle will now cost £2,000, an increase of £200 or 11.1111%.)

(iii) Currency risk can be categorised into translation risk, transaction risk and economic risk.

Translation risk arises because foreign currency-denominated assets and liabilities are translated into the currency of the parent company (here, sterling) for the purpose of presenting consolidated group accounts. The assets and profits of foreign subsidiaries are exposed to a movement in the value of the foreign currency against sterling. Foreign currency assets and liabilities will decline in value when the foreign currency declines in value, affecting reported group results.

Transaction exposure arises from the risk that a movement in the exchange rate will reduce the amount of specific future receipts or payments in the company's domestic currency due to a future change in the exchange rate before the receipt or payment transaction date. In this example, the UK group has about 31% of its borrowings in US dollars and euros, and transactions that might give rise to transaction exposures are interest payments and future repayments of principal, in the currency of the borrowings.

Economic exposures arise from strategic exposures to locating operations in an area of the world whose foreign currency increases in value over time, making the output from the operation relatively more expensive.

(b)

Tutorial note:

This part of the question ought to be straightforward if you are familiar with derivatives and if you had plenty of time to write your answer. However, it is not easy to provide a reasonably complete answer within the limited time available for answering a 12-mark question. A technique that might be useful to practise for the examination is giving competent explanations and descriptions within a restricted time scale!

Derivative financial instruments include futures, options, swaps and forward rate agreements that are derived from instruments and transactions in the 'cash' financial markets, such as loans and foreign exchange transactions.

Some derivatives, such as futures and options on futures, are traded on exchanges as standardised items. Others are negotiated individually 'over-the-counter' and are not exchange-traded.

Derivatives can be used to hedge exposures to an adverse movement in interest rate, exchange rate or market price. A hedge with derivatives is designed so that a profit arises on the derivatives position when there is a loss on the underlying position for which the hedge has been created.

A Forward Rate Agreement (FRA) is an agreement that effectively fixes the rate of interest on a notional short-term loan or deposit, starting at a specified future date. An FRA can be used to fix an effective interest rate on a short-term loan or deposit starting at a future date, usually within the next 12 months. If the interest rate on the underlying position moves adversely, there will be an offsetting gain on the FRA position. (Equally, if interest rates move to the benefit of the underlying loan or deposit, there will be an offsetting loss on the FRA position.) It is unlikely that FRAs would be appropriate hedging instruments for the group in the question, because the liabilities are longer-term.

An interest rate future is similar to an FRA, except that it is a standardised exchange-traded instrument. Derivatives positions can create a hedge against the risk of rising interest rates for a borrower at a floating rate of interest. However, as with FRAs, interest rate futures are appropriate only for short-term exposures, and so are not likely to be appropriate for the group in the question.

Currency futures can be used to fix an exchange rate for a future currency transaction, typically within the next 12 months or so, but are much less commonly used than over-the-counter forward exchange contracts.

Interest rate coupon swaps are used to switch from floating interest rate liabilities (or assets) to fixed rate liabilities (or assets), or vice versa. They could be used by the group in the question, for example, to switch some or all of the sterling floating rate liabilities to fixed rate sterling liabilities, for some or all of the term of the liability. Swaps would be appropriate as a hedge if the group's management believed that interest rates are likely to rise in the future.

Currency swaps can be used to switch from principal and interest liabilities in one currency to principal and interest liabilities in a second currency. The group could use currency swaps to exchange its US dollar liabilities (principal and interest) to UK £ liabilities, and so remove the currency risk for the group by fixing the exchange rate now.

Cross-currency coupon swaps are a combination of interest rate swap and currency swap, and could be used by the group to hedge its floating rate exposures in US dollars and euros, and 'swap' these into fixed rate UK £ exposures.

Interest rate options (with the exception of options on futures) are over-the-counter instruments. They give their holder the right but not the obligation to either borrow or lend a notional amount of principal at a specified rate of interest (the strike rate for the option) for a specified interest period, at a specified date in the future. Interest rate caps can be used to set a maximum interest rate on a floating rate loan. It consists of a series of interest rate options, one for each interest period of the floating rate loan. Caps can be very expensive to buy, and if the group in the question wishes to use options, it might prefer interest rate collars. These effectively fix the interest rate on a floating rate loan between a minimum floor and a maximum cap, but are less expensive than interest rate caps.

45 SK CONSORTIUM

(a) SK Consortium invoices its customers in their domestic currency, but there is no information in the question about the currencies in which it maintains bank accounts. It has offices in the UK, throughout Europe, the Far East and India, which suggests that it has substantial operating expenses in a variety of different currencies.

The 'no hedging' policy has been described as a success, which suggests that there have been profits from favourable movements in exchange rates. This would suggest that net profits are remitted to the UK and converted into UK £, and the exchange rate profits have arisen because UK £ has consistently depreciated in value over time against other currencies.

There are several reasons why this policy might be criticised.

- The currency exposures might be large, and if SK Consortium earns large amounts of money in foreign currencies, the exposures could put the organisation at risk of significant losses from adverse movements in exchange rate in the future, even though not hedging has been profitable in the past.
- If the organisation is growing its business, it seems probable that exposures will increase in amount in the future, and the risks will be greater.
- The board is concerned about currency volatility, which means that presumably investors should be worried for similar reasons. Currency volatility could make profits more volatile, and volatility in earnings and earnings per share could adversely affect the value of SK's shares.
- A corporate governance issue also arises. The board is required (by the UK Combined Code) to satisfy itself that the system of internal control and risk management is satisfactory. In view of currency volatility and its potential effect on the share price, the board may have doubts about the adequacy of the system for controlling currency risks, and require executive management to put in place a system of currency risk monitoring and control.

(b) ***Note:*** Figures are rounded to the nearest £1.

(i) **Not hedging**

The transaction was not hedged. On March, the spot rate was 1.6132 and at this rate, the value of US$875,000 would have been £542,400. However, on 1 June when the receipt was due, the spot rate was1.6080 and actual receipts were £544,154. Actual receipts were higher than the amount that might have been anticipated on 1 March because the dollar has strengthened against sterling over the three-month period.

Forward FX contract

If a forward exchange contract had been arranged on 1 March to sell the US$875,000 receipts on 1 June, the forward exchange rate would have been 1.6038 and the sterling receipts on 1 June would be £545,579.

These receipts on 1 June would be fixed on 1 March by the forward contract.

Currency futures

SK Consortium would want to buy sterling and sell US dollars on 1 June, and if it decided to use futures, it would buy June futures. The price for the futures is 1.5950, and at this rate US$875,000 would have an equivalent sterling value of £548,589.

Each future is for £62,500, and SK would need to buy 8.8 futures. This would be rounded up to 9 futures.

On 1 March, SK would have arranged to buy £562,500 (9 × £62,500) in exchange for US$897,187.50 (£562,500 × 1.5950). The net sterling receipts that would have been expected at 1 March cannot be calculated accurately, because these would depend on the futures price at 1 June.

SK would have to pay an initial margin of £13,500 (9 contracts × £1,500), and the cost of this money invested is assumed to be 3.41% per year.

Interest cost = £13,500 × 3.41% × 3/12 = £115

On 1 June, the position would be as follows:

Sell 9 futures at	1.6085
Purchase price on 1 March	1.5950
Profit per contract	0.0135
Value per tick = £62,500 × $0.0001 per £1	$6.25
	$
Total profit (9 × 135 ticks × $6.25 per tick)	7,594
Receipts in US dollars	875,000
Total income in US$	882,594
Spot exchange rate	$1.6080
	£
Income in sterling	548,877
Interest cost on initial margin 'invested'	(115)
Net sterling receipts	548,762

On the basis of the rates that eventually occurred on 1 June, the policy of not hedging would have been less beneficial than a policy of hedging.

Of the two hedging methods, using futures on this occasion would have been more beneficial than forward exchange contracts, providing net income of £548,762 (compared with £545,579 from a forward contract.)

(ii) The main features of the two hedging methods are as follows:

Forward FX contracts	*Futures*
Arranged 'over-the-counter' with a bank.	Bought or sold on a futures exchange.
Size and settlement dates of contract arranged to suit the company's requirements.	Standard-sized contracts; therefore a perfect hedge might not be possible. Although futures have standard settlement dates, positions can be closed at any time before settlement date.
Contracts are for a fixed maturity, although a bank will agree to alter the settlement date if required – possibly at a cost.	Positions can be closed at any time.

Administratively easy to arrange.	Administratively complex, due to the system of initial and variation margin payments.
It might be difficult to compare rates quoted by different banks, to obtain the best rate available.	Prices competitive in the market.

(iii) Currency futures are more suitable for organisations with large currency exposures and staff who are familiar with futures as hedging instruments, such as large multinationals with centralised treasury departments.

Forward exchange contracts are suitable for all companies with FX exposures, in all traded currencies. Forward contracts are more commonly used because of their simple administrative requirements.

46 IOU

(a) **Forward exchange contracts**

IOU could enter into contracts now to buy the sterling needed to settle the debt interest liabilities as they fall due for payment. It is assumed that the mid-rate applies.

31 October liability

IOU would contract to buy the £725,000 at a cost of \$1,131,073 (= £725,000 × 1.5601), for settlement on 31 October.

31 December liability

IOU would contract to buy the £530,000 at a cost of \$829,715 (= £530,000 × 1.5655), for settlement on 31 December.

Currency options

If IOU Inc used currency options to hedge its currency exposures, it would buy call options, because it needs to buy sterling.

31 October liability

For a perfect hedge, IOU would need to buy 23.2 October call options (= £725,000/£31,250 per contract). This would probably be rounded down to 23 contracts, leaving the remaining £6,250 (= 0.2 × £31,250) un-hedged.

The premium payable now to buy 23 one-month call contracts at a strike price of \$1.57 would be:

23 × 1.32 cents per £1 × £31,250 per contract = \$9,488

Buying these options gives IOU the right to buy 23 × £31,250 = £718,750 in one month's time at a price of \$1.57 to £1.

31 December liability

For a perfect hedge, IOU would need to buy 16.96 December call options (= £530,000/£31,250 per contract). This would probably be rounded up to 17 contracts, which means that £1,250 (= 0.04 × £31,250) is over-hedged.

The premium payable now to buy 17 one-month call contracts at a strike price of \$1.58 would be:

17 × 2.12 cents per £1 × £31,250 per contract = \$11,263

Buying these options gives IOU the right to buy 17 × £31,250 = £531,250 in three months' time at a price of \$1.58 to £1.

Recommendation

In this situation, the appropriate course of action to hedge the currency exposures is almost certainly to arrange forward exchange contracts.

The forward exchange rates available now (30 September) are slightly less favourable than the current spot rate.

	October 31 forward contract	*December 31 forward contract*
Current spot rate	1.5590	1.5590
Forward rate available	1.5601	1.5655
Difference	0.0011	0.0065
Amount to purchase	£725,000	£530,000
Difference in cost	$798	$3,445

The cost of buying call options would be $9,488 to buy sterling at $1.57 on 31 October and $11,263 to buy £530,000 at $1.58 on 31 December. The strike rates in these options are less favourable to IOU Inc than the exchange rate in the forward contract.

To buy the options, IOU would therefore pay substantially more to guarantee worst-possible exchange rates that are less favourable than for forward contracts.

The only circumstance in which buying currency call options would be more beneficial to IOU than forward contracts is if the exchange rate moves in the opposite direction to what is expected, and sterling weakens against the dollar over the next one to three months.

The amount by which sterling would have to weaken to make hedging with options more beneficial can be calculated as follows:

	October 31 forward contract	*December 31 forward contract*
Forward rate available	1.5601	1.5655
Sterling required	£725,000	£530,000
	$	$
Cost of buying sterling forward	1,131,073	829,715
Cost of option premiums	9,488	11,263
Breakeven cost	1,121,585	818,452
Breakeven exchange rate	(/725,000) $1.5470	(/530,000) $1.5442

The current spot rate is $1.5590, and unless the Treasurer believes that the spot rate could fall below the levels shown above – when they are probably expected to move in the opposite direction – hedging with forward contracts would seem to be much more appropriate.

(b) Foreign exchange exposures will arise because the postal and telecommunications organisation will incur net payables to or obtain net receivables from the postal and telecommunication organisations of other countries. These liabilities or assets will be in a foreign currency, the US dollar. Payments between the national organisations of different countries occur periodically.

The postal and telecommunications service of Zorro will be mainly exposed to the following types of currency exposure:

- transaction exposures;
- economic exposures.

(Translation exposures should not arise. These are an accounting problem, and arise either for parent companies that have to consolidate the financial results of foreign subsidiaries, or for companies with long-term foreign-currency denominated assets or liabilities (such as loans).)

Transaction exposures

Transaction exposures arise when there is a future receivable or future payable in foreign currency. In the case of the postal and telecommunication service, transaction exposures arise whenever the organisation agrees the amount of a periodic net receipt or net payment in US dollars with a service in another country, for settlement at a future date. The exposure remains until the payment takes place.

The exposure is to a movement in the exchange rate between Zorro's domestic currency and the US dollar. If Zorro's currency weakens against the dollar, payments to settle US dollar liabilities will be higher. If the US dollar weakens in value, receipts in US dollars would lose value in terms of Zorro's currency.

A policy to reduce transaction exposures would be to net receipts and payments in US dollars, and use US dollar receipts to make US dollar payments. This policy would be made easier if the organisation can open a US dollar bank account with its bank in Zorro. The organisation's exposures would then be reduced to the net receipts or payments in dollars.

The most appropriate way of dealing with the remaining net exposures would be to hedge them, probably using forward exchange contracts.

Economic exposures

Economic currency exposures are longer-term exposures. They occur whenever an organisation will expect to have net receipts or payments in a foreign currency over the long term. Eventually, these exposures will become transaction exposures when they eventually materialise into actual amounts of currency receivable or payable.

Companies with economic currency exposures can hedge their exposures by moving the location of their operations from one country or currency zone to another. In the case of a national postal and telecommunications organisation, this is not possible.

The most appropriate policy for hedging economic exposures might be to pursue policies that achieve a broad balance between outgoing and incoming postal and telecommunications services from and into the country. If this happens, payments and receipts in US dollars will be broadly in balance, and currency exposures will therefore be limited.

Tutorial note:

The answer provided here addresses the specific circumstances of the organisation in the question. You should beware of writing an answer that deals with all types of currency risk (translation exposures are not relevant here). You should also recommend methods of reducing risk that are appropriate to the circumstances, and mention of currency swaps will not be relevant, although currency futures and options might be mentioned as an alternative to forward contracts. It is also unrealistic to suggest that the national postal and telecommunications service of Zorro will be able to persuade the organisations in other countries to settle receipts and payments in Zorro's national currency.

---

47 PONDHILLS

(a) No major change is expected in the £/US dollar exchange rate, therefore the translation exposure for the US company is not significant for its sterling assets, but there is a translation exposure for the dinar.

The current dollar/dinar exchange rate is 246.3. If the dinar were to devalue by 15%, the end-of-year rate would be 283.2 dinars = US$1 (246.3 × 1.15).

The balance sheet translation exposures for Pondhill can be identified in the balance sheet of Ponda SA. The trade receivables are in US dollars, and 50% of the trade payables are in sterling; therefore these are not translation exposures. All the other items in the balance sheet are in dinars, and therefore create translation exposures.

Ponda SA

Balance sheet item		*Exposure*	*In US$ at current exchange rate of 246.3*	*In US$ at rate of 283.2*
		Dinars (millions)	$ million	$ million
Non-current assets		510	2.071	1.801
Cash		86	0.349	0.304
Inventory		380	1.543	1.342
		976	3.963	3.447
Trade payables	50% of 296	(148)	(0.601)	(0.523)
Long-term loans		(500)	(2.030)	(1.766)
		328	1.332	1.158

The expected loss on the translation exposure is therefore $174,000 ($1,332,000 – $1,158,000).

(b) The annual sales revenue is 2,300 million dinars.

The cost of sales is 70% of this amount, 1,610 million dinars.

Of the total cost of sales, 966 million (60%) is in dinars and 644 million (40%) is in dollars or sterling.

	In dinars, at current exchange rate (246.3)	*In dinars, at expected exchange rate (283.2)*	*In US dollars, at current exchange rate*	*In US dollars, at expected exchange rate*
	millions	millions	$ millions	$ millions
Sales revenue (US$)	2,300	2,645	9.338	9.338
Cost of sales:				
Dinars	966	966	3.922	3.411
US$/sterling	644	741	2.615	2.615
Interest (dinars)	60	60	0.244	0.212
Net profit	630	878	2.557	3.100

Since the sales revenue of Ponda SA is entirely in US dollars, but some of its costs are in dinars, Pondhills will benefit from the devaluation of the dinar next year, and its cash flows should be greater. The amount of the expected improvement in profit is \$543,000 (\$3.100 million – \$2.557 million).

This is an example of an economic exposure to currency risk working to the advantage of a company.

(c) On the assumption that the expectation of a devaluation in the value of the dinar is likely to prove correct, the expected change in the exchange value of the dinar is expected to work to the benefit of Pondhills next year. Therefore there would appear to be no reason to hedge the expected exposures. If, however, the dinar were expected to appreciate or revalue against the dollar, the situation would be different. However, Ponda SA does have some dinar assets in cash, and it might be appropriate to remove the exposure to a fall in the value of this cash by arranging to convert the surplus dinars into dollars and hold them in a dollar bank account.

The translation exposure will result in a reported loss in the financial statements, but will not have any effect on the group's cash flows. The problem for Pondhills management is to decide what the effect of a translation loss might be on shareholder sentiment and the share price. If the effect on the share price is not expected to be significant, the exposure can be left unhedged. If the effect might be more serious, Pondhills should consider reducing its translation exposures, probably by increasing its dinar-denominated borrowings to finance more of the investment in the Ponda subsidiary.

(d) The expected effects of the devaluation of the dinar are expected to benefit Pondhills in the short term, by increasing profits next year. The longer-term consequences are more difficult to predict, and will depend to some extent on the measures taken by Pondhills/Ponda management.

(i) If the dinar devalues, a part of the reason could be higher price inflation in the country. The calculations above assume no inflation at all, but if the rate of inflation in the African country is high, dinar-denominated costs will also rise, due to increases in the cost of local raw materials, wages and so on. This will reduce the profitability of the African operation.

(ii) The sales of Ponda are all denominated in dollars, and the devaluation of the dinar will result in a relative rise in the value of the dollar against the dinar. Ponda might decide to keep its dollar prices unchanged, in which sales volume will not be expected to change. Alternatively, Ponda could reduce its dollar prices, in the hope of winning a more sales, and increasing profit through higher sales volume.

(iii) On the other hand, if dollar sales are made in the African country, sales demand is likely to fall after the devaluation, because prices in dinars will be 15% higher. The fall in local sales demand would reduce total sales and profits.

48 TREASURER OF AB

(a) With all three methods of hedging interest rate risk, a time limit has to be decided for the period of the hedge. With a Forward Rate Agreement (FRA) or an interest rate guarantee (option/cap), the time limit must be specific, with an agreed settlement date or expiry date, say six months exactly from the contract/transaction date. With futures, the hedge would be for six months from any date up to the settlement date for the futures, which in this question would probably be September.

It is assumed here that the required hedge is for exactly six months in all three cases.

FRA

An FRA is an over-the-counter instrument that can be arranged with a bank, fixing the interest rate on a notional principal amount for a given period of time, in this case six months. The notional six-month interest period would start from an agreed date in September, in four months' time, so the FRA would be a 4v10 FRA. FRAs are only available for quite large principal amounts (at least $1million) and can be arranged up to about two years into the future.

A company wishing to fix an interest rate for borrowing should buy an FRA. Here, AB should buy a 4v10 FRA on a notional principal amount of £2 million. The bank would specify an interest rate for the FRA, which might be about 7.5% in this case.

The FRA is not an agreement to borrow the funds required. AB must arrange to borrow the £2 million separately. AB will borrow £2 million at the current market rate of interest in September, whatever this happens to be. The FRA would be settled by:

- a payment from the bank to AB if the benchmark interest rate (here probably the six-month LIBOR rate) is higher than the FRA rate; or
- a payment from AB to the bank if the benchmark rate is lower than the FRA rate.

The hedge works because the interest payment on the actual borrowing plus or minus the settlement amount for the FRA should fix the overall effective borrowing cost for AB. For example, if the interest rate does rise by 1.5 percentage points to 9% and AB borrows at this higher rate, it would receive a payment under the FRA agreement worth the equivalent of about 1.5%, thereby reducing the net borrowing cost to about 7.5% (depending on the actual rates that apply).

Interest rate futures

Short-term interest rate futures are exchange-traded instruments. A short sterling future is a notional three-month deposit of £500,000, traded on LIFFE.

A company wishing to fix a rate for borrowing should sell interest rate futures. Since AB wants to hedge the borrowing cost for £2 million for six months, it should sell 8 futures [(£2 million/£500,000) × (6 months/3 months)] and set up a 'short hedge'. It could sell either September or December futures, depending on when the interest period will begin, and when the September futures contract expires during the month.

The interest rate is in the price of the future. Prices are quoted at 100 minus the interest rate, so if AB were to sell September futures, say, at 92.50, this would 'fix' its borrowing rate at 7.5%. As the future approaches settlement date, if the interest rate has risen to 9%, the market price of September futures should have moved to about 91.00. AB could then close its position by buying 8 September futures, and making a profit of 1.50 (150 points) on each contract of its futures dealing. A profit of 150 points on 8 futures would be worth £15,000 (150 points × 8 contracts × £12.50 per point). This is equivalent to interest at 1.5% on £2 million for six months.

AB would borrow £2 million at the market rate. If this is 9%, the net borrowing cost would be 9% less the value of the profit on futures trading (1.5%) giving a net effective interest cost of 7.5%.

Since interest rate futures are only available in standardised amounts and dates, they are less flexible than FRAs, and so possibly less attractive to AB.

Interest rate guarantee

This is a type of borrower's option but with characteristics of an interest rate collar. Unlike an FRA or futures which are binding contracts on both parties, it is not a binding commitment on the option holder. If AB buys this instrument at a cap strike price of 7% (and a notional principal amount of £2 million for six months), for expiry in September, it will exercise its option if the interest rate at expiry is higher than 7%. It will then receive the interest value of the difference (on £2 million for six months) between the actual interest rate (six-month LIBOR) and the cap rate of 7%.

However, in this case, if the interest rate falls below 6%, the option counterparty (a bank) will exercise a floor option, and require AB to pay the difference between the actual interest rate and 6%.

As a result, AB is able to fix the benchmark interest rate between 6% and 7%. So if AB can borrow at, say, LIBOR + 0.50%, the interest rate guarantee would fix its actual borrowing cost between 6.5% and 7.5%, plus the cost of the guarantee.

Arranging this guarantee would cost £2,000 (0.1% of £2 million), which is equivalent to interest of 0.2% on £2 million for six months. The premiums payable on interest rate guarantees can be expensive and must be paid up-front, which can be compared to an FRA on which no premium is payable.

Usefulness of the instruments to AB

All three instruments can help AB to hedge against the risk of a rise in interest rates.

FRAs and futures are binding contracts, so that the hedge effectively fixes the borrowing cost. The interest rate guarantee is a form of option, so that AB can benefit from lower interest rates if they are between 6% and 7%. However, the guarantee has to be paid for.

All three instruments are arranged for a fixed amount and a fixed borrowing period, which means that a hedge might not be perfect. For example, if it turns out that AB needs to borrow £2.5 million for seven months starting in five months' time, none of the hedges would be perfect.

(b) (i) Interest rate swaps can have several uses.

1. They can be used by companies to arrange fixed rate borrowing, when direct access to fixed rate funding (the bond markets) is not possible, for example if the company is too small or would not have a sufficiently good credit rating.
2. Occasionally, they can be used to obtain lower cost borrowing, through interest rate arbitrage. This opportunity exists in the case of RO and AB.
3. They can be used to alter the proportions of fixed and variable rate funding in a company's debt mix without the expense of redeeming existing debt and issuing new debt in its place, and so can be used to manage exposure to risk from possible future interest rate movements.

AB is a larger company than RO, so we see that AB has cheaper borrowing rates in both the floating rate as well as the fixed rate market. However, while RO only has to pay 0.2% more in the floating rate market, it has to pay a full

1.0% more for fixed rate debt. This creates an opportunity to reduce their combined borrowing costs by 0.8% (1% – 0.2%).

AB would prefer fixed rate, while RO would prefer floating rate debt. RO has a comparative advantage in the floating rate market, since its premium there is only 0.2%, so there is no immediate incentive for a swap. No co-operation is therefore possible if AB decides to borrow at a fixed rate and RO chooses to borrow at a floating rate.

However, they could co-operate to their mutual benefit if:

- AB borrows at a fixed rate, since it can borrow comparatively much cheaper than RO (1% less), and swaps into floating rate; and
- RO borrows at a floating rate, where it can borrow comparatively more favourably than at a fixed rate (only 0.2% more), and swap into a fixed rate.

The opportunity for arbitrage is 0.8%, which means that if they share this equally, both will borrow 0.4% more cheaply than if they borrowed directly at a floating rate in the case of AB or at a fixed rate in the case of RO.

A swap could be arranged as follows:

- AB borrows in the fixed rate market at 7.5% and pays LIBOR to RO.
- RO borrows in the floating rate market at LIBOR + 0.5% and pays a fixed rate of 7.6% to AB.

The net effect is as follows:

	AB	RO
	%	%
Borrow at:	7.5	LIBOR + 0.5
Swap		
Pay	LIBOR	7.6
Receive	(7.6)	(LIBOR)
Net borrowing cost	LIBOR – 0.1	8.1

These net borrowing rates are each 0.4% less than AB could borrow at a floating rate or RO could borrow at a fixed rate.

(ii) In practice, most swaps are arranged through banks that run a 'swaps book'. There are several advantages in dealing with a bank rather than directly with another company.

1. In dealing with a bank, there is no problem about finding a swaps counterparty with an equal and opposite swapping requirement. The bank will arrange a swap to meet the specific requirements of each individual customer, as to amount and duration of the swap.
2. In dealing with a bank, the credit risk is that the bank might default, whereas in dealing directly with another company, the credit risk is that the other company might default. Banks are usually a much lower credit risk than corporates.
3. Banks are specialists in swaps, and are able to provide standard legal swaps agreements. The operation of the swap is likely to be administratively more straightforward.

The significant drawback to using a bank is that the bank will want to make a profit from its operations. In practice, it will generally do this by charging different swap rates for fixed rate payments and fixed rate receipts on different swaps. In terms of the RO and AB situation, where there is a credit arbitrage opportunity of 0.8%, if a swaps bank were to be used to arrange a separate swap with each company, it might take a profit of, say, 0.2%, leaving just 0.6% of benefit to be shared between RO and AB.

49 YZ

(a) Assuming that the receipts and payments occur on the same date in each month, the requirement is to make a net payment of €200,000 after one month and to convert net receipts of €400,000 into UK £ after three months.

(i) **Using the forward market**

In 1 month

YZ needs to buy €200,000 in one month.

Spot rate	1.6186
Minus: Forward premium	0.0002
Forward rate	1.6184
Amount to purchase	€200,000
Cost in sterling	£123,579

(Amount rounded to the nearest £1)

In three months

YZ wishes to sell €400,000 in exchange for sterling after three months.

Spot rate	1.6202
Minus: Forward premium	0.0013
Forward rate	1.6189
Income in euros	€400,000
Income in sterling	£247,081

(Amount rounded to the nearest £1)

The payment will occur after one month and the receipt will be after three months.

(ii) **Using the money market**

YZ could wait for one month before hedging its exposure using the money markets. It could then borrow €200,000 for two months and repay this with interest out of the €400,000 received after three months. The exposure from the net receipts at the end of month 3, after repaying the loan with interest, could then be hedged with a forward exchange contract, arranged at the end of month 1 for settlement at the end of month 3.

However, it is assumed that YZ wants to create a hedge immediately.

The end of month 1 payment

- It needs to buy €200,000 in one month in order to make the net payment. It can fix the cost of this now by borrowing enough euros to have €200,000 with interest by the end of month 1.
- The interest rate on euro deposits is 3.00% p.a., which is 0.25% for one month.
- It can obtain €200,000 in one month by depositing €199,501 now (€200,000/1.0025).
- It can obtain €199,501 now by buying spot at 1.6186.

This would cost £123,255 (199,501/1.6186) now.

The end of month 3 receipt

- YZ wishes to sell receipts of €400,000 in exchange for sterling after three months.
- The interest rate on euro borrowing is 3.50% p.a., which is 0.875% for three months.
- It will owe €400,000 after three months if it borrows €396,530 now (400,000/1.00875).
- The receipts of €400,000 after three months can be used to repay the loan with interest.

If it borrows €396,530 now, it can convert the money into sterling at 1.6202 (spot rate), to obtain £244,741.

However, since it is hedging both the payment after one month and the receipt after three months, it can net the cash flows and combine the two hedges into one.

	€
Cost now of month 1 hedge	(199,501)
Income now from month 3 hedge	396,530
Net income	197,029
Spot exchange rate	1.6202
Sterling income	£121,608

This is marginally more profitable than arranging the hedges separately, to earn £244,741 – £123,255 = £121,486.

(iii) **Buy spot when the cash flow arises**

After one month, buy €200,000 spot at 1.6192, at a cost of £123,518.

After three months, sell €400,000 spot at 1.6220, to earn £246,609.

(b) The main advantage of using forward exchange contracts or the money markets is that the exchange rates for the future transactions are fixed now, and all uncertainty about the future movement in exchange rates is eliminated. The exposure to currency risk is therefore hedged. For companies with large quantities of currency receipts or payments, adverse movements in exchange rates can affect profits significantly, and hedging can take away some of the uncertainty and reduce the risk.

With forward contracts, the cash is paid or received when the cash flow occurs. With money market hedging, the cash flows occur when the hedge is set up. Comparing the two methods in this case, we have:

	Forward contracts	*Money market hedge*
Now		Receive £121,608
In one month	Pay £123,579	
In three months	Receive £247,081	

Because these cash flows occur at different times, they are not strictly comparable.

In theory, the net effect should be much the same with both methods of hedging, because money market interest rates and forward exchange rates are closely linked to each other. This theory is borne out by the figures above, which show only small differences between the two methods of hedging.

The disadvantages of hedging are as follows:

- The administrative effort. A company with only occasional currency receipts or payments, or small receipts or payments, might consider the potential benefits not worth the effort involved.
- The cost. A bank will charge a transaction cost for entering into a hedging contract, but no details of the relevant transaction costs are given in the question.
- Hedging is rarely perfect. There is usually uncertainty as to future amounts and future timings of cash flows, but hedging transactions made now have to be based on expectations of amounts and timing.
- Hedging fixes an effective exchange rate for future transactions, so that if the exchange rate moves in the company's favour, the company will not be able to benefit from the favourable movement, since it will be locked into the rate in the hedge.

Not hedging the risk removes the administrative task of having to forecast future currency flows with sufficient accuracy and of arranging the hedge transactions. A further advantage is that if the exchange rate moves favourably up to the time the cash flow occurs, the company will benefit by obtaining a more favourable spot rate for the transaction.

The main disadvantage of not hedging is that exchange rates can move adversely as well as favourably, and if there is a large adverse rate movement, profits on trading transactions can be eroded significantly.

The decision about hedging or not hedging is a matter for judgement.

- If the exchange rate is volatile, and an adverse movement could affect profits significantly, hedging either through forward contracts or the money markets is recommended.
- If the exchange rate is stable, and is expected to remain stable, or if the greater probability is that the exchange rate will move favourably, it might be appropriate not to hedge.

50 LXN (NOV 05 EXAM)

Tutorial note:

(a) Notice that the requirement is *discuss,* indicating that the examiner wants comments on the different factors, and not necessarily any calculations. It is useful initially to check the extent of loans in the company; they are minimal compared to assets and the new project can then be seen as insignificant compared to total assets. However, this does not negate the need to consider interest risk for a relatively small amount.

(b) (i) is a straightforward list of advantages and disadvantages. (ii) again is relatively simple and follows the diagrams in most manuals. Part (c) is strange in the need to *evaluate* the annual saving; it is easy to calculate this, but then less clear what comments can be made on this.

(a) **Initial summary**

LXN currently has €2,000 million of assets and is looking to increase this by €1.5 million (six shops at €250,000 each). The asset base will therefore increase by less than 0.1%, which is a negligible amount.

The amount of loan to be obtained is €1.5 million for the shops plus 20% working capital = €1.8 million in total.

Total debt in euros is €15 million plus €26.3 million (£18 million at €/£0.684) = €41.3 million. Total debt is to be increased by about 4% (1.8 / 41.3).

Factors affecting the choice between fixed and floating rate debt:

Expected changes in interest rates

Obtaining a floating rate loan means a company will be affected by changes in interest rates. If rates increase, then the company will pay more interest on a loan; if rates fall, then the company pays less. If interest rates are expected to rise, then a fixed rate loan may be preferable as the company will not be affected by the rate increase; similarly, if rates are expected to fall, then a variable rate loan will be preferred to take advantage of falling rates of interest.

Amount of time the loan is required

Obtaining a fixed rate loan may be more risky if the loan is for a long period of time as the company will effectively be locked into this rate. Rate changes become more difficult to forecast in the long term. However, a fixed rate again provides certainty as to the amount of interest to be paid. If the loan is for a long period, then various hedging techniques will normally be considered.

Existing mix of fixed and variable loans

The treasurer of LXN may require a portfolio of fixed and variable rates loans simply as a method of hedging risk. Given that the value of variable rate loans is currently higher than fixed loans then this may indicate a preference for fixed rate loan.

Risk appetite

LXN will view the variable and fixed loans as having different levels of risk. If the company's risk appetite is low, then a lower risk alternative will be taken. However, treasurers will normally want a range of financial products to minimise risk for their company.

Loans available in different currencies

LXN currently has fixed and floating loans denominated in euros and sterling. The decision regarding fixed and floating rates will partly be dependent on the range of loans available in different currencies. LXN will need to investigate these options prior to making a decision.

Factors to take into account in deciding whether or not to hedge interest rate exposure:

Cost of hedging

Different hedging options will have different costs associated with them. LXN needs to ensure that the cost of the hedging method is acceptable given the total expected gain from the hedge.

Hedging methods available to the company

Depending on the amount of loan, some hedging methods may be unavailable to LXN. However, given that the total loan requirement is €1.8 million, then most hedging methods including STIRs are available.

For some hedging methods, other suitable companies requiring loan swaps must be available – LXN will have to identify those companies, or obtain assistance from its bank.

Internal hedging techniques available

Even though the treasurer may have access to various external hedging techniques, this does not mean they will be used as there may be various internal strategies for minimising interest rate risks. The exposure of €1.8 million compared to total assets of €2,000 million is not significant and so the treasurer may choose to ignore the risk. Similarly, the increase in loan requirements is only 4% – the treasurer may decide this is immaterial and simply obtain the best 'deal' available without attempting to hedge.

The treasurer may also use internal techniques such as smoothing, matching and netting to minimise risk. The policy of LXN is unclear in this area, and the treasurer will need to ensure that company policy is being followed.

Interest rate movements

If the treasurer believes that interest rates will fall, then a floating rate loan may be taken out anyway, rather than considering different hedging methods.

(b) (i) **Advantages of interest rate swaps**

They can be customised to meet the company's specific requirements in terms of amount of loan and the term of the loan.

There are no premiums to pay compared to, for example, interest rate options.

Useful in hedging long-term exposures (up to 30 years) on bonds and medium-term bank loans.

Disadvantages of interest rate swaps

The agreement is binding on both parties, so neither company will be able to benefit from interest rate movements that may occur in its favour.

There is a high counterparty risk as the actual performance of the contract cannot be guaranteed.

There are no secondary markets making it very difficult to terminate or transfer the contract if the swap is no longer required.

(ii)

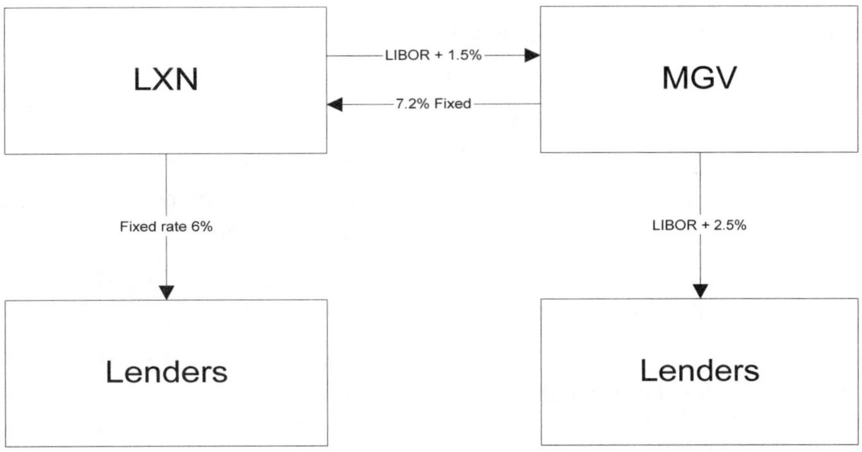

(iii)

	LXN	*MGV*	*Quality spread*
Fixed rate (%)	6%	7.2%	1.2%
Floating rate	LIBOR + 1.5%	LIBOR + 2.5%	1.0%
Quality spread			0.2%

	LXN	*MGV*	
Would pay	LIBOR + 1.5%	7.2%	LIBOR + 8.7%
Could pay	6%	LIBOR + 2.5%	LIBOR + 8.5%
Potential gain			
Split evenly	0.1%	0.1%	0.2%
Expected outcome	LIBOR + 1.4%	7.1%	

Calculation of annual saving

Loan amount €1.8 million

Interest charge using floating rate =	LIBOR + 1.5% × €1.8 million
	6.5% × €1.8 million
	€117,000
Interest charge fixed rate using SWAP	
	LIBOR + 1.4% × €1.8 million
	6.4% × €1.8 million
	€115,200
Net saving	€1,800

The net saving is €1,800 which is relatively minor compared to amount of loans already taken out or total assets.

If total interest charges are:

€15 million at 6% + £18 million at 3% (at €/£0.684)

= €900,000 + €789,474

= €1,689,474

then the savings are about 0.1% of this indicating that the treasurer may choose to ignore hedging.

51 EXPOT

(a) (i) **Method 1: money market hedge**

It is assumed that the three-month interest rate is 0.75% for Swiss francs (3% × 3/12) and 1.5% for sterling (6% × 3/12).

Expot would borrow SFr750,000/1.0075 = SFr744,417 for three months. The amount repayable after three months with interest will be SFr750,000. This can be repaid using the receipts of SFr750,000.

The SFr744,417 borrowed now should be exchanged for sterling at the spot rate of 2.3834, to obtain £312,334.

For comparison with Method 2, it is assumed that this money would be invested for three months to earn 1.5% interest.

	£
Investment now	312,334
Interest for three months (1.5%)	4,685
Value after three months	317,019

Method 2: hedge with forward exchange contract

The receipts of SFr750,000 can be sold forward at a rate of SFr2.3688/£1, to obtain £316,616 after three months.

The money market hedge is more beneficial, by about £500.

(ii) Before deciding whether to hedge the risk, the following factors should be considered:

- The company's attitude to risk. If management are very risk averse, all currency exposures should be hedged wherever possible. If however management are risk neutral, it might be considered appropriate in this situation to keep the currency exposure un-hedged. If the Swiss franc strengthens against sterling in the next three months, selling the SFr750,000 at the spot rate in three months' time might earn more sterling income.
- The costs of the hedge. A commission will probably be payable on setting up the hedge, which must be taken into account when estimating the expected benefits from the hedge.
- The need to hedge, given the Expot group's overall exposure. Elsewhere in the group, there may be a subsidiary with a Swiss franc liability payable in about three months' time. If the group has payments as well as receipts in Swiss francs, it might be appropriate to open a Swiss franc bank account, and make payments in francs out of income in the same currency.
- The materiality of the sums involved. If Expot is such a very large company so that SFr750,000 is not a significant amount, then there is less need to hedge since any anticipated exchange movement will have an immaterial effect on cash flows and profits. Hedging risks is more appropriate when the exposure and the risk are material.
- The cost of hedging using the money markets or forward FX markets, compared to the cost using alternative instruments such as currency futures and currency options.

(b) If Expot is about to invoice a customer in the local currency of a developing country, the risk can be managed in the following ways:

- **Keeping the period of credit offered as low as possible**. For example there is less risk in offering one month's credit than in offering six months.
- **Identifying a proxy currency** in which hedging can take place. The currency of a developing country might move closely with an identifiable major currency. In the past, for example, some South American currencies have followed the US dollar. The local currency position can then be hedged by taking the counterbalancing position in the proxy currency.
- **Borrowing in the local currency**. If no proxy can be identified, the future receivable from the invoice can be hedged by setting up a future payable in the same currency of the same amount. This can be achieved by obtaining a local currency loan that will mature at the same time that the receivable is expected.
- **Creating a netting transaction**. A netting transaction occurs when a receipt in a currency is matched by an equal payment in the same currency at about the same time. Perhaps a netting position might already exist, in which case nothing more needs to be done; however this is unlikely. A netting position can be created by agreeing to purchase goods from a supplier in the same developing country, paying on credit in the local currency, to net off the exposure.

52 WARREN BUFFETT (MAY 06 EXAM)

(a) There is no inconsistency between the views of Warren Buffett and the views of many corporate treasurers. Derivatives such as future contracts, swaps and options enable the holder to manage the risk associated with an underlying position. Thus they can be used to reduce the risk of a position (e.g. if you are due to receive a certain amount of foreign currency on a known date in the future, you can sell it forward and thus fix the amount of the receipt in your own home currency to eliminate the currency risk) or to speculate to increase the risk of a position (e.g. you can buy a financial futures contract for trading purposes, hoping that you can sell it in the future for more than you paid for it). Buffett is concerned about speculators who buy derivatives for trading purposes with no underlying need for them. Corporate treasurers see the value in using derivatives to hedge their risk away, thus reducing their overall risk exposure.

Let us consider Buffett's views in more detail. He has been a long-term investor in the US stock market. As an investor, he would like relevant and reliable financial information on the companies that he is thinking of investing in. In the past, the financial accounting for derivatives has been inadequate throughout the world. Favouring the historical cost convention meant that derivatives were stated at cost in the balance sheet, with any profit or loss only being recognised when the derivative was sold. However the initial cost of a derivative is small or even zero, while its market value at a balance sheet date might be large. It is in this sense that Buffett is correct in having described derivatives as a 'time-bomb', waiting for their profit or loss to be recognised in the future, at a time to be decided by the company holding the speculative position. However, this problem has now been mitigated somewhat by improved standards on financial accounting for derivatives. International Standard IAS 39 (and its US equivalent FAS 133 and UK equivalent FRS 26) now requires all derivatives to be measured at their fair values in each balance sheet. This certainly improves the relevance of the balance sheet, but the volatility of derivative values means that the description of a 'time-bomb' is still appropriate. Things can go wrong very quickly with derivatives, so the fact that they were measured at fair value in the previous balance sheet is of little comfort to the investor who has seen his company suddenly lose a huge sum of money through losing control (e.g. Procter and Gamble lost \$150m in 1994 when speculating on the spread between the German mark and the US dollar).

The opposite view is generally held by corporate treasurers who see derivatives as a means of reducing risk, whether currency risk, interest rate risk or other market risk. Many treasury departments are set up as cost centres and instructed not to engage in speculation. One often sees the statement in companies' Annual Reports that the company does not engage in speculation with derivative instruments. The situation is less clear-cut where the treasury is set up as a profit centre which may choose to take speculative positions within established limits. It is often in these circumstances that the distinction between hedging and speculation becomes blurred in the department's pursuit of profits, and once again the time-bomb can blow up with devastating consequences.

(b) The purpose of accounting standards is to ensure that relevant, reliable, understandable and comparable financial information is made available to users of the financial statements. IAS 39 argues that financial assets and liabilities that are held for trading, and those that are designated to be measured at fair value through profit or loss, must be shown at fair value in each balance sheet in order to present relevant information.

This immediately raises the risk that unreliable information might be presented, due to the tension between relevance and reliability. Many financial assets and liabilities are not exchange-traded, so a company has to use internal means in order to estimate a fair value for the investment at the balance sheet date. Complicated equations such as the Black-Scholes model can be used to estimate the fair value of options, but in practice the reliability of such estimates is questionable.

A further risk is the additional volatility of earnings when fair value accounting is used. The fair value of financial instruments can change rapidly, and since the movement in fair value is recognised in the income statement, there will be much greater changes in reported profits each year using fair value accounting than if traditional historical cost accounting were used. The fear of companies is that analysts will look at the volatile profits record reported by the company, and mark the share price down to compensate investors for the volatility.

(c) (i) Value at Risk (VaR) is a risk model used typically by banks to predict, at a given level of probability, the maximum loss that the bank might expect to suffer on its portfolio in a given time period, assuming that these possible variations in value are normally distributed. From the perspective of a fund manager (e.g. the manager of a pension fund), the VaR gives a statistical measure of the maximum expected loss over a particular time period. Risk-averse managers will seek to reduce the VaR, perhaps by investing more in bonds and less in more volatile equities.

A VaR is bared on two chosen parameters, the confidence level (typically 95%) and the holding period (typically one day for an actively traded fund). Thus a pension fund manager could say that he is 95% certain that the fund will not make a loss bigger than \$1m over the next trading day. The VaR is \$1m.

One commonly observed weakness of the VaR measure is that it is valid only under normal market conditions. If the market has become unusually volatile for some reason, then losses incurred on a fund may be much greater than the calculated VaR.

53 JAPANESE EXPORTER

(a) In the absence of any other information, forward exchange rates are the best predictors of spot rates at the appropriate future point in time.

Forward exchange rates are determined from the interest rates of the two countries concerned, or more precisely from the interest rate differential. In this case the yen is quoted at a premium against the dollar. This indicates that the yen is the strengthening currency and therefore the Japanese interest rate must be less than that of the USA. Given that interest rate differential, if the yen were not quoted at a premium it would be possible to make a profit by covered interest arbitrage. This would involve borrowing yen, converting into dollars at the spot rate, investing in the USA for a period of time and converting back to yen on a forward contract.

If such a transaction results in a gain there must be an imbalance between the interest rate differential and the forward rate. Such a situation cannot be sustained and market forces will ensure that the forward rate is such that neither gain nor loss may occur.

Similarly there is a link between relative interest rates and inflation rates between the countries concerned. This is the so-called 'International Fisher Effect' whereby interest rate differentials equate to inflation rate differentials. Moreover, it is known that inflation is a factor which affects future spot exchange rates due to the necessity of constant purchasing power between two countries.

Therefore we have come full circle: if future spot rates are determined by inflation, if inflation determines interest rates and interest rates determine forward rates, then forward rates must be a good indicator of future spot rates.

This, however, assumes 'ideal' conditions. In reality there will be many other complex economic issues and short-term market factors which will influence to a greater or lesser extent future spot rates.

(b)

	Yen/$
Spot rate	136.45
Minus: 3-month forward premium	1.12
3-month forward rate	135.33

Cost to the importer = 14.4 million/135.33

= $106,406.56

(c) If the importer chose not to take forward cover, he would be compelled to buy the required currency at the future spot rate. This may or may not be favourable, depending upon the currency movement during the period concerned.

(i) **Spot rate = 159.45 yen/$1**

Cost to the importer = 14.4 million/159.45

= $90,310.44

This represents the cost to the importer if the spot rate reflected the dollar's strongest position in the previous year against the yen.

(ii) **Spot rate = 134.20 yen/$1**

Cost to the importer = 14.4 million/134.20

= $107,302.53

This is the cost if the spot rate reflected the dollar's weakest position in the previous year against the yen.

With the benefit of hindsight, it can be seen that if the dollar is at a level equal to its weakest last year, the cost to the importer would be only about $896 more than the cost under the forward contract. However, if the dollar is at a level equal to its strongest last year, the cost to the importer would be substantially less when the dollar is in its strongest position, by about $16,096. However, these comparisons are of doubtful value. The importer should probably hedge the exposure with a forward contract if the risk is considered reasonably significant.

(d) Assuming that the importer has taken out a forward exchange contract to buy the required currency, then in the case of a delay in the payment the forward contract could not simply be cancelled.

A forward exchange contract is binding on both parties. A specified amount of currency must be exchanged on a specified date at the agreed forward rate. Therefore the importer must fulfil his obligations.

As a result of the delay in the payment there are three courses of action open to the importer.

(1) The forward exchange contract may be closed out and a new forward contract set up for the revised expected date of payment. This will involve the importer buying the yen at the rate agreed in the original forward contract, but as the currency is no longer required the bank will buy it back at the spot rate. A new forward contract will be set up at the new appropriate forward rate. Thus depending on exchange rate movements the importer may make a gain or a loss over his original position.

(2) The forward exchange contract may be extended by the bank. In this case the contract is not closed out but renewed with a later completion date but with a new forward exchange rate.

(3) Finally the importer could fulfil the contract by buying the yen and investing them in a yen account until payment is required.

(e) All forward exchange contracts are binding, and represent an obligation to exchange currency at an agreed rate. The difference between the two types of contract lies in the date on which the contract must be fulfilled.

Forward exchange fixed contract

This type of contract must be fulfilled on the one specified future date. Thus a three-month forward exchange fixed contract would have to be settled exactly three months after the date on which the contract was made.

Forward exchange option contract

With this type of contract the option lies in the date of settlement. The contract will specify two dates for settlement, which are the earliest and latest dates between which the contract must be settled, but there is choice of settlement date between these two dates. Thus the trader is protected against uncertainty about the precise date when settlement will be required. The bank's compensating benefit lies in the fact that the exchange rate specified in the forward contract is most advantageous rate for the bank during the option period, irrespective of the actual date for completion eventually chosen by the trader.

54 MNO (NOV 06 EXAM)

(a) We will receive \$1.8m in three months' time.

To hedge the exchange rise with futures we will sell dollars forward.

At the futures price of \$1.690, the dollar receipts are worth:

$$\frac{\$1.8\text{m}}{1.690} = \$1,065,089$$

We therefore need to buy $\frac{1,065,089}{62,500} = 17.04$ contracts.

We will buy 17 contracts (covering 17 × 62,500 = £1,062,500) which leaves £2,589 (or 2,589 × 1.69 = \$4,375) uncovered.

When the dollar income is received, we will close the position by selling our 17 contracts in the futures market.

(i) If the dollar has strengthened, and £1 = \$1.665 when the dollars are received, then we sell our 17 contracts at \$1.665.

Buying price per contract	1.6900
Selling price per contract	1.6650
Loss per contract	0.0250

The loss on future trading is 250 ticks per contract. The value of each tick is £62,500 × \$0.0001 per £ = \$6.25.

Thus the total loss is 250 × \$6.25 × 17 = \$26,562.5.

	£
Income from trading	1,800,000
Loss on futures	(26,563)
Net income	1,773,437

Sterling income, at spot rate = $\frac{\$1,773,437}{1.665}$ = £1,065,127.

(ii) If the dollar has weakened and £1 = \$1.720 when the dollars are received, then we sell our 17 contracts at \$1.720.

Buying price per contract	1.6900
Selling price per contract	1.7200
Profit per contract	0.0300

The total gain is 300 ticks × \$6.25 × 17 = \$31,875.

Income from trading	1,800,000
Profit on futures	(31,875)

Total income	1,831,875

Sterling income, at spot rate $= \frac{\$1,831,875}{1.720} = £1,065,044.$

Subject to rounding, whatever the spot rate happens to be in three months' time, by buying futures contracts, we have fixed the exchange rate for the dollars that will be received to be the futures price of $1.690.

To hedge the exchange risk with options, we will buy a put option to sell dollars forward.

We need to buy options over $\frac{\$1.8m}{1.675 \times 62,500} = 17.19$ contracts.

Again we will buy 17 contracts (covering 17 × 62,500 = £1,062,500). At 1.675 this equates to $1,779,688, leaving $20,312 uncovered.

(i) If the dollar has strengthened to £1 = $1.665, then we abandon the option and sell the dollar receipt for spot in the market.

Sterling receipt $= \frac{\$1.8m}{1.665} = £1,081,081$

(ii) If the dollar has weakened to £1 = $1.720, then we exercise the option to sell the dollar receipt at 1.675.

Sterling receipt $= \frac{\$1.8m}{1.675} = £1,074,627$

Conclusion

Assuming that the option has a nil premium cost, in both cases (i) and (ii) the option gives a higher sterling receipt than the future, so the option should be undertaken. However, the differences in expected receipts are fairly small, so it is a marginal decision that is being taken.

(b) The following problems are encountered in using futures contracts to hedge exchange rate risks:

- Futures contracts are only available in certain currencies. If you are due to receive a currency in the future for which futures contracts are not offered, then you will have to find a different way to hedge the risk.
- Futures contracts are only available for expiry in certain months. If you are due to receive a foreign currency in the future on a date which does not tie in with a contract expiry date, then a perfect hedge will not be possible.
- Futures contacts are available in whole numbers of contracts, for a fixed size. Usually the sum to be hedged will not equate to a whole number of contracts, leaving the fractional amount either unhedged or to be hedged using a different method (e.g. a forward FX contract).
- Margin must be paid on futures contracts, both an initial margin payable immediately that the contract is taken out and a daily variation margin as the value of the contract fluctuates. A company with poor liquidity may therefore prefer a different method of hedging, such as a forward exchange contract on which no margin is payable.

- Futures contracts can be technically difficult to understand, so good training is required for employees if a company is going to start managing risk using futures. Such training is expensive but the risk of disaster if no one understands what is going on is very real, as has been proved over and over in recent history.
- Futures contracts expose the holder to basis risk, i.e. the risk that when a hedge is constructed, the size of the basis when the futures position is closed out is different from the expectation, when the hedge was created, of what the basis ought to be. It would be possible to hold all contracts to their expiry date, knowing that the basis must be zero by that date, but in practice nearly all futures contracts are closed out before expiry, so basis risk will be inevitable.

(c) Small companies are generally owned by their managers and operate mainly in the domestic market. Transactions denominated in foreign currencies are the exception rather than the rule.

Managements of such companies tend to be risk-averse, since it is their own money (i.e. they own the company's shares) that they are dealing with. They do not have highly trained corporate treasurers employed at the company who can advise on the fine detail of risk management techniques. Such companies generally rely on their banks to advise on foreign exchange and interest rate issues. The typical approach is always to take out forward FX contracts whenever foreign currency is to be paid or received in the future, and always to take out fixed interest rate bank borrowings when required. In this way, currency risk and interest rate risk are reduced to a minimum, which is consistent with the low risk appetite of the managers.

In a large company, things are different. Transactions will be routinely carried out in foreign currencies, the appetite for risk will be higher, the resources will exist for highly trained corporate treasurers to be employed, and thus there is the potential for a much wider range of hedging tools to be used. Rather than simply eliminate as much risk as possible, treasurers can actively manage risk profiles in the pursuit of profit. Derivatives will be used extensively, such as futures contracts, options on futures contracts and swaps. A large company can afford the infrastructure necessary to manage its derivative positions, e.g. computer software to match option prices in the market against prices forecast by models such as Black-Scholes. It would be unrealistic to expect a small company to have the resources necessary to carry out this sort of active trading in derivatives.

55 ABC

(a) The procedure for a currency swap is as follows:

- There is either an actual or a notional exchange of principal at spot. This will provide a basis for calculation of interest. The question indicates that in this example, there will be an exchange of principal at the beginning of the swap.
- There is an exchange of interest streams, usually at regular intervals for the duration of the swap.
- Finally, at the end of the swap, the principal will be re-exchanged on terms agreed at the outset. It is usual for the principal amounts to be re-exchanged at the same rate as the original exchange of principal at the beginning of the swap.

With the swap

The project cash flows and exchanges of payments in the swap will be as follows:

(i) At the beginning of the swap, ABC will receive 1,500 million EE marks and in exchange will pay the swap counterparty £100 million (1,500 millon/15 EE marks to £1).

(ii) ABC will invest 750 million EE marks immediately and a further 75 million EE marks after six months.

(iii) Interest is exchanged in the swap after one year, with ABC receiving £12 million (12% × £100 million) and paying 300 million EE marks (1,500 million EE marks × 20%).

(iv) At the end of the swap, the counterparties will re-exchange the principal amounts.

(v) Also after one year, ABC will receive 2,000 million EE marks from the project.

These cash flows can be summarised as follows:

	Receive/(Pay)	
	£ million	EE marks (millions)
At the start of the project		
Initial swap	(100)	1,500
Invest in project		(750)
After six months		
Invest in project		(750)
At the end		
Interest payments	12	(300)
Re-exchange of principal	100	(1,500)
Income from the project		2,000

At the end of the swap, there will be a net cash inflow of 200 million EE marks (2,000 – 1,500 – 300), which will be exchanged into sterling at the spot rate. This net income is exposed to currency risk for the duration of the project. However, the expected spot rate after one year, applying purchasing power parity theory, will be:

18.00 × (1.25/1.03) = 21.85 EE marks to £1.

The expected sterling income from the receipts of 200 million EE marks are therefore £9.15 million (200 milion/21.85).

Summary of sterling returns

	£ million
Sterling from conversion of EE marks	9.15
Sterling interest from swap	12.00
Total sterling returns	21.15
Opportunity cost of tying up £100 million for 1 year in the swap (15%)	(15.00)
Net returns	6.15

Assumptions

The company will hold 750 million for six months until needed for investment in the project, but will be unable to invest it. (An alternative assumption is that the company could invest the 750 million EE marks for six months, or convert the marks into sterling and invest the sterling for six months, and then use the sterling to buy back EE marks after six months.)

The opportunity cost of the sterling is therefore a one-year cost.

Without a swap

If ABC does not enter into the swap, it will buy 750 EE marks spot now and a further 750 million EE marks after six months. It will receive 2,000 million EE marks after one year and convert these into sterling at the spot rate.

The spot rate now is 18 EE marks to £1

The expected spot rate after 1 year is 21.85.

It is assumed that the spot rate after six months would be 19.93 [(18 + 21.85)/2].

	£ million
Cost of initial 750 million marks (at 18.00)	(41.67)
Cost of 750 million marks after 6 months (at 19.93)	(37.63)
Income from sale of 2,000 million marks after 1 year (at 21.85)	91.53
Opportunity cost of £41.67 million for 1 year (15%)	(6.25)
Opportunity cost of £37.63 million for 6 months (15% × 6/12)	(2.82)
Net returns	3.16

Ignoring the different risk exposures of arranging the swap and not arranging the swap, it would appear that the net benefit would be higher with the swap than without it. ABC should therefore agree to the swap, provided that the swap counterparty is an acceptable credit risk.

It is assumed that ABC will undertake the project, having carried out suitable investment appraisal and risk analysis on the business aspects of the investment.

(b) A swap effectively results in the exchange of one stream of cash flows for another, but with different characteristics. Opportunities arise because of differences which can arise between one financial market and another and also because of variable risk premiums on fixed and variable interest rates.

Swaps offer the following benefits to a corporate treasurer:

- Access to capital markets which it is unable to approach directly; for example, low cost fixed interest funds are only available to large companies with good ratings.
- In the example in the question, the currency swap offers ABC an opportunity to hedge much of the currency risk in the absence of a forward exchange market and a formal capital market for the foreign currency.
- Swaps might provide opportunities for favourable interest rates on borrowings.
- Interest rate swaps allow a company to change the structure of a company's loans obligations without having to redeem the loans. For example a treasurer with fixed rate loans who believed that interest rates were going to fall should swap into floating rate loans.
- Foreign currency loans are often cheaper if raised by an institution in the relevant foreign country. A currency swap enables a company to raise funds in its own country and then swap this obligation with a foreign bank into the required foreign currency.
- Long-term foreign exchange risks can be hedged using a currency swap.

The types of risk associated with swaps are as follows:

- **Credit risk.** This is the risk that the counterparty to the swap will default before the end of the swap and fail to carry out their agreed obligations. Such risk is reduced if a reputable bank is used as an intermediary to the deal;
- **Market risk.** This is the risk that interest rates or exchange rates will move unfavourably against the company after it has committed itself into a swap. For example a company may have swapped out of fixed rate debt into floating rate debt when anticipating a reduction in general interest rates, but such rates may actually rise. Market risk is less, the shorter the term of the swap since there is less time for things to go wrong;
- **Sovereign risk.** This is the risk associated with the country in whose currency a swap is being considered. Sovereign risk covers political instability or the possibility of exchange controls being introduced. Sovereign risk may lead to credit risk in a currency swap.

Overall this is a high risk business which should not be undertaken without considerable expertise. However, as long as ABC have a treasurer with experience and knowledge in the area there may be benefits for the company.

56 PS

(a) The Black-Scholes pricing model can be used to calculate the value of a European call option. The five input variables involved are:

- The price of the underlying instrument (current or spot market price).
- The exercise price (the price the holder of the option wishes to buy or sell the share at).
- The risk free interest rate (the rate typically paid on three-month treasury bills) (quoted as an annual rate and as a decimal number).
- The time to expiry of the option (quoted in years).
- The standard deviation of the underlying instrument's returns (i.e. the price volatility).

A decrease in the value of each of these factors will have the following effect.

- *Current market price.* As the current market price of the underlying item falls, the call option will fall in value. The option will become more out-of-the money, or less in-the-money. If the option is exercised, the option holder would be buying an underlying item that is worth less than previously.
- *The exercise price.* The lower the exercise price, the higher is the value of the call option. The option will become more in-the-money or less out-of-the-money, increasing the probability that the option holder will exercise the option.
- *The risk-free interest rate.* A reduction in the risk-free interest rate will reduce the value of a call option. The Black-Scholes model assumes that if a call option is purchased, the money saved by purchasing the option instead of purchasing the underlying item could be invested at the risk-free rate. A reduction in the risk-free rate makes purchasing the call option less attractive, because the interest income will be lower. This reduces the value of the option.
- *The time to expiry of the option.* As the time to expiry of the option becomes less, the value of the option will fall. The 'time value' element of the option is reduced, and at expiry, the time value of a European option is zero.

- *Volatility in the price of the underlying item.* A reduction in the price volatility of the underlying item will reduce the value of an option. This is because lower volatility reduces the probability of extreme movements in price. As a consequence, there is a smaller probability that the option will be in-the-money at expiry (and a lower probability that it will be in-the-money by a large amount).

(b) **Fixed forward contract**

The forward rate for selling US$ in exchange for sterling is:

Spot rate	1.4220
Discount	+ 0.0046
Forward rate	1.4266

The sterling proceeds in three months' time (to the nearest £1) would be:

\$2,350,000/1.4266 = £1,647,273

Option contracts

To hedge the currency risk, the company would buy sterling call options because it will be buying sterling (and selling US dollars).Of the three option prices available, two are in-the-money. PS would therefore be more likely to consider the option at 1.43 that is slightly out-of-the-money.

At a strike price of \$1.43, the sterling equivalent of \$2,350,000 is £1,643,357. Each option is for £31,250, therefore PS would want to buy 52.6 options (£1,643,357/£31,250).

This would be rounded up to 53 or down to 52 contracts.

If PS takes out 52 contracts, it would be exposed to currency risk on \$26,250 of income. The option contracts would be for 52 × 31,250 × 1.43 = \$2,323,750. The under-hedged amount is therefore \$2,350,000 – \$2,323,750 = \$26,250). If the option contracts are exercised in December, the unhedged dollars would be sold at the spot rate.

The premium for the options would be £31,250 × 52 × 1.36 = \$22,100. These dollars would be purchased at the spot rate on 30 September (= 1.4180) and the premium cost in sterling would therefore be \$15,585.

The options will only be exercised if the spot rate on 31 December is worse than 1.43 (higher than 1.43). Suppose for example that the spot rate on 31 December is 1.44. The sterling receipts would be:

	£
52 contracts at £31,250	1,625,000
\$26,250 sold at spot (1.44)	18,229
Total income	1,643,229
Less: Option premium cost	(15,585)
Net receipts	1,627,644

The forward contract will produce higher income if the US dollar weakens between 30 September and 31 December, and the options are exercised. However, exercising the options gives PS a 'worst possible' outcome. The financial benefit of options (compared with a forward contract) arises if the options are not exercised, and PS can sell the dollars at a more favourable spot rate. The 'breakeven point' at which the options would provide higher net income than a forward contract can be calculated as follows:

	£
Income if forward contract is used	1, 647,273
Option premium cost	15,585
Total income	1,662,858
Dollar income	$2,350,000

Breakeven rate: $2,350,000/£1,662,858 = $1.4132

If the spot rate falls below $1.4132, it would be more beneficial to buy call options than to arrange a forward contract.

The final decision will probably be based on views of movements of exchange rates in the future and a company's attitude to risk. PS is risk averse, which probably means that a fixed forward contract would be the better choice.

57 FRAP

(a) An FRA is an over-the-counter agreement between a bank and a customer. A customer can buy an FRA to 'fix' the LIBOR rate for a short-term loan starting at a future date. The FRA relates to a specific borrowing period and a notional amount of capital. In the example in the question, the company can buy a 2v5 FRA on a notional principal amount of $20 million. This will 'fix' the LIBOR rate for the loan at 5.09%. This means that if the company can borrow at LIBOR + 0.5%, the effective cost of borrowing is fixed at 5.59%.

An FRA is settled at the beginning of the notional loan period, by a payment from one party to the other, depending on whether the FRA rate is above or below LIBOR at the settlement date. Since the settlement is at the beginning of the notional loan period, rather than at the end of the interest period, the amount the payment is discounted.

(i) If LIBOR is 7% at settlement of the FRA, the company will borrow for three months at 7.5%. The FRA bank will make a payment to FRAP for the difference between the LIBOR rate and the FRA rate (7% – 5.09% = 1.91% per annum) on $20 million for the three-month interest period, discounted at the LIBOR rate of 7%.

The loan cost, less the amount received from settlement of the FRA, provides a net effective borrowing cost of 5.59% (7.50% – 1.91%).

(ii) If LIBOR is 4% at settlement of the FRA, the company will borrow for three months at 4.5%. FRAP will also be required to make a payment to the FRA bank for the difference between the LIBOR rate and the FRA rate (4% – 5.09% = 1.09% per annum) on $20 million for the three-month interest period, discounted at the LIBOR rate of 4%.

The loan cost, plus the amount paid for settlement of the FRA, provides a net effective borrowing cost of 5.59% (4.50% + 1.09%%).

(b) The current three-month LIBOR rate appears to be about 5%, and if the company wishes to use an option to hedge its interest rate risk, it would probably choose to buy a call option on a $20 million loan for three months, with an exercise date in two months' time and an exercise rate of 5% for three-month LIBOR. The cost of buying this option would be $60,000.

On a three-month loan of $20 million, the effective interest cost of the $60,000 premium is approximately:

[$60,000/$20 million] × [12/3] × 100% = 1.2%.

If, in two months' time, LIBOR is higher than 5%, the company will exercise the option to borrow at 5%. If LIBOR is less than 5%, the company will let the option lapse.

(i) If LIBOR is 7% at the exercise date for the option, the company will exercise the option. The option will be cash-settled, and the bank writing the option will make a payment to FRAP for the equivalent in interest of 2% (7% – 5%) on $20 million for three months. It will borrow in the market at 7.5% (LIBOR + 0.5%).

The effective interest cost would be:

	%
Borrowing cost	7.5
Option premium cost	1.2
From exercising the option	(2.0)
	6.7

(ii) If LIBOR is 4% at the exercise date for the option, the company will let the option lapse and borrow at 4.5% (LIBOR + 0.5%).

	%
Borrowing cost	4.5
Option premium cost	1.2
	5.7

(c) FRAP could seek to reduce the cost of using options by buying a call option at 5% and writing/selling a put option at, say, 4.5%. This would create an interest rate collar, that restricts the effective LIBOR rate to between 4.5% and 5%.

The call option would cost $60,000 and the revenue from the put option would be $45,000, giving a net option cost of $15,000. The effective interest cost of this $15,000 net premium is approximately:

[$15,000/$20 million] × [12/3] × 100% = 0.3%.

(i) If LIBOR is 7% at the exercise date for the option, the company will exercise the call option, and the effective interest cost would be:

	%
Borrowing cost	7.5
Option net premium cost	0.3
From exercising the option	(2.0)
	5.8

(ii) If LIBOR is 4% at the exercise date for the option, the company will let the call option lapse but the put option would be exercised, and FRAP would have to make a payment equivalent to 0.5% (4.5% – 4%). The effective interest cost would be:

	%
Borrowing cost	4.5
Option premium cost	0.3
To settle the put option	0.5
	5.3

(d) An FRA could be described as a single-period interest rate swap. In an interest rate swap, two parties agree to exchange 'interest' payments on an underlying notional principal amount. With a coupon swap, one party might pay LIBOR and receive a fixed rate (the swap rate), and the other party will pay the fixed rate and receive LIBOR.

There are some differences between a swap and an FRA.

(i) A swap is a long-term agreement, whereas an FRA is an agreement over a shorter period of time. (However, a company can arrange to buy or sell a strip of FRAs covering a period up to about two years.)

(ii) With a swap, the interest payment dates for the two parties do not have to coincide.

(iii) With a swap, the settlement of payments is usually at the end of the notional interest periods, rather than at the beginning.

58 NETTING, MATCHING AND POOLING

(a) A company might decide **not** to control its foreign exchange risks for several reasons.

(i) The risk might not be material. If the maximum loss that the group might expect to suffer is low, the benefits from control measures would also be small. Control measures would therefore be unnecessary.

(ii) If the group operates in different currencies whose value fluctuates up and down against other currencies, it might be considered that gains and losses on foreign exchange will cancel each other out, and the net risk is therefore immaterial.

(iii) Since BNM is based in the UK, its main currency might be sterling. If management took the view that the currencies in which it earns income are expected to strengthen against sterling, and the currencies in which it incurs expenditures are likely to weaken against sterling, it might choose not to hedge its FX exposures.

However, there are reasons why an international group should consider hedging its FX risk exposures. The exposures might be large, and if exchange rates are volatile, the risk might be significant. A risk-averse company would want to avoid losses (or gains) on foreign exchange that might have a significant effect on its reported profits. In extreme situations, the trading profits of a company might be eliminated by FX losses. This appears to be the situation that BNM is now in.

(b) (i) Netting is a process of using income in a currency to make payments in the same currency, so that the exposure is reduced to the net amount. For example, if a company expects to receive $400,000 and at about the same time make a payment of $500,000, it could use the income to make most of the payment, leaving a net exposure of just $100,000.

For netting to work successfully, there must be receipts and payments in the same currency at about the same time. Netting might therefore operate on a daily basis, a weekly basis or monthly basis, and would require efficient centralised control, possibly by the group treasury department.

Since receipts and payments do not occur on exactly the same days, there would also have to be currency bank accounts, for temporarily holding currency receipts until they are needed to make payments.

A problem for BNM is that the group has a decentralised management structure, and for netting to be effective, it would probably be appropriate for the cash flows of the subsidiaries to be netted. This will require centralised management.

(ii) Matching is a term that could be used to mean netting. It is also used to describe the practice of matching assets and liabilities, so that if a company or group has an asset in a particular currency, it should seek to have a matching liability in the same currency. Any translation loss on the asset would then be offset by a matching FX translation gain on the liability.

Translation gains or losses are features of financial reporting, rather than a cash flow matter.

However, financing assets with liabilities in the same currency can also reduce actual losses on foreign exchange movements. For example, a subsidiary that operates in US dollars might be financed largely by US dollar-denominated debt, so that income from trading (in dollars) can be used to make the interest payments and debt capital repayments in the same currency, avoiding FX risk.

The capital funding operations of BNM are the responsibility of the central treasury unit, and it should be expected that the unit will use matching principles when deciding on the appropriate currency for any new borrowing.

(iii) Pooling is a system of managing cash. When a business has several bank accounts in the same currency, it might be able to arrange a system with its bank(s) whereby the balances on each bank account in the same currency are swept up into a central account at the end of each day, leaving a zero balance on every account except the central account. Overdraft balances and positive cash balances are all swept up into the central account.

This does not provide a system for hedging against FX risk, but can be an efficient system for cash management. It avoids overdraft costs on individual bank accounts, and it enables the treasury department to make more efficient use of any cash surpluses.

For an efficient system of cash pooling, there needs to be a centralised cash management system. The current organisation allows each subsidiary to operate their own cash management system. Pooling can be organised by each subsidiary. However, it might be even more efficient if subsidiaries operating in the same currencies shared the same pooling system.

(c) A common method of hedging foreign exchange exposures is forward exchange contracts. These can be used to fix the exchange rate for a future purchase or sale of a quantity of currency. In theory, each forward contract would relate to a specific future transaction in the currency, but in practice, large companies might buy or sell large quantities of currency forward without necessarily specifying which forward contracts apply to which trading transaction.

Similarly, a company might use the money markets to hedge its FX exposures, borrowing or depositing foreign currencies 'now' in anticipation of future receipts or payments. Money market hedging can effectively fix a forward rate for a future FX transaction.

(d) An international group will benefit from raising debt capital centrally for several reasons.

(i) If the central treasury has the responsibility for arranging borrowing for the group, a finance subsidiary could be used to raise capital, supported by a guarantee from the parent company of the group. Since debt would then effectively be guaranteed by the group as a whole, the credit rating for any bonds (or the interest rate on any bank loans) will be determined by the credit status of the group. It can therefore use the credit status of the group as a whole to borrow at lower rates of interest.

(ii) A centralised treasury department can raise capital in larger amounts than the individual subsidiaries. This might provide opportunities for the group to use different methods of borrowing that might not be appropriate for individual subsidiaries on their own. For example, the group as a whole might raise capital in the bond market when individual subsidiaries on their own would not require enough capital to make a bond issue worthwhile.

(iii) Raising capital centrally also allows the group to control its debt and capital structure more easily. If individual subsidiaries are allowed to raise capital on their own, without reference to head office, there would be a risk that the group will become excessively indebted, without proper controls being applied to debt risk management.

59 XCV

(a) An interest rate cap is a form of call option on a notional loan. It gives its holder the right, but not the obligation, to borrow a notional amount of principal at a fixed rate of interest, which is the exercise rate for the option, for a succession of interest periods. For example, a cap might give its holder the right to borrow $20 million at 5%, for a succession of notional interest periods of six months up to expiry of the option after, say, four years. In this example, there would be a series of exercise dates for the cap, one every six months, when the option holder can decide whether or not to exercise the right to borrow the notional $20 million for the next six months at the exercise rate of 5%.

The exercise rate is compared with a benchmark or reference rate of interest, such as six-month LIBOR, and the option will be exercised at each exercise date if the reference rate is higher than the exercise rate for the option. If the reference rate is lower than the exercise rate in the cap, the option will not be exercised.

Since a cap is an option on a notional amount of a loan, whenever an option is exercised, it is settled by a cash payment by the option writer to the option holder, for the value of the difference between the reference rate and the strike rate, based on the length of the interest period and the amount of the notional loan.

A cap can be used to set an effective maximum interest rate on a floating rate loan, and this is probably the reason why XCV uses them. When the interest rate rises above the exercise rate in the cap, XCV will pay the higher rate on its actual floating rate loan, but will also exercise the option. The cash received from exercising the option will reduce the effective interest rate to the maximum limit. When interest rates are lower than the exercise rate, XCV will benefit from the lower interest cost in the loan.

The main problem with using a cap to hedge the risk of higher interest rates is the cost of the premium. This can be very high, and it appears that XCV has incurred high costs in the past.

There are two possible ways of reducing the cost.

(i) XCV could arrange interest rate collars instead of interest rate caps. A collar would consist, for XCV, of buying a cap at one exercise rate and selling a floor at a lower exercise rate. The effect of this would be to fix the borrowing cost on a floating rate loan between a maximum rate set by the cap and a minimum rate set by the floor. The advantage of a collar is that the income from selling the floor offsets the premium cost of the cap, and so reduces the cost. However, although a collar protects a borrower against high interest rates, it removes the opportunity to benefit from lower interest rates, and the effect might be to fix the interest rate within a very narrow band.

(ii) It might therefore be more appropriate, instead of arranging interest rate caps or collars, to use a different type of hedging instrument. An interest rate swap could be used to manage XCV's balance between fixed rate and floating rate borrowings. If the risk of rising interest rates becomes higher, XCV could swap some of its floating rate liabilities into fixed rate liabilities, and so manage the risk.

(b) **To:** Treasurer

From:

Date:

Subject: IAS 39: *Financial instruments: recognition and measurement*

Terms of reference

This report sets out the broad rules for reporting financial instruments in the financial statements, and suggests controls for ensuring that the correct accounting methods are used.

The basic rules

IAS 39 defines four categories of financial instrument:

(i) a financial asset (or liability) at fair value through profit or loss. These are financial assets (or liabilities) that are held for trading;

(ii) held-to-maturity investments are financial assets, but not financial derivatives, that have fixed or determinable payments and a fixed maturity date, and the company has a positive intention and ability to hold the investment to maturity;

(iii) loans and receivables are financial assets, but not financial derivatives, with fixed or determinable payments, but which are not quoted in an active market and are not available for sale;

(iv) available-for-sale financial assets are financial assets, but not financial derivatives, that are not in any of the other three categories. This might be the appropriate category, for example, for our investments in quoted company shares.

The four categories are significant for the purpose of financial reporting, because the accounting treatment differs.

(i) Financial assets at fair value through profit and loss must be marked-to-market, and any gain or loss reported in the income statement as a profit or loss for the period.

(ii) Available-for-sale financial assets are also marked-to-market, but any gain or loss is taken directly to reserves and not reported through the income statement.

(iii) Held-to-maturity investments and loans and receivables are reported using a valuation method called 'amortised cost'.

Financial derivatives are always treated as financial assets at fair value through profit and loss, unless the rules in IAS 39 allow hedge accounting to be used. Hedge accounting effectively allows the gain or loss on an underlying position to be offset in the financial statements by a matching loss or gain on the hedge position.

The IAS 39 rules permitting hedge accounting are strict, and a hedge must satisfy certain conditions before hedge accounting is permitted. In practice, it will mean that some hedges the company has arranged against financial risk will not qualify for hedge accounting treatment.

Required controls

Since XCV has a large amount of financial instruments, it must have systems in place so that they can be properly accounted for under IAS 39.

Whenever the company acquires financial assets or incurs liabilities that fall within the scope of IAS 39, it must categorise the instrument into one of the four categories shown above. A record must be maintained of this categorisation. The categorisation process should therefore be continuous and fully documented.

If the company wishes to use hedge accounting to report its hedged positions, it must be able to show that hedge accounting is permitted in the circumstances, and maintain appropriate records.

XCV should have one or more individuals who are familiar with the rules in IAS 39 and so are able to maintain the necessary records. Their supervisor or manager should also be expected to carry out regular checks to make sure that the categorisation and recording systems are operated correctly. Where necessary, advice should be obtained from experts, such as the company's auditors.

Conclusion

This report has described the situation relating to IAS 39 is general detail. Should you need further information, please let me know.

60 SDT PLC (MAY 05 EXAM)

Examiner's comments

This question tests candidates' understanding of the management of financial risk (syllabus section D) and specifically currency risk. A little over one third of the marks go for computational exercises, with the remaining marks allocated for critical commentary on various issues related to foreign exchange risk.

Candidates are expected to understand the pros and cons of currency hedging and be able to interpret spot and forward rate data to estimate revenue flows. Understanding of the limitations of forward contracts is also tested. Additionally, candidates are asked to comment upon the relative risk:return requirements for domestic versus overseas sales.

Common errors that occurred May 05 exam:

Answers to (a) frequently ignored the MD's comments and simply made general points about world events or hedging techniques.

A large number of candidates managed to score full marks for part (b). However, a substantial minority calculated sales values or contribution per unit rather than total contribution as required.

Answers to part (c) were either extremely good or extremely poor, with poor answers demonstrating no real understanding of the matter.

(a) **Market efficiency**

The Managing Director (MD) states that foreign exchange markets are efficient. This is likely to be the case where there are a large number of buyers and sellers. For the currencies traded by SDT, this is likely to be the case. However, for minor currencies, political or other factors may limit trading, making the markets less efficient.

Gains and losses

SDT trades in three major currencies. Therefore given that markets are efficient, the MD's view that the likelihood exchange gains are the same as exchange losses is probably correct. However, the risk of gains or losses depends on the specific portfolio of currencies held. The question indicates that, at present, sterling is likely to weaken; however, the comment could apply to the US dollar or Japanese Yen in the future. Maintaining some diversification does not mean that gains and losses can be ignored. Economic conditions must be monitored and portfolios amended in line with expectations on currency movements.

Currency risk

Currency risk has been hedged by maintaining a portfolio of currencies from different regions of the world. However, SE Asia, North America and Europe are closely linked economically and economic trends tend to be mirrored in all three regions. Other risks such as business risk may not be adequately hedged by investment in three similar areas. Risk diversification may be enhanced by maintaining currencies from other less economically dependent regions in SDT's portfolio.

Benefits of currency hedging

SDT may benefit from currency hedging for the following reasons:

- ensuring future cash flows where transactions are denominated in other currencies;
- improving budgeting as a result of certainty of cash flows;
- reduction in risk by purchasing currency on a futures market.

SDT should therefore continue to hedge foreign currency risks.

(b) (i) *Hedge risk on forward market*

Note answer required in terms of contribution = selling value of units less variable cost

	Company A	*Company B*	*Europe*
Sum due	Y9,487,500	US$ 82,142	€66,181
Two month forward rates	Y200.032	1.7775	1.4784
Sterling receipts =	£47,430	£46,212	£44,765
Units sold =	Y9,487,500 /	US$ 82,142 /	€66,181 /
Amount due / price per unit	632.50	$10.2678	€12.033
=	15,000	8,000	5,500
Variable cost = units × unit variable cost	15,000 × 2.75	8,000 × 4.80	5,55 × 6.25
=	£41,250	£38,400	£34.375
Sterling value of contribution earned = receipts less variable cost	£6,180	£7,812	£10,390

Total contribution with hedging = £24,382

(ii)

	Company A	*Company B*	*Europe*
Sum due	Y9,487,500	US$ 82,142	€66,181
Spot rate in two months	Y202.63	$1.7750	€1.4680
Receipts	£46,822	£46,277	£45,082
Less variable costs	£41,250	£38,400	£34,375
Contribution	£5,572	£7,877	£10,707

Total contribution if sales receipts are un-hedged = £24,156

(iii) *With hedging*

Total receipts from exports = £47,320 + £46,212 + £44,765 = £138,407

Total contribution = £24,382

Average contribution = total sales revenue / total contribution = 17.62%

Without hedging

Total receipts from exports = £46,822 + £46,277 + £45,082 = £138,181

Total contribution = £24,156

Average contribution = total sales revenue / total contribution = 17.48%

Hedging results in a marginally higher average contribution (and total contribution) and therefore SDT should hedge foreign exchange risks.

(c) **Reasons for generating higher returns on export sales:**

Increased risk

Increased risks on export sales include:

- loss or damage in transit due to longer distances involved;
- higher credit risk from lack of knowledge of foreign customers and difficulty of collecting overdue debts;
- transaction risks from foreign exchange movements; and
- delays in payment where electronic payment methods are not sufficiently well developed.

Increased costs

Increased costs result from:

- provision of export documentation;
- increased administration of monitoring foreign debtors;
- expense of contacting foreign customers;
- necessity to obtain insurance against non-payment by foreign debtors.

Increase risk and cost therefore imply that the return expected on foreign sales is higher than for domestic sales. The risk may be mitigated by use of a foreign agent or maintaining an office in the foreign country to deal with the foreign customers directly.

(d) Use of a forward contract by SDT to hedge payment from company B means that SDT is committed to delivering a specific amount of US$ at the end of the contract. If company B pays late, then SDT may not have the funds required to deliver those dollars. There will also be finance costs involved in establishing the forward contract as well as the risk that exchange rate movements will be against SDT.

The risk can be mitigated by:

- Obtaining an option forward contract – although this will have a higher administration charge and the exchange rate used is likely to be less favourable.
- Offering a discount to company B for prompt payment. The discount, however, should not exceed the cost of breaching the forward contract.
- Imposing a late payment penalty. Although this appears attractive, it may be difficult to collect from overseas debtors.

RISK AND CONTROL IN INFORMATION SYSTEMS

61 ERPS AND EIS (PILOT PAPER)

(a) Strategy is concerned with setting targets and formulating plans for the achievement of those targets, in the longer term and the shorter term, as a means of achieving the objectives of the organisation as a whole.

(1) Information Systems strategy is concerned with deciding what information the organisation requires, and for what purposes it is needed. IS strategy supports the business strategy of the organisation, and is concerned with providing management and other users with the information they need to implement business strategies and achieve the business strategy targets. The information systems within the strategy should encompass both non-financial and financial information, competitive information, environmental information. Sources of information should be both internal and external. Essentially, Information Systems strategy is concerned with: 'What information is needed to support business strategy?' and 'Where should the information come from?'

(2) Information Technology strategy is concerned with planning the technological systems for information processing and communication, through which the required information will be provided. IT is concerned with the hardware, communication links and software of systems, and how these will link together to provide IT systems to meet the organisation's current and future information requirements. IT systems can range from simple desk-top computer systems standard application software to sophisticated systems such as ERPS and EIS.

(3) Information Management strategy is concerned with devising the methods by which information should be stored, made available for access and used. A major aspect of IM is the organisation of information on file, such as the use of databases and data warehousing, and the structure of databases. Strategy should also be concerned with ensuring that the information is used, and the ways in which it might be used (for example using data mining methods).

(b) A transaction processing system is designed primarily for processing transactions, often within a stand-alone system for a job-specific application. Management reports are produced from such systems, but these are essentially a summary of the transactions that have been processed or provide an analysis of data on the computer master files. The information produced by transaction processing systems is therefore of operational or tactical value, but not strategic value, and it is used to prepare reports for the line management responsible for the particular area of operations.

An ERPS is a commercial software package that integrates information from a variety of sources, both internal and external. The information is both financial and non-financial. An ERP system might capture transaction data from a number of different transaction systems, as well as information from external sources (such as suppliers). This information can then be used to prepare specially-designed reports for management covering a range of different activities, and of strategic as well as tactical value.

ERP systems can be used to provide performance data for multi-functional activities, rather than specific transactions, and so can be valuable for activity-based costing, balanced scorecard performance analysis and supply chain management.

ERP systems can provide benefits in excess of transaction processing systems because they provide better-quality strategic management information for senior management. The actual value of any particular ERPS obviously depends on the circumstances of each case, but as a general rule, an information system is beneficial if the expected improvements in management decision-making exceed the cost of providing the system.

Executive information systems (EIS) as their name suggests, provide information to senior executives within an organisation, from information sources both inside and outside the organisation. They allow executives to monitor the performance of the organisation and scan general business conditions at any time and in 'real time'. They allow executives to obtain summary performance information, and 'drill down' into further detail if required. They can also be used to make 'one-off' file interrogations to obtain information. Crucially, they are easy to use, and an executive does not have to be an IT expert or systems expert to benefit from using an EIS.

An EIS allows senior management to obtain performance information in 'real time' and should therefore help management to improve their control over the organisation. This is a benefit that transaction processing systems are unable to provide.

(c) Budget allocations for IT in the past have been made using an inefficient system. The system has been to allow a 5% to 10% increase in the budget allocation each year to allow for inflation and system upgrades. This approach to budgeting inevitably builds 'slack' into the budget and encourages wasteful spending.

The system is also weak because it appears to be based on the view that the existing IT systems are more or less satisfactory, and will simply need improving or changing with upgrades from time to time. The budgeting process does not appear to consider whether the IT systems remain adequate for the information needs of the organisation.

The appropriate approach should be to consider the information requirements of the organisation and its management, and the benefits that would be obtained from the information. Costs of providing information should be compared with the potential benefits. New IT system developments should also be considered, in terms of costs and benefits. Instead of following an incremental budgeting approach, an activity-based budgeting approach or a zero-based budgeting approach would probably be more effective in constructing a better budget.

The benefits of an ERPS or EIS are difficult to measure quantitatively. They should provide better management information, and it is important that any new system should be capable of providing the information that management need. To estimate the benefits of a system, it would be appropriate to consider the improvements in management information that the system would provide (more information, more up-to-date information, more accurate information, and so on) and how this should improve the quality of decision-making within the organisation. If an estimate can be made of how decision-making might improve, it should be possible to make a rough estimate of the potential benefits, for example in terms of revenues, cost savings or profits.

62 OUTSOURCING RENEWAL

To: Board of GH

From:

Date:

Subject: Renewal of outsourcing agreement with DF

The contract with DF is due for renewal in six months' time, and GH will have to make a decision whether or not to renew. DF has provided good service for the past six years, and the contract has worked well.

However, we ought to take this opportunity to consider whether outsourcing is an appropriate policy for the future, in view of the changes that have occurred already, and might occur in the future, in our industry.

The most significant change that the board should consider is that:

- the latest signalling systems are complex, and are controlled by computers our customers, the railway companies; but
- the latest prototype system is perhaps even more complex, and might involve the use of GH computer systems.

IT is therefore growing as a significant element of the systems we provide, and in the future we might find that GH has to use its own computer systems to operate the signalling systems. We therefore need to reach a view on whether the maintenance and upgrades for IT hardware and software should be dependent on DF, or whether we ought to bring the operation in-house in order to exercise closer management control.

The benefits and disadvantages of renewing the outsourcing agreement are set out below.

Benefits of outsourcing

Fixed cost contract

One of the major advantages of the contract with DF has been the fixed price arrangement. A fixed annual price means that the cost of the IT service can be predicted with confidence, and DF has to accept all the risk of cost overruns. The arrangement also means that we do not have to monitor internal IT expenditure.

It is also possible that because DF will buy hardware in large quantities, for all its clients, the costs of hardware upgrades will be cheaper using DF than they would be if GH had to purchase the hardware in smaller quantities through an in-house IT department.

Quality of service

DF has provided a good service, and should have a skilled work force that understands our current systems, and can provide a professional maintenance and upgrade service. We should be able to assume that DF would have the ability to learn our new systems, and provide a good-quality support service for them. It might be necessary to give DF staff some training in our new systems, but this should not be a serious problem.

Disadvantages of outsourcing

Increases in cost and cost control

With the growing significance of IT systems within our signalling systems, it seems inevitable that IT costs will increase substantially. DF will therefore increase its annual fixed charge, possibly by a significant amount.

If IT costs rise significantly, GH will find that it has no direct control over them, because of the fixed charge arrangement with DF.

Control over key skills and knowledge

At the moment, although GH develops new signalling systems, it lacks internal expertise in the maintenance of its IT systems. The board of GH should consider whether it is appropriate for such key skills to be outsourced to another organisation.

Although it might be appropriate to outsource standard administration tasks and operations that are not strategically significant, it is a much more risky proposition to outsource critical tasks.

However, since GH does not have any expertise in-house, except in its product development department, the operational difficulties of setting up an in-house operation to replace DF should not be under-estimated.

Control over operations

As IT systems become more significant within signalling systems, we need to consider whether GH should take control of all aspects of IT, in order to improve management control of its operations. However, GH would need to appoint an individual with the experience and skills to manage the operation effectively and efficiently.

Client expectations and relationships

It seems probable that in the future, our clients will expect much closer operational support from GH. We have seen this already, with the proposal by the contracting company in the US to monitor train locations from GH's branch in the US and using GH computers.

We would have to consider carefully the possible effect on client relationships of using an outsourcing service to work with our clients, rather than using our own staff. Using GH staff for this work might help to improve client-supplier relationships, and give GH an additional competitive advantage that it would lack if it used DF staff to do the work.

We would also need to consider whether DF has the operational capability to provide a service to our clients in the US and other countries.

Over-reliance on DF

If we renew the contract with DF, we could become over-dependent on DF for an aspect of operations that is likely to grow in strategic importance. The longer the relationship continues, the more difficult it will be ever to dispense with DF's services.

Conclusion and recommendation

IT systems have grown in importance for our business and will probably continue to grow in importance. There are consequently significant risks involved in failing to exercise close management control over IT, and to outsource the work to DF.

On the other hand, DF currently has the skills and experience that GH lacks.

I recommend that as a matter of some urgency, GH should discuss the problem of contract renewal with DF, indicating the reasons why GH believes that renewing the contract would be against its strategic interests.

GH should seek to establish an in-house team, led by a capable manager, that will take over the operation of the IT services when the contract with DF expires.

However, DF might be willing to assist GH with the transition, by training GH staff or by hiring some staff to GH during the early period of the change-over. DF might even agree to a short extension to the existing contract. Our objective should be to ensure a risk-free transition from a DF-led service to a GH-operated service, and the risks will undoubtedly be reduced if we can obtain the co-operation of DF.

63 HZ HOSPITAL

(a) The characteristics of information provided by the **Management Information System** (MIS) and the **Expert System** (ES) in the HZ hospital are different in every respect. The management information system provides information on the medical history of each patient. It includes factual information on past illnesses and any recurring symptoms as well as the patient's name, address and other personal information. An expert system is used to diagnose an illness.

The differences in the characteristics of the information provided by the two systems can be explained under the following five headings: accuracy, completeness, timeliness, reliability, and security and control.

(i) In terms of **accuracy of information**, the MIS should be accurate and give a true reflection of the medical history of a particular patient. It is the basic record-keeping system for the hospital's patients. It holds the records for each patient including details of past illnesses and symptoms, and has the ability to produce reports either on statistical or individual bases. The hospital uses the MIS to automate the record-keeping and, instead of writing out patients' notes to be kept in a paper-based file, this information is input to the computer system to create an electronic file.

The expert system is unlikely to be as accurate or precise as the MIS. It does not have records and data but comprises a knowledge base and an inference engine, which is a rule set from which the likelihood of illnesses can be inferred. It is used to provide several diagnoses with a range of probabilities and precision can only be increased by entering more symptoms or details about the patient or the illness.

(ii) The MIS must be **complete and up-to-date**. The system depends on inputs made to it following a patient's visit to hospital. The doctor may input information during the consultation with the patient and any medication prescribed would be recorded.

The ES depends on being updated to reflect the latest research findings or expert opinion. There is a very good chance of it being incomplete and out of date and not representing a complete body of knowledge. Also, if the knowledge base was created by the hospital, i.e. the software framework purchased and the information (knowledge) input locally, then there is no guarantee that all the necessary information will be present.

(iii) **Timeliness**. The MIS produces information quickly with typical response times of a few seconds. Most MIS are record-based within a hierarchical or relational database, both types being able to display records quickly at the touch of a button.

In comparison, the ES is very slow because it may need to consider many different combinations of symptoms, rules and information before it can perform a diagnosis. If the patient is showing unusual symptoms, the ES may take a lot longer relatively (i.e. minutes rather than seconds) before it can respond, particularly. This obviously depends on the sophistication of the inference engine and the speed and capacity of the processors used.

(iv) **Reliability**. MIS data is only reliable if it has been input correctly. Even if the information is incomplete, the doctor can see from the screen where the gaps are and, with the patient's help, it should be possible to obtain a good indication of their history. The MIS can therefore offer a degree of assurance that there is control over matching the patient to the information.

In the case of the ES the information should never be considered 100% reliable because the doctor or consultant will not know if all the relevant information has been input. For example, some completely different illnesses are identified by similar symptoms. It is very difficult to diagnose appendicitis because the symptoms are similar to stomach problems, constipation problems and pregnancy problems. When the ES creates its diagnostic inference, it will only pick up the information present and could therefore present a faulty diagnosis.

(v) **Security and control** procedures are much easier with the MIS than the ES. When the records are input, the operating system controls the processing and the information can be prevented from corruption by the database management system (DBMS).

It is more difficult with an ES because of the potential size of its knowledge base and the complexities of its rule-based inference engine. With the hospital ES, there is also a link to the historical records within the MIS. If a link is missing, or a piece of information is incorrect, then the processing could take the completely wrong path towards its goal. The only way this could be tested is by completing every single diagnostic/symptom combination. This would not help because it would create almost an infinite number of possibilities.

(b) **General conditions for the application of an expert system**

Three of the conditions that should be present if a particular domain of knowledge warrants the building of an expert system are:

(i) The expert is capable of explaining how decisions are made in all situations, and the decisions that are reached are consistent. If the expert might reach different conclusions given the same data, or the decision is taken on 'feel', then an expert system is not appropriate. It should be noted that some experts may find it difficult to explain how a decision has been made because their experience enables them to reach a conclusion automatically. An example of this would be in the diagnosis of why a car will not start. The conclusion may be reached that 'the starter motor is jammed'. Although the decision may be instant, it is the result of a series of logical thoughts and therefore is suitable for an expert system. 'The make and model of the car is XYZ, the engine makes a particular noise, the engine does not turn over, therefore the probability is high that the car has a jammed starter motor'. In the situation where the expert finds it difficult to rationalise their conclusion, a skilled knowledge engineer is required to help design the system.

(ii) The expertise that is the basis of the expert system is rare and in demand. This often manifests itself in the situation that the expert is always busy answering the questions of others and cannot do his or her own job properly. In many situations the 'users' are themselves experts in an associated field but sometimes need to augment their knowledge with specialised information. Doctors who are GPs may need to find out if a particular combination of drugs may react together to give bad side effects, or they may need to find out information about a rare speciality. Lawyers or accountants may need to consult about a complex and/or specialised category of law.

(iii) The problem must be one that is worth solving and it must cost less to develop the system than the cost of non-experts making the wrong decision. Examples include:

- when decisions are taken by non-experts ('should a customer be allocated a credit card'); or
- when the cost of making a bad decision is so horrendous that the right decision is vital (this often occurs in legal situations).

(c) **Three advantages of using expert systems**

(i) An expert system may enable a person training in a job to be immediately useful. Expert systems themselves are useful training aids, and if the trainee makes decisions based on the output from an expert system, then the manager can be assured that the right decision is reached despite the trainee's inexperience. This situation is particularly beneficial when there is a high turnover of staff in a particular job. A telephone sales operation is an example of when this benefit is important.

(ii) The expert is released from the mundane task of answering 'routine' queries to work where their expertise is of more value.

(iii) The process of building an expert system can provide significant advantages in understanding the problems to be solved. By going through the disciplines that are vital in building a knowledge base, then the expert is often able to understand their own decision making better, and sometimes to eradicate bad habits that may have crept in to their work.

64 MEASURING COSTS AND BENEFITS

(a) **Cost-benefit analysis techniques**

Techniques of cost-benefit analysis fall into two main categories: those that ignore the time value of money (TVM), and those that take into account the TVM. First, we will consider two techniques, which do not take into account the TVM.

Payback period – this method measures the number of years taken by the project to recoup the initial investment. Obviously, the shorter the payback period the better. Companies use this method frequently because it is easy to apply and comprehend. Use of the payback period does, however, have a number of drawbacks. The determination of the cut-off period is essentially an arbitrary decision. The payback period ignores cash flows which occur after the cut-off date; it also ignores the timing of cash flows within the payback period itself. As a result, viable projects may easily be rejected.

In its favour, the payback period does allow for risk and uncertainty by attempting to recover the initial outlay in as short a period as possible.

Return on investment – using this method, the benefits of the project are expressed as a return on investment in terms of a rate per year.

This technique assumes that the investment is repaid over its economic life in a straight-line way. As with the payback period method, it is easy to apply and comprehend but it, too, does not take into account the time value of money. It does, however, provide a useful indicator; organisations obviously seek to invest scarce resources where they will derive the highest return.

Discounted cash flow (DCF) methods take into consideration the time value of money.

We will consider the two principal DCF methods of project appraisal: Net Present Value (NPV) and Internal Rate of Return (IRR).

Net Present Value – this method takes the discounted present value of the future cash flows generated by the project, less the initial outlay. If the NPV is equal to, or greater than, zero the project should be considered as it will at least attain the required rate of return; when greater than zero it will enhance the value of the firm. When using this method to compare projects the one with the largest NPV should be selected.

Internal Rate of Return – this method identifies the rate of return, which produces an NPV of zero for the project. If the IRR of a project is greater than the firm's required rate of return (usually the cost of capital), it should proceed with the project.

(b) **Measurement of information systems costs and benefits**

Costs – some categories of costs associated with a computer system can be quite precisely ascertained, while others are less easily defined. The main costs related to information systems are those of building the system, installation costs, and operational and maintenance costs.

The costs associated with building the system include staff costs (the average salaries for all levels of staff participating in the project; lost time due to sickness, holidays etc; staff training where the use of new software or hardware is necessary, and travel expenses incurred when making associated trips to suppliers etc) and computer-related costs (computer time incurred during system development, and any new equipment which may need to be bought). Many of these costs cannot be accurately defined, but can only be estimated.

The cost of installing the system, which may include recruitment and training, commissioning and installation, conversion of files, user training, parallel running or phased implementation etc, may be easier to quantify. Operating and maintenance costs, (usually contributing to as much as 70% of the total cost of the system) would include the costs of financing the system, maintenance contracts, etc. These costs are often predetermined, and therefore their measurement is less problematic.

Benefits – tactical benefits are those which enable the company to continue functioning in the same way, but at a lower level of costs, or with increased profits. These can be moderately straightforward to define, although the accuracy of any estimation will be determined by the effectiveness of the new system, and its ability to accomplish the required functions.

Strategic benefits are those that enable the company to enter new markets, either offering a new product/service or reaching new customers, or both. These are of fundamental importance, yet are difficult to predict, or quantify.

The improved system will enable better use to be made of information, which should enhance decision-making and the productivity of managers. Monitoring and quantifying these could present difficulties.

The information system may help in attracting new customers and retaining existing ones; and it should improve inventory and credit control. Again, attempts to quantify and classify these benefits may be problematic.

(c) **Risk analysis of the costs and benefits**

The majority of investments are exposed to at least some element of risk. It may be categorised as systematic (factors that affect all organisations) or unsystematic (events that affect one project).

Most managerial decisions involve an element of uncertainty, and are therefore subject to some level of risk. Identifying, and being able to quantify, the risk factor is of great consequence.

Management want to have their vulnerable assets identified, their security requirements outlined, and protective measures delineated. The costs of safeguarding against risks can then be balanced against the estimated costs, which would be incurred if the event took place. The project may be affected by prices that are higher than anticipated. This may be caused by:

(i) bankruptcy of hardware suppliers;

(ii) high turnover of staff on the project team;

(iii) technology not meeting expectations;

(iv) opportunity being lost;

(v) unforeseen problems with contractors, unions etc;

(vi) inadequacies in the project team;

(vii) instability in the economic environment;

(viii) unforeseen costs/overheads;

(ix) inadequate information from the users with regard to their needs of the system.

The project may equally be affected by anticipated benefits, which do not emerge:

(i) the users may experience difficulties or apprehension in adopting the new system; delays or disruption may ensue as a result;

(ii) projected increases in the market share may not occur;

(iii) the system may not be capable of performing at the level estimated, resulting in lower productivity than predicted;

(iv) the benefits derived from the information being produced by the new system may not be discernible.

Risk assessment often involves scenario-based methodologies, which may involve preparing three scenarios: worst case, best case, and expected case.

65 Q COMPANY

(a) **Report evaluating the four options**

To: Board of Directors of the Q Company

From: Management Accountant

Date:

Subject: **Report evaluating options to improve profitability**

Introduction

The Q company has been in existence for three years and has grown rapidly. There is significant demand for the information provision service you provide. However you are currently considering options of how to improve profitability. This report evaluates each of the options you are considering and recommends which options, if any, you should take. Each option is considered below.

Option 1 – Decrease fixed costs

Advantages

1 By cutting the number of software engineers and administration staff, costs would be decreased. These members of staff are not directly involved in producing the final product so in the short term product quality would be retained and profitability increased.

2 It might be considered that now the software engineers have produced the software it simply needs updating. This will therefore require less ongoing resource and these staff will not be missed.

Disadvantages

1 The quality of software appears to be a key factor in obtaining good quality information. If this is a source of competitive advantage you will need to ensure you have sufficient software engineers to further develop the software as time progresses.

2 Reducing these staff would not be viable if you decide to follow options 2 – 4 below since each requires significant resource.

3 Given that Q is expanding you may need more staff in the future to cope with increased demand – particularly administration staff. If you reduce staff now, you will lose experienced workers and have to train new staff in the future. A better alternative may be to simply avoid employing more people as the business expands.

4 Reducing staff numbers may put extra pressure on existing staff. It may also demoralise staff because they will become worried about their job security and the threat of future redundancies.

Conclusion

On balance, this is not a good option. Given that the company is expanding, the need for staff is likely to increase. Reducing staff numbers will put significant pressure on employees who remain. You might gain short-term benefits, but the longer-term risks would be high.

Option 2 – License out software

Advantages

1 Licensing out software will bring in extra revenues for relatively few extra costs since the majority of the software development will already be undertaken.

2 Customers who could not afford to use the full information provision service may find this a cheaper option since it will not involve paying for the time of an information manager. A new group of customers may therefore be targeted.

Disadvantages

1 Selling software is a very different business from the sale of information. There will be different competitors, different customers and different marketing approaches. This reduces the likelihood of success for this option.

2 It is likely that the software product will require some amendments to ensure that it is user-friendly for non-experts who have not had the training that internal users have had. Also any bugs and errors which might be acceptable in a piece of internally written software would not be acceptable for outside sale. This increases development costs.

3 Software support will be required for the new users. This may, for example, involve setting up help lines and an internet support site, and these would mean additional costs.

4 Existing customers may prefer to buy a licence to undertake their own searches thus reducing income from your current business operations.

Conclusion

The extra costs and possible loss of revenues of this option need to be investigated before a final conclusion can be made. From an initial analysis, this proposal might appear to make good use of existing resources, and have limited risks.

Option 3 – Provide information in graphical format

Advantages

1 Graphical formats can make information easier to understand. This option will therefore improve the overall product offered by Q. This should improve your competitive position and long term reputation. This may result in additional revenue and profitability, but probably in the longer term and no so much in the short term.

2 It may be possible to charge extra for information provided in this format, although this is unlikely. Customers are probably unwilling to pay more for information presented graphically.

Disadvantages

1 There will be extra time spent in developing the software to provide information summaries in graphical format. More IT design staff might have to be employed, so that costs will increase.

Conclusion

Pursuing this option is a good way of improving customer satisfaction in the long term but in the short term it is more likely to result in reduced profit margins. You might wish to consider the benefits of investing for long-term business development, but I recommend that you carry out further research into customer needs before making a decision.

Option 4 – Upgrade Q's internet connection

Advantages

1 The time spent producing information will be reduced. Fewer information managers should be needed and annual fixed costs will therefore be reduced.

2 Information can be provided to customers in a shorter time, thus improving the value added to customers. This may allow slightly higher prices to be charged. Alternatively, a competitive advantage might be gained over competitors, improving the probability of attracting new business and retaining current customers.

Disadvantages

1 'State of the art' facilities may be very expensive to provide.

Conclusion

A cost versus benefit analysis should be undertaken to evaluate the financial merits of this option.

(b) **Developing IS/IT/IM strategies**

The IS, IT and IM strategies might be developed using the following steps:

Step 1

The first step is to define the information systems (IS) strategy. This sets out to provide a long-term direction for the development and priority of information systems throughout the organisation.

Michael Earl said that developing IS strategies should be undertaken in three different ways. Ideally an organisation will employ all three approaches.

(i) *Top down planning – business led*

Top down planning ensures that the IS strategy is consistent with the overall business strategy. Overall business plans can be reviewed for their information needs and ways in which systems can support these. In the case of Q, the strategy might be to provide excellent customer service. In this case options 3 and 4 will support this and development of new graphical presentation systems and an internet site might be prioritised.

The second element of top down planning is to use critical success factors to define key performance indicators – key information required by the business to measure its performance. If a critical success factor is 'accuracy of information provided', a key performance indicator might be the 'number of errors discovered in a quality control check'. Systems must be set up to identify, record and report on the number of errors.

(ii) *Bottom up planning – infrastructure led*

A bottom up planning approach starts with an analysis of current systems, usually by the IT department, and how effective they are. Any problems or gaps in these systems need to be filled. This may involve using new technology to replace or update old systems or could be the rectification of problems being experienced by users of current systems.

(iii) *Inside out planning – mixed*

The problem with bottom up and top down planning is that it may not be creative and may not take advantage of new IT-based opportunities which may exist. This is particularly relevant with IT since new developments are commonplace.

Inside out planning is led by innovative managers in the organisation who spot opportunities to use new technology to improve the business. As part of strategy setting, users should therefore be consulted about their views on systems and how they believe IT could be used to develop the business.

Step 2

The IT strategy follows on from the IS strategy. It is concerned with the development and maintenance of hardware and software to facilitate the overall IS strategy. The next stage is to review the IT requirements of the IS strategy, compare this with current IT and develop a strategy to put into practise development and purchasing programmes to fill any gaps.

Step 3

The Information Management (IM) strategy outlines how the organisation will control and manage information in the organisation. Given the systems and technology from step 1 the best way of developing and managing these in the organisation can be decided.

Many end-user based systems may mean development of an information centre, for example. Outsourcing may be considered the best way of managing user support on the other hand. A full analysis of different options will be needed.

66 RBT

(a) **Intranet**

An intranet is an internal company information system where a wide variety of internal information can be posted for access by staff members. Internal information often includes company news, telephone directories, standard forms, copies of rules and procedures, and so on. In this case of the system under consideration by RBT, the intranet would hold up-to-date information on products and prices, so that sales representatives can download this information to their laptops from a customer's premises and other remote locations.

Advantages

The proposed new system has the following advantages over the old system:

1 **More regularly updated information**

An intranet site is very easy and cheap to update, and product and price information can be kept fully up-to-date by head office. The downloaded product information will therefore be much more up-to-date than the old printed materials, and a better customer service can be provided. All the latest products would be made available to customers and customers would always be given the correct prices.

2 **Reduced costs of producing price lists/brochures**

Regular price lists and brochures will no longer be required, and the production and printing costs of paper-based products should be reduced.

Disadvantages

The intranet site has the following disadvantages compared with the old system:

1 **Slower communication with the production department**

Since the telephone system will be discontinued, the sales people will not have access to production staff to resolve any queries or difficulties with customers. This would be a serious weakness in the system. Good communications between sales and production staff must be maintained.

Solutions

Possible solutions to this problem include:

(i) *E-mail system*

E-mail might provide an efficient way for sales representatives to communicate directly with the production staff, although controls would need to be in place to ensure that the production staff respond promptly to e-mail queries they receive.

(ii) *Maintain telephone access*

Voice telephone access offers immediate communication. A salesperson can get in contact with a member of the production staff and get an immediate reply. Maintaining telephone access for certain queries would be a useful way of ensuring very quick communication where needed.

(iii) *Access to production scheduling system*

Allowing salespeople access to the production scheduling system over the intranet would allow them to estimate a delivery date themselves thus reducing the need for direct contact between production and sales.

2 **Less personal communication with production department**

The intranet is a very impersonal way to communicate with people. It does not allow for two-way conversation, whereas personal contact may be required to resolve difficult issues.

Solution

Both e-mail and a voice telephone system are more personal forms of communication than the intranet. The voice telephone system in particular allows a two-way conversation to take place so that more difficult issues can easily be resolved.

3 **Rejection of new technology**

The sales people may dislike the new technology that they are required to use. At present they do not use IT significantly in their work, and so new skills may be required. Many new systems also have 'teething problems' on implementation, which may also make users dislike the new system.

Solutions

(i) *Training*

Training will be required so people know how the system works and can get the best use from it.

(ii) *Consultation*

Consulting users early in the development process is an excellent way of getting user buy-in to the new system. It will also ensure the system is practical from a day-to-day usage point of view.

(iii) *Testing*

Testing systems well prior to implementation will help avoid the teething problems which may be encountered, particularly if the end users are involved since they know better than anyone else the way the system will be used in practice.

4 **Up-front costs**

The proposed new system will require significant up-front costs both in terms of developing the new systems and training staff. Given the relatively small number of sales representatives (just 20) the investment may not be financially justified.

Solution

A cost benefit analysis can be undertaken to ascertain whether the costs of the investment are justified.

(b) **Information systems – order progress**

Manufacturing system – order tracking

As part of the manufacturing process, progress on orders will need to be recorded. The information recorded will include work done, work still to do and the expected completion date. This information might already exist within the current system or it may need to be input into a database which can be accessed by clients.

EDI or extranet

Using electronic data interchange the customer would be able to log on to RBT's systems to directly access the production data.

An extranet is an extension of an intranet. External parties are allowed to log onto the intranet site and use it to access sections of the intranet. The intranet site would need to be connected to the manufacturing system/database so that up-to-date information was available.

Advantages

1 Clients could access information themselves. This could save staff time and resources in RBT, since there will be fewer customer queries to deal with.

2 An extranet would be relatively easy to provide if the manufacturing system is already linked to the intranet for the benefit of the salespeople.

3 Other information could also be provided to customers (such as past order information, account balances and so on).

Disadvantages

1 There would be a loss of personal contact with customers. The salesperson would not have as many opportunities to make contact with customers in order to build an ongoing relationship. As a consequence, they might identify fewer sales opportunities or find it harder to make a sale because they are less trusted by the customer.

2 External parties would be accessing internal systems. There is a danger that hackers will get into parts of the system that are confidential, and a risk that important information is stolen or damaged. It could also increase the possibility of viruses being brought in which could damage internal systems.

Internet

Alternatively the RBT could put tracking information on a database which is connected to the company's web site. Clients would then be able to access their information through this site.

Advantages

1 Labour cost savings, as described for an extranet.

2 Customers will be familiar with the internet and so find it easier to use than an extranet or internal system accessed via EDI. It also means they will not have to dial in directly to the company's internal network, saving them time and effort.

3 There is less opportunity for hackers or viruses to enter the internal systems using a web site on the internet, since they are not directly accessing internal systems.

4 Other information could also be provided to customers on the internet site.

Disadvantage

The company may not currently have an internet site. This could be a significant extra expense, in terms of designing, creating and maintaining the site.

67 PRINTING COMPANY

The change from a unitary to a divisionalised structure

Each division or profit centre will require its own accounting information and other management information. The accounting system must therefore provide for the recognition of revenues and costs of individual divisions.

There is now a requirement to assess the performance of each division, and the management information system must therefore provide performance reports containing both quantitative and qualitative, and financial and non-financial information

Since each division is a profit centre, the system must provide for a system of transfer pricing for goods or services provided by each division to the other divisions.

Ideally, the management information system will provide benchmarking data, whereby the performance of each division can be compared with the available performance data about similar printing operations in other (rival) companies.

Change from central direction to empowerment of divisional managers

The management information must be capable of providing information to the divisional managers that they need to make decisions. The system should allow each division to extract the data it requires from the company's files for analysis and reporting to management. In addition, local managers should have access to other sources of data external to the company. This might simply be internet access.

Whereas divisional managers will need access to more management information and operational data, the management at head office will need less detailed information. Reports to head office management will monitor the performance of each profit centre, and will also be more strategic in nature. Reports to head office managers will therefore need to be re-designed.

Since authority has been delegated to divisional level and below, new control systems will be required to meet the requirements of the newly empowered team leaders, as well as the requirements of senior management. To ensure consistency in control throughout the company, there should be some standardisation in the nature of the control systems and control information.

The change from internal sourcing of ancillary services to outsourcing

The management information system needs to identify the responsibilities for outsourcing. If outsourcing decisions are taken at divisional level, the costs must be allocated to the division concerned. If outsourcing decisions are taken at head office, individual managers at head office should be made accountable, through a control reporting system.

The information system should maintain a file of external service providers (e.g. approved contractor lists). There should also be a control reporting or monitoring system to ensure that only contractors on the approved list are used.

It will probably also be necessary to establish a system for recording both the costs and the quality and amount of services provided by external suppliers. Outsourcing reports can then be provided to show the total cost and amount of outsourcing, and the cost of individual services. Comparisons between different service providers, and comparisons over time can be reported, for costs, volumes of service and quality.

Use of part-time and temporary employees

The implications for the management information system of using part-time and temporary employees are likely to relate mainly to hours worked and the costs of labour. When all staff are full-time employees, the management information system might report costs per employee. However, when part-time staff are used, it is more appropriate to report costs per labour hour or costs per activity.

Management should also monitor the costs of the various types of employee, to ensure that inefficiencies do not occur. Management reports are therefore likely to include an employee cost report that analyses the costs of each type of employee.

Other aspects of management information might also be affected, such as information relating to the employees themselves (availability in the case of part-time staff, contract termination dates for temporary staff, training records, and so on).

Customers adopting JIT systems

When customers adopt a JIT purchasing system, the supplier becomes responsible for ensuring that customer orders can be met either immediately or very quickly. This has implications for the inventory system of the printing company, and for its production scheduling systems. The information system must be able to recognise JIT customers, and respond instantly to their orders. This might involve maintaining inventories to meet demand, or immediate scheduling of a print run to satisfy the order.

Change from long print runs to high-value low-volume production

The change in the character of customer orders has several important implications for the company's management information systems and order processing systems. First, the order processing system must be capable of handling complex orders. Secondly, there must be a reliable system for measuring the costs of these orders: an entirely different cost and management accounting system might be necessary, based on job costing rather than batch process costing. In addition, due to the complexity of the work, it might be appropriate to analyse overheads differently, perhaps using an ABC costing system. The information system should then be able to estimate prices for customers, if a cost-plus pricing system is appropriate, and also to compare actual and expected job costs for control purposes.

It is also probable that customers for high-value printing will insist on high quality printing, and the management information system should therefore be capable of providing control information about quality standards, and also the costs of achieving those quality standards.

68 STU (NOV 06 EXAM)

(a) As the Head of Internal Audit, I am concerned with carrying out audit assignments to examine and evaluate the adequacy and effectiveness of the controls within the organisation. I will have responsibilities at each of the three phases of the SEM systems implementation.

Design of the system

The new SEM system is being designed and developed in-house, so there will be no access to the knowledge of external exports who are experienced in designing such systems. The risk is that current employees will simply not have the skills necessary to design an effective system on time and to a budget.

Internal audit's first step should be to ascertain the intended objectives of the new system, which will centre around accepting real-time data entry from remote sites, showing the data securely and accessing the data using analytical software tools. A feasibility study has already been carried out, so hopefully the objectives of the system have been agreed and set out in writing. Internal audit should obtain a copy of the feasibility study that the board has approved, to confirm this fact.

The next step is to judge whether the planned system, as set out in the feasibility study, will meet the objectives of the system, and to identify the risks that could frustrate the achievement of objectives. Who will actually do the designing of the components of the new system? Will new employees with skill sets absent amongst current employees have to be recruited? Will existing employees be expected to design the new system on top of all their existing duties, which probably occupy them full-time already? Internal audit can check that the manpower planning for the project is realistic from the start, so that action can be taken at an early stage to bring more resources into the project if that is necessary to bring the project under control.

Designing systems can be an open-ended exercise, taking as much time as is ever available, so internal audit should check that a number of 'milestones' are identified for the design phase, which have to be achieved by particular dates, to ensure proper control of the project is maintained.

Development of the system

Once the new system has been designed by the in-house team, the software should start to be developed. This will be a sensitive time because managers may be perfectly happy using the PC-based databases and spreadsheets that they developed themselves, so they may be relevant to buy into the new system. The key is to ensure that current managers are included in the development phase rather than being presented with a 'fait accompli' at the end of the development phase that they may then be inclined to ignore.

Internal audit should check the means by which current managers are communicated with during the development of the new system. After all, it is senior managers who will be the users of the new system, so their satisfaction with how the system looks and what it produces is paramount. Ideally the front-end of the new system should be developed to mimic as closely as possible the existing systems used by managers whenever this is practicable, to minimise the learning time that manages will have to invest in learning to use the new system.

Once again, in the development phase, internal audit should confirm that mile-stones of progress achieved have been set, and should monitor their actual achievement dates compared with the plan.

Delivery of the system

The board of STU must decide on the implementation strategy for the new system. Internal audit should advise against a 'big-bang' strategy of turning off the old systems one night and hoping to turn on the new system the next morning and to carry on from there. The risk of teething problems is real such that STU cannot afford, in the competitive environment in which it operates, to let down its customers because the new system has failed. STU would be better advised to try a period of parallel running of the old and new systems side-by-side for a period until all the managers have been convinced of the benefits of the new system and it is operating reliably.

Internal audit should visit as many of the remote sites as thought appropriate to test the input of data into the system, should test the security of the data held in the data warehouse, and should confirm that the analytical tools are picking up the data correctly in their operations.

Finally, internal audit should consider whether all relevant laws and regulations are complied with in the new system, for example that any personal data held is stored in accordance with data protection legislation.

(b) (i) There are two possible approaches to auditing computer systems:

- Auditing 'around the computer'
- Auditing 'through the computer'

Auditing around the computer was the old-fashioned approach adopted by auditors in the 1970s and 1980s when computers were being introduced into businesses in a big way. Auditors presumed that they could do their work without having any detailed knowledge of what was happening inside the computer. They looked at the inputs to the computer and the corresponding outputs, checking one to the other, but viewed the computer as a passive 'black box' that they would not go near.

The modem approach is known as auditing through the computer. Auditors check the software processing routines of the system, make sure that the controls in the system are sufficient and that all data is processed correctly. To help with the approach, auditors use computer-assisted audit techniques (CAATs).

The categories of CAATs used in practice are *audit software*, programs used by the auditor to interrogate the files of data held on the company's computers, and *test data*, data input into the company's programme by the auditor to confirm that it is processed correctly. Both audit software and test data can play a valuable role in today's auditing of computer systems.

(ii) The controls that should exist in an IT environment are generally categorised as:

- General controls, and
- Application controls

General controls relate to the whole IT environment. For example, if a company keeps its computer server in a locked room with its own electricity supply and air conditioning unit, this will assist the orderly conduct of all applications run on the system. The purpose of general IT controls is to establish a framework of overall control over the IT activities to provide a reasonable level of assurance that the overall objectives of internal controls are achieved.

Examples of general controls are:

- Organisation and management controls – e.g. segregation of duties
- Application development controls
- Operational controls
- Systems software controls
- Data entry and program controls

Application controls are specific to a particular application, e.g. the payments supervisor may be required to authorise each purchase invoice to be paid. This control is relevant only to the purchase system, so it is an application control. The purpose of application controls is to provide reasonable assurance that all transactions are authorised, recorded and processed accurately and on a timely basis.

Application controls include:

- Controls over input
- Controls over processing and computer data files
- Controls over output

69 AMF (MAY 05 EXAM)

Examiner's comments

This question is designed to test the candidates' ability in relation to risk in information systems in general and outsourcing of IT in particular and show how internal controls and internal audit can mitigate the risk. The syllabus topics being tested are mainly E (Risk and Control in Information Systems). The question meets the learning outcomes by providing a scenario in which an ERPS system is to be outsourced. Candidates are expected to apply their understanding of IT systems, risk and control and to write a report identifying the advantages and disadvantages of outsourcing, evaluating the main risks and recommending appropriate controls.

Common errors that occurred May 05 exam:

A large number of candidates failed to write a report, as requested. In many cases, answers started off in a report format but failed to continue in that style. Clearly, this cost some of the marks offered for presentation.

Answers often dealt with general issues associated with outsourcing, rather than focusing on the specifics of the successful operation of the system as described in the question.

The question clearly asked for a discussion of the transition to a chosen outsourcing company and yet many candidates wrote in some detail about how a company should be chosen.

Report to the Board of AMF
Outsourcing the ERPS system

May 20X0

Introduction

This report has been produced at the request of the board of AMF. The report:

- discusses the advantages and disadvantages of outsourcing;
- identifies the main risks with outsourcing and suggests how these risks might be mitigated through internal controls and internal audit;
- recommends processes and controls that AMF should adopt to manage a project for a successful transition to an outsourcing company.

At the time of writing the board is considering outsourcing the ERPS project. This report will assist the board in making that decision and makes the inherent assumption that the project will go ahead.

Advantages and disadvantages of outsourcing

The main advantages of outsourcing include:

Cost savings

Services are obtained as and when required. This point is particularly relevant where internal staff would not be fully utilised. Costs will also be fixed in a contract providing certainty of IT expenditure.

Overcome skills shortages

The IT/IS function in AMF may not have all the skills necessary for the ERPS project. Outsourcing provides access to the necessary skills without additional costs of hiring and training of staff. The outsourcing company will have access to a larger pool of technical staff than AMF and will therefore be able to meet our company requirements.

Flexibility

Use of external IT providers allows AMF to be flexible in its choice of IT services; services can be bought in as and when required.

Disadvantages of outsourcing include:

Lack of knowledge of AMF

The outsourcing company will not have detailed knowledge of AMF. This may mean that the proposed implementation of ERPS will not focus sufficiently well on AMF's specific system requirements.

Use of Service Level Agreement

The contract with the outsourcer needs constant monitoring. Although AMF will have a group to perform this monitoring, checking service level provision can be difficult where appropriate IT skill and experience is not available in house.

Costs

AMF becomes locked into a contract with the outsourcing company for continued support of the ERPS system. Support may be expensive as the outsourcing company knows it will be difficult to change outsourcing companies.

Evaluation of the risks of outsourcing

Chain of command

Outsourcing implies that the normal chain of command within an organisation is broken. AMF will effectively delegate implementation of the ERPS system to a third party via a contract; AMF therefore have no direct management control over the outsourcer.

Goals and objectives

AMF's goals and objectives are likely to be different than those of the outsourcer. For example, AMF may want to ensure that its IS/IT function remains dynamic and responds to changes in IT technology quickly and efficiently. However, the outsourcer may be more interested in stability and minimal change to try and ensure that costs are kept under control and there is little risk associated with systems upgrade.

Lock-in

AMF will effectively hand over the provision and maintenance of the ERPS system to the outsourcer. If the services of the outsourcer are unsatisfactory leading to the cancellation of the contract, then AMF will have a significant expense of either taking the work back in-house or arranging a new contract with another outsourcing company.

Business / reputation risk

There is an additional risk that the ERPS system will fail to meet customer expectations because the outsourcing company did not sufficiently understand AMF's requirements. If the system is not implemented correctly, AMF could lose customers because its own service provision is unsatisfactory.

Mitigation of risks

The risks noted above can be mitigated using internal controls and internal audit in the following ways:

Chain of command

AMF needs to maintain control over the outsourcing company. It is therefore essential that the review group in AMF have the appropriate knowledge of IT and contract management to control the outsourcing company. Regular meetings with the project management team at the outsourcer will be scheduled and all project plans, systems documentation etc. signed off by managers in AMF prior to implementation.

Goals and objectives

The outsourcer needs to be aware of the objectives of AMF. The main control is to ensure these objectives are included in the contract establishing the outsourcing arrangement and that the outsourcer can demonstrate from their proposal that the objectives will be followed.

The project group with AMF and the internal audit department can then monitor progress of the project against the contractual terms to ensure that the outsourcing continues to meet these objectives.

Lock-in

While lock-in relates to the future, consideration of appropriate controls is appropriate now. Contracts for ongoing support and costs can be agreed prior to the initial installation of the ERPS providing certainty regarding service level and costs. Ongoing costs can be monitored by the internal audit department, with significant variances being identified to management for investigation.

Business / reputation risk

The management team with AMF must ensure that business requirements are included within the contract signed by the outsourcer. Ongoing monitoring of the installation of the ERPS to ensure that requirements are met will also be necessary. Inclusion of penalty clauses in the contract for failure to meet specific performance requirements will also assist in mitigating this risk.

General risk mitigation

The comments above relate to the specific risks identified. Other controls that will be necessary for any systems implementation will include:

- General controls over system development. The outsourcer should be using a recognised development methodology such as SSADM.
- The ERPS application will have to be checked to ensure appropriate controls over the input, processing and output of data. Internal audit can assist in this area by reviewing system designs and ensuring controls are adequate. Internal audit will also ensure that appropriate audit trails are available through the ERPS system to trace all transactions.
- A post completion audit should also be planned to ensure system objectives have been met. Again, internal audit will be able to perform this review.

Processes and controls for transition to an outsourcing company

If an outsourcing company is chosen for the ERPS implementation then there are two main process and control procedures that need to be implemented:

1 Project planning

The outsourcer will become responsible for the implementation of the ERPS system. Processes will therefore be necessary to initially transfer control to the outsourcer and then to monitor the project on a day-to-day basis.

A project team has already been proposed within AMF and this will be essential for the above activities. The team will be involved in managing the project from initial definition of user requirements, through ongoing meetings with the outsourcer to final systems sign-off and user training.

The team will be part of the steering committee which will also include management from the outsourcer and the systems analyst in-charge of the project at AMF. Where possible, users will also be on the steering committee to ensure that their requirements are also met.

2 Systems changeover

Eventually, the existing computer systems will be replaced with the new ERPS system. An implementation plan will be required which will specify the method of systems changeover, including data conversion requirements. In general terms the plan will:

- Confirm the accuracy of processing in the ERPS with test data.
- Set a changeover date.
- Ensure that master file details are up-to-date.
- Manage conversion of the standing master file data onto the new ERPS.
- State provisions for a parallel run to compare output between the old system and the ERPS where possible to confirm accuracy of processing.
- Confirm archiving procedures for old data from the existing systems.
- Finally arrange for removal and secure disposal of old computer equipment, ensuring old data is purged from hard disks and storage media.

Conclusion

The ERPS system is critical to the ongoing business success of AMF. Any outsourcer must be chosen carefully by competitive bidding and then the relationship monitored to ensure contract terms are being adhered to by the outsourcer. Maintenance of appropriate internal controls and involvement of internal audit will be critical to the success of the implementation of the new ERPS system.

Section 5

MAY 2007 EXAM QUESTIONS

SECTION A – 50 MARKS

[the indicative time for answering this section is 90 minutes]

ANSWER THIS QUESTION

QUESTION ONE

ACB is a stock exchange listed company that designs and assembles small passenger aircraft which it sells to regional airlines throughout the world. ACB is highly regarded by its airline customers for the quality of its aircraft. ACB is also recognised for meeting contractual commitments through on-time delivery. The company generates profits before interest and taxes of about 5% of sales. However, due to the depressed nature of the airline industry and competition from foreign manufacturers, the company has modest growth targets. About 60 aircraft are delivered each year.

Competitive Advantage

The company's competitive advantage is its ability to take a standard aircraft design and customise it to the varying needs of its customers. This includes, for example, changes in engine size, passenger capacity, configuration, and electronic equipment. The cycle time from signed order to delivery is about 18 months.

Pricing and Sales Terms

ACB sets the price of its completed aircraft in the customer's currency. The fixed price is converted to ACB's home currency using exchange rates applicable at the time contracts are signed. Progress payments are made on order and throughout the production process, but the balance of approximately 60% of the selling price of the aircraft is made on delivery to the airline. Any delivery delays are classed as a breach of ACB's contract for which it incurs significant financial penalties.

Production and Supply Chain

The manufacture of all the aircraft components has been subcontracted to about 200 suppliers located across several continents. The cost of purchased components constitutes 70% of the final aircraft selling price. Suppliers are selected on the basis of quality, reliability and cost. Contracts with each supplier include prices established in the supplier's currency and incorporate price increases and anticipated efficiency savings over the next two years. This enables accurate forecasting of material costs by ACB. As each component is produced to satisfy the differing requirements of each aircraft, any delay in receipt of any component will delay final assembly. A distribution company has the contract to transport all components to ACB's factory and a combination of bar-coding and satellite tracking technology enables the precise location of all components to be tracked from despatch through to receipt by ACB.

There are five major production operations at ACB's factory: four relate to component assembly and one to final assembly. The four component assembly operations are fuselage, wings, engines, and electronics. All four component assemblies are brought together in a large hangar where the final aircraft assembly takes place. ACB operates its factory on a just-in-time (JIT) basis to minimise inventory. Production scheduling for each of the four component assembly operations must be integrated so that the final assembly can take place on schedule.

IT Support

ACB uses a sophisticated enterprise resource planning system (ERPS) to manage its supply chain, purchase ordering, production scheduling, accounting and performance management, and customer relationship management. The company also relies on an electronic data interchange (EDI) system to track component purchase orders from their despatch by suppliers to receipt at ACB's factory.

Quality Control

Aircraft manufacture is highly regulated with stringent quality control and safety requirements. ACB has always maintained the highest standards. The government's Aircraft Inspection Agency makes regular inspections of component and final assembly quality in order to ensure annual re-licensing of ACB as an aircraft manufacturer.

Costing & Pricing

The cost of each aircraft is estimated from a bill of materials for components and a labour routing, both of which take into account the customisation of each aircraft. Price negotiations follow the cost estimation process and discounts are given for quantity and the significance of the customer to ACB in terms of past and anticipated sales.

Overhead costs are traced to products through an activity-based costing system, based on cost drivers established for eight significant business processes. Profits are calculated for each aircraft and each order (which may be for several aircraft) and customer profitability analysis is used to support future sales efforts.

Risk Management and Governance

The company has a Risk Management Group at senior management level that maintains a register of major risks, carries out risk assessments in terms of their likelihood and consequences, identifies appropriate risk responses, and reports to each meeting of the Audit Committee. IT risks and foreign currency exposures require highly specialised attention and responsibility for these risks is delegated to the IT Department and Treasury Department respectively.

The ERPS and EDI systems are managed by the in-house IT department which has long-serving and highly skilled staff who have developed comprehensive operating procedures and business continuity plans. ACB's Treasury department primarily uses matching techniques to offset foreign exchange exposures in each currency but does use forward contracts where exposures in some currencies are deemed unacceptable.

The Board of Directors emphasises strategy and monitors sales and delivery performance. It aims to ensure that sales are spread evenly over different regions so as not to be disproportionately affected by political or economic changes. The general approach to risk management is to have a portfolio of customers, products and suppliers, so as to minimise sensitivity to any one factor that might jeopardise the company's success. The Board reviews assessments made by the Aircraft Inspection Agency and is actively involved in rectifying any problems identified.

The company's Audit Committee, composed of independent directors, monitors the risk assessments made by managers, ensures that internal controls are adequate and approves the company's internal audit plan each year. The Audit Committee also monitors all monthly financial performance information while the internal audit function spends a considerable proportion of its resources ensuring that financial performance information produced by the ERPS is accurate for management decision-making and financial reporting purposes.

Required:

(a) State the recommended components of any organisation's risk management strategy and evaluate ACB's approach to risk management in terms of those components.

(12 marks)

(b) Identify the major categories of risk facing ACB and evaluate the controls adopted by ACB in relation to each category.

(28 marks)

(c) Risk treatment (or risk response) is an important component of risk management strategy. Explain what is meant by risk treatment and its benefits to a Board of Directors.

(10 marks)

(Total for Question One = 50 marks)

(Total for Section A = 50 marks)

SECTION B – 50 MARKS

[The indicative time for answering this section is 90 minutes]

Answer TWO questions only.

QUESTION TWO

The PKG High School has 900 pupils, 40 teachers, 10 support staff and a budget of $3 million per annum, 85% of which represents salary and salary-related costs. The Local Authority[1] for PKG's area is responsible for 34 schools, of which six are high schools. The Local Authority allocates government funding for education to schools based on the number of pupils. It ensures that the government-approved curriculum is taught in all schools in its area with the aim of achieving government targets. All schools, including PKG, are subject to an independent financial audit as well as a scrutiny of their educational provision by the Local Authority, and reports of both are presented to the school Governing Body.

The number of pupils determines the approximate number of teachers, based on class sizes of approximately 30 pupils. The salary costs for teachers are determined nationally and pay scales mean that more experienced teachers receive higher salaries. In addition, some teachers receive school-specific responsibility allowances.

PKG is managed on a day-to-day basis by the Head Teacher. The governance of each school is carried out by a Governing Body comprising the Head Teacher, elected representatives of parents of pupils, and members appointed by the Local Authority. The principles of good corporate governance apply to school Governing Bodies which are accountable to parents and the Local Authority for the performance of the school.

The Governing Body holds the Head Teacher accountable for day-to-day school management, but on certain matters such as building maintenance the Head Teacher will seek expert advice from the Local Authority.

The Governing Body meets quarterly and has as its main responsibilities budgetary management, appointment of staff, and educational standards. The main control mechanisms exercised by the Governing Body include scrutiny of a year-to-date financial report, a quarterly non-financial performance report, teacher recruitment and approval of all purchases over $1,000. The Head Teacher has expenditure authority below this level.

The financial report (which is updated monthly) is presented to each meeting of the Governing Body. It shows the Local Authority's budget allocation to the school for the year, the expenditure incurred for each month and the year to date, and any unspent balances. Although there is no external financial reporting requirement for the school, the Local Authority will not allow any school to overspend its budget allocation in any financial year.

PKG's budget allocation is only just sufficient to provide adequate educational facilities. Additional funds are always required for teaching resources, building maintenance, and to upgrade computer equipment. The only flexibility the school has in budget management is to limit responsibility allowances and delay teacher recruitment. This increases pupil-contact time for individual teachers however, and forces teachers to undertake preparation, marking and administration after school hours.

---

1 NOTE: A Local Authority (or council) carries out services for the local community and levies local taxes (or council tax) to fund most of its operations. Many of the Local Authority functions are regulated by central government and considerable funding also comes from that source. The range of Local Authority services includes education, community health, refuse collection, and maintenance of footpaths and public parks.

Required:

(a) Explain why the review and audit of control systems is important for the Governing Body of a school such as PKG.

(5 marks)

(b) Evaluate the effectiveness of the Governing Body's control over PKG High School and recommend ways in which it might be improved.

(20 marks)

(Total for Question Two = 25 marks)

QUESTION THREE

Under international accounting conventions, the rules on accounting for employee benefits are based upon the principle that the cost of providing such benefits should be recognised in the period in which the benefit is earned by the employee, rather than when it is paid or payable. The rules laid down in International Accounting Standard 19 (IAS 19) *Employee Benefits* apply to a wide range of employee benefits of which the most common form is pensions.

A significant number of pension plans are classed as defined benefit plans, under which the pension payable by the organisation on the retirement of an employee is linked to his/her salary. The salary used for the calculation of the benefit may be either an average or a final salary, although final salary is still the most common.

Under IAS 19, a company's balance sheet must record the present value of the future benefits payable, net of the value of the pension fund assets. The discount rate used to arrive at a present value for the liabilities is equal to the interest rate payable on AA rated corporate bonds. The valuations are carried out by actuaries, who are required to make a number of assumptions about current economic conditions, life expectancy, the rate of salary increase over time, and the expected rate of return on the pension fund assets.

In the UK, the requirement to put the value of the pension fund's net assets or liabilities on the face of the balance sheet has resulted in a number of companies reporting pension fund deficits in excess of £1 billion and has led to concerns over a 'pensions crisis'.

Required:

(a) A company has a pension fund deficit equal to ten per cent of its market capitalisation. Explain and discuss the nature of the risks posed to **both** the company and its current employees by the existence of such a substantial pension fund deficit.

(10 marks)

The Finance Director of a UK listed company is concerned about the sensitivity of the company's pension fund deficit to changes in life expectancy. If the company's advising actuaries use the most up-to-date life expectancy table, the company's pension deficit will increase by 30%, to approximately 60% of its market capitalisation. The Head of Financial Reporting is therefore considering requesting the actuaries to continue using tables which are now deemed out of date.

Required:

(b) (i) Discuss the proposal to request the actuaries to use out-of-date tables.

(8 marks)

(ii) Identify the internal and external financial reporting controls that could be used to prevent the manipulation of the liability valuation in the manner suggested by the Head of Financial Reporting. **(7 marks)**

(Total for Question Three = 25 marks)

QUESTION FOUR

You work in the new product development division of a USA based global consumer electronics company. You are employed as the accountant responsible for costing and project appraisal of all new product proposals. All costs and revenues are based on information provided by the electronic engineers and marketing staff responsible for each individual project. It is assumed that all development is fully completed prior to initial marketing, and so no redesign costs are allowed once a product is launched. The rapid rate of technological change within the industry has led the company to assume a maximum product life of seven years.

The tables below give details of the company-wide incremental cash flows for two new consumer products. All cash flows are assumed to occur at the year end. Regulatory constraints mean that the company cannot invest in both developments. The company-wide hurdle rate for capital investments is 7.5% per year but the Finance Director is considering introducing risk-adjusted rates, which would give a discount rate of 8.5% per year for Product 1 and 10% per year for Product 2. The net present values generated by each of the products, using both the standard hurdle rate and the risk-adjusted hurdle rates, are also given in the tables.

Product 1 would be manufactured and assembled in China and transferred to company-owned retail outlets in the USA. Product 2 would be assembled in the Czech Republic from components shipped in from Taiwan and then sold to third party distributors across Western Europe.

Product 1	*Year(s)*	*Annual Sales Revenue $ Million (based on ex factory prices)*	*Design and Development Costs $ Million*	*Annual manufacturing and distribution costs $ Million*
	1	Nil	200	Nil
	2	Nil	400	Nil
	3	280		120
	4 – 7	420		180
NPV at 7.5% p.a.	$244 million			
NPV at 8.5% p.a.	$217 million			

Product 2	*Year(s)*	*Annual Sales Revenue $ Million (based on ex factory prices)*	*Design and Development Costs $ Million*	*Annual manufacturing and distribution costs $ Million*
	1	Nil	6,400	Nil
	2	1,250	Nil	600
	3	2,000	Nil	750
	4 – 6	3,500	Nil	1,200
NPV at 7.5% p.a.	$430 million			
NPV at 10% p.a.	($45 million)			

Required:

(a) Recommend three ways of improving your company's internal control systems to ensure better management of risks throughout the product life cycle.

(10 marks)

(b) Prepare a memo for your Head of Division recommending which product your company should support. You should clearly explain and justify your recommendations in the context of risk management.

(15 marks)

(Total for Question Four = 25 marks)

QUESTION FIVE

You are the newly appointed treasurer of VQR Ltd, a medium sized importing and exporting company based in Singapore. The company imports goods from Australia and New Zealand and exports these goods to the United States. A subsidiary company, based in Sydney, Australia, is partly financed by an Australian dollar denominated floating rate bank loan. VQR uses the forward or money markets to hedge its foreign currency risk. Most customers are allowed, and take, three months' credit.

You need to respond to the points raised in the following memo from your Chief Executive Officer:

From: **CEO**

To: **Treasurer**

Date: **24th May 2007**

I have been reading the financial section of the local business press and note the following in respect of interest rates and other economic data:

Exchange rates	*Singapore$/US$*	*Australian$/US$*
Spot	1.565	1.311
1 month forward	1.562	1.312

	Singapore	*USA*	*Australia*
Annual inter-bank offer rate	3.44%	5.38%	6.2%

Annual inflation for Singapore over the next twelve months is forecast at 0.5%, compared with forecast rates of 1.3% for Australia and 1.86% for the USA.

I have a number of questions:

(i) As interest rates are higher in the USA than here in Singapore, surely the US dollar should be trading forward at a premium to the Singapore dollar, not a discount?

(ii) The newspaper did not quote a 3 month forward rate. We have recently sold goods to a customer in the USA to the value of US$ 3 million. What 3 month forward rate of exchange is implied by the information we do have, and therefore what will be the receipt in Singapore dollars in three months' time?

(iii) Can we save money by buying Australian dollars on the spot market as and when we need them to pay for imports, rather than taking out forward contracts, and are there any disadvantages to this strategy?

(iv) Would it be in our interest to borrow Singapore dollars and use the proceeds to pay off our Australian dollar loan given that rates of interest in Australia are higher than those in Singapore?

Please respond to these questions by the close of today.

Required:

Produce a response to the CEO.

Note: Your response should include a brief explanation of theories and appropriate calculations to support your discussion. Five marks will be allocated for **explanation** of appropriate theories. The balance of twenty marks is for **application** of those theories and relevant calculations.

(Total for Question Five = 25 marks)

(Total for Section B = 50 marks)

Section 6

ANSWERS TO MAY 2007 EXAM QUESTIONS

QUESTION 1

(a) An organisation's risk strategy defines its approach to managing risks and provides a basis for the implementation of risk management. Key components of the strategy are:

- A statement about why the organisation manages risk. This should include recognition that it may be necessary to undertake activities which involve an element of risk in order to make best use of opportunities.
- A definition of the organisation's risk appetite – that is the level of risk exposure which is considered to be acceptable.
- Objectives of the risk management strategy based on the objectives and business strategy of the organisation. Risk management should be part of the strategic planning cycle of the organisation so that business objectives provide the context and parameters within which risks are managed.
- A statement of the organisation's expectations of its staff in relation to risk management, which is built on an awareness throughout the organisation of the importance of risk management and the way in which it affects everyone's role.
- Responsibilities for risk strategy and management.
- The framework within which risk management will be carried out – that is the activities which the organisation will undertake to assess risks and determine the appropriate response.
- The different options which the organisation is prepared to use to manage risks.
- Performance criteria for measuring the effectiveness of risk management.

Risk management within ACB

A risk management group has been established at a senior level within ACB which reports to the Audit Committee. However, this group does not appear to consider IT or treasury risks which are key issues for ACB. There is no evidence that anyone within the company has responsibility for ensuring that the board has an overview of all the risks facing the business or that there is comprehensive identification or assessment of risks. Risk management appears to be a very reactive activity.

There is no mention of the organisation's risk appetite or consideration of alternative methods of responding to risks. The main approach seems to be to undertake a portfolio of projects as a way of spreading the risk, rather than trying to minimise the impact of risks on the organisation by reducing, avoiding or transferring them.

The board does review annual assessments from the regulator and rectify those problems; however, in general, its focus seems to be on sales and delivery performance. There is no obvious link between the business strategy and risk management.

There is a risk register, but again this does not include IT or financial risks and therefore is not comprehensive.

The Audit Committee does not oversee the management of risks relating to IT and treasury activities as it should. In addition the Audit Committee and internal audit both appear to focus too much on financial information. The Audit Committee does agree the internal audit programme, but there is no evidence that this programme focuses on the risks facing the company.

The IT department does have a business continuity plan which is important as the company is so dependent on the IT systems. However, it does not appear that this covers any other activities within the company or that it is regularly tested.

The treasury department takes responsibility for management of financial risks. However, it appears that the same methods of risk management are always used – the methods should be reviewed regularly to ensure that the best option has been selected.

(b) There are a number of areas which present major risks to the company:

Exchange rate risk

There are two sources of exchange rate risk which present a major risk to the company. Firstly, supplies of components are priced (and presumably paid for) in the supplier's currency. In addition, prices for finished aircraft are set in the customer's currency at exchange rates applicable at the time the contract is signed, which is around 18 months before the final payments are received. The company is therefore subject to a risk due to exchange rate fluctuations in the intervening period. These risks may add to or offset one another depending on the variations in exchange rates.

The company undertakes limited management of these exchange rate risks. They could consider making more use of risk management methods such as increased numbers of forward contracts, or invoicing in ACB's home currency.

Additionally, the treasury should be accountable to the Audit Committee and report regularly on the company's exposure to exchange rate risk.

Supply chain risk

The company is heavily dependent on its suppliers, both component manufacturers and the distribution company used to transport components. Delays in delivery of components would delay delivery of finished aircraft and cause ACB to incur substantial fines. In addition, poor quality components could cause the company to fail the Aircraft Inspection Agency inspection and lose its licence, which could be disastrous for the company.

Although the company uses sophisticated systems to track components in transit from suppliers, there is no information about quality inspection of incoming goods or monitoring and review of the quality of suppliers after contracts are agreed. The company should also consider dual-sourcing suppliers for components and for distribution.

IT risk

The effective operation of its IT systems is critical for ACB. The EPRS system manages the supply chain, and all operations within the company from purchasing through to delivery of finished aircraft. A failure of this system would leave ACB unable to carry out any of its manufacture, which would result in delays and significant penalties, as well as damage to the company's operations. It also appears that the company is reliant on the system for supplier and customer management. There are risks to ACB both in terms of hardware or software failure and in terms of data quality. In addition, as the systems are managed in-house the company will be heavily dependent on key staff.

The IT department has drawn up business continuity plans and operating procedures; however there is no evidence that these are regularly tested and reviewed. The managers of the IT department should also be accountable to the Audit Committee for the management of these risks.

Reputation risk

Failure of ACB's aircraft to meet the strict industry safety standards could result in the loss of its licence as a manufacturer. This would cause serious damage to ACB's reputation and the company might not be able to re-establish its position in the very safety-conscious airline industry. Quality problems could occur either through failures in the manufacturing process or in components purchased from external suppliers. Whilst ACB does maintain high standards and resolve problems identified in the inspection reports, there is no evidence of quality control of incoming components or internal quality control systems.

In addition, the risks already identified within the supply chain and internal operations, which could result in delays in delivery of finished aircraft, could also damage the company's reputation.

Cost control

As prices are fixed at the start of an 18-month cycle time, there is a significant risk that costs will change over that period. Although cost increases do appear to be built into suppliers' prices, it is not clear how increases in labour and overheads, or the additional costs due to customisation, are taken into account. Initial estimates are based on a bill of materials and labour routings, but even if these are accurate at the time the estimate is made, there should be a process of monitoring costs and reviewing their accuracy. There is also no mention of overhead cost control.

Economic and political risks

The market in which ACB operates is depressed and competition is fierce, and ACB faces the possibility of declining sales over time. Apart from the use of conservative growth estimates for planning purposes, ACB appears to have no strategy for dealing with a declining market.

In addition, there is increasing concern about the environment and fuel costs which could have a significant effect on the market for aircraft manufacture. Again, ACB appears to have no plans to address this, which could be done perhaps by diversification into different products using its existing skills or looking at the possibility redesigning its aircraft to improving fuel efficiency and reduce the environmental impact.

(c) Risk treatment or response is the process of analysing risks on an individual basis, identifying the possible ways of reducing the risk to an acceptable level, and then choosing the best alternative.

There are four main methods of responding to risks:

- Risk avoidance

  An organisation might choose to avoid a risk altogether. However, since risks are unavoidable in business ventures, they can be avoided only by not investing (or withdrawing from the business area completely).

- Risk reduction

  This includes operational measures designed to reduce the probability of a loss or reduce the size of the impact of the adverse event.

- Risk transfer

  In some circumstances, risk can be transferred wholly or in part to a third party, so that if an adverse event occurs, the third party suffers all or most of the loss. A common example of risk transfer is insurance.

- Risk acceptance

  Where no action is taken to avoid, reduce or transfer the risk, the possibility that the event will occur is accepted and the risk is retained in the organisation. This should always be a deliberate decision taken because no other response was assessed as being more attractive or there is no other practical option. However, it often happens by default when a risk is not recognised because there is no effective risk management.

Risk treatment involves:

- Identifying risks and the likely impact and probability of occurrence. This should enable the organisation to determine a priority for the risk as one among many.
- Specifying its attitude to the risk and the objectives of the organisation's response. (This should take account of its priority).
- Identifying possible options for responding, including the cost of the response and the extent to which it will reduce the impact of the risk, and choosing the preferred option.
- Identifying responsibilities for managing the risk and the management processes involved.
- Performance measures to assess the effectiveness of the response
- Plans for dealing with the adverse event if it does occur.

Advantages of the process of risk response to the board are:

- A better understanding of the risks facing the organisation
- A decreased likelihood of adverse events occurring and an improvement in the organisation's ability to respond when they do.
- An organisation which is better at making good use of opportunities
- That the costs and benefits of managing risks will be better understood.
- That the organisation will be able to identify where risks are not being dealt with, provided the risk identification and assessment process is comprehensive.

QUESTION 2

Key answer tip:

At this level, to get a good mark for a question like this, it is not sufficient to answer in general terms – you need to discuss specific controls which the school could or should have in place.

(a) The Governing Body of the school is responsible for good governance of the school in exactly the same way as the board of directors of a company are responsible for corporate governance. This means that the governors need to ensure that an effective system of internal control is in place, that they are working with the Head to identify risks and that they put in place procedures and policies to ensure that these risks are managed.

The main areas of risk for the school are that the school would overrun on its budget and that it would fail to provide an education of an adequate standard to the pupils. The governors therefore need to ensure that the school's internal control system effectively manages these risks. An independent audit also needs to be carried out to investigate the operation of the controls and review their effectiveness. The governors will then need to take action to resolve any problems identified by the audit.

(b) Although the local authority is responsible for reporting on the standard of the educational provision and monitors expenditure on an annual basis, the Governing Body needs to provide assurance that the controls necessary to ensure that educational standards are as high as possible and that spending is controlled are in place. The annual reporting by the local authority is insufficient to allow the governors to identify and correct any problems which are emerging during the year. It is also unlikely that the reports will contain all the information which the governors need in order to carry out their role.

The governors receive a monthly financial report. However, this only gives the expenditure on a monthly basis and for the year to date, and details of unspent balances. There is no indication that the reports include an analysis of trends, any phasing of the budget or forecasting of actual expenditure to the end of the year, without which the Governing Body's ability to control the budget will be limited. The accuracy of the reporting and financial data also needs to be independently audited.

There are a number of specific items of expenditure which the governors need to pay attention to:

- The level of expenditure which the Head can make without prior agreement is $1,000. In order to ensure that this is not abused, the spending should be monitored using a system of retrospective approval, or at least reviewing items on a sample basis.
- Although the Head seeks advice from the Local Authority on issues such as buildings maintenance, as this still forms part of the school's expenditure the governing body needs to ensure that it is aware of the levels of expenditure and the impact on the budget, and include forecasts of expenditure in its budgetary planning.
- School-specific responsibility allowances will affect the budget and it is important that these are regularly reviewed to ensure that they are still applicable and that the system is not being abused.

The governors could consider an increase in class size above 30; if the number of class sizes remained the same, this would increase the budget available to the school as funding is based on numbers of pupils. Alternatively if the number of classes in each year was decreased, this would allow for flexibility in the use of the teaching staff. However this could also have an impact on the effectiveness of teaching and this should only be done with careful monitoring.

There is no mention of any monitoring by the Governing Body of the educational performance of the school except for the annual report from the Local Authority. However this is unlikely to show all the information necessary – the governors should also be considering trends throughout the year and specific indicators in areas where performance needs to be improved. There is also a need for more information to enable an audit of performance or value-for-money.

The governors are responsible for the strategic direction of the school and ensuring that its activities meet the needs of stakeholders such as the local authority, parents, pupils and employees. However, there does not appear to be any form of strategic planning in place.

A major proportion of the budget for the school will be the payment of staff. In addition, the quality of the workforce will have a significant effect on the educational performance of the school. The governing body is responsible for appointment of staff – however it is not clear how involved the governors are in the recruitment process and to what extent decisions are delegated to the Head. There are a number of points to be made:

- The monthly report includes details of teacher recruitment – however there needs to be some form of workforce planning. The governing body should also be involved in the recruitment process, such as decisions about the job requirements and the person specification, and possibly involved in the interview process.

- The level of experience of staff will have an impact on the salary costs. However, if too many newly-qualified teachers are employed this could have a detrimental effect on the standard of education. Ensuring an appropriate balance between experienced and newly-qualified teachers needs to form part of the workforce planning process.
- There is no evidence of governing body involvement in the appointment of support staff – however they form a significant part of the workforce. The governors need to monitor the levels of support staff to ensure that there is not more staff than necessary and that the support roles support the school's activities.
- Staff morale is very important, but could be affected if teacher recruitment is delayed in order to meet the budget. This needs to be closely monitored.

QUESTION 3

(a) The issue facing employers and employees from a pension fund deficit is that, although there may not be an immediate risk, the deficit means that the long-term liabilities of the fund exceed the value of the assets. If this deficit remains, in the future the fund may be unable to fund pension payments which fall due and which are a commitment for the fund.

Pension fund deficits of as much as ten part cent of market capitalisation, as is the case here, can significantly affect the company's value because of the need to correct the deficit for the future. Indeed, pension fund deficits have become an issue in a number of takeover attempts as the extent of the deficit and the need for long-term funding to close the gap have come to light.

In the long-term the company, which is one of the parties responsible for closing the gap, has no choice but to take action to reduce and eventually eliminate the deficit. This may be done through a one-off contribution or in a number of increments. With a deficit of this size it is likely to be done through multiple payments.

Whichever choice the company makes, the payments will have the effect of reducing reserves and increasing the expenses of the company. This will therefore have and impact on the income statement, and in turn will reduce the value of the company as that reflects the value of the future cash flows. In addition to the impact on reported profits, funds used to reduce the pension fund deficit will not be available to fund the main activities of the business and will limit the company's ability to make new investments. This could have operational implications and also limit the company's potential for growth, harming its reputation and presenting a risk to the achievement of strategic objectives.

There will also be a number of risks facing the employees. There is a serious and long-term risk to them that their own pension rights may be jeopardised if the deficit remains. Pension funds receive contributions from both employers and employees and with a deficit of the magnitude here the employees may be asked to agree to make additional contributions in order to provide sufficient funds.

The pressure on company resources due to increased company contributions will also affect the employees in the short-term as there will be fewer funds available for salary increases and bonuses, training and development budgets. Damage to the company's reputation and poor company performance may also threaten their long-term career prospects.

There may also be a risk to the employees of reduced pension levels in the future if there is no agreement to increase contributions and the deficit remains. This may either be through a reduction in their benefits or a closure of the scheme. Closed schemes may be replaced by schemes with reduced benefits or which are no longer defined-benefit schemes but are linked to the value of the fund's investments. These schemes place the risk with employees whose future benefits are no longer certain.

There will also be a risk that future employees will be affected as a part of the agreement reached on reducing the deficit, as even if the scheme is not closed to current employees, there will often be a new scheme for future employees.

(b) (i) It is a generally accepted principle underpinning accounting standards that accounting statements should be based on a 'true and fair view'. This means that they need to be based on reliable information. In the case of the valuation of the pension fund deficit it should be based on the most up-to-date tables which are available. If the old tables are used, the valuation in the company's reporting statements will not be reliable and will not present a 'true and fair view'. The valuation will be understated in the short-term, which may reduce the immediate pressure on the company, but in the long-term the problem cannot be avoided.

For the Head of Financial Reporting to request the actuaries to use tables which are known to be out-of-date is to deliberately give a misleading view. The deficit will appear to be a lower percentage of the market capitalisation and readers of the accounts who are not aware that the tables are not valid will be misled into thinking that the value of the company is higher than is really the case. The action of the Head of Financial Reporting is unethical at best and could be regarded as fraudulent. This activity would go against the fundamental principles which professional accountants should follow.

(ii) In order to ensure that the liability valuation does present a true and fair view a number of controls should be in place:

- Such calculations should not be carried out by one individual but should be double-checked by another individual in the organisation.
- The company should ensure the qualifications of any external advisors such as the actuarial advisors in this care are checked before their appointment. Their work should be monitored, checked and verified by the company's internal auditors.
- Figures of this importance could be checked by an external independent third-party to ensure that they have not been manipulated.
- A deficit of this size would be material and therefore would form part of the company's external audit.
- Any checks carried out internally or externally should examine the validity of the calculation, including the data used to make the estimate. This would include checking that actuarial tables used are valid and up-to-date.

QUESTION 4

Answer tip:

The question only asks for three ways of improving internal control. More are given here for completeness.

(a) A number of controls could be introduced to ensure better management of risks throughout the product life cycle.

- Information provided by electronic engineers and marketing staff on product costs and sales forecasts should be verified. Supporting documentation should be checked to ensure that the forecasts are reasonable and that estimates are not over-optimistic. It could also be valuable for a finance manager to work alongside the engineers and marketing staff as the forecasts are being developed to ensure the reliability of figures used.

- The criteria used to judge projects should be formalised and documented to ensure that all projects are assessed on a similar basis and that comparisons can be made between projects in order to prioritise expenditure.
- Criteria other than NPV should be introduced for the appraisal of new development projects which take account of the wider impact of proposals. For example, the launch of a new product may have an impact on sales of existing products which it may replace or complement, or there may be implications for purchasing if it is necessary to find new suppliers.
- The assessment of proposals should include sensitivity analysis and scenario planning to ensure that the appraisal reflects any uncertainty about the outcome. The use of such techniques will enable specific risks associated with the project to be assessed to ensure that the decision reflects the risks.
- The appraisal of projects is based on the assumption that there are no redesign costs once a product has been launched. This may not be a valid assumption and makes no allowance for the possibility of minor redesigns after launch to prolong a product's life or improve profitability. Redesign costs and lifecycles need to be monitored and reviewed after launch to test the validity of the assumption and to inform cost estimates on future projects.
- There should be a process of post-project review and audit which monitors the cost, sales and profit of products after launch and for some time afterwards and compares them with the initial estimate. This would be used to inform and improve the appraisal process in general and the estimates for specific products.
- An alternative costing method such as target or life cycle costing could be introduced. Target costing considers the entire life-cycle of the product, so that total costs to the manufacturer are minimised. It also begins very early in the development phase of new products, as decisions made at this stage generally determine a high proportion of the costs of any product. The use of life cycle costing would also ensure that the costs of the product over the entire life cycle are considered.

(b)

MEMORANDUM

To: Head of Product Development Division

From: Finance Manager

Subject: Appraisal of investments in new product developments

Date: May 2007

Firstly, considering these two proposals from a financial perspective, the decision as to which product to support depends on whether the company continues to use the standard hurdle rate for projects, or whether the decision is taken to introduce a risk adjusted rate. If the standard hurdle rate is used and the decision is based on NPV then Product 2 should be chosen as it gives a much higher NPV. However in order to achieve this return Product 2 does require very high development costs, which does make it a more risky investment.

If the risk-adjusted rate is used, Product 1 becomes more attractive as the NPV for Product 2 becomes negative using the relevant risk-adjusted rate. It may be sensible to calculate an IRR for this product in addition to the NPV.

However there are other issues to consider:

- No information is available on the total level of funding that is available to invest in new product development. If funding is limited, then we also need to consider what other possible uses there are for the money, particularly in the light of the high investment required for Product 2. The opportunity cost of other possible uses for the money should be built into the project costs.

- If it is the case that funds are limited, projects could be compared on the basis of the return per dollar of design and development funding. This would give a figure of 40.7% for Product 1 and 6.7% for Product 2, using the NPV calculated with the standard hurdle rate. On that basis, Product 1 is significantly more attractive.
- Both products would be manufactured overseas, but Product 1 would be sold through our own outlets. However Product 2 will use components purchased from Taiwan and sold through distributors in Europe rather than through our own stores here in the US. This combined with the sums of money involved in the manufacture and distribution of Product 2 would mean considerable foreign exchange risk for the company.
- There are a number of non-financial issues which also need to be considered:
  - How do these two products fit into the company's overall strategy?
  - Are there other benefits from producing these products, for example do we need more products to take up spare capacity in our company's stores?
  - The high design and development cost of Product 2 may be because it is a more innovative product. We may need this product in the market for other reasons, for example in order to appeal to new groups of customers or improve or maintain the reputation of the company.
  - Do we already know the suppliers of components for the two products and are they reliable, or will we have to find new suppliers?

The risk-adjusted hurdle rate may take into account some of these issues already – certainly the rates given suggest that Product 2 is considered to be more risky that Product 1. However in the absence of information on the assumptions which have been used to calculate the rates it is not possible to confirm that all the issues above have been considered. If the risk-adjusted rates are used, from a financial perspective the choice should be to produce Product 1. However, depending on the risk appetite of the company, the decision could be made to undertake the development of Product 2 in order to increase the possible returns, while managing the risks associated with this project. Having said this, in the absence of further information, and until it is possible to confirm how the risk-adjusted rates have been calculated, my recommendation would be to develop Product 1 based on the results of the financial analysis based on the analysis of results using both the standard and risk-adjusted hurdle rates and the return on development expenditure.

QUESTION 5

Key answer tip:

There are only 5 marks available for explanations of the theories, so you need to ensure that you cover them briefly and concentrate most of your time on the application of the theories to the specific examples in the question. Note that you could answer part (ii) using just one of the available models, but as the question asks you to consider the relationship between interest rates, inflation rates and exchange rates, to gain full marks you should demonstrate that you can apply both the interest rate parity theory and the purchasing power parity theory.

MEMORANDUM

To: Head of Product Development Division

From: Treasurer

Subject: Queries regarding foreign exchange policy

Date: May 2007

In response to your queries raised earlier today, I will begin by outlining the main theories concerning the relationship between exchange rates, interest rates and inflation rates. It is these theories, together with an understanding of the inefficiencies of financial markets which underpin the company's foreign exchange policies.

Interest rate parity

The interest rate parity theory suggests that there is a relationship between exchange rates and interests rates, and that spot exchange rates will move towards the level at which there is parity in real interest rates. If there is a difference in interest rates, then a currency with a lower interest rate will sell at a premium in the forward market to the currency with the higher interest rate. This is because a lower interest rate implies a lower inflation rate and a stronger economy. Future spot rates can be predicted from the differences in nominal interest rates between the two currencies.

Purchasing power parity

The purchasing power parity theory suggests the exchange rate should in some way be determined by the relationship between prices, or the inflation rate, in the two currencies. Purchasing power parity implies that exchange rates will always be adjusted so that there is only one 'real' price for goods in countries between which there is relatively free trade.

Changes in the exchange rate will result from different rates of inflation in each country. If a country has a higher rate of inflation, its currency will fall in value against the currency of a country with a lower rate of inflation. The future spot exchange rate can be predicted from the current spot rate and the expected rates of inflation in each country.

In response to your specific questions:

(i) As discussed above in terms of the interest rate parity model, a higher interest rate in the USA than in Singapore implies a weaker economy in the USA, and that the US dollar should be trading forward at a discount to the Singapore dollar, as is indeed the case.

(ii) The interest rate parity model can be used to forecast the 3 month forward exchange rate according to the formula:

Predicted spot rate (Singapore \$/US\$) =
Current spot rate (Singapore \$/US\$) $\times (1 + r_s) / (1 + r_u)$

Where r_s is the interest rate for the three month period in Singapore
And r_u is the interest rate for the three month period in the USA.

We do not have a three month interest rate for either country. However this can be calculated from the annual interest rate using the relationship:

$(1 + r)^4 = (1 + R)$ where r is the 3 month interest rate and R is the annual rate.

Thus for Singapore, the three month rate is given by:

$\sqrt[4]{(1.0344)} - 1 = 0.85\%$

For the USA, the three month rate is given by:

$^4\sqrt{(1.0538)} - 1 = 1.32\%$

Thus using the interest rate parity formula, the predicted spot rate is given by:

$1.565 \times 1.0085 / 1.0132 = 1.5577.$

If we assume that the three month forward rate is equal to the spot rate, then the US$ 3 million receipt in three months time will be mean that the value of the receipt will be Singapore$ 4.673 million. This compares with the value if we received the payment today which would be Singapore$ 4.695 million; this difference demonstrates the foreign exchange risk which we are exposed to by pricing in US dollars rather than in Singapore dollars.

The purchasing power parity model could also have been used to calculate the three month spot rate, using the following formula:

Predicted spot rate (Singapore $/US$) =

Current spot rate (Singapore $/US$) × $(1 + i_s) / (1 + i_u)$

Where i_s is the forecast inflation rate for the three month period in Singapore
And i_u is the interest rate for the three month period in the USA.

Again, we need to derive 3 month inflation rates from the annual rates which are available.

Thus for Singapore, the three month rate is given by:

$^4\sqrt{(1.005)} - 1 = 0.0124\%$

For the USA, the three month rate is given by:

$^4\sqrt{(1.0186)} - 1 = 0.462\%$

And the predicted spot rate is given by:

$1.565 \times 1.00124 / 1.00462 = 1.5597.$

The two answers are close to one another – differences are likely to result from difficulties in making accurate forecasts, particularly in inflation rates.

(iii) To answer this question it is necessary to calculate rates for the Singapore$ to the Australian$.

At the current spot rates, one Singapore dollar is worth Australian$ 0.838 (1.311/1.565). At the one month spot rates, one Singapore dollar would be worth Australian$ 0.840 (1.312/1.562). This suggests that the Australian dollar is depreciating against the Singapore dollar, and it would appear that we could save money by buying Australian dollars on the spot market when we need to pay for imports, but this is risky and would require a high level of forecasting skill. The reason for taking out forward contracts is to minimise this risk.

(iv) The higher rates of interest in Australia make it tempting to think about borrowing Singapore dollars to pay off the Australian dollar loan, but interest rate parity theory suggests that exchange rates will move so that the real rate of interest in both countries is the same. The implication of this is that because of the higher interest rate in Australia, the exchange rate will change so that the Australian dollar depreciates against the Singapore dollar and that when the loan falls due it will cost less than it would if in Singapore dollars. There is also a transaction cost associated with taking out any loan.

In addition, taking out a loan in Australian dollars would add to our exposure to fluctuations in this currency as we already have some exposure due to purchases from Australian suppliers. If we were to consider taking out an overseas loan, it would be better to borrow US$ as we could then match that liability against receivables in US dollars from our US customers. Hedging to manage foreign exchange risks by matching assets and liabilities in the same foreign currency is a common technique.

Section 7

NOVEMBER 2007 EXAM QUESTIONS

SECTION A – 50 MARKS

[The indicative time for answering this section is 90 minutes.]

Answer this question

QUESTION ONE

The NOP Group is one of the world's largest clothing retailers and had a turnover in excess of £2,000 million for the year ended 30 September 2007. The group's clothes are sold in Europe, East Asia, North America and Australia and New Zealand. The clothes are made for NOP by a number of approved contractors in China, Sri Lanka, Thailand and India. The clothes are designed by employees of NOP at the company's headquarters in London, England. The designers base their ideas on what has attracted them when they have attended the previews of the latest styles at the fashion shows presented by the world's leading fashion houses. NOP operates to a four month lead time which runs from the start of the design process through to the first appearance of the new styles in the retail stores.

NOP's clothes are targeted at the mid to high priced sector of the market and are sold under several brand names. NOP tries to match brands to differing customer profiles, and in doing so recognises that its customers' ages are an important factor. Within the 18-25 year customer age group, brands are 'uni-sex'.

NOP operates across four geographic business units, with each managed as a profit centre. The group has differing arrangements for its retail outlets across the world, as shown below:

Business unit	**Outlet arrangement**
Europe (UK, France, Italy)	Group owned shops
USA and Canada	Franchise agreements
Asia (Japan, Thailand, China, Singapore)	Joint ventures with department stores
Australia and New Zealand	Joint venture with a distributor

The Group is a signatory to an ethical code of conduct (see extracts in the additional information below) which has been developed for use within the clothing sector, and it produces a separate social and environmental report which it views as complementary to its annual report. As part of its environmental protection policy, NOP has also declared a commitment not to send waste to landfill sites from 2008 onwards and will make arrangements for all company waste to be recycled.

The Group's Treasurer regards NOP as highly exposed to currency risk, and therefore requires that all open positions with an equivalent value in excess of £100,000 are hedged. Responsibility for hedging arrangements lies with the Finance Director of each of NOP's four regional business units.

Capital gearing is kept at a low level compared to NOP's competitors, and the market value of debt equalled just 30% of the market value of equity at the balance sheet date of 30th September 2007. The Group Directors' remuneration, as detailed in Note 3 below, is linked to medium term financial targets.

The Group's shares are listed on both the London and the New York stock exchanges. NOP's share price has fallen by 15% over the last six weeks, compared with an average fall of 10% for the general retail sector, and 8% for fashion retailers. A meeting of the Board of Directors has been called to address the problem.

The Group Finance Director thinks that a share price recovery could be stimulated by a well targeted cost cutting exercise. The production and transportation costs being charged by suppliers are considered too high, as they amount to 75% of the cost of goods sold. Initial estimates suggest that there is scope to reduce each of these costs by around 5%. Profit is further eroded by high employee costs, especially in Europe, where they equal 18% of sales, compared to an industry average of 12%. The Group Finance Director believes that increasing the proportion of part-time sales staff could bring employee costs in line with the industry average.

The Group Marketing Director proposes an alternative solution, as he believes that a new advertising campaign would stop the decline in the share price. The campaign would focus on the group's most glamorous product ranges and would use international film stars to promote the clothes. The average gross margin on all clothes sales across the group varies significantly. For some products in the UK and Japan it is 45%, but it is as low as 6% for some products in Thailand and Singapore. The glamour ranges earn an average gross margin of 22% and sales of these ranges account for 15% of group revenue, but it is thought that the advertising campaign could significantly boost global sales of these high mark-up products with no accompanying sales loss elsewhere.

Additional information

1 **Extracts from key financial statistics for the preceding two years**

	2005	*2006*
	£million	£million
Sales*	2,400	3,120
Gross profit (excluding joint ventures)	480	625
Distribution costs	72	50
Profit/loss from joint ventures	(350)	180
Net Interest payable	24	22
Dividend yield on year end share price	1.5%	1.5%
UK Share Price (year end)	465 pence	490 pence
Price index for UK retail shares (Base 100 in 1997)	680	782

The current (November 2007) share price is 480 pence

*Sales are split across the regions as follows: Europe 60%; USA & Canada 20%; Asia 12%; Australia and New Zealand 8%

2 The Ethical Code of Conduct covers conditions and terms of employment within NOP and in NOP's suppliers, and includes the following requirements.

- Payment of the legal minimum level of wages (or industry average) whichever is higher.
- No use of forced labour, and freedom for employees to join a trade union and/or engage in collective bargaining.
- Safe and hygienic working conditions.
- A commitment not to use child labour, that is, aged below 15.
- Working hours kept to normal national levels or local industry standards.

3 **Remuneration of Group Executive Directors**

In addition to a fixed, market based salary, plus pension and health scheme benefits, group directors are entitled to performance related pay. The performance related pay usually represents over 50% of each director's annual remuneration and is based upon the following terms.

- A variable bonus is payable if performance meets or exceeds pre-determined annual targets for NOP's profit before tax. Achieving target performance earns the directors a bonus of 55% of their annual salary, and this rises to a maximum of 150% for performance more than 20% above the target level.
- Half of the variable bonus is granted in cash, and the rest is paid in shares, which must be held for a minimum of three years.

4 **Remuneration of business unit directors and other senior managers**

In common with the executive directors, other senior managers in NOP are paid partly on the basis of performance. Senior staff can earn bonuses paid in shares, which carry no minimum holding period requirement. The bonus rates are dependent upon performance relative to earnings per share growth targets set by the Board of Directors and in recent years have ranged between 50% and 220% of annual salary.

Required:

(a) Discuss the extent to which **each** of the following characteristics of NOP creates potential risks for the company's shareholders.

(i) Branding and marketing strategy.

(ii) Design and procurement strategy.

(iii) Remuneration of senior management and executive directors.

(iv) Corporate Treasury function.

(v) Social and environmental policies. **(30 marks)**

(b) Prepare a report to be presented at the board meeting that:

- explains why the principle of risk ownership at board of director level is a vital form of control, especially in extremely large companies such as NOP; **(5 marks)**
- discusses the relative merits of the Finance Director's and the Marketing Director's proposals. (Your discussion should be from a risk management perspective, and should therefore focus on the risks created by the share price fall and the impact of each proposal on the group's overall risk profile.) **(15 marks)**

(Total: 50 marks)

(Total for Section A = 50 marks)

SECTION B – 50 MARKS

[The indicative time for answering this section is 90 minutes.]

ANSWER *TWO* QUESTIONS ONLY

QUESTION TWO

X is a small company based in England. The company had the choice of launching a new product in either England or France but lack of funding meant that it could not do both. The company bases its decisions on Expected Net Present Value (ENPV) and current exchange rates. As a result of this methodology, and the details shown below, it was decided to launch in England (with an ENPV of £28,392) and not France (with an ENPV of £25,560).

England		*France*	
	Probability		*Probability*
Launch costs		Launch costs	
£145,000	0.1	£190,000	1.0
£120,000	0.9		
Annual cash flows		Annual cash flows	
£65,000	0.4	£90,000	0.5
£42,000	0.4	£70,000	0.2
£24,000	0.2	£30,000	0.3

The annual cash flows are based on contribution margins of 10% for England and 20% for France where it is expected that sales volumes will be lower. It is thought that the product will sell for four years only.

The monetary values are expressed in the home currency of the company and have been converted (where necessary) at the current exchange rate of €1.47/£1.

The company has discounted the cash flows using a cost of capital of 10% per year.

Required:

(a) It has now been forecast that the Euro is likely to strengthen against sterling by 5% in each of the next four years.

Calculate and briefly comment upon the revised Expected Net Present Value if the product is launched in France. **(5 marks)**

(b) Identify the different risks associated with each launch option and discuss how these may be managed by the company. **(8 marks)**

(13 marks)

(c) Company X wishes to raise a £500,000 fixed rate bank loan to fund the product launch and additional capital investments. Company X is able to obtain fixed rate finance at 8.5% or a variable rate loan at LIBOR + 0.5%. Using its bank as an intermediary, Company X has been offered a swap arrangement with HTM, a smaller company that wishes to borrow at a fixed rate. HTM has been quoted a rate of 10.5% for a fixed rate loan or LIBOR + 1.1% for a floating rate loan. The bank charge for arranging a swap is 0.2% of the principal, and it is assumed that the net benefits will be shared equally between Company X and HTM.

Required:

(i) Briefly discuss the potential benefits and hazards of interest rate swaps as a tool for managing interest rate risk. **(6 marks)**

(ii) Show the transactions involved, the bank charges and the interest terms payable if X and HTM agree to the swap. **(6 marks)**

(12 marks)

(Total: 25 marks)

QUESTION THREE

VWS is a company manufacturing and selling a wide range of industrial products to a large number of businesses throughout the country. VWS is a significant local employer, with 2,500 people working out of several locations around the region, all linked by a networked computer system.

VWS purchases numerous components from 750 local and regional suppliers, receiving these components into a central warehouse. The company carries about 10,000 different inventory items, placing 25,000 orders with its suppliers each year.

The Accounts Payable Department of VWS has six staff who process all supplier invoices through the company's computer system and make payment to suppliers by cheque or electronic remittance.

Required:

(a) Discuss the purposes and value of an internal control system for Accounts Payable to a company like VWS. **(10 marks)**

(b) Identify the information systems controls that should be in place for Accounts Payable in a company like VWS. **(10 marks)**

(c) Explain the risk of fraud in a computerised Accounts Payable system for a company like VWS and how that risk can be mitigated. **(5 marks)**

(Total: 25 marks)

QUESTION FOUR

EWC is a large company in an unregulated sector of the telecommunications industry. It has ambitious plans for sales growth and increased profitability. In support of these goals, senior management has established a flat management structure. Budget targets place employees under considerable pressure but success in achieving and surpassing sales and profitability targets is rewarded by bonuses and share options. Employees who do not achieve their targets do not remain with the company for long.

Performance targets exist for expanding EWC's customer base, sales value and profitability per customer, and geographic and product-based expansion. EWC zealously pursues cost reduction with continual efforts to drive down suppliers' prices. The company aims to eliminate any wasteful practices in management and administration. EWC considers any expenditure that does not lead directly to sales growth to be wasteful and the company minimises its corporate policies and procedures. As a result, EWC has tended to overlook unscrupulous practices in its employees' dealings with customers, competitors and suppliers in the pursuit of its goals. The company is unlisted and reports its profits to shareholders once per year.

Required:

(a) Identify the major types of risk facing EWC that arise from its style of management. Give reasons to support your answer. **(10 marks)**

(b) Explain the significance of the control environment in EWC. **(5 marks)**

(c) From the perspective of a newly appointed non-executive director, evaluate the financial, non-financial quantitative, and qualitative controls in EWC in the context of EWC's goals and the risks facing EWC. **(10 marks)**

(Total: 25 marks)

QUESTION FIVE

Required:

'Effective internal control, internal audit, audit committee and corporate governance are all inter-related'.

Discuss this statement with reference to:

(a) How internal audit should contribute to the effectiveness of internal control; **(7 marks)**

(b) How an audit committee should contribute to the effectiveness of internal audit; **(9 marks)**

(c) The role of an audit committee in promoting good corporate governance. **(9 marks)**

(Total: 25 marks)

(Total for Section B = 50 marks)

Section 8

ANSWERS TO NOVEMBER 2007 EXAM QUESTIONS

QUESTION 1

(a) Any potential event which could prevent the company from achieving its objectives creates a risk for the shareholders. These risks could be due to the possibility of an event or set of circumstances which threaten the company's profitability or revenue and which could reduce potential dividends or share price. Alternatively any adverse event could lead to a worsening in the stock market's opinion of the company and hence a drop in the share price. This would restrict the capital returns available to the shareholders and impair the company's ability to raise finance for new projects, threatening its long term growth and again presenting a risk to the shareholders.

(i) There are a number of risks which are associated with the branding and marketing strategy:

- There is a significant exchange risk as the company has a large number of stores outside the UK. Indeed the geographical spread of outlets indicates that the majority of sales could be in currencies other than sterling. This will be discussed further under the Corporate Treasury function.
- The company is selling in some countries at a very low margin, particularly Asia. There is a risk that if the margins drop the company could make a loss on these sales – indeed it is possible that this is already the case.
- NOP is making use of franchise arrangements in the US and Canada. Although this reduces the financial risk to NOP as most of the cost of these operations is transferred to the franchisee, NOP is dependent on the franchisee to maintain the brand image and there is a risk that poor franchisees may damage the company's reputation.
- Again, the company has joint ventures in a number of countries with department stores. Again, the risk of establishing outlets in these countries and the costs of the operation and the financial risk are shared with the joint venture partner, but there is a risk that the actions of the partner could cause problems for NOP. It is particularly difficult to manage such relationships when joint venture partners are based in different countries. It can be seen from the financial statistics that in 2005 significant losses were made from joint venture operations (nearly 15% of sales revenue), although in 2006 there was a profit.
- The company sells different clothes to different age groups under different brand names. Although it may be appropriate to market the clothes in different ways to different groups of customers, there is a risk that if customers have loyalty to one brand, if they do not associate the other brands with the same company they may not continue to buy from NOP as they become older.

(ii) Risks associated with the design and procurement strategy

- The company uses suppliers in a number of developing countries. NOP is dependent on these suppliers to maintain the required ethical standards. If they do not, there is a risk to NOP's reputation. This will be discussed further under the heading of social and environmental policies.
- The company has suppliers in a number of different Asian countries. This is a source of exchange risk unless the suppliers are happy to be paid in sterling (see also under treasury management).
- There is no evidence of a link between the designers and the customers when developing new ranges. It appears that the designers attend fashion shows and then design the clothes which they like. There is a risk that these designs will not meet the requirements of NOP's customers, with the result that sales revenues drop.
- There is a lead time of just four months from the start of the design process to having to have the goods in stores. This is a short timescale, particularly given that suppliers are oversees, and there is a risk that any delay could cause the clothes to be late in arriving in shops, which could reduce sales. This is particularly important with clothes which need to be fashionable where different styles and materials are needed for different seasons of the year.

(iii) The remuneration of senior management and executive directors

- It is essential to ensure that any remuneration package ensures that the directors and managers have a stake in doing a good job for the shareholder and are motivated to improve performance. At NOP there is a performance related element of remuneration, and it appears that the bonus could potentially reach a very high level if the company performs well. This could focus the directors on achieving a high profit in absolute terms, leading to attempts to amend the financial statements to increase profit.
- The granting of share options means that the directors have the right to buy shares at the exercise price in a number of years' time. If the price of shares has increased, then the directors will make a profit based on the difference between the two share prices (exercise and the future price). Options appear to be a good method of rewarding long term performance as they are normally granted for periods in excess of three years. However, there remains the issue that directors may attempt to increase share price near the option date.
- If the bonuses paid to directors and managers reach very high levels as they have done in recent years, this will have the effect of increasing staff costs significantly and reducing the returns to shareholders.
- It is not clear how many directors and senior managers are covered by the performance-related scheme. If the number is large, the risks due to the scheme could be very significant.
- The reward system is based purely on financial measures. Although this is not uncommon, there is a risk that this could divert managers' attention from other areas of performance such as quality.

(iv) Risks associated with the corporate treasury function

- As the majority of the company's markets are outside the UK and all its suppliers are in Asia there are considerable currency risks to be managed. However it appears that the management of these exposures is left to the Finance Directors of the individual business units. If they do not have the necessary expertise to manage the currency risk effectively NOP could be very exposed to changes in exchange rates.

- The finance directors are only expected to hedge open positions in excess of £100,000. There could be a number of positions which are just below this level which combined across the company may amount to large sums which are not hedged.
- There does not appear to be any attempt to manage currency exposures on a company-wide basis. For example, if suppliers are paid in US dollars it might be possible to match these payments with receipts from the USA. This could lead to more effective currency risk management.

(v) Social and environmental policies

- As has already been mentioned, even though NOP has a clear statement of ethical standards, it is dependent on overseas suppliers in developing countries to maintain those standards. NOP needs to devote resources to managing and monitoring standards of its suppliers as a failure by a single supplier could cause major difficulties to NOP. For example, recently the clothing retailer Gap, which has had a clear ethical policy for a number of years, received very bad publicity when it was reported in the media that some of its clothes were being produced in sweat shops. Customers are looking increasingly for clothes which they can be confident have been ethically sourced.
- The ethical standards are based on keeping working hours and pay to minimum local standards. Depending on the norms in the countries in which suppliers are based, these standards could still be below those expected by NOP's customers.
- The environmental policy may have the effect of improving NOP's reputation with its customers. However recycling all its waste may increase costs and lower profitability.

(b) To: The board on NOP

Date: November 2007

(i) **The board's ownership of risk**

Enterprise risk management is an element within enterprise management, and also has two dimensions. In their joint report on Enterprise Governance in 2004 CIMA and IFAC (the International Federation of Accountants) said: 'The role of risk management has historically been a largely peripheral one in many organisations. Focused on the prevention of physical and financial loss at an operational level, the formal consideration of risk was far removed from key decision-making. However, recent high-profile corporate failures have identified that failure to identify and appropriately manage risk at a strategic level has a far greater potential impact on organisational fortunes than insured or tightly-controlled operational risk'.

If risks are to be identified and managed at a strategic level this must be led by you as a board. You need to demonstrate your commitment to managing risks to the rest of the organisation. This will ensure that risk management is aligned with NOP's strategic objectives and encourage managers and staff within the organisation to play their own role in this. There are a number of key areas identified by CIMA and IFAC which you as the board need to take responsibility for:

- In relation to the organisation, its specific objectives and the risk environment within which it operates, there should be a statement about the 'value proposition' for risk management. This recognises the need to take risks to achieve objectives.
- The risk appetite of the organisation should be defined.
- Based on the objectives and business strategies of the organisation, define the objectives of the risk management strategy.

- Make a statement of the culture that the organisation requires (and the behaviour the organisation expects from individuals) with regard to risk-taking.
- Responsibilities for the application of risk management strategy should be assigned to managers throughout the organisation.
- The strategy should identify or refer to the risk management framework or system that will be used to deliver these requirements. (For example, the strategy should refer in some way to the internal control system, with regard to the control of risks through conformance.)
- Performance criteria should be defined for reviewing the effectiveness of risk management within the organisation in delivering the risk management objectives.

(ii) **The Finance Director's and Marketing Director's proposals**

The share price fall is a source of concern for NOP as it could have an impact on NOP's strategic objectives. It could:

- Limit your ability to raise new finance and in the long term limit the growth of the company.
- Increase the risk that the company could be taken over.
- Have an impact on the company's reputation.

It is not clear why the share price has fallen as there is limited information available on the current performance of the company. If the sales revenue for the last year was in excess of £2,000 million, this is still significantly below the previous year's level when sales revenue exceeded £3,000 million. If costs such as employee salaries have not decreased at the same time there may have been a drop in profitability. This could be the cause of decreased confidence in the stock market in the company with a consequent drop in the share price. If this is the case, the company needs to consider taking action to improve sales and profitability.

The Finance Director's proposal

The focus of this proposal is on the reduction of costs and hence the improvement of profitability. If the impact of the Finance Director's estimates are compared with the costs of sales at the 2005 level, which is closest to the current level and gives a more conservative estimate:

Cost of sales = sales – gross profit = £1,920
Supply costs = 75% = £1,440
Saving 5% = £72 million.

Reducing employee costs will have a greater impact:

if a saving of 6% of sales is made this amounts to a saving of £144 million.

However this proposal will have no impact on the level of sales turnover and is not without risk:

- Pressure on the suppliers to reduce costs could mean that they are more likely to compromise standards in order to reduce costs. This could increase the risk that they will use unethical practices in manufacture. It could cause there to be a risk of poor product quality which would cause customer dissatisfaction and could lead to a decrease in sales.
- It is not clear how the finance director proposes to move from using full-time staff in the stores to making more use of part-time staff. If the majority of staff are employed on a full-time basis then it is unlikely that this could be changed in the short-term without making staff redundant which would be costly and risks demotivating staff (leading to lower productivity) across the company. Such actions could also cause increased reputation risk.

The marketing director's proposal

This proposal from the marketing director considers actions to improve the sales in the glamour market. If the margin on these sales is estimated based on sales at the 2005 level:

Total sales = £2,400
Sales in glamour market = 15% of total = £360 million
Gross margin 22% = £79.2 million.

The marketing director has not provided estimates of the impact of his proposals on the level of sales in this area and the increase would have to be significant to bring sales back up to the level in 2006.

Other issues:

- This proposal does not include any activities aimed at increasing sales of other ranges. Indeed there is a risk that it could divert attention from the marketing of other higher margin ranges.
- A marketing campaign such as the marketing director suggests using high profile film stars would be very costly. There is a risk that if it does not succeed the company's costs and profitability would be worse for the next year.
- The need to produce new designs to back up the campaign and drive to increase sales would put increased pressure on the design team and increase the risks in this area.
- As the company sells products under different brand names to different segments of the market this activity is unlikely to damage those sales – however it will not have a positive impact on them either.

Conclusion

Both proposals must address the need to improve sales and profitability. However neither is without risk and should not be undertaken by you without proper consideration of the risks and how they could be managed.

QUESTION 2

Tutorial note:

You could answer part (a) of this question by adjusting each year's cash flow at each of the three possible levels for the change in exchange rate, but the most straightforward way to answer the question is to calculate the expected value of the annual cash flow at the original sterling figure and then adjust that figure for the change in the exchange rate before calculating a revised expected present value.

The launch costs could vary with the exchange rate as at least some of these costs are likely to be incurred in France. However as they are all incurred in Year 0 any such costs will be unchanged as they would still be calculated at the current exchange rate.

(a) If the Euro strengthens against sterling then the company will receive more £ for the Euro receipts from France and the value of the annual cash flows in sterling will increase.

Expected value of £k annual cash flows at current exchange rate is:

$90 \times 0.5 + 70 \times 0.2 + 30 \times 0.3 = £68k$

If the Euro strengthens by 5% each year the expected value of the cashflows increases as follows:

Year 1	£68,000 / 0.95	= £71,579
Year 2	£68,000 / $(0.95)^2$	= £75,346
Year 3	£68,000 / $(0.95)^3$	= £79,312
Year 4	£68,000 / $(0.95)^4$	= £83,486

To calculate revised expected net present value:

	Year 0	*Year 1*	*Year 2*	*Year 3*	*Year 4*
Launch costs (£)	(190,000)				
Expected value of cash inflow (£)		71,579	75,346	79,312	83,486
Discount factor @ 10% per year		0.909	0.826	0.751	0.683
Expected present value (£)	(190,000)	65,065	62,236	59,563	57,021

Expected net present value = £53,885.

The effect of revising the cash flows to reflect the forecast strengthening of the Euro is to increase the expected net present value of launching the product in France so that it is considerably higher than the expected net present value of a launch in England. If the decision was made on the basis of this calculation the company would have decided to launch in France instead of England. However:

- This calculation is based on a forecast of changes in the exchange rate which may or may not occur. It is impossible to forecast changes in exchange rates accurately, particularly over a number of years. If the Euro does not strengthen as much as forecast the receipts would be lower than forecast and the calculation of expected net present value would not be valid.
- This methodology takes no account of the risks associated with the two different options such as the exchange rate risk of a French launch. The discount rate used for both options is the same although the launch of the product in France is likely to be more risky than to launch in England. The company could use a higher discount rate for the cash flows from France to reflect the increased risk, which would result in a lower expected net present value.

(b) There are a number of different risks associated with the two different options. Purely based on the financial estimates, it appears that although the potential returns are higher (on the revised estimates from part (a) above) with a launch in France, launching in England is a lower risk, as there is a lower spread of possible annual cash flows. The launch costs are also lower, and the company would have committed fewer funds in launch costs if the product failed.

There are a number of other risks, as follows:

Risks common to both options

- **Product quality**

  Whether the product is launched in France or England there is a risk that the quality will be poor due to problems in manufacturing, particularly relevant with a new product. This could have the effect of increases in costs due to returned product or damage to the company's reputation. If the company's main market is England, a problem with this product could have a greater impact on sales of other products. This risk can be mitigated by careful planning of production and monitoring of production processes and output.

- **Sales revenue**

  There is a risk that customers will not buy the new product and it will not reach the required volumes or that take up will be lower than expected. Although this is a risk in both countries it is likely to be higher in France if the company is less well-known there. The company can manage this by ensuring that market research is thorough or through activities such as test marketing before a full launch.

- **Technology (Materials) risk**

  There is a risk that technology will change and that the product will become obsolete before the end of its four year life. The company needs to ensure that it reviews its products regularly and develops product enhancements and variations to cater for new technical requirements.

Risks relating to launch in France

- **Exchange rate risk**

  As discussed in part (a) above, the company faces an exchange rate risk if it launches in France as receipts and possibly some costs will be in Euros. There are a number of techniques which the company can use to manage this exposure such as forward exchange contracts.

- **Contribution margin**

  There is a risk that the product will not achieve the required price and contribution margin. Although this risk is common to both options, it is greater with a launch in France as the required margin is higher. The company should address this both through its marketing activities and also by ensuring that costs are controlled.

(c) (i) **Benefits of interest rate swaps**

Interest rate swaps have several uses.

- A company can use swaps to manage the mix of its fixed rate and floating rate debt obligations, without having to change the underlying loans themselves.
- Swaps can be customised to meet the company's specific requirements in terms of amount of loan and the term of the loan
- A swap can allow a company to borrow at an effective fixed rate when it cannot do so directly in the bond markets because it is too small to make a bond issue.
- There are no premiums to pay compared to, for example, interest rate options.
- Transaction costs for Swaps are lower than redemption costs (in relation to existing borrowing)

Hazards of interest rate swaps

- The agreement is binding on both parties, so neither company will be able to benefit from interest rate movements that may occur in its favour.
- There is a risk that interest rates or exchange rates will move unfavourably against the company after it has committed itself into a swap. For example a company may have swapped out of fixed rate debt into floating rate debt when anticipating a reduction in general interest rates, but such rates may actually rise.
- There is a high counterparty risk as the actual performance of the contract cannot be guaranteed. This is the risk that the counterparty to the swap will default before the end of the swap and fail to carry out their agreed obligations. Such risk is reduced if a reputable bank is used as the other party to the deal.

- There are no secondary markets making it very difficult to terminate or transfer the contract if the swap is no longer required.

(ii)

Tutorial note

The question as written was impossible as both parties wanted fixed rate loans. In the exam you needed to recognise this and make a reasonable alternative assumption.

Assuming that the question should have stated that X wanted to borrow at a variable rate and HTM fixed:

- X can borrow both at fixed and variable rates cheaper than HTM
- However, a SWAP can be arranged that benefits both parties if each company borrows where they have the greatest comparative advantage:
  - X borrows at a fixed rate of 8.5%
  - HTM borrows at a variable rate of LIBOR + 1.1%
- The overall benefit from the swap = 2.0 – 0.6 = 1.4%. Given that the bank wants 0.2% commission, that leaves 0.6% each for X and HTM.
- There are many ways of setting up the final swap – here is one example:

Cash flows	*Bank*	*X*	*HTM*
	%	%	%
X borrows fixed at 8.5%		(8.5)	
HTM borrows at LIBOR + 1.1%			(L+1.1)
X pays the bank LIBOR + 0.3%	L+0.3	(L+0.3)	
The bank pays HTM LIBOR + 0.2%	(L+0.2)		L+0.2
HTM pays the bank fixed at 9.0%	9.0		(9.0)
The bank pays X fixed at 8.9%	(8.9)	8.9	
Net	0.2	(L-0.1)	(9.9)

QUESTION 3

(a) Internal management control refers to the systems of control implemented by management in a company to ensure that the company's objectives are achieved and that risks in terms of factors which will stop a company obtaining those objectives are identified and guarded against.

The APB in the UK provides guidance to auditors with specific reference to the implementation of International Standards on Auditing. A definition of internal controls from the APB is: 'The internal control system … includes all the policies and procedures (internal records) adopted by the directors and management of an entity to succeed in their objective of ensuring, as far as practicable:

- **The orderly and efficient conduct of its business, including adherence to internal policies**

  Systems in place to ensure that all transactions are recorded (so the business is conducted in an orderly manner) through to following policies such as provision of good customer service.

- **The safeguarding of assets**

  Assets in this case include buildings, cars, cash, etc. (e.g. those things that can be touched) through to other assets including the intellectual property of the company (e.g. those things which cannot be touched but are still an asset of the business).

- **The prevention and detection of fraud and error**

  This will include fraud and error at the operational level through to the strategic level.

- **The accuracy and completeness of the accounting records**

  Again, ensuring that all transactions are recorded – so liabilities are not 'hidden' and assets are not overstated.

- **The timely preparation of financial information.**

  This will include information for internal and external purposes.

In the specific case of Accounts Payable, effective internal controls will ensure that:

- all transactions are recorded accurately
- all records relating to inventory are accurate
- purchases are properly authorised
- payments to suppliers are paid promptly and that the sums paid are correct. This will have the added benefit of ensuring that relationships with suppliers are maintained.
- There are no duplicate payments
- Accurate and timely information on purchases, prices and materials used, are available for management accounting reports
- The ability of the company to detect instances of fraud or theft relating to supplied goods and inventory is improved.

In a company such as VWS with a very large number of suppliers and orders internal controls are essential as it is not possible to manage the accounts payable without an effective system.

(b) Controls which should be in place for the accounts payable information system include:

- All documentation relating to the purchase should have the purchase order number on. This number should be used as the primary identifier for a given purchase.
- Payments should not be made unless the invoice has been authorised by an authorised signatory or the appropriate budget holder. The authorisation should include the identification of the payment to the appropriate cost centre.
- When goods are received the details of the goods received note must be entered on the system to confirm that the goods have been received and are of acceptable quality.
- Anyone receiving an invoice must ensure that the invoice is checked to ensure that it is accurate before being passed to the relevant signatory and then, once authorised, passed to the accounts payable department.
- No payment should be processed without appropriate documentation including:
  - Purchase order
  - Goods received note
  - Invoice
- Once all the relevant documentation is received the invoice can be processed for payment.
- In addition there may be information collected to monitor the effectiveness of the accounts payable department such as:
  - Time between receipt and payment of invoices
  - Invoices processed per month

(c) There is a risk of fraud in any accounts payable system, particularly when the control environment is poor and internal controls are weak. Fraud may consist of the theft of cash or other assets or false accounting, which includes concealing or falsifying accounting records with a view to personal gain or providing false information that is misleading or deceptive.

Examples of the way in which the accounts payable system could be used to commit fraud are:

- Covering-up internal theft by altering, falsifying or deleting purchase records
- Gaining unauthorised access to details of bank accounts of suppliers in order to transfer funds
- Collusion with suppliers to pay for more goods than were actually received and using the system to cover up the collusion.

In particular employees with IT expertise have the skills necessary to commit fraud, and those who work unsociable hours unsupervised, for example to catch up with processing of payments have the opportunity.

There are a number of ways in which the company can mitigate this risk:

- Physical security measures to prevent (or monitor) physical access to assets, documents or IT systems, to ensure that there is no loss or unauthorised use. All assets and documents should be held securely, and access should be restricted to authorised individuals. Assets include computer terminals, cheques, cash and purchase order forms and other documents.
- Defined levels of authority for making changes to the system.
- Segregation of duties, for example separating responsibilities for authorising expenditure and making the payments.

- The system should provide an audit trail, so that all transactions can be traced through the system from start to finish. Audit trails assist with the detection of fraud, and are also used to review the effectiveness of controls.
- A culture within the company where fraud is recognised and punished, and a plan for identifying and responding to fraud when it occurs.

QUESTION 4

(a) There are a number of risks which face EWC arising from its style of management:

- Managers who are rewarded for achieving very high targets may take excessive risks to achieve the targets, without proper planning or assessment of the risks associated with their actions.
- The loss to the company of capable managers who do not achieve the targets set for no fault of their own – there does not appear to be any analysis of performance to identify reasons for failure (which may be out of the control of the employee) before punishing them.
- Reputation risk due to the company overlooking unscrupulous practices. Increasingly, customers, suppliers and shareholders expect companies to behave ethically. If these practices become public then this could severely damage the company's reputation and lead to lost customers and suppliers.
- Litigation risk. The company leaves itself open to the possibility of legal action by overlooking unscrupulous practices which could actually be illegal.
- There could be a risk of fraud by employees who are underperforming and whose jobs may be under threat. The lack of company policies and procedures and the lack of direct supervision make it easier for employees to commit fraud, and less likely that the fraud will be detected. In addition the type of employee who is unscrupulous in dealing with customers is more likely to be prepared to defraud an employer.
- There is a risk that product quality could be compromised as the suppliers are under pressure to reduce costs, leading to poor quality of components purchased. In addition the focus on cost reduction could lead to managers cutting corners, leading to poor product quality. Poor product quality could lead to losses in sales and further damage to the company's reputation.
- In general, the lack of internal controls other than the use of financial targets means that the company could fail to see emerging problems until its too late. It is also possible that the company could fail to spot opportunities in the market place.

(b) The control environment is sometimes referred to as the 'tone at the top' of the organisation. It describes the ethics and culture of the organisation, which provide a framework within which other aspects of internal control operate. The control environment is set by the tone of management, its philosophy and management style, the way in which authority is delegated, the way in which staff are organised and developed, and the commitment of the board of directors. The control environment provides the discipline and structure for the achievement of the primary objectives of the system of internal control. The control environment includes the following elements:

- integrity and ethical values
- management's philosophy and operating style
- organisational structure
- assignment of authority and responsibility
- human resource policies and practices
- competence of personnel.

In the case of EWC, the culture of the organisation is one in which unscrupulous practices are allowed, and where the senior management show by the way they behave and the way in which they value sales growth at any cost. It is almost inevitable in such an environment that staff will do whatever it takes to achieve sales, whether their actions are ethical or not.

Simply imposing more controls in this environment will not change the behaviour of employees. If the company wants to change the behaviour of staff then it will be necessary to develop a new culture in which senior managers demonstrate that they value integrity and ethical behaviour.

(c) It appears that the company have very few controls. The existing control system consists of the reward system which is based on sales and profitability targets and an aggressive system of cost control. This has led to a number of risks which could be addressed by an improved internal control system.

Financial controls

As has already been said, the company does have a system of cost control. However there seems to be an over-emphasis on cost control which means that other areas have been neglected. In addition, this intense pressure to reduce costs means that administrative procedures and policies are virtually non-existent, which means that there are a number of areas of the business which are not managed at all.

There is no evidence of reporting of financial performance, except for an annual report to shareholders. The company should introduce regular reporting of performance to the board, including reports on costs, profitability and growth as well as other costs such as staffing. I am concerned for example that there may be costs which are not being recognised related to the high staff turnover as employees who do not reach their targets leave and have to be replaced.

There is also no evidence of controls and procedures relating to expenditure. The company needs to introduce controls on spending such as authorisation and approval procedures.

Non-financial quantitative controls

The company has a performance management system which incorporates targets relating to sales growth and profitability. However this does not include any measures which relate to other aspects of performance which may actually have a significant impact on sales. The reporting of performance needs to include other measures such as customer satisfaction and levels of repeat business, which would enable us to see whether the way in which the company does business is having a detrimental effect on our customers and causing them to move their business.

The collection of additional data should be analysed using an information system which includes a range of reports such as trend analysis which would enable us to spot problems early, and to assess the reasons behind failures to meet targets to identify whether it was due to circumstances beyond the control of the manager.

Qualitative controls

The company needs to establish formal controls throughout the organisation to protect the company's assets, protect against fraud and ensure that information is timely and accurate. These controls will include authorisations, verifications, reconciliations, approvals, segregation of duties, performance reviews and asset security measures. These need to be documented and disseminated throughout the company.

I would like to see the development of an ethical approach to doing business which is established from the top of the organisation. This could include a statement of ethical principles, which senior managers are seen to follow, and should be backed up by measures to eradicate unscrupulous practices. It is important that the board is seen to be identifying and dealing with such practices.

The development of unethical practices is in part due to the way in which the company rewards employees for reaching targets at any cost. The company needs to consider other performance indicators which reward the achievement of targets in other areas such as product quality and building good relationships with our customers to encourage a change in behaviour.

The company needs to consider other aspects of human resource management, such as the recruitment of new employees who would support an ethical approach to business. There will also be a need to train existing employees in the operation of the new internal controls.

Whilst there are advantages in having a flat structure in terms of increased flexibility of the business, I would like to see closer supervision of managers to ensure that the new company procedures are being followed.

Finally, there is no evidence of risk management or audit of the company's activities. I would like to see the introduction of a programme of risk management and internal audit which is overseen by an Audit Committee.

QUESTION 5

(a) **The contribution of internal audit to the effectiveness of internal control**

One method of assessing internal controls is to carry out planned audits. The audits might be conducted by an internal audit section or department or this activity could be outsourced to an external organisation with internal audit expertise, such as a firm of auditors.

Internal audit is 'an independent appraisal activity established within an organisation as a service to it. It is a control which functions by examining and evaluating the adequacy and effectiveness of other controls' (CIMA). An internal audit function therefore acts as an internal control, to ensure that the internal control system is operating effectively.

The Institute of Internal Auditors (IIA) defines internal audit activity as 'a department, division, team of consultants, or other practitioner(s) that provides independent, objective assurance and consulting services designed to add value and improve an organisation's operations. The internal audit activity helps an organisation accomplish its objectives by bringing a systematic, disciplined approach to evaluate and improve the effectiveness of risk management, control and governance processes.'

An internal audit function might undertake its own programme of investigations into controls and control systems, and also carry out special investigations into an aspect of control, at the specific request of management. Its work might cover the following areas:

- Reviewing elements of the accounting and internal control systems, on a continuous and ongoing basis. These reviews should:
  - assess the design of the system and individual controls (both financial and non-financial)
  - monitor the implementation and operation of the system (through detailed testing or system analysis)
  - recommend improvements
- Examining financial and operating information, for example testing it for reliability and accuracy.
- Reviewing the economy, efficiency and effectiveness of operations (value for money audits).
- Reviewing compliance with laws and external regulations, or compliance with internal rules and procedures.
- Assisting with the identification of significant risks.

- Special investigations, for example investigations into suspected fraud.

It is important to recognise that the scope of internal audit should be broader than a review of internal controls, and internal audit should cover:

- risk assessment processes
- the control environment
- control activities
- information and communication
- the effective application of control activities.

(b) **The contribution of the audit committee to the effectiveness of internal audit**

In the UK and many other countries, it is recognised that an audit committee should provide an effective way of ensuring an effective system of internal controls. An audit committee with suitable responsibilities and authority provides a formal channel for the transparent discussion and resolution of financial reporting and auditing issues. In UK listed companies, for example, the audit committee is a committee of the board of directors consisting entirely of independent non-executive directors (three, in larger companies).

Responsibilities of the audit committee which relate to internal control include:

- to monitor the integrity of the financial statements of the company
- to review the company's internal financial controls
- unless this responsibility is delegated to a separate risk committee of the board, to review all the company's internal control and risk management systems
- to monitor and review the effectiveness of the internal control function, of which internal audit is an important part.

The audit committee should monitor and review the effectiveness of the company's internal audit function. If the company does not have an internal audit function:

- the committee should consider annually whether there is a need for an internal audit function and make a recommendation to the board, and
- the reasons for the absence of an internal audit function should be explained in the relevant section of the annual report.

Where a company does have an internal audit function, the audit committee has an important role in preserving the independence of the internal audit function from pressure or interference.

The audit committee should:

- approve the appointment or termination of appointment of the head of internal audit
- ensure that the internal auditor has direct access to the board chairman and is accountable to the audit committee
- review and assess the annual internal audit work plan
- receive a report periodically about the work of the internal auditor
- review and monitor the response of management to the findings of the internal auditor
- monitor and assess the role and effectiveness of the internal audit function within the company's overall risk management system.

(c) **The role of the audit committee in promoting good governance**

Corporate governance refers to the way in which companies are governed. Voluntary codes and laws and regulations on corporate governance are concerned with achieving a good standard of governance. A company should be governed in the best interests of its stakeholders, and particularly its shareholders (the owners). However, consideration should also be given to other stakeholders, such as employees, lenders and the general public (for example, with regard to social and environmental issues). There is a strong conformance element, and the key issues in corporate governance relate to compliance with rules or principles.

The main areas of concern in corporate governance differ to some extent between countries, but are broadly as follows:

- The role of the board of directors and whether the directors fulfil their role successfully and properly.
- The reliability of financial reporting, and issues such as the role of the auditors (both external and internal auditors) and the effectiveness of the system of internal controls.
- The role and influence of the company's owners (shareholders) over the direction the company is taking and its policy-making.

The key roles of the audit committee are 'oversight', 'assessment' and 'review' of other functions and systems in the company. As such the audit committee is key in ensuring that the company achieves good governance. The audit committee should review the significant financial reporting issues and judgements in connection with the preparation of the company's financial statements. Management is responsible for preparing the financial statements and the auditors are responsible for preparing the audit plan and carrying out the audit. However, the oversight function can sometimes lead to more detailed analysis. For example, if the audit committee is not satisfied with the explanations of the auditors and management about a particular financial reporting decision, 'there may be no alternative but to grapple with the detail and perhaps seek independent advice.'

The audit committee needs to satisfy itself that the financial statements prepared by management and approved by the auditors are acceptable. It should consider:

- the significant accounting policies that have been used, and whether these are appropriate
- any significant estimates or judgements that have been made, and whether these are reasonable
- the method used to account for any significant or unusual transactions, where alternative accounting treatments are possible
- the clarity and completeness of the disclosures in the financial statements.

The committee should listen to the views of the auditors on these matters. If it is not satisfied with any aspect of the proposed financial reporting, it should inform the board. The committee should also review the financial-related information that accompanies the financial statements.

The audit committee should also review the company's internal financial controls. Unless the task is taken on by a separate risk committee or the full board, the audit committee should also review all the company's internal control and risk management systems, and give its approval to the statements in the annual report relating to internal control and risk management. Management is responsible for:

- identifying, assessing, managing and monitoring risk
- developing, operating and monitoring the system of internal control
- providing assurance to the board that this has been done.

In addition, however, the audit committee should receive:

- reports from management about the effectiveness of the control systems they operate, and
- reports on the conclusions of any tests carried out on the controls by the internal or external auditors.